MANAGEMENT BUY-OUTS AND VENTURE CAPITAL

Management Buy-outs and Venture Capital

Into the Next Millennium

Edited by

Mike Wright

Professor of Financial Studies and Director, Centre for Management Buy-out Research, University of Nottingham Business School, UK

Ken Robbie

Senior Research Fellow and Deputy Director, Centre for Management Buy-out Research, University of Nottingham Business School, UK

Edward Elgar

Cheltenham, UK • Northampton, MA, USA

Published by
Edward Elgar Publishing Limited
Glensanda House
Montpellier Parade
Cheltenham
Glos GL50 1UA
UK

Edward Elgar Publishing, Inc.
6 Market Street
Northampton
Massachusetts 01060
USA

A catalogue record for this book is available from the British Library

Library of Congress Cataloguing in Publication Data
Management buy-outs and venture capital : into the next
millennium / edited by Mike Wright, Ken Robbie.
Papers based on a two-day symposium held to
celebrate the 10th anniversary of the Centre for
Management Buy-Out Research (CMBOR),
University of Nottingham Business School, UK.
Includes bibliographical references.
1. Management buyouts—Forecasting—Congresses.
2. Venture capital—Forecasting—Congresses
3. Management buyouts—Europe—Forecasting—
Congresses. 4. Venture capital—Europe—Forecasting—
Congresses. 5. Twenty-first century—Forecasts—
Congresses. I. Wright, Mike, 1952– II. Robbie,
Ken. III. Centre for Management Buy-out Research.
HD2746.5.M282 1999
658.1'6—dc21 98–27890
CIP

ISBN 1 85898 999 X

Printed and bound in Great Britain by Biddles Ltd, Guildford and King's Lynn

Contents

Figures

Tables

Contributors

Amy Beekman, Researcher, University of South Carolina

Martin Binks, Senior Lecturer in Economics and Entrepreneurship, University of Nottingham Business School

Hans Bruining, Associate Professor and Director, Dutch Management Buy-out Research Unit, Erasmus University, Rotterdam

Bill Bygrave, Frederick C. Hamilton Professor of Free Enterprise, Centre for Entrepreneurial Studies, Babson College

Brian Chiplin, Professor of Industrial Economics and Director, Centre for Management Buy-out Research, University of Nottingham

David Citron, Lecturer in Accounting, City University Business School

Philippe Desbrières, Professeur of Finance, Universite de Bourgogne

Zbigniew Dudzinski, Technical University of Lublin, Poland

Mark Dibben, Researcher, University of Aberdeen

Christine Ennew, Professor of Marketing, University of Nottingham Business School

Richard Harrison, Professor of Strategy and Organisation Development, University of Ulster Business School

Michelle Haynes, Research Assistant, Department of Economics, University of Nottingham

Arthur Herst, Professor of Finance, University of Limburg

Judit Karsai, Research Fellow, Institute for Industrial Economics Research, Academy of Science, Budapest

Benoît Leleux, Assistant Professor, Centre for Entrepreneurial Studies, Babson College

Sophie Manigart, Assistant Professor, Vlerick Management School, University of Ghent

Colin Mason, Professor of Economic Geography, Department of Geography, University of Southampton

Falconer Mitchell, Professor of Management Accounting, Department of Accounting and Business Method, University of Edinburgh

Jan Morovic, President, City University of Bratislava, Slovakia

Dan Muzyka, Professor of Entrepreneurship, INSEAD

Gavin Reid, Professor of Economics and Director, CRIEF, University of St. Andrews

Ken Robbie, Senior Research Fellow and Deputy Director, Centre for Management Buy-out Research, University of Nottingham

Harry Sapienza, Associate Professor, University of South Carolina

Carole Singleton, Lecturer, University of Nottingham Business School

Barbara Summers, Research Associate, Credit Management Research Group, Leeds University Business School

Nicholas Terry, Senior Lecturer in Finance, University of Edinburgh Business School

Steve Thompson, Professor of Managerial Economics, Dept. of Economics, University of Leicester

Jeffry Timmons, Professor of Entrepreneurship, Centre for Entrepreneurial Studies, Babson College

Koen de Waele, Research Assistant, Vlerick Management School, University of Ghent

Nicholas Wilson, Professor of Credit Management, Credit Management Research Group, Leeds University Business School

Mike Wright, Professor of Financial Studies and Director, Centre for Management Buy-out Research, University of Nottingham

Preface

This book analyses the prospects for management buy-outs and venture capital into the next millennium. The collection of papers it contains is based on a two-day symposium on this theme held to celebrate the 10th Anniversary of the Centre for Management Buy-out Research (CMBOR).

There has been a growing debate that traditional venture capital is now at a crossroads. Although venture capital has usually been associated with investments in early stage ventures, management buy-outs increasingly play an important role in the activities and performance of UK and European venture capital firms. As we move towards the millennium, venture capital markets worldwide are facing changing conditions, notably: greater funding availability; increased competition between venture capital firms; increasing pressure on venture capital firms to perform from their institutional funds providers; increasing exits from initial venture capital investments and growing prospects for investment in serial entrepreneurs; increasing pressure in certain market segments from non-domestic venture capital firms; and developments in competing sources of funds such as relationship banking and informal venture capitalists. For the first time the broader scope of the issues facing the venture capital market are brought together through the contributions in this volume.

We hope that the contents of this book will be of interest to and stimulate further debate among practitioners, researchers and policy makers in the area of the financing and management of growing and restructuring firms.

We would like to thank the contributors for participating in the conference on which the papers in this volume are based. Financial support from the Chartered Institute of Management Accountants for the CMBOR 10th Anniversary Conference, from Barclays Private Equity and Deloitte & Touche Corporate Finance for CMBOR and from the British Venture Capital Association for the survey work on which some of the material in Chapters 3 and 9 are based, is gratefully acknowledged. We would also like to thank David Quysner for leading a discussion about venture capital at the 10th Anniversary Conference and Margaret Burdett for administrative support.

Mike Wright
Ken Robbie

1. Introduction

Mike Wright and Ken Robbie

Introduction

Venture capital is typically defined as the investment by professional investors of long-term, unquoted, risk equity finance in new firms where the primary reward is an eventual capital gain, supplemented by dividend yield. An analysis of the US industry by Bygrave and Timmons in 1992 argued that traditional venture capital was now at a crossroads. Similarly, Murray's (1995) analysis of the UK venture capital industry considered the issues to be faced by a mature industry. These previous studies were undertaken at the time of a recession. As we move towards the millennium, venture capital markets generally face changing conditions which are likely to shape the future of the industry.

Although venture capital is typically associated, especially in the US, with investments in early stage ventures, the activity and performance of venture capital firms is increasingly expected to focus on later stage investments undergoing radical restructuring, such as buy-outs. Early stage and start-up funds account on average for only about 6.5 per cent of the annual value of European venture capital investments (EVCA, 1995 and Chapter 3), with management buy-outs and buy-ins accounting for about 44.5 per cent of funds invested. There has hitherto been a general neglect of the broader issues raised by firms involved in buy-outs and buy-ins which go well beyond those usually encompassed by the term venture capital. Given the growing importance of these enterprises to venture capital industries internationally it is appropriate to bring together contributions which address the new issues they raise. Different markets internationally also display varying levels of development and differ in their operation of the various stages of the investment screening and monitoring process. Awareness of these differences is important for the development of the strategic entry of venture capital firms into non-domestic markets.

The importance of buy-outs as an investment vehicle for private equity has been highlighted by recent studies in a number of countries of the performance of venture capital firms (see Chapter 3). Buy-outs and other late stage investments which account for the majority of deal activity in the UK, for example, are found to earn superior returns to start-ups and early stage investments traditionally seen as the focus of venture capital. These studies therefore raise questions about the risk–reward trade-offs of different types of venture capital investment. In the context of these returns, there has been increasing pressure on venture capitalists from their institutional funds providers to enhance performance in an environment of transparency of comparative performance. This has major implications for the behaviour of venture capital firms and for the restructuring of venture capital industries. Indeed, the recession of the early 1990s provoked rationalization and strategic reorientation within the industry which still continues. In some countries, such as the US and the UK, greater availability of funds in the mid-1990s has contributed towards greater competition among venture capital firms to find attractive investments and/or new markets beyond their domestic ones.

Venture capital firms also face increasing pressure in some segments of their market from competing sources of funds as banks develop closer monitoring relationships, one of the main strengths of venture capital, with their clients. Although the leveraged buy-out (LBO) market, especially in the US, has focused on high levels of debt, there is growing recognition of the role of private equity in such transactions. Informal venture capitalists also increasingly offer both competition for and complementarity with formal venture capitalists.

In the light of all these emerging issues it is timely to examine new developments in this area and their implications for both venture capital practitioners and researchers. This chapter outlines a framework for the analysis of a venture capital market which provides a context for the main body of the book. The chapter analyses the issues involved in venture capital at two interrelated levels, that is, from the industry/market level and the venture capital firm level (Figure 1.1). Accordingly, the chapter is structured as follows. The first section reviews the literature at the industry and market level. This involves issues concerning the structure and interaction of venture capital competitors, the power of suppliers of funds to the industry, the power of customers in demanding and searching for venture capital, the importance of substitute products (especially informal venture capital, LBO associations and banks), and the role of new entrants. The second section reviews existing literature at the firm level. This section focuses on the governance of venture capital firms by their funds providers and the process of venture capital investment in investee companies. The latter raises issues concerning deal generation, initial and second screening (pre-contracting problems), deal valuation and due diligence, deal approval and structuring, post-contractual (general and restructuring and failure), investment realization and entrepreneurs' exit and assessment by venture capitalists and post-exit monitoring and recontracting. The final section presents conclusions. The analysis in this chapter and in the main body of this volume encompasses the range of investment stage activities undertaken by venture capitalists, which includes development and replacement capital, management buy-outs (MBOs) and management buy-ins as well as early stage investments.

Industry and market level

From major initial developments in the US, there has been a diffusion of venture capital market growth first to the UK and then throughout Europe and beyond.[1] Tyebjee and Vickery (1988) note the variation in maturity of different venture capital markets in Europe, while Roure, Keeley and van der Heyden (1990), Ooghe, Manigart and Fassin (1991) and Murray (1995) argue that market development is likely to be associated with greater competition, reduced rates of return and a shift to later stage investments.

Developed capital markets face a number of challenges relating to their ability to generate high returns, to identify attractive new investments, pressure to focus on later stage and buy-out investments, their ability to add value to transactions, and so on. In Chapter 2, Bygrave and Timmons, authors of a major book in this area, revisit the principal issues they raised at the beginning of the 1990s concerning the future of venture capital. They examine first the development of primarily the US market since the early 1990s and consider to what extent the issues they raised then have been addressed. Second, they look forward, considering the prospects for the venture capital industry to the year 2000 and beyond. In Chapter 3, Robbie and Wright review trends in the development of venture capital and buy-out markets in both the UK and Europe. The emerging markets of Central and Eastern Europe (CEE) present a number of problems for the development and operation of a venture capital market. Using the framework outlined in this chapter, Karsai, Wright, Dudzinski and Morovic in Chapter 4 examine the issues concerning the development of a venture capital market in CEE in general and provide evidence of the operation of such markets in the cases of Hungary and Poland, two of the most developed markets currently in CEE, and Slovakia, a less well-developed market. Using original research by the authors, the chapter highlights issues that need to be addressed for the development of a venture capital market to be achieved in such circumstances and draws contrasts and comparisons with developed 'Western' markets. Bruno (1986) shows that Porter's (1980) competitive forces model provides a framework for reviewing industry level issues as it directly analyses the ability of an industry to sustain long-term profitability by reference to the degree of inter-firm rivalry, the power and roles of customers and suppliers, new entrants and providers of substitute products and services. The following subsections review industry level issues following this framework (see Figure 1.1).

Rivalry between firms

In analysing competition between formal venture capitalists it is important to consider the investment stages they target since this provides an important segmentation of the industry. In terms of investment stages, it has been suggested that late-stage investors, especially investing in smaller buy-outs, should not be considered venture capitalists (for example, Bygrave and Timmons, 1992), though given that many such venture-backed transactions can involve considerable product and organizational innovation this argument seems debatable (Wright, Robbie and Ennew, 1997). There is growing recognition of the need to consider the portfolio mix of investment stages adopted by venture capitalists (see, for example, Elango et al., 1995), a point to which we return below. Moreover, industry statistics encompass in the term venture capital all stages of investment. While some venture capitalists do invest across the range of investment stages, others only invest in later stage projects. In 1996 later stage financings represented 95 per cent of the total value of investments and 82 per cent of the total number of financings made in that year by members of the British Venture Capital Association (BVCA, 1997).

Power of suppliers

Sourcing of funds used by venture capitalists can be divided into two principal areas. 'Captive' venture capitalists, which are part of banks or insurance companies, do not have to raise capital from third parties (Abbott and Hay, 1995). In the UK they are often viewed as investing primarily in later stage projects such as development capital and management buy-outs and buy-ins. 'Independent' firms tend to be seen as the more traditional type of venture capitalist, though in the UK at least many of these may only engage in later stage transactions. They are typically funded through limited-life closed-end funds, with funding coming from pension funds, foreign investors, and so on, and are more committed than captives to generating a return for investors through realizing a capital gain within a more clearly specified period of time; the latter are more likely to place a higher emphasis on the income stream from their investments. In 1996 independent venture capitalists accounted for 63 per cent of new funds invested, a sharp increase on the 47 per cent recorded the previous year (BVCA, 1997). Murray (1995) notes the increasing power of funds providers in a maturing market as evidence becomes available on the nature of the performance of venture capitalists in investing previous funds (we return to the evidence on performance in chapter 3). Recent funding developments, however, have meant that traditional captive institutions have become more hybrid (or semi-captive) as they source funds from outside to add to those provided by their parent bank or insurance company.

McNally (1994) provides an analysis of the role of corporations both as direct (that is, through corporate venturing) and indirect (that is, through funds) investors in venture capital and suggests that problems relating to mis-matches in expectations between corporations and other parties in relation to investment timescale and control mechanisms in particular have resulted in major difficulties in the development of this source of finance.

Power of customers

There has been relatively little attention to demand side issues although Bruno and Tyebjee (1985) refer to the cost to the entrepreneur of the equity relinquished, the effects of the long time that may be taken to raise venture capital finance and the chances of raising venture capital from another supplier when rejected by an initial venture capital firm. An important area is the potential role of intermediaries. Hustedde and Pulver (1992) examined the role of different types of intermediaries in securing venture funds for their entrepreneurial clients. Their results showed that entrepreneurs who failed to seek advice were more likely to be less successful in acquiring equity finance, but that those using bankers or public agencies were likely to increase their chances of failure. While providing interesting insights, the study focused primarily on entrepreneurs seeking finance for early stage projects.

Evidence from Murray et al. (1995), relating to management buy-outs shows that management generally takes the dominant role in the venture capital identification process and, particularly, the final choice decision. Given the considerable uncertainty of the process and the acknowledged inexperience of most managers in respect of obtaining venture finance, it is surprising that most managers in smaller deals (but not in larger ones) only involve their key advisers late in the process, if at all.

These findings provide interesting insights into the relative power of customers and have clear implications for both industry and, as will be seen below, firm levels since they suggest an asymmetry in bargaining to the advantage of the venture capitalist in respect of smaller transactions.[2] A further issue is raised in the particular context of venture capital backed management buy-outs of divisions of larger firms where the divestor is seeking to obtain the maximum price for the disposal through an auction process.[3] In such circumstances, incumbent managers may or may not be able to exercise power over the venture capitalist, depending on their specific contribution to the firm and the skills the venture capitalist possesses in being able to replace them if necessary. These issues link to the firm-level problems concerning deal generation and screening to be considered below.

Threat of new entrants

Manigart (1994) finds support for a population ecology approach to the entry of firms into venture capital markets, with the major influences on the overall founding rate being the density of the industry. Interestingly, institutional changes were not found to be influential. Wright, Thompson and Robbie (1992) in examining the MBO sector of the overall venture capital market suggest that institutional changes are important at least in the initial stages of market development, but that subsequently new entrants are encouraged by evidence that attractive returns are being earned. Roure, Keeley and van der Heyden (1990) also show that greater market maturity is associated with entry by a greater variety of funds providers, especially by pension funds and insurance companies. Ooghe, Manigart and Fassin (1991) support this view and in addition find that public sector funds providers are more likely to exit.

Relatively little attention has been directly addressed to the influences on new entrants to markets from other countries. However, Wright, Thompson and Robbie (1992) and Murray (1995) find evidence from UK venture capitalists that they are attracted to enter new markets in other countries because of declining opportunities in their original market, their accumulated expertise and perceived comparative advantage over domestic competitors in new markets in seeking out and taking advantage of emerging opportunities. These authors also consider the appropriateness of differing entry strategies and suggest that a major problem is insufficient attention to developing an understanding of the workings of new markets with, in particular, little regard to the need to recruit local executives with the necessary market expertise. There is, however, little systematic evidence as yet as to whether entrants' behaviour is dynamic in the sense that they adapt their entry strategies according to previous experience and differing market conditions.

Threat of substitutes
In addition to the comparisons between mutual funds and venture capitalists seen in the previous section, three other competing funders are of particular interest, informal venture capitalists (or business angels), LBO associations, and banks.

(i) *Informal venture capitalists* Informal venture capitalists, or 'business angels' are individuals who seek to invest a part of their personal wealth in, typically, a minority equity stake in an entrepreneurial venture.[4] Evidence by Landstrom (1993) shows that there are marked international differences between the involvement of informal investors in their investee companies. In terms of transaction screening, investors in the UK devote little attention whereas in the US it is moderately high and in Sweden high. Post-transaction in the UK, such investors are generally passive, in Sweden they are generally active, whilst in the US they are active and highly involved in day-to-day activities. US informal investors take the highest risk in their portfolio of investments. Contrary to views that informal investors are less constrained by the need to earn returns in a specified period, Landstrom finds their exit horizons were usually less than five years. There is also some evidence that informal venture capital markets are inefficient in terms of the communications channels between investors and entrepreneurs (Harrison and Mason, 1992; Freear and Wetzel, 1990).[5]

There has been little systematic empirical analysis in the informal venture capital literature surrounding the process of investment rather than the outcomes of that process. Dibben, Harrison and Mason in Chapter 5 aim to address these gaps in the literature. First, they develop a framework for the elucidation of the concepts of swift trust and swift cooperation and in so doing develop the generally passing references to trust in the entrepreneurship and venture capital literatures. Second, they derive an operational framework for analysing trust and cooperation which is applied to the informal investment decision process. Using verbal protocol analysis they examine the role of trust and cooperation in the investors' initial screening of potential investment opportunities.

An important theoretical issue concerns the extent to which agency theory applies as well to informal as it does to formal venture capitalists. Landstrom (1992), finds little evidence that the involvement of business angels in monitoring their investments will vary according to the level of agency risk and suggests that the agency framework is inappropriate. He argues that the assumptions applicable in agency theory which concern rational economic maximizing behaviour, asymmetric information and conflicting objectives are not valid in the case of informal investors since they are more motivated by non-economic factors, have a desire to make a value-added contribution and are able to mitigate asymmetric information problems through the prior relationships and close involvement in the business.

However, it is necessary to understand the differing approaches of the two types of venture capitalists towards two types of risk. Fiet (1995b) finds that formal venture capitalists attach more importance to market risk than agency risk and vice versa and argues that formal venture capitalists are less concerned about agency risk because they protect themselves from it through stringent contracting which enables them to replace underperforming entrepreneurs. Informal venture capitalists who screen very few deals per year have access to comparatively limited information and place more emphasis on agency risk, that is finding the 'right' entrepreneur who will be able to address market risk. Fiet (1995a) also shows that formal venture capitalists make greater use of formal informant networks and that they prefer their own due diligence to reliance on informal networks.[6]

There is also evidence (Ehrlich et al., 1994) of significant differences between formal and informal venture capitalists in respect of investee monitoring, with the former providing more difficult targets and greater feedback and involvement in monitoring, especially when the firm is experiencing problems. These differences may arise because private investors neither have the time, expertise nor flexibility to engage in close monitoring, so that formal venture capitalists may be more appropriate for entrepreneurs with high technical but low managerial skills, and vice versa for private investors. These arguments suggest that agency theory is also of importance for informal investors, but that greater emphasis is placed on ex ante rather than ex post issues. To trust an investee entrepreneur to manage market risk, the informal investor will have had to develop skills for dealing with adverse selection problems. In the absence of these skills business angels may react by not investing ('virgin angels') despite screening large numbers of potential investments.

(ii) *LBO associations* There is some considerable degree of overlap between specialist providers of funds to buy-outs (LBO associations, Jensen, 1993) and venture capitalists (Sahlman, 1990). Both invest funds on behalf of other institutions and although there is a degree of heterogeneity in the forms they take, both are often, especially in the US, organized as limited partnerships. Both cases involve relationship investment with management, managerial compensation is oriented towards equity and there are likely to be severe penalties for under-performance. The principal differences concern the nature of the relationship between investor and investee and that in investments by LBO associations most of the funding required to finance an acquisition is through debt. Sahlman (1990) in comparing LBO associations with venture capital firms notes that executives in the former may typically assume control of the board of directors but are generally less likely than venture capitalists to assume operational control. Investments by venture capitalists, which especially in Europe may also involve buy-outs as well as start-ups and development capital, make greater use of equity and quasi-equity.[7] These differing relationships and financing instruments may be used to perform similar functions in different types of enterprise, so widening the applicability of the active investor concept within the Anglo-American system of corporate governance (Wright et al., 1994).

Covenants attached to the debt in MBOs provide an additional monitoring mechanism for the providers of finance to add to the monitoring by equity providers. While these mechanisms may be an important means by which financiers can initiate bankruptcy proceedings, they also offer the potential for a flexible range of actions according to differing levels of financial distress of the investee company. Baker and Wruck's (1989) detailed case study shows that breaches of covenants may lead to renegotiation of the terms of the loan or waiver where such a breach is not the result of a financial problem. Citron and colleagues in Chapter 7 examine the operation of debt covenants as a monitoring device in management buy-outs using evidence from the authors' surveys in the UK and Holland. The evidence is that MBO loan agreements contain more covenants than general purpose corporate lending agreements, monthly management accounts and telephone communication are more frequent first indicators of distress than are accounting based covenant breaches, lenders with specialist MBO lending units are more likely to waive covenant breaches and less likely to recall loans in default than those without such units, and relationships between MBO lenders and customers appear to be closer in the UK than in Holland.

(iii) *Banks* While the overall need of small and growing firms to have bank finance has been widely researched, Chan, Siegel and Thakor (1990) raise the issue of the need to explore the conditions which lead to the simultaneous existence of banks and venture capitalists.[8] They suggest that venture capitalists may have advantages over banks in providing finance in settings where entrepreneurial skills are highly uncertain at the outset and the role of close monitoring is potentially significant. As banks begin to develop close long-term relationships involving detailed information flows with their corporate customers (Ennew and Binks, 1995; Holland, 1994), there would appear to be increasing convergence with the approach adopted by venture capitalists. Moreover, the problems faced by venture capitalists in respect of adverse selection and their response in terms of increased price versus refusal to fund is analogous to issues concerning the so-called finance gap (De Meza and Webb, 1987).

While collateral is a means of counteracting the information asymmetries which lead to credit rationing, the development of a close working relationship is an important means of enhancing the flow of information. Binks and Ennew in Chapter 6 examine the nature of the banking relationship, paying particular attention to the idea of relationship participation and the benefits which accrue to both parties as a result of participation. Using data from over 3000 UK small firms, it is possible to identify four broad relationship types based on the degree to which the bank and business participate in the relationship. A comparison across different relationship types suggests that there are considerable benefits associated with more participative relationships.

New and smaller firms may face particular problems in obtaining longer-term forms of finance, especially that provided by venture capitalists. For these firms, trade credit is an important source of funds. Its use has been the subject of vigorous policy debate concerning the cash flow problems caused by the late payment if commercial debt. Empirical evidence that isolates the factors determining the demand for trade credit and other forms of short-term finance is scarce but will have an important bearing on the credit rationing debate. In Chapter 8, Wilson, Singleton and Summers use evidence from a study of small owner-managed businesses in order to model the demand for trade credit. The chapter suggests that trade credit is often used as a premium-priced source of short-term finance for small and growing firms that are rationed by institutional lenders.

Firm level

In examining firm-level issues, venture capitalists and funders of buy-outs can be viewed as facing a two-level principal-agent relationship between themselves and their providers of capital and between themselves and the managers of the companies in which they invest (Sahlman, 1990). First, in respect of the relations between venture capital firms and their funds providers, the previous section has shown that venture capital firms obtain their funding from a range of sources each with their own objectives. However, the availability of alternative outlets for funds and evidence from performance with previous tranches of funds provides a measure of power in the dynamic context where venture capital firms need to raise second and subsequent rounds of funds to invest in further projects. Not only does this raise issues as to whether or not funds providers will extend funds, it also raises issues concerning their governance of venture capital firms in order to help ensure that their objectives are met. Hence, as agents, venture capital firms may be faced with the risk that if they do not perform satisfactorily they will fail to attract further funding. Second, venture capital firms as principals face problems in screening potential investments due to both uncertainty and adverse selection problems and moral hazard problems in the post-investment monitoring of their investee companies. Reid, Terry and Smith (1995) show that venture capitalists attempt to manage the risks involved in their activities, first, through fine filters on proposals, high hurdle rates of return and being strongly resistant to downside risk exposure to address adverse selection, and second, through tight monitoring and an unwillingness to bear all the risk in order to address moral hazard issues. Each of these two firm-level aspects is considered in turn.

Governance of venture capital firms

A pioneering study by Sahlman (1990) examines the nature of the principal–agent relationship between funds providers and the venture capitalist and identifies the mechanisms used to help minimize these problems, which include incentives for mutual gain, the specific prohibition of certain acts on the part of the venture capitalist which would cause conflicts of interest, limited life agreements, mechanisms to ensure gains are distributed to investors, expenditure of resources on monitoring the venture capitalist and the regular provision of specific information to the funds providers by the venture capitalist. The terms of the contract both communicate the expectations of funds providers and filter out those venture capitalists who are unable to meet these requirements. Venture capitalists' remuneration is typically based on an annual management fee plus some percentage of the realized profits ('carried interest') from the fund. Sahlman points out that good venture capitalists by accepting a finite funding life and performance dependent compensation are signalling their quality in relation to weak ones, but that the funds provider has to invest in intensive screening in order to guard against false signalling.

Gompers and Lerner (1996) find evidence that the use of covenants in the contracts between funds providers and venture capital firms is both a means of dealing with agency problems but also a reflection of supply and demand conditions in the industry.

Robbie, Wright and Chiplin in Chapter 9 examine the changing nature of the monitoring of venture capital firms by their funds providers. The chapter draws on evidence from the authors' survey of venture capital firms to examine the nature of the monitoring role of funds providers; the targets they set venture capitalists; the type, extent and frequency of information reporting they require for monitoring purposes; and the nature of the monitoring actions they undertake.

A significant agency problem may also arise in the valuation of investments for the purposes of reporting to providers of funds. It is venture capitalists as agents who are responsible for such valuations and on which their performance will be judged (Fried and Hisrich, 1994). However, since it may take many years for a venture capital investment to come to fruition, considerable subjectivity surrounds the valuation of investments in any particular year before the investment is realized. In the absence of clear and 'complete' rules, management may have the scope and incentive to report biased interim investment values. The valuation rules used by venture capital firms in the UK are discussed in Chapter 3.

The deal process

The stages in the venture capital and buy-out funding, assessment and monitoring process have been analyzed in a number of studies (for example, Bygrave and Timmons, 1992; Fried and Hisrich, 1994; MacMillan, Siegel and Subbanarasimha 1985; Tyebjee and Bruno, 1984; Sweeting, 1991b; Sahlman, 1990). These stages have been identified from direct analysis of the operation of venture capitalist's operations and have been based on approaches which have sought to develop an understanding of what it is that venture capitalists and funders of buy-outs do (Figure 1.1). The following subsections review evidence relating to each stage in the deal process in turn.

(i) *Deal generation* At the beginning of the process it is crucial to obtain access to viable projects which can be funded at entry prices which will generate target rates of return. The difficulties faced by venture capitalists because of entrepreneurs' search and decision processes, and increases in competition between venture capitalists noted earlier, serve to highlight the importance of a deal generation strategy. While there has been attention to these issues by practitioners, there has been relatively little academic research.

Deal generation is closely linked at the strategic level to venture capitalists' preferences with respect to investment stages and deal size, as well as to the availability of information and the recruitment of venture capitalist executives with the specific skills to seek out transactions (Murray, 1995; Bygrave and Timmons, 1992). There is some evidence from both the US and the UK which draws attention to the implications for deal generation of differences between the regional locations of venture capitalists and those of potential investees (Murray et al., 1995). As seen earlier, problems here link back to an understanding of the dynamics of the power of customers in differing segments of the market. Operationally, issues are raised which concern the comparative net benefits of proactive versus reactive approaches. In an environment of increasing competition

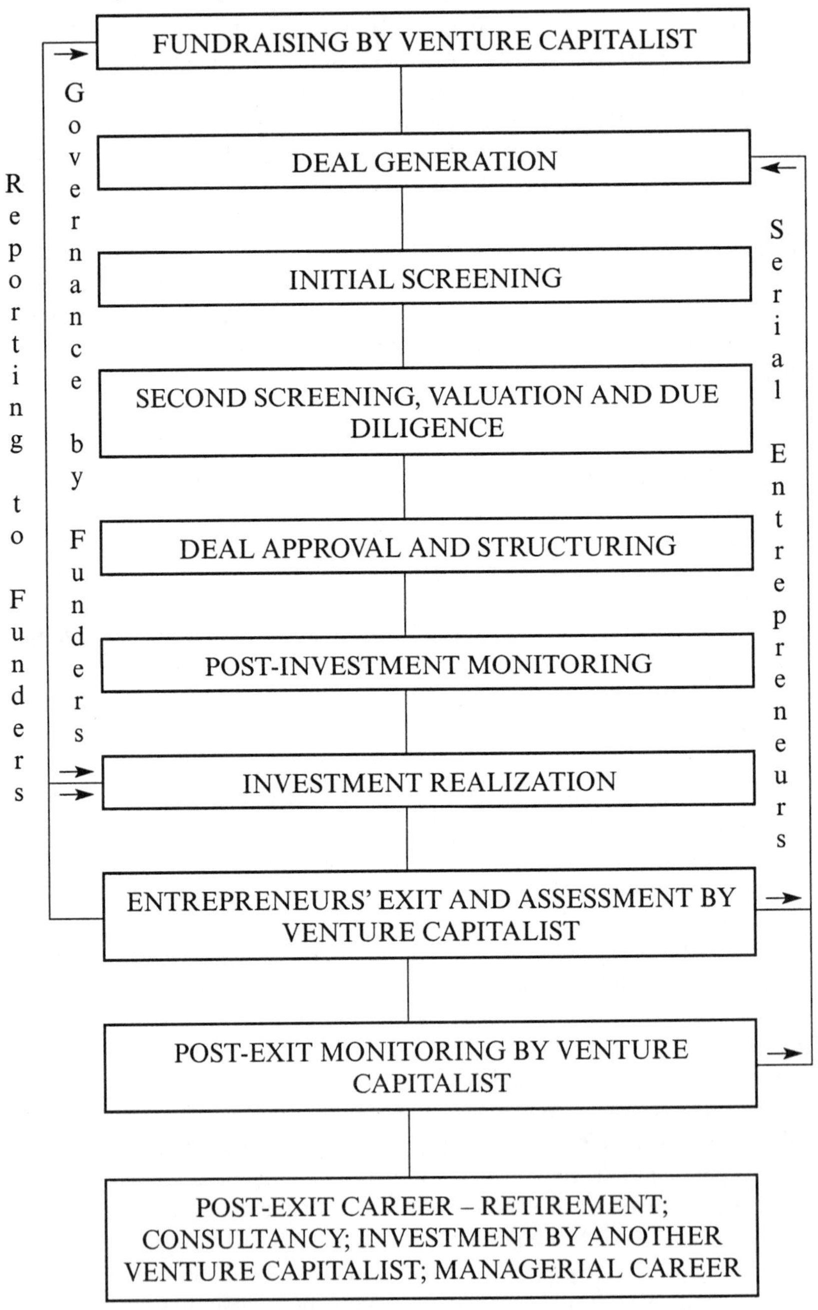

Figure 1.1 Venture capitalist fundraising, deal appraisal monitoring and serial entrepreneurs

for deals there appears to be a move towards more proactive approaches, even though this involves increased costs and may require greater technical as well as financial skills, which may only be possessed by certain segments of the market.

In the case of. buy-outs, agency cost problems in corporations quoted on stock markets have been identified as a major antecedent to the generation of such transactions (for example, Jensen, 1993). The ability to reduce agency cost problems through the introduction of performance enhancing governance and incentive mechanisms is argued to be a major factor in the creation of buy-outs. However, the agency cost perspective offers a rather restrictive view of the factors influencing the generation of buy-out deals. Wright, Dial and Hoskisson (1997) argue that a number of theoretical perspectives help explain the generation of buy-out transactions, including agency theory, environmental change and adaptation, transactions cost economics, resource dependency theory, entrepreneurship theory, leadership succession and employee motivation. Environmental change factors relevant to the generation of buy-outs predominantly involve capital market innovations and taxation incentives. Shleifer and Vishny (1992) argue that increased liquidity in the market for corporate assets in the 1980s helped increase debt capacity and made many highly leveraged transactions possible; the decline in the market in the late 1980s being attributable to a combination of exogenous factors and investor concerns that asset markets would become less liquid. The introduction of new financial instruments, notably 'junk bonds', made it possible to fund more highly leveraged and riskier transactions than previously (Kaplan and Stein, 1993). The possibility for taxation savings to be achieved from the financing of corporations with debt as opposed to equity are also argued to have had an important influence on the generation of buy-outs of quoted companies in particular (Lowenstein, 1985). Divestment buy-outs are often considered to be generated where there are control problems and underperformance relating to peripheral subsidiaries in conglomerate firms. However, where trading relationships exist, the parent may prefer a buy-out over selling to a competitor or supplier, especially where the former subsidiary is more heavily dependent on its former parent than vice versa (Wright, 1986).

Buy-outs may also be generated following the perception by incumbent managers of unexploited entrepreneurial opportunities (Wright and Coyne, 1985). Concerns that incumbent management who take such initiatives may be exploiting informational advantages *vis-à-vis* existing owners has led to the introduction of auctions and other mechanisms aimed at establishing performance-contingent prices (see, for example, Jones and Hunt, 1991; Wright, Thompson and Robbie, 1993 for discussion). Leadership succession problems (Kets de Vries, 1977) may be particularly important in the generation of buy-outs of family/privately owned businesses. The need to introduce direct equity ownership to gain employees agreement to a transfer of ownership and to motivate them afterwards are important influences on the generation of employee buy-outs (Long, 1978; Bradley and Nejad, 1989; Pendleton, Wilson and Wright, 1997). Employee ownership in buy-outs has been a particularly important feature of transactions generated by governmental privatisation programmes (Wright, Thompson and Robbie, 1993).

Management buy-outs arising on divestment developed as attractive investments for venture capitalists as they provided risk–return trade-offs that were often better than could be obtained from investing in earlier stage transactions. Increasing competitive pressure on venture capitalists has led them to become proactive in identifying potential divestment candidates, rather than reacting to proposals brought to them from divisional management or intermediaries. At the same time, corporate divestors have become reluctant to give preference to incumbent management when subsidiaries are divested because of concerns about their exploitation of asymmetric information advantages. The development of investor-led buy-outs (IBOs) is one important recent innovation in the market which has resulted from these influences (Wright and Robbie, 1996b). To effect such actions has meant an increasing need on the part of venture capitalists and buy-out specialists to understand the divestment process. In Chapter 10, Thompson, Wright and Haynes contribute to this understanding through an examination of the characteristics of refocusing firms with particular emphasis on the divestment process. Using divestment data, the study examines the importance of internal governance mechanisms, firm profitability, firm size, diversification strategy and leverage on corporate refocusing. The results indicate that firms with high leverage and poor performance are more likely to divest. Firm size and diversification strategy are positively correlated with divestment activity, while board composition, management equity interests and a change in top management have no effect on the divestment decision.

(ii) *Initial and second screening – pre-contracting problems* At the time that a venture capital investment is being considered, institutions are faced with a potential adverse selection problem in that they are unable to gauge the manager's performance in the enterprise prior to deal completion (Amit, Glosten and Muller, 1990b). Adverse selection issues also raise crucial problems in the potential effectiveness of post-transaction monitoring by institutional investors (Stiglitz and Weiss, 1981). To the extent that these problems lead investors to misjudge the situation, a deal and accompanying financial structure may be agreed which is inappropriate and possibly unviable. As a result, the control mechanism introduced by the commitment to meet the cost of servicing external finance may lead to suboptimal decisions.

Amit, Glosten and Muller (1990a) develop a model which examines the nature of the adverse selection problem for venture capitalists. The general assumption is made that the entrepreneur knows his own ability level, whereas the venture capitalist does not. In an initial case it is assumed that the entrepreneur is risk neutral and no new investment is needed. In such conditions, only entrepreneurs with below average ability will choose to involve a venture capitalist who, because of the absence of information, makes a bid to fund a project on the basis of the average ability level. This will result in a negative net present value investment and because of the severity of the adverse selection problem the market breaks down. Relaxing this assumption to allow for risk averse entrepreneurs may still mean that only low-ability entrepreneurs accept the venture capitalists' bid while the high ability ones develop ventures on their own.[9] This model may go some way to explaining the phenomenon that subsequently successful ventures may initially have been refused venture capital finance, together with the relatively low amounts of venture capital funding of early stage investments where information asymmetry problems are most serious.

Sweeting (1991b) points out that venture capitalists have been particularly proactive in deal generation in an attempt to reduce adverse selection problems by becoming more involved with entrepreneurs at an earlier stage. The nature of the adverse selection problem may not be constant with all entrepreneurial ventures, but may vary with the stage and sector of an investment. In a buy-out, investing institutions may be guided by the incumbent management's experience in the post and their knowledge of the business, though management may have an incentive not to reveal full information in an attempt to obtain the most favourable terms. In a buy-in, as the entrepreneur comes from outside there may be problems of asymmetric information, both in relation to their true skills and an inability to observe the manager in post ex ante (Robbie and Wright, 1996). In development capital situations it may be difficult to judge whether the entrepreneur's previous performance will continue in the future where his/her equity stake is diluted by the introduction of venture capital. The informational asymmetry problems may also be more intractable in the case of complex high-tech ventures than for more straightforward ventures using existing technology, which raise issues concerning the specialist skills of both the entrepreneur and the venture capitalist.

Empirical studies examining venture capitalist investment criteria have evolved from descriptive studies of the variables taken into account to those which attempt to identify the relative importance of various criteria using a variety of rating and ranking scales and principally focused on start-ups (for example, Bruno and Tyebjee, 1985; MacMillan, Siegel and Subbanarasimha, 1985; MacMillan, Zemann and Subbanarasimha, 1987; Hall and Hofer, 1993; Rah, Jung and Lee, 1994).

MacMillan, Zemann and Subbanarasimha (1987) show that the most important criteria used by venture capitalists in screening investment proposals were entrepreneurial personality and experience, with lesser dependence being placed on market, product and strategy. In a replication study, Fried, Hisrich and Polonchek (1993), show that six years on venture capitalists were more concerned with market acceptance and less demanding of high potential rates of return and quick exit, which these authors see as a more realistic view of venture potential. Fried and Hisrich (1994) suggest that venture capitalists use three generic criteria for screening investments – the viability and novelty of the project; the integrity, track record and leadership skills of management; and the possibility for high returns and an exit – before proceeding to detailed evaluation. The focus on management raises important issues concerning the different characteristics and motivations of the entrepreneurs involved with investment projects at different stages and the link between these factors and performance. Woo et al. (1991) discuss typologies of entrepreneurs, while Ennew et al. (1994) show that although entrepreneurs display heterogeneous characteristics, there are significant differences between the mean attributes of novice start-up entrepreneurs, buy-out entrepreneurs and buy-in entrepreneurs. Buy-out entrepreneurs on average appear to be less opportunistic than either buy-in or start-up entrepreneurs. Muzyka et al. (1995) emphasize that venture capitalists have to make trade-offs between various criteria in their screening of investments, and that previous approaches fail to take this into account. Using conjoint analysis, Muzyka, Birley and Leleux (1995), conclude that venture capitalists would prefer to select an opportunity which offers a good management team and reasonable financial and product market characteristics, even if the opportunity does not meet the overall fund and deal requirements.

These last results are consistent with Wright and Robbie (1996a) who show that venture capitalists place considerable emphasis on the specific attributes of a potential investee company both in relation to assessment of its value and the rate of return to be expected from it. While accounting information is an important element in deal screening and in arriving at a valuation and a target rate of return, venture capitalists place most emphasis on very detailed scrutiny of all aspects of a business, typically including sensitivity analysis of financial information, discussions with personnel and accessing considerably more information of an unpublished and subjective kind. There is some debate in the US literature about the extent to which the use of non-accounting information varies between stage of investment (Elango et al., 1995; Fried and Hisrich, 1994). There appears to be greater consensus that later stage investors will be more interested in market acceptance of a product. Early stage investors emphasize a range of product strength and market growth characteristics, particularly as early stage transactions are technology based with little available data on market acceptance.

(iii) *Valuation and due diligence* Discounted cash flow (DCF) and discounted dividend yield methods whilst theoretically correct (Brealey and Myers, 1996) pose particular problems in a venture capital investment context. With the DCF approach it is difficult to forecast future cash flows in the typically highly uncertain environment of a start-up, so that the expected error of the forecast will increase. It may be difficult to apply the dividend yield method to early stage investments which rarely pay significant dividends.

Evidence suggests that venture capital projects are typically valued by applying one or more valuation techniques to the financial and accounting information relating to the potential investee typically contained in the business plan submitted by management to the venture capitalist (Wright and Robbie, 1996a). Similarly, DeAngelo (1990) shows that in the case of arriving at fair valuation opinions in LBOs/MBOs investment banks typically use a variety of techniques, including DCF methods, asset and earnings-based methods, comparisons with transaction prices in the same sector, and so on, to establish a range of valuations. Forward looking information in the business plan may be subject to sensitivity analysis both by management and their advisers and by the venture capitalist according to the expected influence on future performance of other information. Most importance appears to be attached to price–earnings multiples-based valuation methods (Wright and Robbie, 1996a), particularly among later stage investors. The process is likely to involve several iterations based on assumptions about the future trend in performance to test the robustness of the point at which the proposed venture meets an acceptable internal rate of return (IRR), the most common measure of performance used in the industry (Murray, 1991). Dixon (1991) using data relating to the buoyant economic conditions of the late 1980s suggests that little scrutiny of information to assess risk and adjust target IRRs takes place. However, Wright and Robbie (1996a) indicate that by the early-mid 1990s venture capitalists were undertaking widespread assessment of risk. Moreover, Murray and Lott (1995) show that venture capitalists perceive technology-based projects to be more risky than alternative later stage projects and use a higher target rate of return in assessing them, but also that the stage of financing is significantly more important in determining project risk than the state of technology involved.

It has been argued that the valuation of venture capital and buy-out investments may not be independent of the relative buoyancy of these markets. Gompers and Lerner (1997) examine the valuation of investments by venture capital funds in the US and find that the growth in money committed to new venture funds is associated with an increase in the price paid by venture investors. They argue that these findings are consistent with suggestions that competition for a limited number of good investments may be responsible for rising prices. In respect of US buy-outs, Kaplan and Stein (1993) find evidence of price rises between the early and late 1980s consistent with overheating in the buy-out market. A similar picture emerges with UK buy-outs and buy-ins (Wright, Thompson and Robbie, 1996). Years in which higher prices are paid for apparently more marginal transactions subsequently result in significantly greater failure rates (see below). These findings have implications for the buoyant venture capital and buy-out market conditions which emerged again in the late 1990s, notably that if previous behaviour patterns are repeated, funds which harvest their investments in the next millennium are likely to display reduced performance.

Approaches to valuation may also be expected to vary according to the nature of the economic system in different countries as well as the stage of development of different venture capital markets. In Chapter 11, Manigart and colleagues examine the issues concerning the valuation of investment projects using the authors' evidence from the US and Europe.

A variety of issues broadly categorised as time restrictions, cost constraints and situational factors, may directly impact the level of due diligence during an acquisition process (Harvey and Lusch, 1995). Evidence from buy-ins (Robbie and Wright, 1996) identifies a major problem related to the ability to obtain adequate up to date information concerning the target company. While due diligence is expected to be undertaken in a thorough manner, its cost in relation to transaction value in smaller buy-ins and time constraints in negotiations, meant that this ideal was difficult to achieve. There are indications that venture capitalists have adapted to such asymmetric problems through recent developments involving hybrid inside and outside management and investor buy-outs, where there is direct negotiation between vendors and venture capitalists.

(iv) *Deal approval and structuring* Appropriate structuring of venture capital investments has important implications for the ability of venture capitalists to earn their target rates of return. Sahlman (1990) shows that venture capitalists use various mechanisms to encourage entrepreneurs both to perform and to reveal accurate information.[10] These mechanisms include staging of the commitment of investment funds, convertible financial instruments ('equity ratchets') which may give financiers control under certain conditions, basing compensation on value created, preserving mechanisms to force agents to distribute capital and profits, and powers written into Articles of Association which require approval for certain actions to be sought from the investor(s). Theoretical work by Chan, Siegel and Thakor (1990) provides a two-period agency model to explain the nature of these venture capitalist contracts.

An important feature of many venture capital investments, especially early stage ones, is the staggering of financing into several rounds. Staging of investments, however, can lead to myopia and over-investment where initially entrepreneurs and subsequently first round venture capitalists as insiders present misleading information to outsiders in an attempt to persuade them to invest.

An important issue arises which concerns how contracts are to be structured under these conditions of multi-stage investment decisions (Cooper and Carleton, 1979; Admati and Pfleiderer, 1994). Analysis by Admati and Pfleiderer (1994) shows that a contract in which venture capitalists continue to maintain the same fraction of equity in the various rounds of financing a project can neutralize a venture capitalist's incentive to mislead. With entrepreneur-led financing this situation does not hold as there does not exist a fully revealing signalling equilibrium which would resolve asymmetric information problems. Relaxing the assumption of risk neutrality in the case of venture capital financing requires the contract design to address risk-sharing issues.

Syndication in the first stage of the project can also be a means of sharing risk; the lead venture capitalist as inside investor being given a fixed-fraction contract and making the continuation decisions, while syndicate members are given securities which reduce the risk of the entrepreneur. Admati and Pfleiderer argue that this analysis is consistent with the notion that venture capitalists often form syndicates with different types of contracts and different responsibilities with respect to monitoring for different capital providers. Bygrave (1988) finds that an important reason for syndication is to share information to reduce uncertainty and that this may be as important, if not more important, than the spreading of financial risk. Lerner (1994a) also finds support for this view and for the argument that typical later-round syndication involves less experienced venture capitalists investing in a deal begun by established organizations. Given issues relating to effecting post-contractual monitoring, to which we return below, the extent and nature of syndication may be dynamic. Venture capitalists may in effect search over time for a network of syndicate partners with whom they are able both to complete transactions and undertake effective monitoring. Since monitoring is costly and cannot be performed continuously the venture capitalist will periodically check the project's status and preserve the option to abandon at each stage. An examination of the factors influencing syndication in UK buy-outs and buy-ins (Chiplin, Robbie and Wright, 1997) identifies investee risk characteristics, venture capital firm and control factors which influence the syndication decision.

Gompers (1995) and Gompers and Lerner (1996) examine agency and monitoring costs in the staging of venture capital investments. They find evidence to support the view that the monitoring process provides valuable information which enables the venture capitalist to cut off new financing in the light of negative information about future returns and provide more financing and a greater number of rounds of financing in the more successful transactions. However, they also note that though venture capitalists periodically check up on entrepreneurs between capital infusions, entrepreneurs still have private information about the projects they manage. Hence, the nature and effectiveness of the monitoring process, which we examine below, is of considerable importance.

Little attention has been devoted to the range of financial instruments used by venture capitalists. Norton and Tenenbaum (1992) find that venture capitalists favoured the use of preference shares regardless of the presence or absence of deal specific influences, and that the use of debt was consequent on expectations that the investment would shortly generate taxable income, would have collateralizable assets, would have products resistant to the economic cycle and that the investment was more likely to be later stage. A follow-up study (Norton and Tennenbaum, 1993b) examines the link between financing structures, financing stages and venture capitalists' characteristics. They find that smaller less diversified venture capitalists make greater use of ordinary equity instruments, but the use of preference shares did not increase in higher risk (early) stage investments nor did investors who were subject to greater amounts of unsystematic risk make greater use of preferred instruments.

The importance of innovations in financing structures and financial instruments has been highlighted in discussions of buy-outs (Jensen, 1993), notably the use of vertical strip financing and 'junk bonds'. The unbundling of assets post-buy-out in order to pay down debt which cannot be serviced from cash flow is also an important feature of buy-out financial structures. The difficulties faced by many highly leveraged transactions resulting from excessive leveraging of marginal transactions, problems in disposing of assets at predicated prices and problems in servicing debt when apparently stable cash flow became adversely affected by recessionary conditions (Shleifer and Vishny, 1992; Kaplan and Stein, 1993) have led to a reassessment in practice of the degree of leverage in buy-outs and the reliance on the disposal of assets to reduce debt. However, there are concerns that the resurgence in the buy-out market from the late 1990s onwards may lead to similar problems as before. Although there is some evidence that buy-out financiers are aware of and anxious to avoid these problems (CMBOR, 1997), the continuing incentives and pressures on them to complete transactions may mean that such difficulties become inevitable.

The importance of debt in buy-out structures emphasizes the need for financing structures to include different and more comprehensive debt covenants than are found in general lending. As noted earlier these issues are discussed in Chapter 7. The different risk characteristics of buy-outs and buy-ins noted earlier raise issues concerning the effects on financial structures. Evidence suggests that although the financial structures of buy-ins have on average slightly lower leverage than in buy-outs this is not statistically significant (Wright, Thompson and Robbie, 1996). Similarly, the extent and tightness of debt covenants also appears to be the same in both types of transaction (Citron, Robbie and Wright, 1997).

A particular theoretical and practical problem in buy-out and venture capital investments concerns the consequences of the financial backer and the entrepreneur failing to agree on the degree to which the venture will be profitable, with consequent implications for the split between the equity stake attributable to each. Such differences may arise because of differing views of an uncertain situation and because of the agency cost problem when entrepreneurs own less than all the equity (Jensen and Meckling, 1976). Chua and Woodward (1993) suggest that this problem can be addressed through the use of stock options in the financing structure which provides entrepreneurs with an incentive to perform since they increase the cost to the entrepreneur of excessive consumption of perks. Similar devices have been used extensively in practice, termed 'equity ratchets' in the UK. Available evidence from UK buy-outs, where such instruments are widespread, suggests that they may pose major problems in terms of specifying (relatively) complete contracts concerning the definition of financial performance to be used, manipulation of information by managers and the timing of their crystallization[11] (Thompson and Wright, 1991). These problems may lead to major relationship difficulties between the venture capitalist and the entrepreneur.

(v) *Post-contractual monitoring – general* As noted above, post-contractual asymmetric information problems have major implications for the nature and effectiveness of venture capitalists' monitoring of investments. The agency theory perspective adopted above focused on the contractual structures involved in monitoring. However, an important aspect of monitoring concerns the relative roles of contractual mechanisms and processes.

Barney et al. (1989) examine the influences on the degree to which elaborate governance mechanisms are used by venture capitalists and find that high agency risks and business risks were associated with more elaborate governance structures. In a complementary paper, Sapienza and Gupta (1994) focus on the processes of monitoring by venture capitalists. In an important and innovative study, which used matched pairs of lead venture capitalists and Chief Executive Officers (CEOs) of investee companies, they find using US data that the frequency of interaction between the two parties depends on the extent of the CEOs' new venture experience, the venture's stage of development, the degree of technological innovation being pursued and the extent of goal congruence between the CEO and the venture capitalist. Contrary to expectations they find that the degree of management ownership had no impact on the frequency of interaction. This study's findings are of interest since it shows that even with goal congruence, in an uncertain new business environment, signals regarding the appropriate course of action may be weak, leading to expectations of disagreements between investors and investees and a need for greater exchange of information to identify the appropriate course of action. Moreover, the finding concerning the effect of management ownership suggests that where a high level of managerial ownership is present, there is little reason to expect incentive-related shirking so that further adjustments to incentive mechanisms may be ineffective. The need for interaction is emphasized as the idiosyncratic knowledge possessed by the venture's founders may be virtually irreplaceable (we return to this issue in the next subsection). A subsequent four country study which included the US data plus data from the UK, France and the Netherlands suggests that some of these results may be country specific (Sapienza, Manigart and Vermeir, 1996), thus emphasizing the need to understand the interlinkages between the nature of the venture capital environment and appropriate monitoring mechanisms and processes.

A number of other studies have examined the links between the process of monitoring and the choice of the venture capitalist, the demands of a particular investment situation, the skills level of venture capitalists and the stage of the investment.

MacMillan, Kulow and Khoylian (1989) show that differing levels of involvement in venture capital investments were not related to the nature of the operating business but to the choice exercised by the venture capital firm itself as to the general style it wished to adopt. Sapienza (1992) provides evidence that there is less involvement by venture capitalists in monitoring activities which are more developed and presumably less risky. Elango et al. (1995) identify three levels of assistance by venture capitalists in their investees, but surprisingly, they find that this involvement is not primarily related to the stage of investment.

Sweeting (1991a) and Mitchell, Reid and Terry (1995) show that part of the contractual measures adopted by venture capitalists are accounting information demands which are designed to deal with moral hazard and information asymmetry problems and provide safeguards through bonding arrangements. Accounting information flows were typically required on a more regular and more detailed basis than are statutory requirements for quoted companies. In general, there has been relatively little attention to the changes in the information systems of venture-backed firms. Mitchell, Reid and Terry in Chapter 12, examine the origins and characteristics of developments in the accounting information systems (AIS) of firms which are in receipt of venture capital funds. The consequences of venture capital intervention for the entrepreneurial firm are explored using matched investor–investee cases ('dyads'). The study finds evidence of extensive changes in accounting information systems (AIS).

MacMillan, Kulow and Khoylian (1989) find no significant differences in the performance of businesses subject to differing levels of venture capitalist involvement. However, there are major variations in the amount of time spent and severity of actions taken by different venture capitalists on problem investees (Elango et al., 1995). Barry (1994) cites evidence that venture capitalists intensify their monitoring activities as the need dictates. Venture capitalist representation on the board is found to increase around the time of chief executive turnover, while the number of other outsiders remains constant, according to evidence from the bio-technology industry, that is, an early stage sector (Lerner, 1995).

Rosenstein, et al. (1993) find that the value added by venture capitalists on the investee's board was not rated significantly higher by CEOs than that of other board members and that entrepreneurs valued venture capitalists with operating experience more than those with purely financial expertise. However, Murray (1994a) shows that finance was the only area where venture capitalists skills were judged by entrepreneurs to be greater than those of other parties. Indications are that the general type of skills possessed by venture capital executives varies between types of venture capitalist, with those employed by captive funds tending to be more financial skills oriented whilst those employed by independents tend to have greater industrial skills (Beecroft, 1994).

Sweeting (1991a) and Hatherly et al. (1994) for the UK and Fried and Hisrich (1995) for the US provide evidence of the importance of flexibility through personal relationships in the governance of venture capital and buy-out investments and that formal power needs to be used sparingly and almost only when things go wrong to be effective. However, this may be because of inertia rather than a deliberate policy. While venture capitalists may take control when things go seriously wrong, such action has to be exercised with care since to act precipitously may destroy carefully nurtured relationships and commit the venture capitalists to unknown amounts of time to put matters right. We return to the issues in dealing with problem investments below.

Similarities but also differences emerge in the operation of active investor governance in venture-backed buy-outs and buy-ins. UK evidence from both buy-outs and buy-ins shows that board representation is the most popular method of monitoring investee companies with venture capitalists also requiring regular provision of accounts (Robbie, Wright and Thompson, 1992), but that there is a greater degree of control exercised by institutions over management buy-ins than for buy-outs especially in the form of greater requirement for regular financial reports and greater use of equity ratchets. Evidence from smaller buy-ins suggests that even where they have non-executive directors institutions may not be as active in responding to signals about adverse performance as might have been expected (Robbie and Wright, 1996) and that relationships between entrepreneurs and investors had not developed to the extent that potential crises could be identified and understood by the venture capitalist. These problems reflect the high cost of monitoring and control in relation to the value of investments. In larger buy-ins there is evidence of extensive and repeated active monitoring (see Wright et al., 1994). This difference illustrates the comparative cost–effort–reward trade-offs involved in the active monitoring of large and small investments.

Evidence from buy-outs has examined the effectiveness of the differing mechanisms used to enhance performance. Comparisons of leveraged recapitalizations, which simply substitute debt for equity in publicly traded companies, and buy-outs show that the greater increases in shareholder value found in the latter result from the increase in managerial equity ownership active investor involvement which they encompass but which are not found in the former (Denis, 1994). Insider management's equity holdings in buy-outs are found to have a greater positive impact on performance than enhanced commitments to service debt (Thompson, Wright and Robbie, 1992; Phan and Hill, 1995). Moreover, the performance of inside management in buy-outs is generally significantly greater than that of incoming management (Robbie and Wright, 1996; Kaplan, 1991; Lichtenberg and Siegel, 1990; Harlow and Howe, 1993).

A major remaining issue concerns the appropriate theoretical lens through which to examine monitoring issues. There is now some debate about the extent to which agency theory is the most appropriate theoretical tool for understanding the monitoring relationships between entrepreneurs and venture capitalists, or whether it requires some adaptation given the particular conditions of venture capital investments. In general, legal forms are able to facilitate exchange relationships. Thus contract law specifies a general set of arrangements under which goods and services are exchanged for money. The universal recognition of these norms, backed up by sanctions, economizes on the costs of writing complex contracts. A potential complementary development to principal–agent theory associated with contracting problems is offered by procedural justice theory (Korsgaard, Schweiger and Sapienza, 1995). Procedural justice is concerned with exchange relationships in which one party does not have control over decisions. The essential argument is that regardless of the outcome of decisions, individuals react more favourably when they feel the procedure used to make them was fair. The theory has clear parallels to the situation faced by the indirect involvement by venture capitalists in the operations of investee firms. Though venture capitalists may make considerable contributions to investee firms through the presence of non-executive directors and other monitoring devices, it is the entrepreneurs who control the way in which funds are used, who develop the strategies to achieve the returns that venture capitalists are seeking and who possess intimate inside information on the operation of the business. The venture capitalist seen as a principal may not therefore be in a position to control the nature and level of governance over the entrepreneur as agent.

Procedural justice can also be viewed as an important influence on the development of trust and commitment in relations between venture capitalists and entrepreneurs. This perspective links to agency theory in that the development of relationships may reduce uncertainty and ameliorate the need for costly monitoring as it reduces the need for formal mechanisms in the management of exchange relationships and may also reduce the perceived need to scrutinize data offered openly. This relationship may be considered in the context of the timeliness of information flows from an entrepreneur to the venture capital monitor. An absence or a persistent delay in the provision of information may be perceived by the venture capitalist as an unfair violation of an investment agreement and to undermine the investor's trust in the entrepreneur. Sapienza and Korsgaard (1996) use a procedural justice perspective to examine the impact of entrepreneurs' management of information flows on entrepreneur–investor relations. They find that the more entrepreneurs share information, the more likely are investors to eschew monitoring, to trust that the entrepreneurs will be honest, to support the entrepreneurs' decisions and be more willing to reinvest.

A procedural justice approach goes some way to overcoming some of the oversimplified assumptions of formal theoretical models which address agency problems, such as perfectly revealed information or no information. However, procedural justice theory focuses on the process of monitoring, not the outcome.[12] There may be considerable trust, but performance may be suboptimal. In addition, evidence from agency theory perspectives concerning the link between perceptions about entrepreneurs' skills and the nature of monitoring have so far been omitted from procedural justice approaches.

A further critique of the agency cost approach to modelling entrepreneur–venture capitalist relationships is provided by Cable and Shane (1997) who point out that such an approach is unduly restrictive given the potential for opportunistic, non-cooperative actions by both parties. Adopting a game-theoretic framework they argue that the probability of cooperative entrepreneur–venture capitalist relationships will increase with: increased time pressure; increased pay-offs from cooperation; greater quality and frequency of communication; the existence of a previous positive social or business relationship; demographic similarities, work value congruence and perceived power equality; the posting of bonds by both parties; multiple stage performance evaluation; the degree of generosity shown by one party toward the other; and the use of penalties against non-cooperative behaviour.

In the light of this discussion there appears to be scope for multi-theoretic perspectives on the nature of the venture capitalist–investee monitoring process. A possible way forward is suggested in an interesting and insightful study by Fiet et al. (1997) which investigated venture capitalists' dismissal of new venture team members and found that agency theory, procedural justice theory and power theory offer complementary perspectives into the roles of venture capitalists.

Restructuring and failure

Particular importance has been attached to the governance role of active investors in cases where venture capital investments require restructuring. Ruhnka, Feldman and Dean. (1992) find that 'living dead' investments, that is, investments which are viable but fail to achieve adequate growth and returns, arise usually because of problems with management and markets. Ruhnka, et al. find that successful turnaround, which occurs in only 56 per cent of cases is influenced by the nature of the problem and the ability of venture capitalists to control them.

Subsequent research (Wright et al., 1993) has distinguished between 'Living Dead' and 'Good Rump' investments, where the former essentially involve enterprises where the business collapses with little prospect of turnaround and the latter are capable of being turned round, but the effects of restructuring have yet to be seen. A problem of enforcing restructuring is that it may be difficult to obtain consensus with other parties, both entrepreneurs and co-investors, as to what form it should take. In smaller investments, since management are usually important majority shareholders great care is needed in taking action. If institutions are a controlling shareholder, as is usually the case in larger buy-outs and buy-ins, making changes is theoretically straightforward. However, in cases with large syndicates of financiers, restructuring may be delayed or take a particular direction because of differences in the attitudes of syndicate numbers.[13]

Problems in the screening and control of venture capital investments may be expected to be closely associated with business failure. The influences on likelihood of failure in buy-outs in the UK was examined by Wright et al. (1996) who found that while positive managerial motives for buy-outs and greater levels of restructuring undertaken expeditiously at buy-out are associated with survival, direct investor monitoring *per se* was found not to be significant. Kaplan and Stein (1993) in the US and Wright, Thompson and Robbie (1996) in the UK also find that overpricing of buy-out type transactions in over-heated market conditions are significantly associated with failure.

(i) *Investment realization* Issues surrounding the exit or realization of venture capital and buy-out investments concern the timing and nature of such actions. As regards venture capital, different investment stages are generally seen to have differing life-cycles. In respect of buy-outs, there is considerable debate as to whether they are a long-term (Jensen, 1993) or transitory (Rappaport, 1990) form of organization. Realization may be through initial public offering (IPO), full or partial sale to a third party, secondary buy-out/buy-in or receivership, with there being considerable variance around the mean period of investment in a venture capital project. Buy-outs are also found to have a heterogeneous life-cycle, with some, especially larger ones, changing their ownership structure within a short period while most last for periods in excess of six years (Kaplan, 1991; Wright et al., 1995; Wright et al., 1994; Wright et al., 1993).

An important point to emerge is that the timing and form of realization of venture capital investments requires the objectives of all parties to be satisfied (Relander, Syrjanen and Miettinen, 1994; Wright et.al., 1994). Barry et al. (1990) indicate that venture capitalists have several mechanisms to ensure firms go public at times perceived to be optimal, including board seats and informal advice. Wright et al. (1994) writing in the context of venture backed management buy-outs suggest that institutions' desire for realization in order to achieve their returns, may influence the nature of corporate governance to achieve a timely exit. In order to achieve timely exit, institutions are more likely to engage in closer monitoring of their buy-out investments and to use exit-related equity-ratchets on management's equity stakes (Wright et al., 1995). Both quantitative and case study evidence suggests that the greater the conflicts in the objectives of the parties which had to be suppressed at the time of the transaction, the more the governance structure has to be able to respond and be flexible. Even so, exit arrangements will largely be influenced by the relative bargaining power between venture capitalists and entrepreneurs.

In the context of venture capital investments generally, most attention has focused on exit through IPO. Barry et al. (1990) show that successful timing of a venture-backed IPO provides significant benefits to venture capitalists in that taking companies public when equity values are high minimizes the dilution of the venture investor's ownership stake. Barry (1994) cites evidence that venture capitalists' governance may be biased where they have incentives to offer bad advice to their investees in the matter of premature IPO timing. Such a potential reverse principal–agent conflict may arise where venture capitalists seek a premature IPO in order to gain profile and report prior performance in the raising of new funds.[14] Lerner (1994) shows that seasoned venture capitalists appear to be particularly good at taking companies public near market peaks, though of course this does not necessarily mean that such timing is appropriate from the point of view of the company itself (Wright et al., 1994).[15]

While there is evidence that unseasoned IPOs generally result in significant underpricing (see, for example, Ibbotson, Sindelar and Ritter, 1988 for a review), Megginson and Weiss (1991), however, do show that there is less underpricing in venture-backed IPOs, a finding consistent with a recognized role for venture capitalists as monitors.[16] Moreover, Jain and Kini (1995) whilst supporting this evidence, go further and show that venture capitalist-backed IPO firms have superior post-issue operating performance compared to non-venture capital backed IPO firms over a three year post-issue period. Importantly, they also show that the extent of superior performance is positively associated with the quality of venture capitalists' monitoring.

The valuation of venture capital investments at the time of exit may be particularly problematic since as Lam (1991) has shown, a venture capitalist may not be able fully to realize the value of an investment in a low information environment because of the existence of estimation risk, that is the incremental variation in the predictive return distribution that is attributable to investors' ignorance of the parameters of its true return distribution.[17] Estimation risk may be expected to decline as more information becomes known about the firm's performance. Thus, if part of the estimation risk is transitory and can be dissipated in the aftermarket following IPO then it is worthwhile for the venture capitalist to adopt a graduated policy towards the realization of cash gains.

European secondary markets appear to have failed as providers of capital for emerging growth companies. Conventional explanations focus on the supply side of the market, blaming over-regulation, complex listing requirements, the absence of an equity culture, weak competition between national markets and a shortage of growth companies for the failure. In Chapter 13, Leleux and Muzyka highlight significant underperformance in long-term IPO returns in European markets, possibly affecting demand by investors. Alternative demand-side factors, such as constraints on institutional investments in small cap stocks and the lack of supporting analysts are also discussed.

Despite the emphasis on realization through IPO, venture capitalists maintain a flexible approach to the timing and form of exit (Wright et al., 1993; Relander, Syrjanen and Miettinen, 1994). Sale to a third party is often the most commonly preferred and actual form of exit. Relander et al., using European evidence, show that although in principle IPOs may be the preferred realization route, in practice sale to a third party is the most common form used, principally because a threshold for an IPO is not reached or because an attractive but unforeseen acquisition proposal is received. Wright et.al. (1993) show that venture capitalists' attitudes to exit are not homogeneous between European countries.[18] Petty, Bygrave and Shulman (1994) examine trade sales as an exit route for US venture capitalists and find that although it provides more immediate full liquidity of an investment than is possible in an IPO, the objectives of the entrepreneur may not be satisfied. Murray (1994a) in a study of exit possibilities from early stage investments shows that venture capitalists rank trade sale as their preferred route with IPO third. Exit by sale to a next stage venture capitalist was ranked only fourth, despite early stage investors' expressed preference for such a form of finance. Murray expresses concern that young, growing firms may be faced by a second equity gap. Such companies may represent rather small acquisitions for trading groups seeking to obtain economies of scale and/or scope, though they may be attractive where purchasers are seeking to gain access to new technology or product innovations.

(ii) *Entrepreneurs' exit and serial recontracting* The existence of entrepreneurs who are exiting from venture capitalists' own portfolios raises interesting theoretical and empirical issues concerning recontracting. To date, the available literature has not addressed this dynamic aspect of venture capital investment. Although the screening literature in section (ii) above refers to previous entrepreneurial experience, it has not directly examined the problems faced by venture capitalists in assessing entrepreneurs who have exited from their own (and indeed others portfolios). As venture capital markets mature, and increasing realization of investments is likely to be followed by exits by entrepreneurs, this would appear to be an area of growing importance.

Studies which have specifically examined cases of habitual entrepreneurship, for example, Birley and Westhead (1994) and Kolvereid and Bullvag (1993) generally find little difference in characteristics and performance between novice and experienced entrepreneurs. Starr and Bygrave (1991) suggest that although there is a danger that experienced entrepreneurs may become fixated on repeating past behaviour, the positive experience of previous entrepreneurial ventures should make it easier to raise start-up financing *per se* and in larger amounts. At the initial investment stage, venture capitalists may be able to negotiate relatively advantageous terms compared to entrepreneurs who are inexperienced in dealing with such situations, using their screening expertise as discussed earlier.[19]

In recontracting with entrepreneurs who have exited from their own portfolio, venture capitalists are potentially faced with a situation in which the entrepreneur is more aware of the effectiveness of the venture capitalist's monitoring and of how (dis)advantageous was the initial contract. Though the skills of the entrepreneur have been revealed to the venture capitalist, at least more so than in the first venture, assumptions about the nature of the entrepreneur's objective function (for example, risk neutral/risk averse) may need to be amended since the outcome of the first project may affect the entrepreneur's motivations about subsequent ones. There is essentially a multi-period game whereby serial entrepreneurs and venture capitalists will seek to change either the invest/not invest decision and/or the nature of the contract in the light of information which has been revealed in the first project. As a result, venture capitalists may be cautious about reinvesting in entrepreneurs from their own portfolios.

Empirical evidence on recontracting with exited entrepreneurs presented by Wright, Robbie and Ennew in Chapter 14 shows that venture capitalists do indeed identify major differences between novice and serial entrepreneurs in the negotiation process as a result of their experience with the venture capital process. With respect to entrepreneurs who have exited from other venture capitalists' portfolios, the contracting problem is more complicated as the entrepreneur now has knowledge about the venture capital negotiating process in general, though not of the venture capitalist to whom an approach is being made for the first time. While venture capitalists may know the entrepreneurs who have exited from their own portfolios, they are still faced by potential adverse selection problems in respect of entrepreneurs exiting from others' portfolios. Hence, venture capitalists may be more cautious about investing in such entrepreneurs because of both contracting problems relating to asymmetric information and the entrepreneur's knowledge of the negotiation process. In general, there would appear to be scope for further theoretical modelling of the recontracting process where venture capitalists are considering reinvestment in serial entrepreneurs.

An understanding of why entrepreneurs may cease to be entrepreneurs also has important implications for venture capitalist's strategies to monitor entrepreneurs post-exit. Ronstadt (1986, 1988) specifically cites evidence which suggests that at least some may have the potential for undertaking further ventures. Whilst this provides general evidence of the reasons for entrepreneurial exit, there is a need to examine more directly the implications for venture capitalists.

Conclusions

This introductory chapter has emphasized the need, as we move into the next millennium, to examine the wider range of investment activities undertaken by venture capital firms which covers early stage through to buy-out type transactions. The chapter has presented an integrated framework for analysing both industry/market and firm levels issues in order to provide a fuller understanding of the full spectrum of venture capital markets.

The discussion presented in the chapter has implications for further research. Although there is considerable work on various aspects of the venture capital process, there is relatively little work at the industry/market level. In this context, further research which analyses aspects of competing and complementary sources of finance appears warranted. There has also been relatively little attention to explicit examination of the inter-linkages between the industry/market and the firm level issues.

There has been considerable focus on venture capitalists' screening processes and on the nature of venture capitalist–investee relationships. However, particular gaps where further research could make an important contribution concern, for example, the modelling of perfect versus imperfect revelation of information at the screening and post-contractual monitoring stages, the costs of information search by the venture capitalist, the development of appropriate forms of managerial and financial control systems, the development and testing of approaches to the valuation of venture capital investment, the use of performance contingent contracts as a means of dealing with asymmetric information, the consequences of venture capitalists not being able to control production if the entrepreneur is replaced, and the development and testing of bargaining models of contract negotiation.

The literature reviewed in this chapter also signals the beginnings of a broadening out of the conceptual underpinnings of both venture capital and buy-outs which emphasizes the restrictiveness of the principal–agent approach. The recent development of procedural justice and game theoretic-based approaches provide potentially important additions to the theoretical framework for analysing the role of venture capitalists. Similarly, the application of entrepreneurial and transactions cost-based theories to the study of buy-outs provides insights which are not available from a principal–agent perspective. Further research is required which both develops the differences and complementarities between various theoretical insights and also provides empirical tests of the relative explanatory power of these approaches.

Three particular features of current developments in practice also stand out as having important implications for the next millennium. First, changing pressures on funds providers and transparency of evidence on venture capital returns have important implications for the future monitoring of venture capital firms by their funds providers. Second, changes in funding availability and other aspects of the behaviour of venture capital firms have important implications for the syndication of financing in venture capital investments. Third, the dynamic and maturing nature of venture capital markets introduces issues concerning recontracting by venture capitalists with entrepreneurs in whom they have previously invested. Although some research is beginning to appear in these areas, none of these aspects of venture capital markets is as yet well understood.

Consideration of the above issues appears to be an important aspect of the future research agenda given the dynamic nature of venture capital markets and the implications for the behaviour of venture capital firms. Differences between venture capital markets in individual countries also stress the future importance of international comparative studies. The contributions in this volume represent initial attempts to address a number of these issues facing practitioners in both developed and developing venture capital markets.

Notes

1. Prior to this more recent substantial market growth it needs to be borne in mind that the world's largest venture capital institution, 3i, based in the UK has, however, been investing since the mid-1940s (Coopey and Clarke, 1995) whilst Charterhouse and other banks provided venture capital at least a decade earlier.
2. This can lead, for example, to an overemphasis on equity stakes by entrepreneurs with the venture capitalist making counter-balancing adjustments in other aspects of the contract that an inexperienced entrepreneur may not fully appreciate, and to insufficient search on the part of the entrepreneur for an appropriate venture capitalist. This is consistent with notions that entrepreneurs finding themselves in unfamiliar situations under-search for information as they fail to appreciate fully the issues involved or their complexity.
3. This is particularly an issue in the recent development of investor-led buy-outs (IBOs) where venture capitalists are proactive in seeking and completing deals. While this may to some extent reduce the power of incumbent entrepreneurs/managers in obtaining large equity stakes from the venture capitalist, venture capitalists are faced with potential problems arising from paying higher prices to invest and asymmetric information problems where they may have full unbiased information on the investee (see Wright and Robbie, 1996b for discussion).
4. Different types of business angels can be identified according to their behaviour and characteristics (see, for example, Harrison and Mason, 1992).
5. It is not clear, however, how representative these studies are. For example, 'more informed' informal investors may utilize their links with banks to identify investment opportunities rather

than using 'marriage bureaux' and such entrepreneurs may therefore not be fully represented in these studies.

6. Wright and Robbie (1996a) who examined only formal venture capitalists also find a high degree of importance is attached to own due diligence.
7. Though the LBO industry in the US is typically seen to be distinct from the venture capital industry, venture capitalists are extensively involved in funding buy-outs especially smaller ones (see, for example, Malone, 1989). In the UK, there is probably much greater overlap between venture capitalists and what may be seen as LBO Associations (Wright, Thompson and Robbie, 1996). Moreover, although there has been some reference to the rehabilitation of the US LBO post the problems of the late 1980s this has been a much stronger and persistent feature of the UK buy-out market where venture capitalists play a significant role. Venture capital widens the emerging literature on corporate restructuring which has hitherto tended to focus on debt forms of finance (Jensen, 1993), in particular in relation to the balance between the reduction of agency costs and the stimulation of growth and entrepreneurial actions. Although the corporate restructuring debate has tended to emphasize the former, there is evidence that a large number of management buy-outs in both the US and the UK make extensive use of venture capital and engage in significant R&D and investment expenditure (see, for example, Zahra, 1995; Wright, Thompson and Robbie, 1992).
8. For example, in the UK management buy-out market, venture capitalists are involved in funding around a half of smaller transactions, with banks fully funding the rest (Wright and Robbie, 1995).
9. Hustedde and Pulver (1992) examine the important roles of different types of intermediaries in securing venture capital funds for their clients and finds that entrepreneurs who failed to seek advice had a significantly lower chance of success.
10. In this respect, venture capital has an important contribution to make to the corporate governance debate as the involvement of venture capitalists in investee companies has implications for both performance and accountability simultaneously (Lorenz, 1989). Sykes (1994) also draws attention to the contribution that active investors in MBOs may have to the corporate governance debate.
11. Performance may be in terms of profits over a given period, market value on flotation, and so on. Flotation at a date prior to that expected in the ratchet contract may provoke disputes about the extra amount of equity to which management are entitled where a sliding scale operates.
12. This parallels other behavioural research relating to the link between job satisfaction and performance.
13. See Lerner (1994a) for discussion of syndication of venture capital investments.
14. This issue also raises further governance problems in relation to conflicts between venture capitalists and their investors.
15. Evidence from IPOs of buy-outs in the UK also indicates a marked increase in activity at times of market buoyancy (see Wright and Robbie, 1995).
16. Parallel evidence from reverse LBOs (DeGeorge and Zeckhauser, 1993) shows they outperform comparable firms in terms of operating profitability pre-flotation but not post; a finding consistent with the view that managers and their institutional supporters wait for a good year before coming to market. However, evidence that despite this change in relative performance reverse LBOs do not underperform the share price of non-LBOs suggests that the market anticipates such a change.
17. Estimation risk has transitory and permanent components. The former may be eliminated as more information becomes available while the latter is due to the random nature of asset return parameters.
18. However, it is worth emphasizing that 40 per cent of IPOs in the UK in the period 7/92 to 12/95 were venture capital-financed companies according to the British Venture Capital Association.
19. Although some entrepreneurs mitigate this problem with the use of intermediaries, there is evidence to suggest that intermediaries become involved at a late stage, especially in smaller transactions (Murray et al., 1995).

References

Abbott, S. and M. Hay (1995), *Investing for the Future*, London: FT-Pitman.

Admati, A. and P. Pfleiderer (1994), 'Robust financial contracting and the role of venture capitalists', *Journal of Finance*, 371–402.

Amit R., L. Glosten and E. Muller (1990a), 'Entrepreneurial ability, venture investments and risk sharing', *Management Science*, 1232–45.

Amit, R., L. Glosten and E. Muller (1990b), 'Does venture capital foster the most promising entrepreneurial firms?', *California Management Review*, **32** (3), 102–11.

Baker, G. and K. Wruck (1989), 'Organizational change and value creation in leveraged buyouts: The case of O.M. Scott & Sons Company', *Journal of Financial Economics*, **25** (2), 163–90.

Barney, J., L. Busenitz, J. Fiet and D. Moesel (1989), 'The structure of venture capital governance: an organisational economic analysis of relations between venture capital firms and new ventures', *Academy of Management Proceedings*, 64–8.

Barry, C. (1994), 'New directions in research on venture capital finance', *Financial Management*, **23** (3), 3–15.

Barry, C., C. Muscarella, J. Peavy and M. Vetsuypens (1990), 'The role of venture capitalists in the creation of public companies: evidence from the going public process', *Journal of Financial Economics*, **27**, 447–71.

Beecroft A. (1994) 'The role of the venture capital industry in the UK' in N. Dimsdale and M. Prevezer (eds), *Capital Markets and Corporate Governance*, Oxford: OUP, 195–208.

Birley, S. and P. Westhead (1994), 'A comparison of new businesses established by "novice" and "habitual" founders in Great Britain', *International Small Business Journal*, **12** (1), 38–60.

Block, Z. and I. MacMillan (1993), *Corporate Venturing*, Boston, MA: Harvard Business School Press.

Bradley, K. and A. Nejad (1989), *Managing Owners – The NFC Buy-out*, Cambridge: Cambridge University Press.

Brealey, R. and S. Myers (1996), *Principles of Corporate Finance*, 5th edition, New York: McGraw-Hill.

Bruno, A. (1986), 'A structural analysis of the venture capital industry', in D. Sexton and R. Smilor (eds), *The Art and Science of Entrepreneurship*, Cambridge: Ballinger.

Bruno, A. and T. Tyebjee (1985), 'The entrepreneur's search for capital', *Journal of Business Venturing*, **1**, 61–74.

BVCA (1997), *Report on Investment Activity 1996*, London: BVCA.

Bygrave, W. and J. Timmons (1992), *Venture Capital at the Crossroads*, Boston, MA: Harvard Business School Press.

Bygrave, W. (1988), 'The structure of investment networks of venture capital firms', *Journal of Business Venturing*, **3**, 137–57.

Cable, D. and S. Shane (1997), 'A prisoner's dilemma approach to entrepreneur–venture capitalist relationships', *Academy of Management Review*, **22** (1), 142–76.

CMBOR (1997), Trends in management buy-outs', *Management Buy-outs – Quarterly Review from CMBOR*, CMBOR, University of Nottingham, Spring.

Chan, Y., D. Siegel and A. Thakor (1990), 'Learning, corporate control and performance requirements in venture capital contracts', *International Economic Review*, **31** (2), 365–81.

Chiplin, B., K. Robbie and M. Wright (1997), 'The syndication of venture capital deals: buy-outs and buy-ins', paper presented at Babson Entrepreneurship Conference, Babson College, Wellesley, MA, April.

Chua, J. and R. Woodward (1993), 'Splitting the firm between the entrepreneur and the venture capitalist with the help of stock options', *Journal of Business Venturing*, **8** (1), 43–58.

Citron, D., K. Robbie and M. Wright (1997), 'Debt covenants in UK MBOs', *Accounting and Business Research*, forthcoming.

Cooper, I. and C. Carleton (1979), 'Dynamics of borrower–lender interaction: partitioning final payoff in venture capital finance', *Journal of Finance*, **34** (2), 517–29.

Coopey, R. and D. Clarke (1995), *3i-Fifty Years Investing in Industry*, Oxford: Oxford University Press.

DeAngelo, L. (1990), 'Equity valuation and corporate control', *Accounting Review*, **65** (1), 93–112.

DeGeorge, F. and R. Zeckhauser (1993), 'The reverse LBO decision and firm performance: theory and evidence', *Journal of Finance*, **48** (4),1323–49.

De Meza, D. and D. Webb (1987), 'Too much investment: a problem of asymmetric information', *Quarterly Journal of Economics*, **102**, 281–92.

Denis, D. (1994), 'Organizational form and the consequences of highly leveraged transactions: Kroger's recapitalization and Safeway's LBO', *Journal of Financial Economics*, **36** (2),193–224.

Dixon, R. (1991), 'Venture capitalists and the appraisal of investments', *Omega*, **19** (5), 333–44.

Ehrlich, S., A. DeNoble, T. Moore and R. Weaver (1994), 'After the cash arrives: a comparative study of venture capital and private investor involvement in entrepreneurial firms', *Journal of Business Venturing*, **9**, 67–82.

Elango, B., V. Fried, R. Hisrich and A. Polonchek (1995), 'How venture capital firms differ', *Journal of Business Venturing*, **10** (2), 157–79.

Ennew, C., M. Wright, K. Robbie and S. Thompson (1994), 'Small business entrepreneurs and performance: evidence from management buy-ins', *International Journal of Small Business*, **12** (4), 28–44.

Ennew, C. and M. Binks (1995), 'The provision of finance to small business: does the banking relationship constrain performance', *Journal of Small Business Finance*, **4** (1), 69–85.

EVCA (1995), *EVCA Yearbook 1995*, Zaventem: European Venture Capital Association.

Fiet, J. (1995a), 'Risk avoidance strategies in venture capital markets', *Journal of Management Studies*, **32** (4), 551–74.

Fiet, J. (1995b), 'Reliance on informants in the venture capital industry', *Journal of Business Venturing*, **10** (3), 195–223.

Fiet, J., L. Busenitz, D. Moesel and J. Barney (1997), 'Complementary theoretical perspectives on the dismissal of new venture teams', *Journal of Business Venturing*, **12** (5), 347–66.

Freear, J. and W. Wetzel (1990), 'Who bankrolls high-tech entrepreneurs?', *Journal of Business Venturing*, **5**, 77–90.

Fried, V. and R. Hisrich (1994), 'Towards a model of venture capital investment decision making', *Financial Management*, **23** (3), 28–37.

Fried, V. and R. Hisrich (1995), 'The venture capitalist: a relationship investor', *California Management Review*, **37** (2), 101–13.

Fried, V., R. Hisrich and A. Polonchek (1993), 'Research note: venture capitalists' investment criteria: a replication', *Journal of Small Business Finance*, **3** (1), 37–42.

Gompers, P. (1995), 'Optimal investment, monitoring, and the staging of venture capital', *Journal of Finance*, **50** (5), 1461–89.

Gompers, P. and J. Lerner (1996), 'The use of covenants: an empirical analysis of venture partnership agreements', *Journal of Law and Economics*, **39** (2), 463–98.

Gompers, P. and J. Lerner (1997), 'The valuation of private equity investments', *Harvard Business School*, mimeo.

Haar, N., J. Starr and I. MacMillan (1988), 'Informal risk capital investors: investment patterns on the east coast of the USA', *Journal of Business Venturing*, **3**, 11–29.

Hall, J. and C. Hofer (1993), 'Venture capitalists' decision criteria in new venture evaluation', *Journal of Business Venturing*, **8**, 25–42.

Harlow, W. and J. Howe (1993), 'Leveraged buy-outs and insider nontrading', *Financial Management*, **22** (1), 109–18.

Harrison, R. and C. Mason (1992), 'International perspectives on the supply of informal venture capital', *Journal of Business Venturing*, **7**, 459–75.

Harvey, M. and R. Lusch (1995), 'Expanding the nature and scope of due diligence', *Journal of Business Venturing*, **10**, 5–21.

Hatherly, D., F. Mitchell and J. Innes (1994), 'An exploration of the MBO–financier relationship', *Corporate Governance*, **2** (1), 20–29.

Holland, J. (1994), 'Bank lending relationships and the complex nature of bank–corporate relations', *Journal of Business Finance and Accounting*, **21** (3), 367–93.

Hustedde, R. and G. Pulver (1992), 'Factors affecting equity capital acquisition: the demand side', *Journal of Business Venturing*, **7** (5), 363–80.

Ibbotson, R., J. Sindelar and J. Ritter (1988), 'Initial public offerings', *Journal of Applied Corporate Finance*, Summer, **1**, 37–45.

Jain, B. and O. Kini (1995), 'Venture capitalist participation and the post-issue operating performance of IPO firms', *Managerial and Decision Economics*, **16** (6), 593–606.

Jensen, M.C. and W. Meckling (1976), 'The theory of the firm: managerial behavior, agency costs and ownership structure', *Journal of Financial Economics*, **3**, 305–60.
Jensen, M.C. (1993) 'The modern industrial revolution: exit, and the failure of internal control systems', *Journal of Finance*, **48**, 831–80
Jones, T. and R. Hunt (1991), 'The ethics of leveraged management buyouts revisited', *Journal of Business Ethics*, **10** (11), 833–40.
Kaplan, S.N. (1991), 'The staying power of leveraged buyouts', *Journal of Financial Economics*, **29**, 287–313.
Kaplan, S.N. and J. Stein (1993), 'The evolution of buyout pricing and financial structure in the 1990s', *Quarterly Journal of Economics*, **108**, 313–57.
Keeley, R. and L. Turki (1995), 'A venture capital price index', in W. Bygrave et al. (eds), *Frontiers of Entrepreneurship Research*, Wellesley, MA: Babson College, pp. 381–93.
Kets de Vries, M.F.R. (1977), 'The entrepreneurial personality: a person at the crossroads', *Journal of Management Studies*, **14**, 33–55.
Kolvereid, L. and E. Bullvag (1993), 'Novices versus experienced founders: an exploratory investigation', in S. Birley and I. MacMillan (eds), *Entrepreneurship Research: Global Perspectives*, New York: Elsevier Science Publishers, pp. 275–85.
Korsgaard, M., D. Schweiger and H. Sapienza (1995), 'The role of procedural justice in building commitment, attachment and trust in strategic decision-making teams', *Academy of Management Journal*, **38**, 60–84.
Lam, S. (1991), 'Venture capital financing: a conceptual framework', *Journal of Business Finance and Accounting*, **18** (2), 137–49.
Landstrom, H. (1992), 'The relationship between private individuals and small firms: an agency theory approach', *Entrepreneurship and Regional Development*, **4**, 199–223.
Landstrom, H. (1993), 'Informal risk capital in Sweden and some international comparisons', *Journal of Business Venturing*, **8**, 525–40.
Lerner, J. (1994a), 'The syndication of venture capital investments', *Financial Management*, **23** (3), 16–27.
Lerner, J. (1994b), 'Venture capitalists and the decision to go public', *Journal of Financial Economics*, **35**, 293–316.
Lerner, J. (1995), 'Venture capitalists and the oversight of private firms', *Journal of Finance*, **50** (1), 301–18.
Lichtenberg, F. and D. Siegel (1990), 'The effects of leveraged buy-outs on productivity and related aspects of firm behavior', *Journal of Financial Economics*, **27** (1), 165–94.
Long, R. (1978), 'The relative effects of share ownership vs. control on job attitudes in an employee owned company', *Human Relations*, **31**, 753–63.
Lorenz, T. (1989), *Venture Capital Today*, 2nd edition, Cambridge: Woodhead-Faulkner.
Lowenstein, L. (1985), 'Management buyouts', *Columbia Law Review*, **85**, 730–84.
MacMillan I., D. Kulow and R. Khoylian (1989), 'Venture capitalists involvement in their investments: extent and performance', *Journal of Business Venturing*, **4**, 27–47.
MacMillan, I.C., R. Siegel and P.N.S. Subbanarasimha (1985), 'Criteria used by venture capitalists to evaluate new venture proposals', *Journal of Business Venturing*, **1**, (1), 119–28.
MacMillan, I.C., L. Zemann and P.N.S. Subbanarasimha (1987), 'Criteria distinguishing successful from unsuccessful ventures in the venture screening process', *Journal of Business Venturing*, **3**, 123–37.
Malone, S. (1989), 'Characteristics of smaller company leveraged buy-outs', *Journal of Business Venturing*, **4**, 349–59.
Manigart, S. (1994), 'What drives the creation of a venture capital firm', *Journal of Business Venturing*, **9**, 525–41.
McNally, K. (1994), 'Sources of finance for UK venture capital funds: the role of corporate investors', *Entrepreneurship and Regional Development*, **6**, 275–97.
Megginson, W. and K. Weiss (1991), 'Venture capitalist certification in initial public offerings', *Journal of Finance*, **45**, 879–903.
Mitchell, F., G. Reid and N. Terry (1995), 'Post investment demand for accounting information by venture capitalists', *Accounting and Business Research*, **25** (99), 186–96.
Murray, G. (1991), *Change and Maturity in the UK Venture Capital Industry 1991–95*, London: BVCA.

Murray, G. (1994a), 'The second equity gap: exit problems for seed and early stage venture capitalists and their investee companies', *International Small Business Journal*, **12** (4), 59–76.

Murray, G. (1994b), 'The European Union's support for new technology-based firms: an assessment of the first three years of the European seed capital fund', *European Planning Studies*, **2** (4), 435–61.

Murray, G. (1995), 'The UK venture capital industry', *Journal of Business Finance and Accounting*, **22** (8), 1077–106.

Murray, G. and J. Lott, J (1995), 'Have venture capitalists a bias against investment in new technology firms', *Research Policy*, **24**, 283–99.

Murray, G., B. Nixon K. Robbie and M. Wright (1995), 'Managements' search for venture capital in smaller buy-outs and the role of intermediaries', Paper presented at 6th EFER Conference, Ghent, Belgium, November.

Muzyka, D., S. Birley and B. Leleux, B (1995),'Trade-offs in the investment decisions of European venture capitalists', *Journal of Business Venturing*, forthcoming.

Norton, E. and B. Tenenbaum (1992), 'Factors affecting the structure of venture capital deals', *Journal of Small Business Management*, **30** (3), 20–29.

Norton, E. and B. Tenenbaum (1993a), 'The effects of venture capitalists' characteristics on the structure of the venture capital deal', *Journal of Small Business Management*, **31** (4), 32–41.

Ooghe, H., S. Manigart and Y. Fassin (1991), 'Growth patterns in the European venture capital industry', *Journal of Business Venturing*, **6**, 381–404.

Pendleton, A., N. Wilson and M. Wright (1997), 'The perception and effects of share ownership: empirical evidence from employee buy-outs', University of Bradford Management Centre, mimeo.

Petty, J., W. Bygrave and J. Shulman (1994), 'Harvesting the entrepreneurial venture: a time for creating value', *Journal of Applied Corporate Finance*, **6**, 8–58.

Phan, P. and C. Hill (1995), 'Organizational restructuring and economic performance in leveraged buy-outs: an ex post study', *Academy of Management Journal*, **38**, (3), 704–39.

Rah, J., K. Jung and J. Lee (1994), 'Validation of the venture evaluation model in Korea', *Journal of Business Venturing*, **9**, 509–24.

Rappaport, A. (1990), 'The staying power of the public corporation', *Harvard Business Review*, **68** (1), 96–104.

Reid, G., N. Terry and J. Smith (1995), 'Risk management in venture capital investor–investee relations', Paper presented at ESRC Conference on Risk in Organisational Settings, University of York.

Relander, K.-E., A.-P. Syrjanen and A. Miettinen (1994), 'Analysis of the trade sale as a venture capital exit route', in W. Bygrave, M. Hay and J. Peeters (eds), *Realizing Investment Value*, London: FT-Pitman, pp. 132–62.

Robbie, K. and M. Wright (1996), *Management Buy-ins: Entrepreneurship, Active Investors and Corporate Restructuring*, Manchester: Manchester University Press.

Robbie K., M. Wright and S. Thompson (1992), 'Management buy-ins in the UK', *Omega*, **20**, 445–56.

Ronstadt, R. (1986), 'Exit stage left: Why entrepreneurs end their entrepreneurial careers before retirement', *Journal of Business Venturing*, **1**, 323–38.

Ronstadt, R. (1988), 'The corridor principle', *Journal of Business Venturing*, **3**, 31–40.

Rosenstein, J., A. Bruno, W. Bygrave and N. Taylor (1993), 'The CEO, venture capitalists and the board', *Journal of Business Venturing*, **8** (2), 99–114.

Roure, J., R. Keeley and T. van der Heyden (1990), 'European venture capital: strategies and challenges in the 90s', *European Management Journal*, **8** (2), 243–52.

Ruhnka, J., H. Feldman and T. Dean (1992), 'The "living dead" phenomenon in venture capital investments', *Journal of Business Venturing*, **7** (2),137–56.

Sahlman, W.A. (1990), 'The structure and governance of venture-capital organizations', *Journal of Financial Economics*, **27**, 473–521

Sapienza, H. (1992), 'When do venture capitalists add value?', *Journal of Business Venturing*, **7**, 9–27.

Sapienza, H. and A. Gupta (1994), 'Impact of agency risks and task uncertainty on venture capitalist-CEO interaction', *Academy of Management Journal*, **37** (6),1618–32.

Sapienza, H. and M. Korsgaard (1996), 'Procedural justice in entrepreneur–investor relations', *Academy of Management Journal*, **39** (3), 544–74.
Sapienza, H., S. Manigart and W. Vermeir (1996), 'Venture capitalist governance and value added in four countries', *Journal of Business Venturing*, **11**, 439–69.
Shleifer, A. and R. Vishny (1992), 'Liquidation values and debt capacity: a market equilibrium approach', *Journal of Finance*, **47** (4), 1343–66.
Starr, J. and W. Bygrave (1991), 'The assets and liabilities of prior start-up experience: an exploratory study of multiple venture entrepreneurs' in N. Churchill et al. (eds), *Frontiers of Entrepreneurship Research 1991*, Wellesley, MA: Babson College.
Stiglitz, J. and A. Weiss (1981), 'Credit rationing in markets with imperfect information', *American Economic Review*, **71**, June, 393–410.
Sweeting, R. (1991a), 'Early-stage new technology-based businesses: interactions with venture capitalists and the development of accounting techniques and procedures', *British Accounting Review*, **23**, 3–21
Sweeting, R. (1991b), 'UK venture capital funds and the funding of new technology based businesses: process and relationships', *Journal of Management Studies*, **28**, 601–22.
Sykes, A. (1994), 'Proposals for internationally competitive corporate governance in Britain and America', *Corporate Governance*, **2** (4), 187–95.
Thompson, S. and M. Wright (1991), 'UK management buy-outs: debt, equity and agency cost implications', *Managerial and Decision Economics*, **12** (1),15–26.
Thompson, S., M. Wright and K. Robbie (1992), 'Management equity ownership, debt and performance: some evidence from UK management buy-outs', *Scottish Journal of Political Economy*, **39** (4), 413–30.
Tyebjee, T. and A. Bruno (1984), 'A model of venture capitalist investment activity', *Management Science*, **30** (9), 1051–66.
Tyebjee, T. and L. Vickery (1988), 'Venture capital in Western Europe', *Journal of Business Venturing*, **3**, 123–36.
Woo, C., A. Cooper and W. Dunkelberg (1991), 'The development and interpretation of entrepreneurial typologies', *Journal of Business Venturing*, **6**, 93–114.
Wright, M (1986), 'The make–buy decision and managing markets: the case of management buy-outs', *Journal of Management Studies*, **23** (4), 434–53.
Wright, M. and J. Coyne (1985), *Management Buy-outs*, Beckenham: Croom-Helm.
Wright, M. and K. Robbie (1995), 'Managerial and ownership succession and corporate restructuring: the case of management buy-ins', *Journal of Management Studies*, **32**, 527–50.
Wright, M. and K. Robbie (1996a), 'Venture capitalists and unquoted equity investment appraisal', *Accounting and Business Research*, **26** (2), 153–70.
Wright, M. and K. Robbie (1996b), 'The investor-led buy-outs: a new strategic option', *Long Range Planning*, **29** (5), 691–702.
Wright M., S. Thompson and K. Robbie (1992), 'Venture capital and management-led leveraged buy-outs: a European perspective', *Journal of Business Venturing*, **7**, 47–71.
Wright, M., K. Robbie, S. Thompson, Y. Romanet, R. Joachimsson, J. Bruining and A. Herst (1993), 'Harvesting and the longevity of management buy-outs and buy-ins: a four country study', *Entrepreneurship: Theory and Practice*, **18** (2), 89–110.
Wright, M., S. Thompson and K. Robbie (1993), 'Finance, accountability and control in privatisation by management buy-out', *Financial Accountability and Management*, **9** (2), 75–99.
Wright, M., K. Robbie, S. Thompson and K. Starkey (1994), 'Longevity and the life cycle of MBOs', *Strategic Management Journal*, **15**, 215–27.
Wright, M., S. Thompson, K. Robbie and P. Wong (1995), 'Management buy-outs in the short and long term', *Journal of Business Finance and Accounting*, **22** (4), 461–82.
Wright, M., S. Thompson and K. Robbie (1996), 'Buy-ins, buy-outs, active investors and corporate governance', *Corporate Governance*, **4** (4), 222–34.
Wright, M., J. Dial and R. Hoskisson (1997), 'A multi-theoretic perspective on leveraged buyouts', Texas A&M University, mimeo.
Wright, M., K. Robbie and C. Ennew (1997), 'Venture capitalists and second time entrepreneurs', *Journal of Business Venturing*, **12** (3), 227–49.
Zahra, S. 1995, 'Corporate entrepreneurship and financial performance: the case of management leveraged buy-outs', *Journal of Business Venturing*, **10** (3), 225–47.

2. Venture capital: predictions and outcomes. *Venture Capital at the Crossroads* and *Realizing Investment Value* revisited

William D. Bygrave and Jeffry Timmons

Introduction

In keeping with the theme 'Venture Capital and Management Buy-outs into the Next Millennium', we will examine the predictions and prescriptions for the professional venture capital industry that we made earlier in the 1990s. Those predictions were published in two books, *Venture Capital at the Crossroads* (Bygrave and Timmons, 1992) and *Realizing Investment Value* (Bygrave, Hay and Peeters, 1994). The first book was the culmination of ten years of research into the US venture capital industry. The second book resulted from a 1992 conference, 'Realizing Enterprise Value: IPOs, Trade Sales, Buybacks, MBOs and Harvests' that was organized by the European Foundation for Entrepreneurship Research (EFER). In this chapter, we will examine what we predicted and prescribed for the US venture capital industry, and what we were brash enough to recommend for Europe.

Venture Capital at the Crossroads

When we embarked at the start of the 1980s upon our concerted research into the US venture capital, the industry was shrouded in secrecy and replete with folklore. For example, two of the most widely held beliefs were that the annual return rate on venture capital was 40 per cent or higher, and that by far the most important influence on the flows of venture capital was a favorable capital gains tax.

Venture Economics has data on the US venture capital industry that goes back to the late 1960s.[1] By accessing that historical data and tracking new data as the industry evolved throughout the 1950s, we were able to analyze longitudinal data sets spanning 20 years. Over that period the industry went from being red-hot at the end of the 1960s to almost an ember by 1974; it rekindled in the late 1970s until it was white hot by 1983; then from 1987 it began to cool off.

There were many factors that could have influenced the flows of venture capital (Figure 2.1). Among the more important ones were changes in public policy, including income tax, interest rates, pension fund regulations, and Securities Exchange Commission (SEC) rules; the health of public stock markets, especially

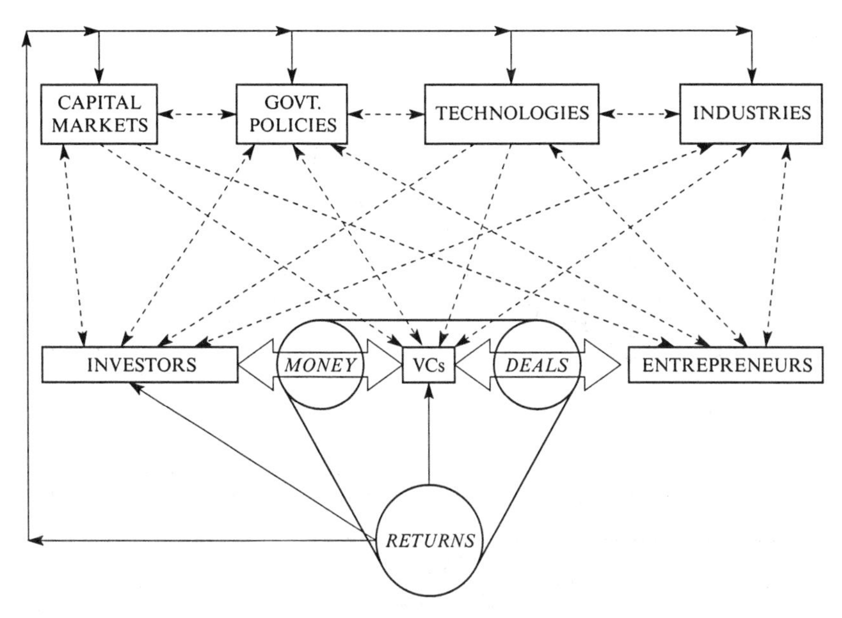

Figure 2.1 Factors influencing the flows of venture capital

the National Association of Securities Dealers Automated Quotations (NASDAQ) market for small-cap flotations; commercialization of new technologies such as personal computers, biotechnology, and communications; and fundamental changes in the structure of some existing industries, for example, deregulation of the telephone and airline industries. All those factors influence the financial return, which of course is the ultimate influence on the flows of venture capital (Figure 2.1).

Actual rates of return on US venture capital (Figure 2.2) peaked in 1983 and then declined for the remainder of the 1980s. The top quartile of funds actually peaked briefly above the folklore return of 40 per cent, and the capital-weighted average of all funds peaked slightly above 30 per cent. Unfortunately, returns slipped from those peaks to low teens and single digits by 1989. We found there was a very close correlation between those returns and the return on small cap stocks. In Figure 2.3, we have plotted the difference between the returns on NASDAQ small-cap stocks and Standard & Poor (S&P) 500 stocks held for a ten-year period. We chose a ten-year period because most venture capital is invested in ten-year limited partnerships. On the same graph we have plotted the returns of the top quartile of venture capital funds. It shows that from 1974 through 1989 there was a very strong correlation between performance of small-cap stocks and the returns of venture capital. That is because the preferred harvest for a venture capitalist is an initial public offering of a portfolio

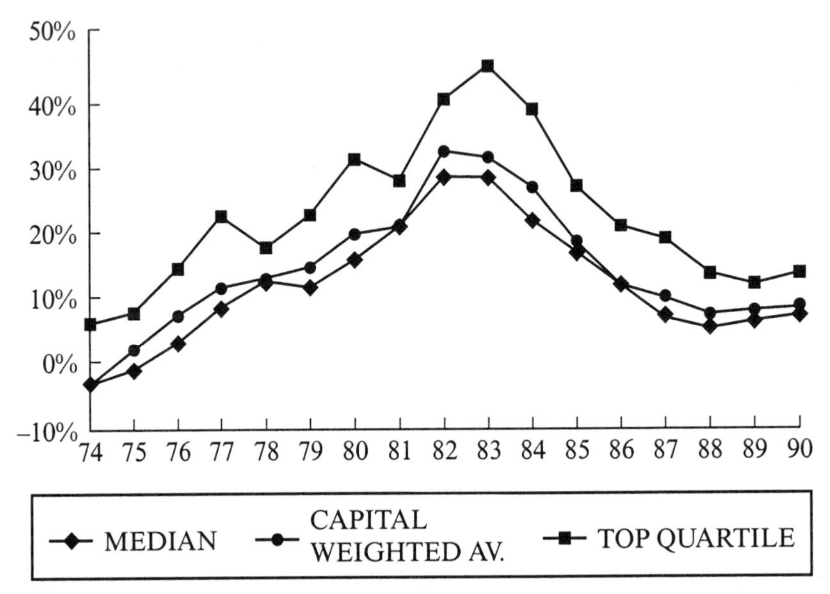

Source: Venture Economics.

Figure 2.2 Overall rates of return

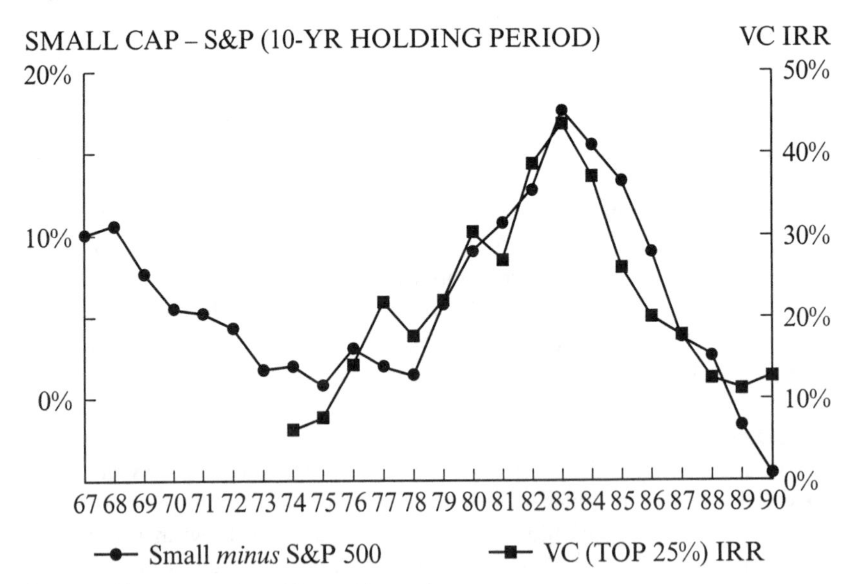

Source: Ibbotson Associates: Venture Economics.

Figure 2.3 Small-cap minus S&P 500 venture capital returns

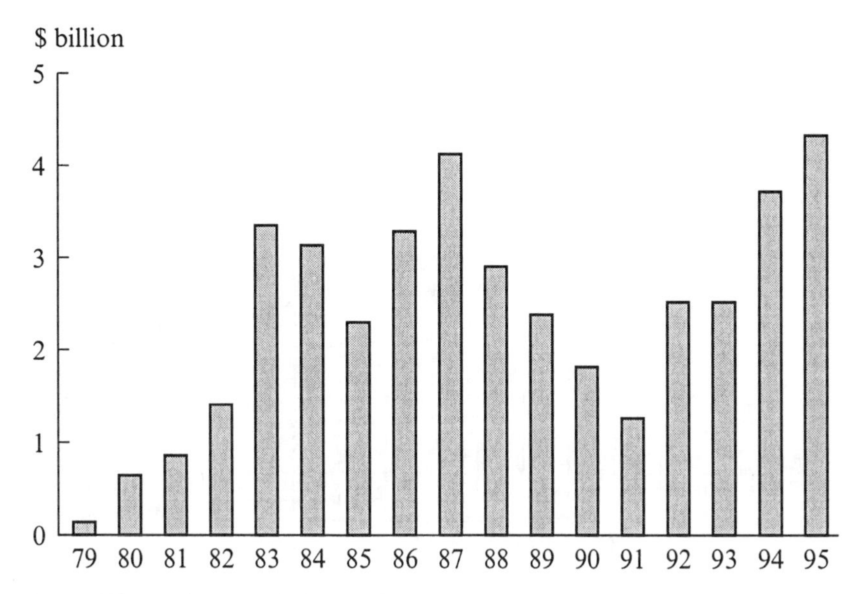

Note: VC commitments excluding SBI family groups, and corporate affiliates.

Source: Venture Economics.

Figure 2.4 *USA venture capital commitments to independent private funds*

company. The offering is almost always made on the NASDAQ market, so when the NASDAQ small-cap market is strong, it is easier to float an IPO and – what's more – at a higher offering price than when it is weak.

When we were writing *Venture Capital at the Crossroads* in 1990–1991, the venture capital industry in the USA was in the doldrums. The decline of the returns to the limited partners that had invested in venture capital funds had taken their toll. Commitments of new money to venture capital funds, which had grown rapidly in the early 1980s, peaked in 1987 at more than $4.2 billion, and then steadily declined to $1.3 billion in 1991 (Figure 2.4); and over the same period venture capital disbursements to portfolio companies declined from $4.0 billion to $1.4 billion (Figure 2.5). The total number of portfolio companies receiving venture capital dropped from 1740 in 1987 to 792 in 1991. The drop in the number of new portfolio companies – that is companies receiving venture capital for the first time – was more steep; 712 in 1987 compared with 173 in 1991 (Figure 2.6). But what was causing the most concern was the precipitous dive in the number of seed-stage and early-stage investments from 384 in 1997 to 126 in 1991.

As we looked ahead in 1991, this is what we predicted for venture capital in the decade of the 1990s.

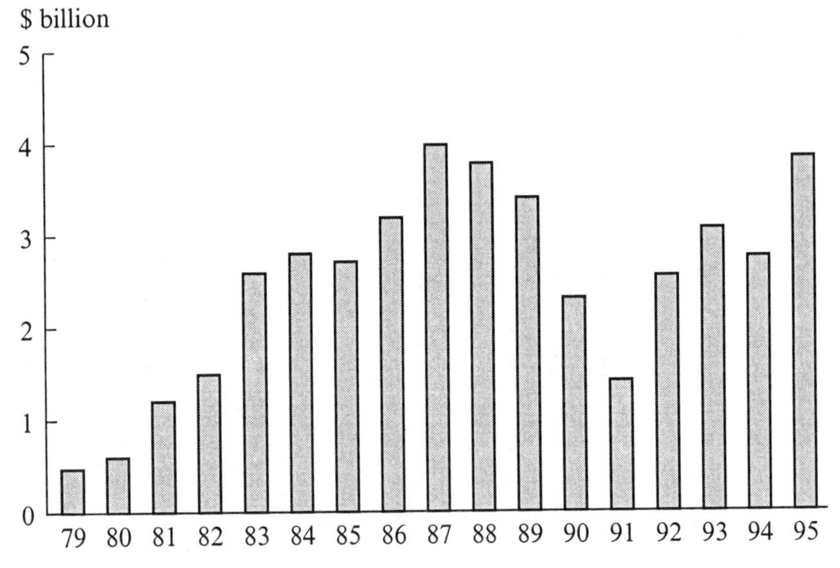

Source: Venture Economics.

Figure 2.5 Venture capital disbursements to portfolio companies

- In the USA, a white-hot IPO market will be needed to restore returns to acceptable levels.
- On average, about 140 venture-capital-backed IPOs per year will be necessary for healthy returns if the annual number of first-round investments stays approximately level.
- Market mechanisms will cull underperformers from the industry. The US shake-out will end by the mid-1990s, with about 40 or so top performers earning returns higher than 20 per cent.
- Mergers with strategic partners – like those pioneered by biotechnology companies – will become the harvest of choice because IPO markets are too unpredictable.
- More and more, seed-stage companies will be built with the intent of merging with giant corporations rather than going public. As a result, they will concentrate on building R&D assets rather than quickly generating revenue and profits.
- The 1980s style of merchant capital will steadily lose ground to creative financial strategies and alternative sources of capital.
- Increasingly well-informed entrepreneurs will seek only the 50 to 75 venture capital firms known for value-added skills and a commitment to structuring deals in ways that equitably share the risks and rewards with management.

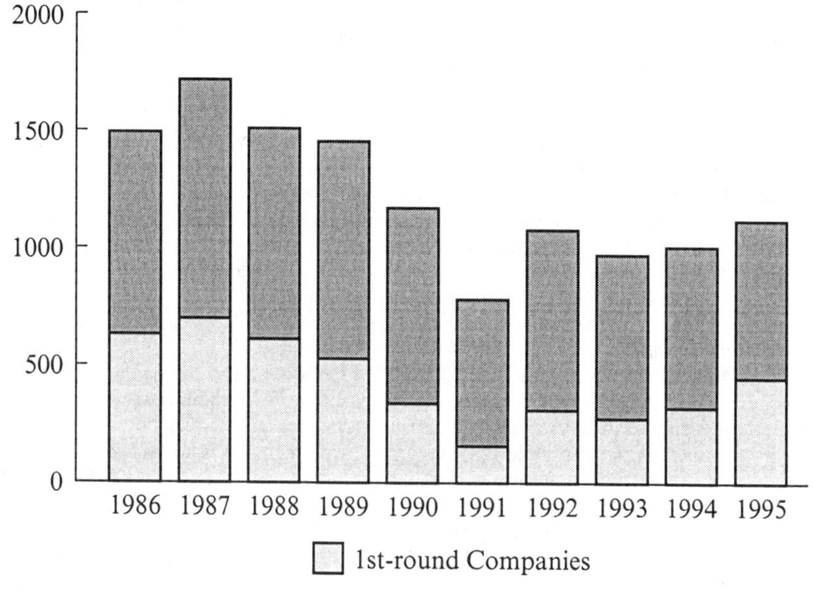

Source: Venture Economics.

Figure 2.6 Companies receiving venture capital: total number of companies

- A new technology wave (parallel to the microprocessor and biotechnology wave of the late 1970s and early 1980s) will precipitate a surge in early-stage and startup investing.
- Competition for deals, capital, and venture capital know-how will become global.
- The US industry with $45 to $50 billion under management will rank third behind Europe and Japan.
- A shake-out will begin in the European venture capital industry that will mirror what happened in the USA five or so years earlier.
- A unique form of venture capital will emerge in the post-communist European nations with links to western venture capital and investment banking, especially in Germany.

Realizing Investment Value

In 1992, soon after the publication of *Venture Capital at the Crossroads* one of the authors spent a year in Europe at INSEAD. The European venture capital industry was concerned about the paucity of venture-capital-backed IPOs on the national second-tier markets. The author led an eight-nation European study of venture-capital-backed entrepreneurs' attitudes towards different forms of exit. Simultaneously, a conference was held at the London Business School in

December 1992 to examine exit mechanisms in Europe. The work presented at that conference was the basis for *Realizing Investment Value*. Here is what we wrote in the introduction to that book:

> One of Britain's leading venture capitalists recently stated that liquidity of funds is the biggest issue facing the European venture capital industry in 1993 (Onians 1993). To be precise, it is illiquidity that has become a major concern as opportunities for successful exits of venture capital investments have become less abundant in Europe. Nowhere is that more apparent than for flotations. With the major European secondary stock markets in the doldrums, initial public stock offerings by venture-capital-backed companies – indeed, by small and medium-sized enterprises in general – are relatively infrequent. Hence, perhaps the most important issue facing not only venture capitalists but all investors in private businesses is how can they realize the value in their investments?
>
> The organized venture capital industry in Europe is not much more than ten years old; in contrast the US industry is just three years short of its 50th birthday. True, there were a few players in Europe before 1980, most notably the UK firm now-named 3i, and at least one American-style venture capital firm – which was not a success – that was set up in the 1960s. But it was during the entrepreneurial era of the 1980s that European venture capital grew explosively. From 1984 through 1992, the venture capital funds under management in Europe grew from ECU 3.6 billion to ECU 38.5 billion (EVCA 1991, 1992, 1993). Today, the total capital under management in Europe rivals the USA
>
> However, unlike the USA, where divestments and investments have been roughly in balance, the amount of money being invested in portfolio companies by European venture capital funds far exceeds the amount being divested. For instance, over the five years 1988 through 1992, ECU 21.2 billion was invested in portfolio companies but only ECU 9.4 billion was divested. Consider these numbers, divestments actually declined slightly from ECU 2.06 billion in 1990 to ECU 2.00 billion in 1991, then increased to ECU 2.3 billion in 1992, whereas investments increased from ECU 4.13 billion in 1990 to ECU 4.63 billion in 1991, and increased again to ECU 4.7 billion in 1992. Of course, some of that imbalance is because the total pool of venture capital continues to grow. But that is only a partial explanation because the amount of new funds raised has been declining since it peaked in 1989. If the 1990–92 trend continues, a logjam of unrealized investments is building up.
>
> By the end of 1992, the European venture capital industry reluctantly acknowledged that much of that investment–divestment imbalance was due to the relative scarcity of successful realizations. European venture capitalists will have to improve their realizations if they are to earn a respectable return on the ECU 20.4 billion in their portfolios at the end of 1992.
>
> It is estimated that as many as 17 000 European companies received equity venture capital over the past decade (Batchelor, 1992). The majority of those investments have yet to be harvested, and the entrepreneurs and their venture capital backers will be looking to realize their investments. Of course, not all of them will be seeking a flotation, but flourishing stock markets will be essential for putting a price on these businesses. The secondary markets in Amsterdam, Brussels, London, Paris, and other European financial centers have been struggling to maintain and even establish viable trading volumes. London scrapped its third market in 1990 and has announced its intention to close down its USM (Batchelor, 1992).
>
> One of the important reasons for the decline of secondary markets is simply economics: the promoters, market makers, and stockbrokers cannot make an adequate

profit on the low trading volumes. Hence, they cannot afford to provide the level of support post-IPO that the CEOs expect (Onians, 1992).

While European stock markets for small capitalization stocks are floundering in Europe, NASDAQ in the USA is thriving with the NASDAQ index hitting all time highs. It lists 4000 stocks. It has on average 12 market makers for each one of its stocks. And 98 percent of its top 2200 companies are subject to regular analysts' reports (Wall, 1992). In the last couple of years, it has set new records for initial public offerings. It appears that NASDAQ is trying to meet the concerns expressed by the CEOs in our survey. Small wonder that more and more European venture-capital-backed companies are having stock flotations on NASDAQ rather than on their national markets in Europe. NASDAQ now lists 181 European stocks. NASDAQ has tried to establish links with European exchanges, but has been unsuccessful because it has not found a local partner who did not see it as a threat, according to its executive vice president, John Wall (1992).

NASDAQ has proven that a nationwide electronic stock market can be a huge success. It seems to us that the time has come to set up the European equivalent of NASDAQ. Our survey shows that CEOs of venture-capital-backed companies are interested in a Pan-European stock market. The venture capital industry would welcome it. Perhaps its time for European policy makers in Brussels to take the initiative.

The final chapter of *Realizing Investment Value* culminated in a plea for the establishment of a European Electronic Market for Entrepreneurial Companies modeled after the NASDAQ. Ronald Cohen (1993) suggested that the market should be called EASDAQ, the European Association of Securities Dealers Automated Quotations.

Outcomes

Now we will look at the state of the US venture capital at the end of 1995, and where appropriate, compare it with our forecasts. After the decline in the late 1980s, the venture capital industry began to recover in 1992. Since then, both commitments of new capital to private venture capital funds and the disbursements of that capital to portfolio companies have grown (Figures 2.4 and 2.5). However, after adjusting for inflation, both the commitments and disbursements in 1995 were below what they had been in 1987. Moreover, fewer portfolio companies received venture capital in 1995 than in 1987 (1128 vs 1511) and there was a corresponding drop in the number of rounds of financings (1485 vs 2075). The number of first-round investments – that is companies receiving venture capital for the first time – bottomed out in 1991 and recovered somewhat by 1995 but was still substantially below the 1987 level. The proportion of early-stage financings increased from 33 per cent in 1991 to 42 per cent in 1995 (Figure 2.7).

There can be little doubt that the renewed vigor of the US venture industry was caused by the improvements in the returns (Table 2.1). Those improvements can be seen more easily in Table 2.2, which shows the average returns for 700 funds in Venture Economics data base. The four-year annualized return through December 31, 1995 was 23.5 per cent. Furthermore, the one-year return for 1995

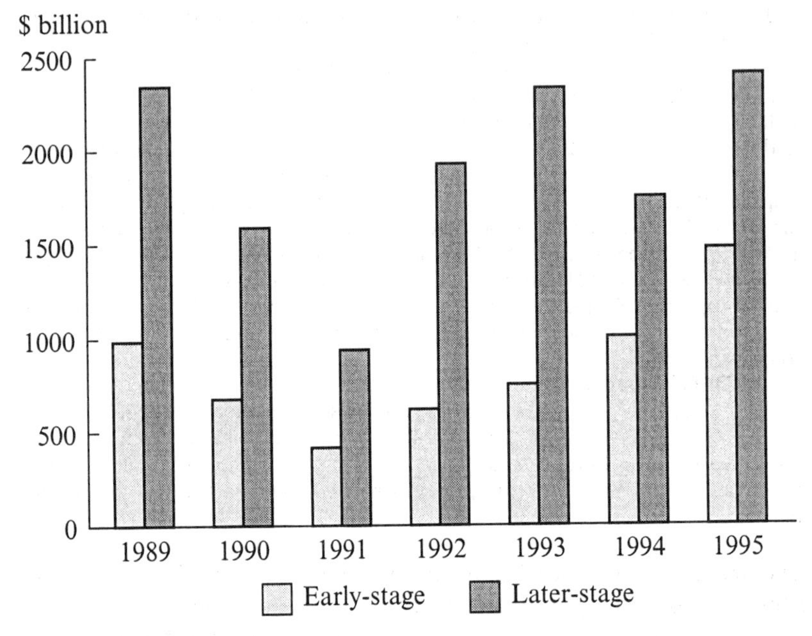

Source: Venture Economics.

Figure 2.7 Dollars invested by stage

was 50.7 per cent for all types of funds, with early-stage funds returning 51 per cent. To put these returns in perspective, we have listed the returns from the S&P 500 and two of Fidelity's select mutual funds, computers and electronics, which are two industries where venture capitalists have substantial investments. It shows that venture capital returns for the period 1992–95 handily outperformed the S&P 500 and approximately matched the returns on the two Fidelity funds (Table 2.2).

Venture capital returns from 1992 through 1995 confirmed what we had observed in the 1970s and 1980s. When the IPO market for small-cap stocks is robust, venture capital returns are healthy. The number of venture-capital-backed IPOs jumped to a record high in 1991 and continued to climb through 1995 (Figure 2.8). As the number of IPOs increased, the number of acquisitions declined (Figure 2.9).

How have our 1991 predictions for the US industry fared? First and foremost, the IPO market from 1991 through 1995 was indeed white hot. It was so hot that the average number of IPOs for the 1992–95 period was 147 compared with the 140 that we believed would be necessary to restore returns to a healthy level. Underperforming venture capital firms were culled out because they were unable to raise follow-on funds. and in a few instances ran out of money and

Table 2.1 *US venture capital industry composite holding period returns as of December 31, 1994*

Annualized IRR for Holding Period Ending December 31, 1994					
Portfolio of funds formed:	1-Year Return (%)	3-Year Return (%)	5-Year Return (%)	10-Year Return (%)	20-Year Return (%)
1969–1990	16.2	16.0	13.8	10.0	11.5
1980–1990	16.2	16.0	13.9	10.0	11.6
1981–1990	16.5	15.5	13.2	10.0	
1982–1990	16.5	15.4	13.3	9.7	
1983–1990	16.6	15.6	13.4	9.8	
1984–1990	17.5	16.6	14.3	10.1	
1985–1990	18.5	17.5	15.5	10.2	
1986–1990	19.1	18.2	15.8		
1987–1990	22.9	19.9	16.9		
1988–1990	22.8	20.8	17.7		
1989–1990	25.9	20.8	16.4		

Source: Venture Economics.

Table 2.2 *Returns on US venture capital funds and public stocks: '1995 was an excellent year'*

	Venture Capital (700 Funds)	S&P 500	Fidelity select Computers	Mutual funds Electronics
To Dec 31, 1995	1-Year	1-Year	1-Year	1-Year
All Stages	50.7%	37.6%	51.8%	69.0%
Early-Stage	51.0%			
Late-Stage	56.0%			
To Dec 31, 1994	1-Year	1-Year	1-Year	1-Year
All Stages	16.2%	1.3%	20.5%	17.5%
To Dec 31, 1995	4-Years	5-Years	5-Years	5-Years
All Stages	23.5%	16.0%	26.9%	31.7%
Early-Stage	18.0%			
Late-Stage	37.7%			
To Dec 31, 1995	26-Year	10-Year	10-Year	10-Year
	14.0%	13.8%	14.9%	21.9%

Note: Returns are annualized IRRs for the specified period.

Sources: Venture Economics; Fidelity Insight.

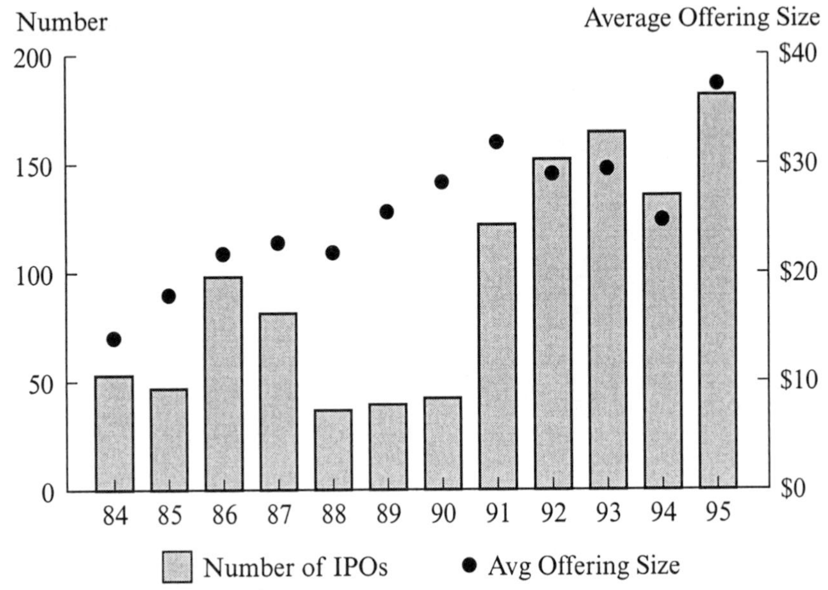

Source: Venture Economics.

Figure 2.8 Venture-capital-backed IPOs 1984–95

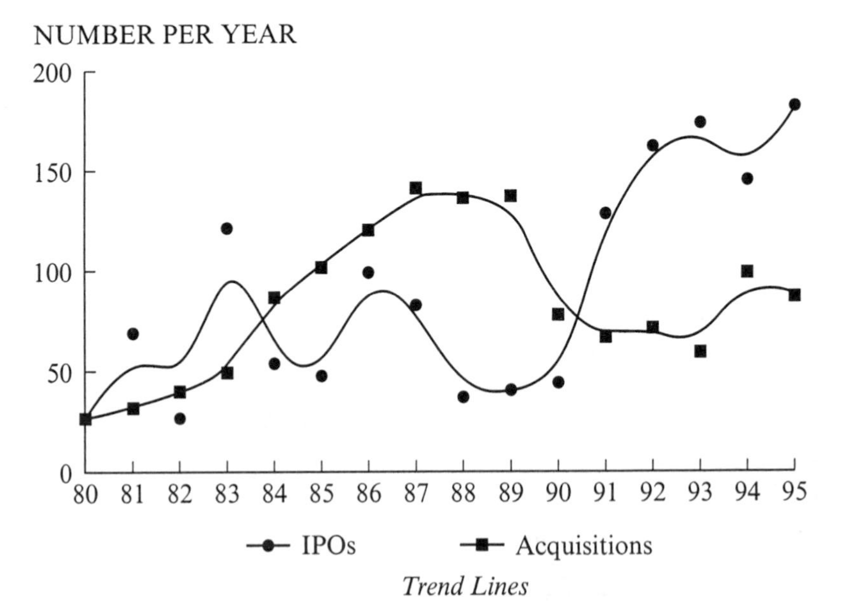

Source: Venture Economics.

Figure 2.9 Number of IPOs and acquisitions: venture-capital-backed companies

had to be merged with other funds. Between 1993 and 1994 the number of firms decreased from 637 to 591. The top performers earned returns better than 20 per cent. Those top performers dominate the industry with just 41 venture capital firms managing 48 per cent of the total pool of venture capital. In fact, our first three predictions were right on the mark.

But we were off the mark with our prediction that mergers with strategic partners would become the harvest of choice because the IPO market was too unpredictable. The sustained IPO market – the best there has ever been – that began in 1991 and continues today (September 1996) has restored the IPO as the harvest of choice for venture-capital-backed companies.

In *Venture Capital at the Crossroads* we coined the term 'classic' venture capital for investment in early-stage companies and the term 'merchant' capital for investment in late-stage and mature companies, especially buyouts. While there is not much evidence that merchant capital is declining, there is evidence that classic venture capital is growing. But classic venture capital has not yet climbed back to where it was almost ten years ago, because, as we expected, it has to compete with other sources of risk capital, including corporations and 'professional' angels.

The World Wide Web has turned out to be the new technology wave that we predicted. In just two years since it burst on to the computer-communications scene, the World Wide Web has propelled a new wave of technology-driven products that have stimulated consumers in a way that rivals the personal computer revolution at the start of the 1980s. It reached a fever pitch among investors in August 1995 with the initial public offering of Netscape Communications Corp, a two-year-old venture-capital-backed company. Four months after the IPO, the price of Netscape's stock had increased 500 per cent. Returns of that magnitude stimulated a surge of seed-stage and startup venture capital investments in World Wide Web companies.

There is evidence that competition for deals, capital, and venture capital know-how is becoming global. For example, Japanese corporations and venture capital firms are actively investing in early-stage companies in the USA.

While the pools of venture capital have grown in Europe and Japan, the US pool of $34 billion has not grown in real dollars in the 1990s. Commitments will have to be at record levels for the remainder of the decade if the US pool is to grow to the $45 to $50 billion that we forecast for 2000. However, our prediction that the venture capital pool in Japan would be bigger than the US pool by 2000 is way off target because in 1994 the Japanese pool of investment capital was only $8.5 billion (MITI, 1996). Granted, the same Japanese venture capital firms also managed a loan pool of $12.7 billion, but it was not really risk capital. The European venture capital pool is already larger than the US pool, but there are definitional problems because the European Venture Capital Association includes buyout capital in its statistics while Venture Economics excludes almost all buyout capital in its US statistics. In terms of classic venture capital, the US pool is still larger than the European pool.

As to the last two predictions in *Venture Capital at the Crossroads*, it is too early for us to judge the extent of the shake-out of the European industry, or for us to claim that a unique form of venture capital has emerged in Europe's post-communist nations. But the plea in *Realizing Investment Value* for a Pan-European small-cap electronic stock market has been heeded: the EASDAQ began trading in September 1996.

State of the industry in 1996

In September 1996, the US venture capital industry is euphoric. Returns are at highs that have not been seen since the hot IPO market of 1982–83. The industry is growing fast. New commitments in the first half of 1996 are up 31 per cent over the same period of 1995; and first-half disbursements are up almost 100 per cent in 1996 compared with 1994. Pre-money valuations are soaring. The average deal size in 1995 was 36 per cent bigger than in 1994, but fewer firms are participating in each syndication. Venture-capital-backed IPOs set a blistering pace in the first half of 1996. Strategic buyouts are competing with IPOs and pushing up valuations.

Highly specialized targeted funds are being raised to focus on the World Wide Web and software. Some corporations have venture funds targeted at specific industries. The best performing funds are 'dictating' terms to limited partners when raising new funds. Some are even in a position to select their limited partners; for them it is almost investing by invitation only. Other funds are asking for a 25 per cent carried interest instead of the prevailing rate of 20 per cent. Could the peak of the venture capital cycle be close at hand'?

Japanese policy makers and other observers of the US venture capital market are concerned that Japan is falling behind the USA in technology, especially the World Wide Web and software because of a lack of classic venture capital. They are considering what Japan must do to stimulate more venture-capital-backed entrepreneurs.

The next millennium

Before we make predictions for the venture capital industry at the beginning of the next millennium, let us look at a graph showing the influences on the flows of new venture capital that we first presented in *Venture Capital at the Crossroads*. We have updated it with six more years of data from 1990 to 1995 (Figure 2.10). Events since 1990 have reinforced convictions we had when we wrote that book. The most important determinant, by far, of the health of the venture capital industry is the condition of the IPO market. All other factors pale in comparison. For example, as we wrote earlier, in 1980 there was a widespread belief that a favorable capital gains tax was essential for a healthy venture capital

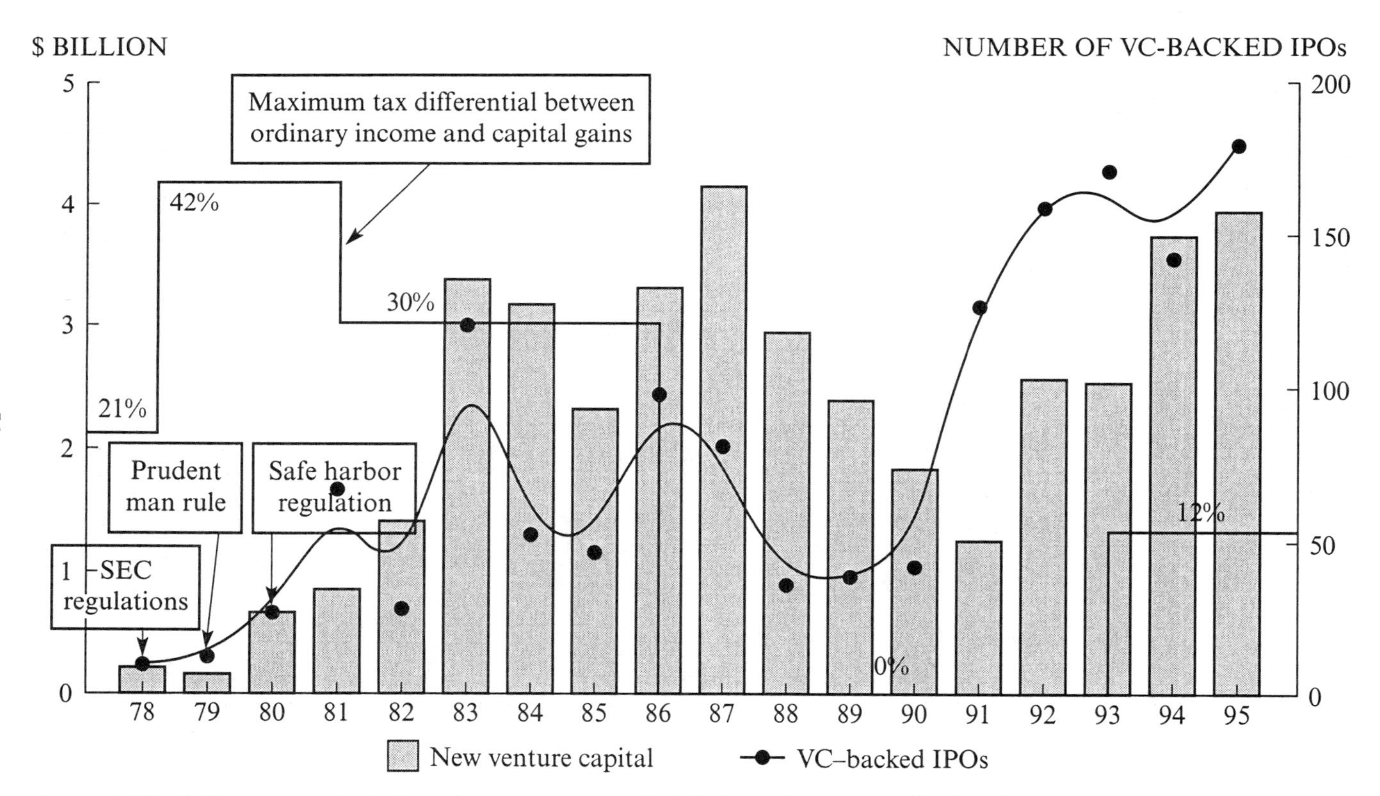

Figure 2.10 Influences on the inflow of new venture capital: independent private funds only

industry. So certain was the industry of this belief that it established the Steiger award in honor of the congressman who introduced the amendment to the 1978 tax bill that reduced the capital gains tax. Well . . . since 1978 there have been three major changes in the capital gains tax rate and there appears to be no correlation between that rate and the flows of venture capital. Which probably should not be a surprise because less than ten per cent of the formal venture capital in the USA comes from individuals and families that pay capital gains taxes. Of course, informal venture capitalists, usually called angels, are directly affected by that tax.

Predictions and prescriptions for the next millennium

In Figure 2.11, we have applied Porter's five-force model to analyze the US venture capital industry in 1996. Here are our forecasts for the US industry in the year 2000 and, in some cases, beyond.

- The flows of venture capital will continue to go through cycles linked to IPO cycles.
  Venture capital returns are closely linked to the small-cap IPO market. Investment managers are strongly influenced by short-term returns, even though the venture capital funds in which they invest have ten-year lifetimes.
- The influence of investment advisers – gatekeepers – will continue to grow.
  More than 70 per cent of venture capital comes from pension funds, insurance companies, endowments, and foundations. Investment managers in those type of organizations take comfort from another layer of due diligence that gatekeepers provide. And furthermore they do not have sufficient staff to carry out investigations and research as thoroughly as gatekeepers. At the end of 1995, gatekeepers controlled $9.6 billion for 174 clients (Deger 1995).
- The top 40 or so firms will continue to control at least 50 per cent of the venture capital pool.
  The successful firms will get bigger because gatekeepers will continue to select them in preference to new firms with no track record.
- As more money flows into venture capital funds from US pension funds, which are regulated by government rules, there will be increasing pressure to treat venture capital as a separate asset class and to require full disclosure of information, especially on returns.
  One reason that gatekeepers are so powerful is that they have their own standardized methods of computing returns on venture capital funds. And because they manage portfolios of venture capital funds, they know the returns of many individual funds. That information is not available elsewhere. Venture Economics has 700 or so US funds in its data base but

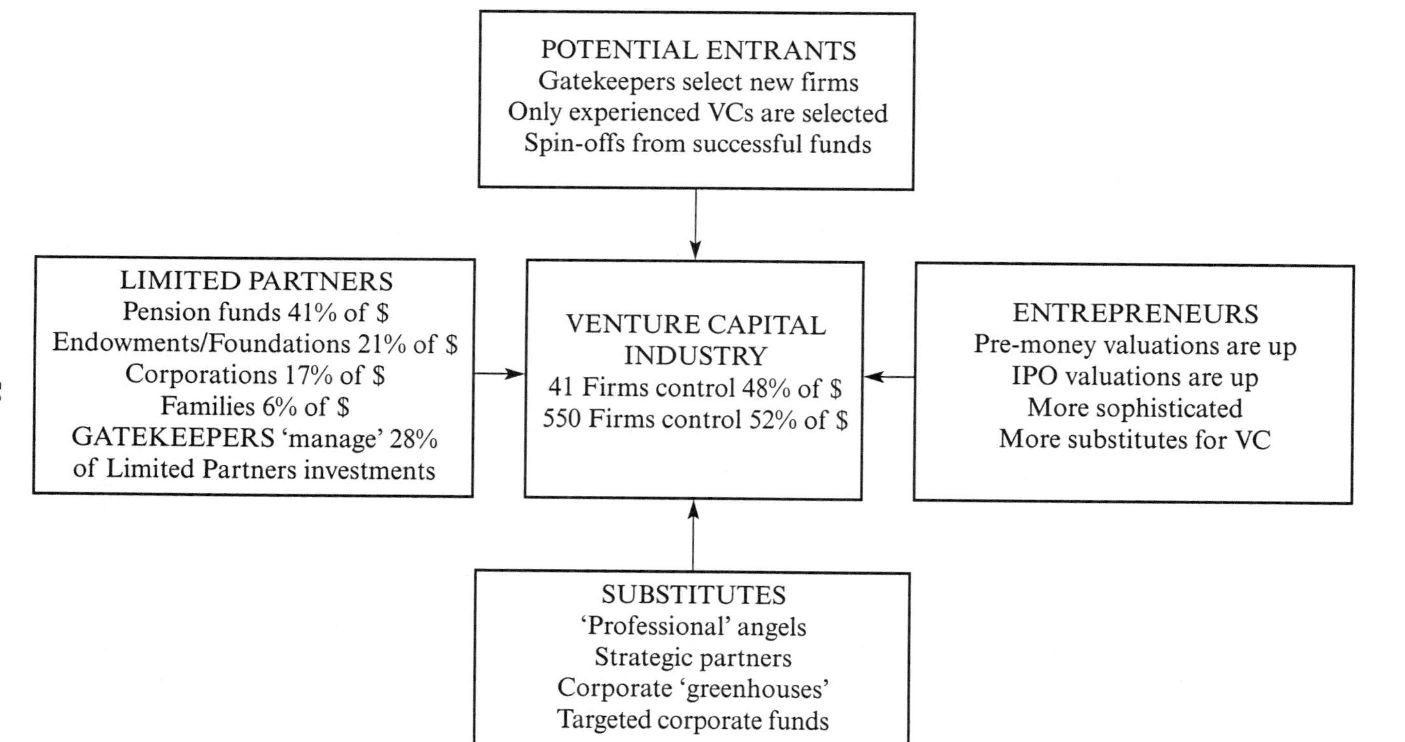

Figure 2.11 Porterian view of US venture capital industry, 1996

the returns performance of individual funds is a closely guarded secret. Likewise, those venture capital associations in Europe that now have information on returns are not releasing information on the performance of individual funds. Of all the assets in institutional investors' portfolios, private equity – venture capital in particular – is the only class that lacks standardized measurements.

- Formal venture capitalists will face increasing competition from substitute sources of capital, including 'professional' angels, strategic investors, corporate 'greenhouses', and targeted corporate funds.
  The booming US stock market of the last few years has substantially increased the wealth of many very wealthy angels. More and more they are investing some of their wealth in seed and startup companies in industries that they know something about. They are behaving more like formal venture capitalists, hence we call them 'professional' angels. Corporate 'greenhouses' are back in fashion. One of the most successful is at Thermo-Electron, where internal entrepreneurs are funded as separate startup corporations by the parent company. Some high-tech corporations have their in-house venture capital funds that invest in seed and startups with technologies related to the corporations' interests.
- Entrepreneurs will continue to be increasingly sophisticated in their negotiations with venture capitalists.
  Private equity investing is no longer shrouded in total secrecy. There is no longer as much asymmetry in the information available to venture capitalists compared with entrepreneurs. Entrepreneurs are quite likely to seek capital from multiple sources besides formal venture capitalists, such as 'professional' angels and targeted corporate funds. As a result, pre-money valuations will continue to rise. 'Professional' angels, for instance, do not have to pay 20 per cent of any capital gain plus a 2 to 3 per cent annual management fee when they invest as individuals rather than as limited partners in a venture capital fund. Hence, when investing as angels they can afford a higher pre-money valuation and still get the same return that they would have received by investing in the same company as a limited partner of a venture capital fund.
- There will be changes in the capital gains tax, but it will not have a significant positive effect on the formal venture capital industry. On the contrary, it might have a negative effect.
  The percentage of formal venture capital that comes from individual investors continues to decline as the percentage from institutions that are not subject to the capital gains tax continues to increase. So a reduction in the individual capital gains tax will have only a marginal effect on formal venture capital. However, it will have a noticeable effect on angel

investors; none more so than 'professional' angels, who will be more likely to realize some of their gains in public stocks and reinvest that money in young, private companies. Hence, they will compete with venture capitalists for investment deals.

- There will be even more emphasis on classic venture capital in all industrial nations.
  The success of US venture-capital-backed companies is envied by other industrial nations and they are seeking to emulate it.
- More nations will realize that a thriving small-cap stock market is crucial for a thriving venture capital industry. Just as NASDAQ was the model for EASDAQ, so too it will become a model for other nations.
  NASDAQ clones will be set up in other nations. The Internet and the World Wide Web will facilitate the use of those electronic trading systems. In addition they will facilitate their interconnection. It seems inevitable that a global electronic stock market that never closes will evolve – let's call it GLASDAQ.
- New technologies will continue to trigger waves of entrepreneurship.
  We don't know what that technology will be nor when it will occur. But we do know that venture capital will play a key role in accelerating its commercialization.

We will end with this thought: Today, finance and economics gurus are frequently using the term Anglo-Saxon capitalism to explain what has happened to the US and UK economies in recent years (for example, *Business Week*, 1997). Since the bulk of venture capital resides in Anglo-Saxon nations and some that resides in other nations is actually managed by Anglo-Saxon firms, what are the special features of Anglo-Saxon economies that foster a climate that is favorable for venture capital investing?

Note

1. We will forever be deeply grateful to the encouragement and assistance that we received from the staff at Venture Economics.

References

Batchelor, C. (1992), 'Enterprise looks for a way out', *Financial Times*, 22 December, p. 7.

Boylan, M. (1982), 'What we know and don't know about venture capital', American Economic Association Meetings, December 28, 1991, National Economist Club, January 19, 1982.

Business Week (1997), 'A continent at the breaking point', February 24, pp. 50–51.

Bygrave, William D. and Jeffry A. Timmons (1992), *Venture Capital at the Crossroads*, Boston, MA: Harvard Business School Press.

Bygrave, William D., Michael Hay and Jos B. Peeters (eds) (1994), *Realizing Investment Value*, London: Financial Times/Pitman.

Cohen, R. (1993), Presentation at EVCA symposium on Ten Years of Venture Capital, Brussels, June.

Deger, R. (1995), 'Barbarians at the gate', *Venture Capital Journal*, **35** (11), November, 45–8.

EVCA (1991), *Venture Capital in Europe: 1991 EVCA Yearbook*, Zaventem, Belgium: EVCA.
EVCA (1992), *Venture Capital in Europe: 1992 EVCA Yearbook*, Zaventem, Belgium: EVCA.
EVCA (1993), *Venture Capital in Europe: 1993 EVCA Yearbook*, Zaventem, Belgium: EVCA.
MITI (1996), *Venture Capital in Japan*, MITI Small and Medium Enterprise Agency.
Onians, R. (1992), Presentation at the EFER 92, London, December.
Onians, R. (1993), 'A European secondary market', Presentation at the EVCA business seminar on Exiting in Europe, Venice, 11–12 February.
Wall, J. (1992), Presentation at the EFER 92, London, December.

3. The venture capital and buy-out markets in the UK and Europe

Mike Wright and Ken Robbie

Introduction

The European venture capital and buy-out markets have experienced considerable growth since the early 1980s, though this development has been uneven between countries. Among European countries, the UK has the largest and longest established venture capital and buy-out markets. By 1996, the UK market had raised a cumulative total of ECU 25.7 billion, which accounted for 43.7 per cent of the European total venture capital raised (EVCA, 1997). Similarly, the UK buy-out market is as large as that for Europe combined (Initiative Europe/CMBOR, 1997). Given its importance, this chapter focuses primarily on an analysis of the UK venture capital and buy-out market. Developments in Continental Western Europe are analysed in comparison with the UK position. The highly competitive market conditions of the late 1990s, especially in the UK, in an environment of a plateauing of the growth in demand for venture capital from entrepreneurs, increasing attention by funds providers for high returns on their investments and an emphasis on buy-out type investments, highlights the importance of analysing the trends and prospects for the industry as the millennium approaches.

The chapter draws on a number of sources of information, which include both secondary data sources and literature as well as original field research. Extensive use is made of analyses provided for the authors by the British Venture Capital Association of trends in the UK market and of the authors' own monitoring of management buy-outs and buy-ins which form a significant part of venture capital activity in both the UK and Europe. In addition, the authors conducted a series of in-depth face-to-face interviews with 25 senior UK venture capitalists in mid-1996 in order to address strategic aspects of the industry into the next millennium.

The chapter first identifies the principal trends in and structure of the UK venture capital market including analysis of both the value and the number of venture capital investments over time by different types of venture capital firms, trends in the relative importance of investment in different stages, industries and countries, and exits. The third main section considers issues relating to suppliers of finance to venture capital firms and business angels. This analysis of the UK is followed by a comparative analysis of developments in venture capital and buy-outs in the rest of Western Europe. Finally, some implications for the future development of the market are presented in the concluding section.

The development of venture capital

The growth of venture capital

After the 1980s which saw rapid growth in UK venture capital (Lorenz, 1989; Murray, 1991), the first half of the 1990s saw marked changes. While the recession of the early 1990s had a marked effect on the industry, the mid-1990s have seen a resurgence of activity. The number of BVCA members peaked at the height of the last recession (Table 3.1). In the early 1990s the number of BVCA members fluctuated a little but by 1996 had fallen to 103. The total number of companies financed in any one year peaked in 1989 and has since declined by about a quarter. However, the average size of investment has increased substantially over this period. Following an initial peak in 1989, annual total amounts invested in nominal terms fell during the recession but from 1994 onwards record levels were set in successive years.

Table 3.1 Investment activity and fundraising

Year	Number of BVCA members (full)	Number of companies financed	Amount invested (£M)	Independent funds raised (£M)
1984	34	479	190	n.a.
1985	50	635	433	n.a.
1986	65	708	584	n.a.
1987	77	1298	1029	645
1988	90	1527	1394	492
1989	107	1569	1647	1964
1990	120	1559	1394	759
1991	121	1386	1153	390
1992	115	1297	1434	413
1993	113	1202	1422	588
1994	117	1208	2074	2551
1995	115	1163	2535	749
1996	103	1200	3239	2445

Source: BVCA, *Report on Investment Activity*, various issues.

The growth in venture capital activity over the last decade has been achieved with marked increases in amounts invested by both independent and captive firms. Greatest growth has occurred among independents, which invested £140 million in venture capital in 1985, rising to an initial peak in 1989 of £1,030 million. After halving during the recession of the early 1990s, annual funds invested again increased, reaching £1,765 million in 1996. By comparison, captives invested approximately the same amount as independents in 1985, but achieved an initial peak of only £390 million in 1989. Decline in the recession of the early 1990s was accompanied by the growth of semi-captives, so that by 1996 captives invested £237 million as against £804 million by semi-captives.

The past few years have seen several major traditional captives accessing external sources of funds through, for instance, acquisition of venture capital fund management companies or contracts for external portfolio management. Some venture capital firms belonging to large financial groups have become more independent in their management, effectively acting as independents. It is anticipated that this blurring of the traditional distinction between independent and captive venture capitalists will continue. For captive venture capitalists, raising independent funds provides scope for more effective rewarding of executives, the ability to raise larger amounts of funds for buy-outs beyond the internal restrictions imposed by parents, and it enables bigger deals to be funded. These moves have implications for existing independents. Some independents may face increasing difficulties in obtaining funds, especially if they are not strong performers.

Generally until 1995 there had been less exit from the industry than anticipated at the start of the 1990s (Murray, 1991), not least because firms whose funds were invested could continue to manage them during the life of the fund. Ten year limited partnership structures can produce a surprising inertia to change. Relationships built over years with investors can result in finance being provided for successor funds despite poor performance. Nevertheless the mid-1990s saw several significant changes including spin-offs from financial groups and acquisitions by captives of independents.

Investment behaviour

Investment stage The majority of venture capital investments have consistently been in the expansion area (Tables 3.2 and 3.3). From the peak seen in 1989, the proportion of investments going into early stage projects has generally fallen sharply and accounted for little more than a sixth of the total in 1996. In contrast, the proportion of investments involving management buy-out and buy-in transactions is now at its highest ever level at 33 per cent. Similarly, the share of the total value of annual investments involving management buy-outs and buy-ins is also at a record at just below three quarters of the total, having risen from a little over a half at the time of the previous analysis of the industry in 1991.

Table 3.2 Investment by funding stage (% of number of investments)

Year	Early	Expansion	MBO/MBI	Total
1984	31.8	54.5	13.7	100.0
1985	27.6	49.7	22.7	100.0
1986	29.8	49.6	20.6	100.0
1987	26.8	55.0	18.0	100.0
1988	28.0	51.0	21.0	100.0
1989	38.0	37.0	25.0	100.0
1990	26.0	48.0	26.0	100.0
1991	22.0	55.0	23.0	100.0
1992	17.0	57.0	26.0	100.0
1993	19.0	62.0	19.0	100.0
1994	15.0	58.0	27.0	100.0
1995	16.0	53.0	31.0	100.0
1996	18.0	49.0	33.0	100.0

Source: BVCA.

Table 3.3 Investment by funding stage (% of amount invested in UK)

Year	Early	Expansion	MBO/MBI	Total
1984	27.1	52.1	20.8	100.0
1985	19.1	44.0	37.0	100.0
1986	22.4	32.4	45.2	100.0
1987	12.9	32.1	55.0	100.0
1988	10.0	34.0	56.0	100.0
1989	15.0	24.0	61.0	100.0
1990	12.0	36.0	52.0	100.0
1991	6.0	39.0	55.0	100.0
1992	6.0	29.0	65.0	100.0
1993	6.0	32.0	62.0	100.0
1994	5.0	28.0	67.0	100.0
1995	4.0	23.0	73.0	100.0
1996	5.0	21.0	74.0	100.0

Source: BVCA, *Report on Investment Activity*, various issues.

This overall pattern of the relative importance of different investment stages masks an important distinction in the UK venture capital industry between those firms which do and those which definitely do not invest in early stage projects. It might be argued that firms which do not invest in early stage projects ought not to be considered venture capitalists. However, later stage projects including management buy-outs and buy-ins may be in high-tech areas and involve significant entrepreneurial action beyond straightforward financial engineering, as will be seen in more detail below when performance issues are discussed.

Competitive pressures for deals were overwhelmingly seen by senior venture capitalists we interviewed to be greatest at the larger buy-out end of the market with smaller non-focused buy-out players likely to experience the greatest pressures. As a result, there are strong expectations that venture capital firms will become more proactive in deal origination, especially for investor buy-outs and management buy-ins. Vendor auctions became important in the late 1990s, especially for buy-outs and buy-ins. Although such a trend may contain cyclical elements, it is expected to continue as the twin factors of pressures on corporate divestors to maximize disposal proceeds and competition between venture capital firms are likely to remain.

Investment by industry sector and country Reflecting the emphasis of the UK venture capital industry on later stage investments, the principal industrial sectors have consistently been consumer related, industrial products, services and other manufacturing (Table 3.4). Sectors typically associated with early stage innovative projects, such as computing, electronics and medical/health/biotechnology accounted for about a fifth of companies invested in by the UK venture capital industry over the period 1984–95. This share, however, is inflated somewhat by data relating to the period 1984–86 when buy-outs, which generally do not involve firms in these sectors, were not included in the figures. Latterly, less than a fifth of investments have in general been in these sectors, with a low of a sixth (16.4 per cent) being recorded in 1992. In terms of actual numbers of investments, there has been a sharp fall in respect of the consumer related sector since 1991. The annual number of investments in the electronics and medical/health/biotechnology sectors has fluctuated markedly over the period, with the former being at its lowest for a decade in 1995 while the latter reached its highest ever level. This pattern of investment activity has led some to argue that the UK venture capital industry has a bias against investment in new technology (Murray and Lott, 1995), although it may simply be a rational response to earning high returns in a market characterized by high uncertainty and difficulties in obtaining objective information.

Both by number and value, the vast majority of investments by UK venture capital firms take place within the UK. There was some initial growth in activity in Continental Europe in 1989 and 1990, but recession and the problems

Table 3.4 UK investment by number of companies by industry sector

Year	Consumer related	Computer related	Electronics related	Industrial products	Medical health biotec	Communi- cation	Energy	Transport	Construction	Financial services	Other services	Other manu- facturing	Total
1984*	59	51	31	25	24	20	19	10	8	n.a.	35	23	305
1985*	96	71	39	16	44	34	7	20	19	14	33	31	424
1986*	112	64	35	35	32	28	3	23	9	24	64	24	453
1987	259	117	73	125	58	53	14	53	55	36	190	141	1 174
1988	305	127	68	155	52	37	19	62	58	126	109	208	1 326
1989	329	139	81	132	58	30	16	67	82	25	147	196	1 302
1990	305	156	61	130	51	20	14	90	75	55	91	173	1 221
1991	270	114	80	155	42	13	20	43	58	29	204	170	1 198
1992	282	82	59	177	48	20	15	30	58	23	202	151	1 147
1993	242	84	77	158	64	20	9	44	52	34	143	139	1 066
1994	209	80	71	164	48	23	11	33	59	42	149	212	1 101
1995	226	83	51	152	68	31	20	64	61	26	75	173	1 030
Total	2694	1 168	726	1 424	589	329	167	539	594	434	1 442	1 641	11 747

Notes:
Membership changes annually.
1984* Figures exclude buy-outs and acquisitions.
1985* Figures exclude buy-ins/outs and acquisitions.
1986* Figures exclude buy-ins/outs, acquisitions and secondary purchases.
* 12,030 Total number of companies in receipt of venture capital in UK – including those deals omitted in 1984–86 in this table.

Source: BVCA.

arising from investment in new markets meant a retrenchment of interest in the early 1990s. In 1994 and 1995 there was some recovery in the share of investment value taking place in Continental Europe, although this eased again in 1996. Continental Europe was seen by respondents to our survey as the most attractive opportunity for UK venture capital over the next five years. The interview responses enabled a more precise identification of promising opportunities with Germany, followed by France, being considered the most attractive areas for European expansion. Viable entry strategies may vary according to the positioning of different players. Some respondents took the view it was necessary to have a good network of relationships with a London-based international team able to conduct transactions, while others considered that the only approach was through direct offices who had the same aims as the London base. Our interviews with leading venture capitalists indicate some resistance in the UK at present to significant investment in Central and Eastern Europe until major areas of uncertainty are addressed.

Exiting As an initial attempt to provide a means for smaller firms to access the capital markets, the Unlisted Securities Market (USM) was introduced in 1980. The market reached its peak in 1989 with 438 firms quoted. However, problems of liquidity of shares, reduced differentials between the terms of listing on the main market and the USM and the increasing tendency for the more successful firms to opt for an initial main market quotation rather than using the USM as an intermediate stage, meant that the market declined in the first half of the 1990s. The USM was closed to new entrants in December 1994. The short-lived Third Market existed between 1987 and 1990 and offered less stringent conditions for flotation than the USM. During this period, 91 companies joined the market, five of which were management buy-outs. As a result of the problems of liquidity of shares in the aftermath of the stock market crash of 1987 and the onset of recession, the Third Market merged with the USM at the end of 1990.

The Alternative Investment Market (AIM) was introduced to provide an attractive route for growing companies which are too small or not yet in a position to achieve a full stock market listing to obtain equity finance. Unlike the main stock market, AIM imposes no minimum on the percentage of shares in public hands, no minimum market value and no minimum trading record. In addition, new companies entering AIM do not require a sponsor who would normally be a stockbroker of a merchant bank which scrutinizes the accounts and prospectus on behalf of investors. The Stock Exchange authorities do not scrutinize a candidate's prospectus, rather this task is carried out by nominated advisers approved by the Exchange who must be retained while the company is quoted on AIM. Firms opting for an AIM listing rather than a full listing obtain certain taxation benefits, notably in respect of income tax relief where Enterprise

Investment Scheme funds are a potential source of capital and in respect of capital gains tax through Venture Capital Trusts and as a result of the ability of firms to claim re-investment relief which allows a gain to rolled over into a new investment so deferring the tax charge. These benefits were not available to firms quoted on the USM. In general, these differences enable companies quoted on AIM to maintain many of the taxation benefits available to private companies while gaining the benefits of a degree of liquidity in their shares and access to new sources of finance.

At the end of December 1995, 121 companies were trading on AIM. By the end of August 1997, 291 companies had come to the AIM with a combined market capitalization at this date of £5.5 billion. A total of £1378 million of new funds had been raised by these companies, ranging from about £0.4 million to £20 million. As is to be expected, the FTSE–AIM Index is considerably more volatile than the FTSE–All Share Index. The FTSE–AIM Index began in January 1996 and taking this date as 100 for both indexes, the FTSE–All Share Index had risen to 114 while the FTSE–AIM Index had increased to 105 by May 1996. Almost a half of companies in terms of both numbers and market capitalization are from the service sector, though companies from this sector account for almost two thirds of funds raised. The general industrial sector accounts for a tenth of companies by number, and a fifth by market capitalization, but accounts for less than a tenth of funds raised. Companies in the financial sector account for over a quarter of companies by number while the consumer goods sector accounts for a tenth of market capitalization.

An important aspect of the role of AIM is, of course, the attitudes towards it of venture capital firms. Our interviews with senior venture capitalists suggest that while there is a positive stance towards AIM, reservations exist over such aspects as the market not having been tested as yet by adverse economic conditions or major problem cases, and that there is still a need to attract the active interest of more market makers than at present if it is to achieve sufficient liquidity. There are also issues concerning the quality of companies entering AIM and of the intermediaries who were bringing them to market. There is clearly a trade-off between introducing strong regulation which means only high quality companies come to AIM and which helps to develop investor confidence and looser regulation which allows a greater flow of new entrants but carries the dangers of alienating potential investors. Liquidity is also a potentially significant problem in exiting from venture capital investments via AIM and on entering AIM venture capitalists may need to give up important control rights while still retaining a significant holding.

Although the classic view of exit from a venture capital investment is often seen to involve a stock market flotation (IPO), UK venture capitalists both prefer and use the sale to a third party as the most frequent means of realization (Wright et al., 1993 and Table 3.5). This is principally because a threshold for an IPO is not reached or because an attractive but unforeseen acquisition proposal is received.

Table 3.5 Exits from UK venture capital portfolios

Type	Amount (£m) 1992	No. 1992	Amount (£m) 1993	No. 1993	Amount (£m) 1994	No. 1994	Amount (£m) 1995	No. 1995	Amount (£m) 1996	No. 1996
Write-off	268	524	184	437	121	371	142	215	117	269
Trade sale	158	285	432	748	312	316	495	283	729	456
Flotation	247	86	377	190	495	176	619	132	359	158
Other	58	303	68	256	122	591	114	264	206	369
Total	731	1198	1061	1631	1050	1454	1370	894	1411	1252

Note: Numbers refer to number of investments not number of companies.

Source: EVCA Yearbook (various).

The period 1992–96 saw a dramatic shift in the pattern of exits from UK venture capitalists' portfolios (Table 3.5). In particular, up to 1994 there was a sharp fall in the number and value of write-offs, as the economy came out of recession and a marked increase in both trade sales and stock market flotations. In 1996, divestments from venture capital portfolios at cost in the UK amounted to £1411 million, representing over a sixth (17.4 per cent) of the total portfolio at cost at the beginning of the year. New investments at cost during the year amounted to £2417 million. In 1995, the extent of trade sale and flotation activity eased before rising again in 1996.

The pattern of exits from management buy-outs is also an important feature of the UK venture capital market. Although some buy-outs may float on a stock market or be sold within a very short period of time, even ten years after the transaction nearly half remain as buy-outs (Wright et al. 1994, 1995). Venture-backed buy-outs are more likely to exit sooner and at a greater rate than non-venture backed buy-outs. Reflecting expectations that venture capitalists are likely to invest in riskier ventures than providers of debt, venture backed exits are more likely to be both highly successful (that is, stock market flotation) and, at the other extreme, unsuccessful (that is, receivership). CMBOR's long-term monitoring of a sample of buy-outs completed between 1983 and 1986 shows that a decade after the deal, 46 per cent of venture backed buy-outs had exited through trade sale or flotation and a further tenth had entered receivership. In contrast, only a tenth of non-venture backed deals had exited by trade sale or flotation.

It was anticipated by the senior venture capitalists we interviewed that there would be a broadening of exit options over the next five years, with the balance between trade sales and stock market flotations continuing to depend on economic conditions. There was a strong view among respondents to our survey that inter-institutional sales and secondary buy-outs would increase in importance and acceptability. EASDAQ was seen as having the potential to provide a useful exit route for a minority of investments. The respondents to our survey, however, considered that the pressure to focus on IRRs within the constraints imposed by fund lives had an important impact on the time horizons of investments even though venture capital firms may prefer to remain with good investments to generate a greater cash return.

Performance of venture capital firms and buy-outs

Evidence of the target rates of return sought by venture capitalists ex ante (Wright and Robbie, 1996a) shows that in the UK, the overall average internal rate of return sought on venture capital investments is around 29 per cent and that these target returns vary according to the stage of the investment, and the size and the degree of technology risk involved in the project.

A review of the main US literature to 1987 by Bygrave (1994) concludes that 'contrary to the folklore figure of 30–50 per cent, actual venture capital returns have most often been in the teens, with occasional periods in the 20–30 per cent range and rare spikes above 30 per cent'. Bygrave's own study of the performance of funds formed in the period 1969–85 shows that the median internal rate of return (IRR) peaked in 1982 at 27 per cent and that early stage funds had higher returns than later stage ones.

Kleiman and Shulman (1992) examine the comparative performance of publicly traded venture capital firms and government sponsored small business investment companies and find that for the period 1980–86 the latter demonstrate significantly greater total and unsystematic risk and greater returns on a risk-adjusted basis, but significantly less systematic risk, than the former. However, this difference disappears for later years.

An analysis of 33 quoted European venture capital firms during the period 1977–91 (Manigart, Joos and De Vos, 1993) showed only eight of the sample with a return higher than the market return although the systematic risk was lower than the market risk. Venture capital companies specializing in a specific investment stage had a higher return. In Europe, the sensitivity of returns information has led to analyses being conducted by national venture capital associations. Though these studies provide some data there is a lack of transparency in the process of analysis. Dutch venture capitalists earned an average annual return on investment of 13 per cent for the period 1986–90. However, these figures are based on realizations only and ignore the value of portfolio companies which have not been realized and which may be expected to lower these returns. The Dutch analysis, in contrast to US evidence, showed that early stage finance was on average loss-making (–3 per cent annual return) compared with the much less riskier management buy-outs which earned a high positive return of 25 per cent per year.

It is clear that returns depend to a great extent on the stage of investment and the timing of the raising of the fund and have generally fallen internationally since the market began to develop significantly from the early 1980s. Moreover, it is also the case that the bulk of returns are earned on the top quartile. In Bygrave's study, the top quartile funds peaked at a rate of return of 44 per cent. It is notable that funds involving the lowest risk categories, such as buy-outs, earned the highest returns. It is also notable that the actual returns earned are somewhat below the target returns sought by venture capital firms as noted above.

Buy-outs have been shown to be the strongest performing element of the UK venture capital industry. Analysis of the longer term returns of funds launched between 1980 and 1992 shows an overall annual return to end December 1996 of 14.2 per cent. Large MBO funds produced the highest returns at 25.4 per cent, with mid-sized MBO funds generating an annual return of 16.2 per cent. In comparison, early stage investments earned an annual return of 4.3 per cent, while development stage investments achieved an 8.1 per cent annual return. Funds raised in 1986 and 1987 were the worst performers while the best ones were raised in 1985, 1990 and 1991, reflecting the effects of differing market conditions notably the entry price/earnings ratios paid for investees. Unlike the Dutch study, but in line with US approaches, the UK analysis was based on all investments not just exited ones and relates to the performance of funds not companies.

In the UK market, the performance of management buy-outs and buy-ins is of especial importance. Most available studies concerning post buy-out performance changes have concerned the short term after the transaction and generally show substantial improvements in profitability, cash flow and productivity measures over the interval between one year prior to the transaction and two or three years subsequent to it (see Jensen, 1993; Thompson and Wright, 1995, for reviews). A CMBOR survey of 182 MBOs completed between 1983 and 1986 indicated that two thirds showed clear improvements in profitability (Wright, Thompson and Robbie, 1992). In this study improvements in working capital management and productivity appeared to be important identified sources of improved performance. The performance of management buy-ins has, however, been generally less strong than for buy-outs (Robbie and Wright, 1996). Coming from outside with less detailed knowledge of the business than is the case in buy-outs, it has often proved more difficult than expected for management and investors to achieve enhanced short-term profitability. Evidence about longer-term performance shows that over years three to five after the change in ownership, buy-outs on average perform significantly better than comparable non-buy-outs on both return on total assets and profit per employee measures (Wright, Wilson and Robbie, 1996).

Though there is some concern that flotations occur at the peak of the gains from buy-outs, those which have come to market tend on average to generate greater performance relative to the market. The CMBOR Index of buy-outs which have floated shows a 151.7 per cent increase between the end of 1990 and the end of February 1997 compared with an increase in the Hoare Govett Small Companies Index of 106.5 per cent over the same period.

Sources of capital for venture capital firms

It is difficult to estimate the amount of funds available for investment by captive venture capital firms. The amount of independent funds raised is much clearer, with the breakdown of sources shown in Table 3.6. The amount of independent funds raised varies considerably from year to year, with 1994 displaying significant growth over previous years as confidence of investors increased following several years of recession. Pension funds are the largest single source of finance for independent funds, ranging from over two thirds in 1991 to a little under a third in the peak year of 1994. Although pension funds increased their contributions to venture capital funds by more than threefold in 1994, the increases shown by banks, insurance companies and corporate investors are remarkable. The growth of interest by corporate investors is of particular interest in the light of a recent study of the behaviour and experience of corporate investors which suggested that conflicting objectives and unsatisfactory returns were likely to continue to produce a reluctance on the part of such enterprises to participate in the UK venture capital industry (McNally, 1994). In general, the largest single source of contributions to independent UK venture capital funds is the UK, the exception over the last five years being North America in 1993. Indeed, North America was consistently the main source of funds from outside the UK in the period 1991–95.

Table 3.6 UK independent funds raised by source (£m)

By source	1991	1992	1993	1994	1995	1996
Banks	14	10	45	592	49	221
Pension funds	251	157	232	796	361	1253
Insurance companies	34	72	106	368	143	325
Corporate investors	20	50	37	424	50	80
Private individuals	22	38	19	96	47	176
Government agencies	1	5	3	35	17	138
Academic institutions	6	0	21	10	50	
Others (includes investment trusts)	20	14	17	230	32	252
Total (rounded)	368	347	479	2551	749	2445

Source: BVCA.

As regards future developments in sources of funds, our interviews with senior venture capitalists show that in the UK market established funds providers are increasingly concentrating their investments on fewer key relationships with well-known venture capitalists in whom they had previously invested. In a market such as the UK, increasing transparency about the performance of individual venture capital firms in relation to industry averages is likely to increase rationalization but would mean that good performers would have little difficulty in raising funds. In cases of good performance, institutional investors may be more likely to commit a larger amount to a particular fund and particularly for sources outside the UK may be looking for an international perspective. Correspondingly, there are fewer domestic funds providers to whom venture capitalists can market their funds, partly as a result of some exiting the market, partly because some had externalized their fund management and partly because of mergers and acquisitions. A potentially important issue in the UK is the role of venture capital as an investment class within institutional investors' portfolios. The separate identification of venture capital as an asset class may encourage pension funds to increase their allocations to this sector, especially to firms generating good returns. Apart from making efforts to increase the performance of funds as a means of improving their fund raising ability, venture capital firms may place increasing emphasis on enhancing the service they provide to suppliers of funds in order to differentiate themselves in the market place.

Business angels (informal venture capitalists)

Business angels, or informal venture capitalists, involve private individuals with significant amounts of funds to invest directly in the form of equity in unquoted companies and projects with which they have no prior connection. There is some debate about the extent and nature of business angel activity in the UK (Mason and Harrison, 1997). A survey of 85 business angels in the UK (Mason and Harrison, 1996) found that in the previous three years these informal venture capitalists had identified 2500 investment opportunities, out of which 17 per cent had been considered seriously and investments had been made in 8 per cent (172 ventures) for a total amount of £3.1 million.[1] In contrast to this study, Stevenson and Coveney (1994) in a survey of 484 business angels found that the median amount invested was £40 000 with an average investment of £120 000. On this basis the total cumulative funding generated by informal venture capitalists up to the mid-1990s is estimated to range from £2 billion to £4 billion. In contrast the formal venture capital industry, as seen earlier, invests in excess of £1.5 billion per year.[2]

Investments in young companies accounted for a third of investments in the Mason and Harrison study, pre-start-up cases accounted for nine per cent of investments, start-up and early stage accounted for around forty per cent, with the balance being established companies. The manufacturing sector accounted for a third of investments, nearly half of which were in high-technology firms. Including service sector cases, some 37 per cent of investments were in technology-based ventures.

Although it is sometimes argued that informal venture capitalists are likely to be more patient investors than formal venture capitalists, the Mason and Harrison study found that a little over a half of business angels expected to exit from their investments in 3–5 years, and a little under a quarter expected to hold their investments for 6–10 years. The most frequently cited expected exit route was a trade sale (29 per cent) followed by stock market flotation (25 per cent), although 17 per cent were undecided. The Stevenson and Coveney study found that the timeframe before exit was six years.

A major issue in developing the informal venture capital market in the UK concerns the problem of matching investors and investees. Since 1993 the BVCA has published an annual directory of business introduction services in the UK. Between the first and the third edition the number of listed services rose from 17 to 37. An analysis of 30 of the 37 services listed in the 1995 directory shows that they were involved in investments in 173 companies in which 330 business angels invested over £16 million. On a like-for-like basis, the number of investments increased by 51 per cent and the amount invested increased by 32 per cent between 1993/4 and 1994/5. Networks have been established by public sector and not-for-profit organizations. The Mason and Harrison survey of UK informal venture capitalists found that organized referral sources were the least efficient sources of information in investment opportunities. Although the most frequent source of referral were informal sources, investors were most likely to invest in investment opportunities which arose from the less frequently used referral sources. A second generation type of business network now seems to be developing which involves private sector rather than public sector initiatives, national scale of operation and the use of alternative matching and presentational technologies.

In general, informal venture capitalists or business angels can be viewed as providing a useful complementary role to that of formal venture capitalists. Where they do present a competitive challenge this is generally only at the edges of the market for very small deals which meet the investment criteria of few venture capitalists. They may provide early stage or seed capital for deals that would be of future interest to formal venture capitalists. The potential for links with business angels to provide deal flow for formal venture capitalists may be restricted by the approach of venture capitalists towards rewarding the input made to early stage projects seeking later stage financing. This suggests that business angels may have insufficient incentive to approach formal venture capitalists where they see early stage development being inadequately rewarded and their interest being heavily diluted at the next stage.

Mezzanine debt

Mezzanine finance can take various forms. Most notably it involves unsecured or subordinated debt, but it may also be considered to involve various forms of preference shares. Many venture capitalists see themselves as effectively providing mezzanine finance either through their preference share instruments or through subordinated debt provided as part of an overall financial structure. Mezzanine debt tends to become more important in the UK market when the market is overheated and there is an emphasis on large buy-out deals. This was particularly the case during the first peak of the UK buy-out market in 1989. The market began to appear in 1985 when, according to the authors' own monitoring, only five deals with a total transaction value exceeding £10 million included mezzanine debt to a value of £92 million out of a total funding level of £421 million. By 1989, 35 deals with a transaction value exceeding £10 million could be identified by the authors, with mezzanine debt accounting for £933 million of a total funding of £5859 million. After this date, the advent of the recession and the collapse of the large buy-out market, meant that the use of mezzanine finance fell sharply reaching the lowest point since 1986 in 1994 at £110 million before beginning to rise again in 1996 to £336 million as large deals in the UK buy-out market began to re-emerge. In terms of the percentage of buy-out and buy-in financial structures which are accounted for by mezzanine debt, the authors' monitoring shows that for transactions with a value of at least £10 million, it peaked in 1989 at 12.8 per cent, subsequently falling to a low of 4.6 per cent in 1993, before recovering to 5.7 per cent in 1996. For buy-outs and buy-ins with a transaction value below £10 million, the share of mezzanine debt in financial structures is typically much lower, peaking in 1989 and 1990 at just below 9 per cent and subsequently fluctuating downwards to reach a low of 1.7 per cent in 1995 before recovering to 3.1 per cent in 1996.

In the context of venture capital firms, it is important to recognize that where specialist mezzanine providers combine with venture capital firms to put together a financial structure, problems may arise because of conflicts of interest with mezzanine providers particularly in respect of the returns being sought and in dealing with problem cases. While mezzanine has so far been limited to buy-out and buy-in investments, there is growing interest in the possibilities of using mezzanine for expansion funding where venture capital terms may not be considered attractive by owner managers. In addition, although a US-style quoted 'junk bond' market (Altman, 1990; Molyneux, 1990) did not develop in the UK in the late 1980s, there are signs in the late 1990s that this is changing. In addition, a number of UK and European deals completed in 1997 issued junk bonds on the US market (Initiative Europe/CMBOR, 1997).

Venture capital trusts (VCTs)

VCTs were introduced in April 1995 and provided various taxation incentives to invest in small unquoted companies. VCTs aim to invest in a range of companies, so enabling investors to spread their risk. Companies are able to raise up to £1 million per year from a VCT. Companies must be unquoted or listed on AIM and have assets of less than £10 million. Individuals subscribing to VCTs obtain 20 per cent income tax relief on purchase of the shares. In addition it is possible to postpone the payment of capital gains tax by re-investing in a VCT gains which would otherwise be chargeable. 'There is no income tax payable on any dividends. Gains made within a VCT can be distributed as tax-free dividends. The maximum total investment allowed in each tax year in VCTs is £100 000. In order to qualify for the taxation benefits it is necessary for the shares to be held for at least five years and for the investment rules of the scheme to be followed. VCT losses can be set against capital gains. Up to August 1996, £162 million was raised through 13 VCTs according to the BVCA. However, while VCTs may become important at smaller and earlier stages before formal venture capital firms become involved, their ability to select good investments remains to be seen.

Comparisons with Continental Europe

There are considerable variations in the size of venture capital markets in individual European countries, both in absolute terms and with respect to the relative size of each country (Table 3.7). In terms of cumulative funds raised, a measure of a market's maturity, and actual investment activity the UK market dwarfs that of all other European countries. France, Germany and Italy, three of the largest economies in Continental Europe also display the largest amounts of funds raised, but the actual amount of investment activity in Italy remains relatively low. The number and value of investments in Germany increased rapidly in the mid-1990s.

In relation to GDP, the UK also has the largest market. However, the relative importance of the venture capital markets in the other large countries in Europe is much less than in some smaller countries, notably the Netherlands and Sweden. In these relative terms, the German market appears to be no more developed than that in Spain.

The percentage of investment portfolios divested in any particular year reflects both market conditions as well as the maturity of a market. In general, the more mature markets, such as the UK, France, Netherlands and Sweden, have the highest divestment rates in terms of the percentage of the cost of portfolios disposed of in 1996. High divestment rates are also evident in Italy, Portugal and Spain, largely reflecting the effects of the exits of a few large transactions from small overall portfolios.

The relative contributions of early stage investments and buy-outs to venture capital markets varies considerably across Europe (Table 3.8), a reflection of the relative maturity of individual markets as seen in Chapter 1. Most notably, in the mature UK market, over seven tenths of the value of venture capital investments in 1996 related to buy-outs, compared with two fifths of the number of investments. Among the other large countries, the share of the value of the French venture capital market accounted for by buy-outs dropped sharply in 1996 from the fourth largest in Europe to eighth. In Switzerland and Sweden, buy-outs accounted for the second and third largest shares of venture capital market value.

Table 3.7 Venture capital in Europe

Country	Cum. funds raised (ECU m)	Amount investments 1996 (ECU m)	No. investments 1996	Investment as % of GDP 1996	Divestments (% of portfolio at cost 1996)
Austria	75	1	4	0.0001	5.3
Belgium	1429	109	158	0.05	9.2
Denmark	456	34	38	0.02	9.7
Finland	331	40	111	0.04	10.2
France	11 697	849	1 186	0.07	17.3
Germany	5 168	715	769	0.04	12.9
Ireland	574	38	65	0.07	2.6
Italy	4 884	510	198	0.05	16.6
Netherlands	3 271	593	320	0.19	17.0
Norway	502	83	154	0.07	11.9
Portugal	475	34	74	0.04	17.1
Spain	1 396	193	158	0.04	17.8
Sweden	1 862	420	172	0.21	14.2
Switzerland	789	127	32	0.04	6.5
UK	25 653	2 973	1 715	0.33	17.4

Source: EVCA (1997).

The European buy-out market has been dominated by that of the UK for the last 15 years. For the decade from the mid-1980s, the period for which it is possible to provide comparative data across Europe, the number of deals completed in the UK has exceeded the total for other main European countries combined in each year. The difference between the value of the UK and Continental European buy-out markets is less marked. Apart from the exceptional years at the beginning and end of the period, when the UK experienced a small number of mega-deals, the total value of Continental European deals was generally a little above that for the UK.

Table 3.8 Comparison of investment stages in Europe (1996)

Country	Early stage (% of inv. value)	Early stage (% of inv. no.)	Buy-out (% of inv. value)	Buy-out (% of inv. no.)
Austria	30.6	50.0	0.0	0.0
Belgium	18.7	32.2	2.9	3.2
Denmark	6.8	18.4	22.2	13.2
Finland	22.5	50.4	12.0	9.0
France	11.5	14.4	12.1	15.7
Germany	13.3	36.5	21.1	7.9
Ireland	8.0	20.0	6.7	4.6
Italy	8.9	28.3	30.2	12.1
Netherlands	15.5	27.8	31.2	22.5
Norway	6.9	11.6	1.0	2.6
Portugal	3.4	5.4	10.3	4.1
Spain	6.2	26.6	6.1	3.8
Sweden	1.3	17.4	43.7	8.1
Switzerland	4.2	25.0	56.5	34.4
UK	1.4	6.1	71.7	40.9

Note: Early stage = seed and start-up.

Source: EVCA (1997).

Within Continental Europe, there are major differences between the size and stage of development of buy-out markets (Figure 3.1). A buy-out market requires four sets of positive conditions to be present if it is to develop. These concern the demand for managers to undertake a buy-out; the supply of businesses suitable for buy-outs from willing vendors; the infrastructure to complete transactions; and opportunities for the investors in buy-outs to realize their gains. As shown by Wright, Thompson and Robbie (1992), across Europe the impact of these factors on the development of buy-out markets varies markedly. These conditions may change over time so that underdeveloped markets begin to display growth and previously active markets experience a learning and adaptation process. As a result of these changes, some well-established markets began to show growth again in the late 1990s, while the long awaited surge in others appeared at last to have arrived. France was consistently the largest market in Continental Europe in terms of numbers of transactions from the mid-1980s. The relatively mature Dutch market saw a modest increase

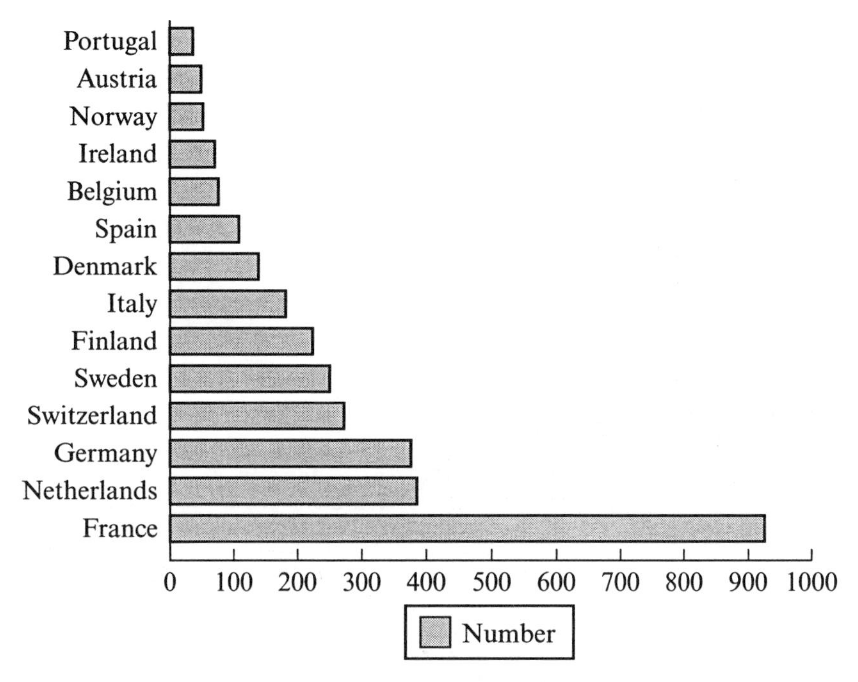

Source: Initiative Europe/CMBOR (1997).

Figure 3.1 European buy-outs (number) 1989–96

in deal completions in the mid-1990s, but the growth in deal numbers in both Germany and Switzerland in this period is particularly noticeable.

In terms of the value of transactions, France had also been the major market until 1996, when for the first time it was exceeded by Germany (Figure 3.2). France is likely to see significant market growth in 1997, but Germany moved into second place in terms of the total value of transactions in the period 1989–96 with a doubling in the size of its market value in 1996, to exceed the equivalent of £1 billion for the first time. Compared to pre-1993 trends, the long-established Dutch market has also experienced strong transaction values in the past three years as average deal size has increased. However, Italy and Switzerland showed the strongest performance increases in 1996, both achieving record transaction values. Although both deal volume and value have increased in Switzerland with some of the largest recent European deals being located there, there are no marked signs of strong growth in deal volume in Italy.

The important economic contribution of buy-outs is reflected in comparisons with the level of GDP. For example, in the UK buy-outs accounted for over 1 per cent of GDP in 1996, whilst the shares in France and Germany were 0.1 per cent and 0.07 per cent, respectively. Expressing the value of transactions as a

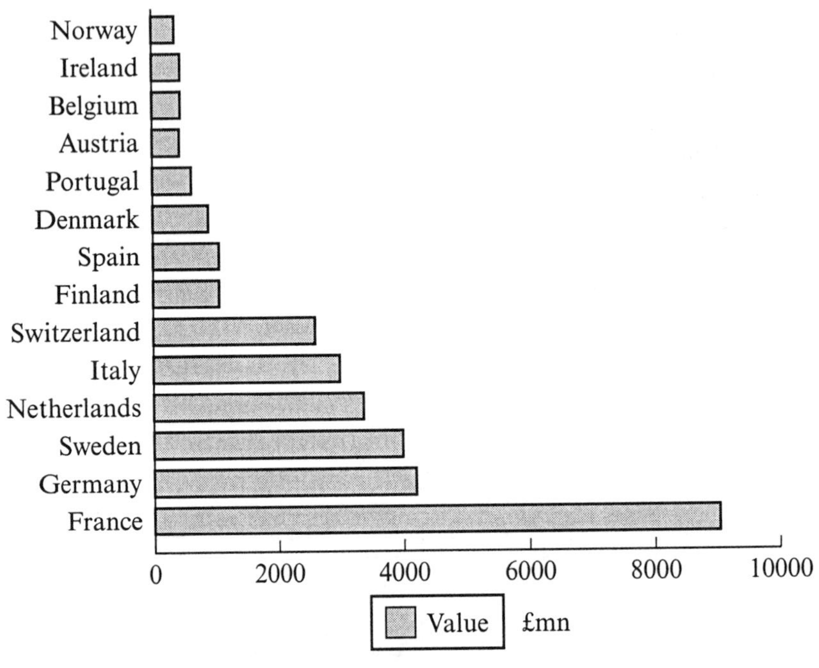

Source: Initiative Europe/CMBOR (1997).

Figure 3.2 European buy-out markets (value) 1989–96

percentage of GDP alters the relative sizes of buy-out markets quite dramatically. While the UK remains clearly the largest market, Switzerland becomes the second largest, followed closely by Finland. The rankings of the buy-out markets of all the large Continental European economies, that is France, Germany, Spain and Italy, on this basis are considerably lower than would be expected from their relative GDP rankings. France, the second largest market in absolute terms, falls to tenth place. Third-placed Germany moves to twelfth position.

Reflecting the differing ownership structures of firms, there are marked differences in the sources of buy-outs and buy-ins both between Europe and the US and within Europe (Initiative Europe/CMBOR, 1997). Although leveraged buyouts of companies quoted on a stock market are often seen as epitomising the US market, they accounted for little more than five per cent of transactions during the period 1991–96. On average, of course, they are considerably larger than buy-outs from other sources. In continental Europe, buy-outs of quoted companies account for a higher share of the Swedish market than they do in the US. These buy-outs tend to be smaller than their US counterparts, with significant stakes generally being held by family shareholders. However, the considerable number of quoted companies across Europe with substantial family shareholdings (for example, France) indicates considerable scope for further buy-outs of this kind as families seek to deal with succession problems.

In both the US and most of the major markets in Europe, buy-outs involving subsidiaries or divisions of larger groups account for the majority of transactions. The share of deals arising on divestment is particularly marked in Finland, the Netherlands and Sweden, where upwards of three-quarters of deals are from this source. In clear contrast, little more than two-fifths of French and Italian buy-outs involve divested assets. Rather, sales to management of privately-held family businesses are relatively more important in these two countries. In France, about a half of deals are from this source, while in Italy over two-fifths of buy-outs are of family businesses.

The UK market has seen a regular stream of buy-outs which involve the privatisation of modest sized parts of larger state and local government owned enterprises. There have been modest numbers of privatization buy-outs in Continental Europe but this remains an undeveloped source of deals. As privatization programmes gather pace, such transactions are likely to become an important part of buy-out markets in several European countries.

Conclusions

The discussion in this chapter highlights a number of key expected developments in venture capital and buy-out markets into the next millennium. Particularly important areas concern the generation of new transactions, the scope for the development of Continental European markets, accessing sources of funds and the impact of competing and complementary sources of finance.

The increase in competition among venture capital firms emphasizes the need for them to be more proactive in creating transactions and in identifying new types of deal. In this regard, investor-led buy-outs (IBOs) are expected to become an even more important part of the market. A further feature of the increasing pressure on venture capital firms to find novel investment opportunities where added value can be achieved is the emergence of build-ups. These involve the identification of an initial buy-out transaction which will act as the locomotive to which further companies can be added, typically through the acquisition of related enterprises, to create a larger group of companies.

Pressure and incentives for closer relationships between venture capital firms and investees stem partly from the greater need to add value in an environment where competition for deals means the payment of full entry price–earnings multiples. The lessons of the problems created by insufficient monitoring of buy-ins and highly leveraged transactions are also being learnt. These developments also require more operationally-oriented venture capitalists. There remain, however, concerns about future poor returns on recent investments where venture capitalists are unable to generate sufficient added value especially where there is overpayment in buy-out auctions. While there is evidence that venture capital firms are seeking to learn from past problems in carefully developing their strategies, competitive pressures to invest the substantial amounts of funds raised during the latter half of the 1990s may be difficult to resist.

After slow beginnings, the environment for growth in the buy-out markets of some of the largest European countries is now in place. Greater corporate restructuring in the face of greater pressures to generate shareholder value, the growth in privatization programmes and pressure to address succession problems all mean an increasing willingness of owners to sell across Europe. There remains some resistance by family owners in countries like Germany to the notion of turning second tier managers into owners.

The crucial question concerns the speed with which the factors conducive to the growth of buy-outs and buy-ins will lead to actual deal completions. The extent of new fundraising in the late 1990s in major European countries such as France and Germany, together with the substantial amounts of funds available elsewhere for cross-border deals, suggests that if positive economic conditions prevail there will be significant market growth into the next millennium. In late 1998, however, macroeconomic conditions began to look less positive.

An important feature of the growing maturity of venture capital and buy-out markets is the increase in exits from investments. Accompanying the exits by venture capitalists from deals is the exit by the management entrepreneurs. An emerging key issue is the extent to which it will be possible to find opportunities to reinvest in these individuals to create serial entrepreneurs. Difficulties in exiting large numbers of investments through more conventional IPO and trade sale routes are also likely to give rise to the development of more novel forms of exit such as secondary buy-outs and buy-ins. Both serial entrepreneurs and serial buy-outs are discussed in more detail in Chapter 14.

The European venture capital and buy-outs markets have seen an increasing number of cross-border deals, often involving divisions of larger groups with activities spread across several countries. The generally larger size of these kinds of buy-outs and the typically complex issues they raise mean that relatively few institutions are able to lead them. Although a number of large cross-border deals have been led from a base of expertise located in one country, important differences in market conditions in individual countries emphasize the need for networks of local offices and contacts throughout Europe. It is anticipated that with the benefits of learning from the mistakes of those institutions who entered other European markets in the late 1980s, there will be further extensive entry by non-domestic players, especially from the UK.

With respect to obtaining funds for investment, the evidence in this chapter suggests venture capitalists are increasingly seeking to identify ways in which they can make themselves attractive to funds providers and that funds providers are placing increasing emphasis on previous performance and focusing investment in a few large funds. The industry has already made significant progress towards being seen as an asset class by funds providers and the importance attached by independent firms in particular to such recognition further emphasizes the need for carefully developed strategies which will enable venture capital firms to demonstrate that their investments yield attractive and reliable returns which compare favourably with other asset classes. The further development of co-investment rights may also be an important aspect of meeting the needs of funds providers. Venture capital firms display significant awareness of the implications of expected increases in monitoring by funds providers and are engaging in major efforts to identify the monitoring needs of funds providers as a means of differentiating themselves in the market place. These issues are discussed further in Chapter 9.

Business angels were seen as providing a complementary service to venture capital firms which was as yet underdeveloped. The recognition of important complementarities with business angels and entrepreneurs exiting from venture-backed investments suggests opportunities to develop further links in this area. The skills and size base of informal venture capitalists may see them as best placed to nurture newly established businesses while formal venture capital firms become involved at the next round of financing. Developed in a formal way which also provides for the fair valuation of earlier stage investments, this may offer possibilities for addressing the needs of this part of the market.

The extent to which all these avenues develop and the success they are likely to achieve will depend greatly on the availability of attractive investment propositions as the venture capital market moves into the next millennium.

Notes

1. This appears to suggest a higher investment rate than for formal venture capitalists, although this does not necessarily mean that informal investors are identifying better opportunities or making better investment decisions.
2. The differences between these two studies may in part be accounted for by the nature of the samples used in the two surveys, with the Mason and Harrison survey containing a greater proportion of business angels who were members of public sector networks while the Stevenson and Coveney survey had a higher proportion of business angels who were or had been members of the private sector VCR network.

References

Altman, E. (1990), 'Setting the record straight on junk bonds', *Journal of Applied Corporate Finance*, **39** (2),82–95.

BVCA (1996a), *Report on Investment Activity*, London: BVCA.

BVCA (1996b), *BVCA Performance Measurement Survey*, London: BVCA.

Bygrave, W. (1994), 'Rates of return from venture capital', ch. 1 in W. Bygrave, M. Hay and J. Peeters (eds), *Realizing Investment Value*, London: FT-Pitman, 12–38.

EVCA (1997), *EVCA Yearbook*, Zaventem: European Venture Capital Association.

Initiative Europe/CMBOR (1997), *Europe Buy-out Review*, 8th edition, London: Initiative Europe.

Jensen, M. (1993), 'The modern industrial revolution: exit, and the failure of internal control systems', *Journal of Finance*, **48**, 831–80.

Kleiman, R. and J. Shulman (1992), 'The risk–return attributes of publicly traded venture capital: implications for investors and public policy', *Journal of Business Venturing*, **7** (3), 195–208.

Lorenz, T. (1989), *Venture Capital Today*, 2nd edition, Cambridge: Woodhead-Faulkner.

Manigart, S., P. Joos and D. De Vos (1993), 'The performance of publicly traded European venture capital companies', in N. Churchill et al. (eds), *Frontiers of Entrepreneurship Research 1992*, Wellesley, MA: Babson College.

Mason, C. and R. Harrison (1996), Informal venture capital: a study of the investment process, the post-investment experience and investment performance', *Entrepreneurship and Regional Development*, **8**,105–25.

Mason, C. and R. Harrison (1997), 'Business angels in the UK: a response to Stephenson and Coveney', *International Small Business Journal*, **15**, 83–90.

McNally, K. (1994), 'Sources of Finance for UK venture capital funds: the role of corporate investors', *Entrepreneurship and Regional Development*, **6**, 275–97.

Molyneux, P. (1990), 'US high yield debt and the case for a European market', *National Westminster Bank Quarterly Review*, Feb., 2–15.

Murray, G. (1991), *Change and Maturity in the UK Venture Capital Industry 1991–95*, London: BVCA.

Murray, G. and J. Lott (1995), 'Have venture capitalists a bias against investment in new technology firms', *Research Policy*, **24**, 283–99.

Robbie, K. and M. Wright (1996), *Management Buy-ins: Entrepreneurship, Active Investors and Corporate Restructuring*, Manchester: MUP.

Stevenson, H. and P. Coveney (1994), 'Survey of business angels: fallacies corrected and six distinct types of angel identified', *Venture Capital Report*, Henley on Thames.

Thompson, S. and M. Wright (1995), 'Corporate governance: the role of restructuring transactions', *Economic Journal*, **105**, May, 690–703.

Wright, M. and K. Robbie (1996a), 'Venture capitalists and unquoted equity investment appraisal', *Accounting and Business Research*, **26**, 153–70.

Wright M., S. Thompson and K. Robbie (1992), 'Venture capital and management-led leveraged buy-outs: a European perspective', *Journal of Business Venturing*, **7**, 47–71

Wright, M., K. Robbie, S. Thompson, Y. Romanet, R. Joachimsson, J. Bruining and A. Herst (1993), 'Harvesting and the longevity of management buy-outs and buy-ins: a four country study', *Entrepreneurship: Theory and Practice*, **18** (2), 89–110.

Wright M., K. Robbie, S. Thompson and K. Starkey (1994) 'Longevity and the life cycle of MBOs', *Strategic Management Journal*, **15**, 215–27.

Wright, M., S. Thompson, K. Robbie and P. Wong (1995), 'Management buy-outs in the short and long term', *Journal of Business Finance and Accounting*, **22** (4), 461–82.

Wright, M., N. Wilson and K. Robbie (1996), 'The longer term performance of management buy-outs', *Journal of Entrepreneurial and Small Business Finance*, **5** (3), 213–34.

4. Venture capital in transition economies: the cases of Hungary, Poland and Slovakia

Judit Karsai, Mike Wright, Zbigniew Dudzinski and Jan Morovic

Introduction

The countries of Central and Eastern Europe (CEE) are now deep into a long-term process of transition to a market economy. The creation of market oriented enterprises is a crucial element of this transition and has been taking place both through the establishment of new businesses (Lane, 1995; Roman, 1991; Gibb, 1993) and the privatisation of state-owned firms either through sales to other companies or to incumbent management and employees (Karsai and Wright, 1994). While these developments have already led to a significant private sector throughout much of CEE, a number of major problems need to be addressed before transition to a fully functioning market economy is achieved (Grosfeld and Hare, 1991). The development of entrepreneurship was severely constrained under the regimes in existence prior to 1989 and although there has been extensive creation of new businesses since then, considerable progress still needs to be made in the development of entrepreneurial skills (Filatotchev et al., 1996b). Similarly, although much of the state-owned enterprise sector has been transferred to the private sector, major problems remain in converting them into commercially viable enterprises, not least because of problems with the age and vintage of productive capacity and the level of managers' commercial skills.

Developing a successful private sector also faces two further major problems. The first concerns access to finance. Roman (1991) in a survey of entrepreneurs in 214 Hungarian small and medium-sized enterprises (SMEs) found that access to finance was one of the major problems they faced, with this being a particular constraint on their ability to increase the level of technology in their enterprises. State-owned enterprises which have been acquired by incumbent management and employees, which account for a significant proportion of privatizations throughout the region, also face financial problems. These problems arise whether the enterprises have been privatised through voucher schemes (Boycko et al., 1993), as in Russia, or through the purchase in a manner similar to Western European and US experience, as in Hungary and Poland (Filatotchev et al., 1996a). Enterprises privatised through vouchers are effectively given away and do not directly involve the introduction of new finance.

Enterprises sold as buy-outs, as in Hungary, typically involve the taking on of debt, but problems in the banking system severely constrain access to equity finance for innovation and growth (Estrin et al., 1992).

The second problem concerns corporate governance. Newly created enterprises with entrepreneurs inexperienced in a commercial environment and with little if any commitments to servicing outside finance may possess shortcomings in their corporate governance mechanisms. Similarly, the simple transfer of state-owned enterprises to the private sector does not necessarily enhance governance, especially where transfer is to incumbent management and employees, there is no commitment to service outside finance and there are few if any outsiders represented on enterprise boards (Boycko et al., 1993; Frydman et al., 1993; Filatotchev et al., 1996a, b).

These two problems are closely inter-linked since access to finance may be necessary for effective governance and effective governance may be a condition for access to finance. These problems may be addressed in CEE with the introduction of closely involved investors such as venture capitalists who can help to solve the dual problem of an inadequate system of corporate governance and a lack of long-term finance for restructuring and investment. They offer a form and style of financing which is not provided elsewhere in the spectrum of financial services available in CEE so far, in respect of its combination of a certain length of commitment with greater involvement and a degree of influence over the companies in which equity stakes are taken (Beecroft, 1994).

This chapter examines the initial development of venture capital in CEE by focusing on the cases of Hungary, Poland and Slovakia. The first two began the transformation process somewhat earlier than other countries and now have two of the most significant venture capital industries in the region; the third began the transformation process later and has a venture capital industry at a considerably earlier stage. The chapter utilises both desk research of secondary data as well as the results of the first surveys of Hungarian, Polish and Slovak venture capital firms using face-to-face interviews and a mail questionnaire. The following section discusses the theoretical issues influencing the development of a venture capital market, both in general and in relation to Hungary, Poland and Slovakia. The third section summarises the development of the venture capital industries in each country in the context of the elements of the general model of the development and operation of a venture capital market discussed in Chapter l. The fourth section outlines the methodology used for the survey of venture capitalists and the fifth section presents the results. The final section presents some conclusions.

Theoretical issues

As seen in Chapter 1, in general the development and operation of a venture capital market will be influenced by the interactions between factors affecting the general cultural, legal and institutional environment; competitive forces at the industry level; the incentives and governance mechanisms in place in individual venture capital firms; and the process by which firms make their investments (Wright et al., 1992; Bruno, 1986; Roure et al., 1990). These themes are now discussed in relation to the three countries examined here.

Cultural, legal and institutional factors

These have been shown to involve such issues as the factors which influence the generation of investment opportunities, including the willingness of entrepreneurs to use venture capital; legal and taxation frameworks, which may include particular measures to favour or not disfavour certain types of investment; the ability to use a range of financing instruments, and the ability of non-domestic funds to enter markets without (undue) legal and taxation barriers; institutional factors which include the availability of networks of intermediaries and the existence of developed stock markets and markets in corporate assets (Wright et al., 1992). In the three countries examined, considerable efforts are required to introduce legal and institutional frameworks appropriate to the functioning of a market economy. The extent to which these factors are becoming more conducive to the development of venture capital markets may be expected to vary between the three countries.

Industry level

As shown by Bruno (1986), Porter's (1980) competitive forces model provides a framework for reviewing industry level issues as it directly analyses the ability of an industry to sustain long-term profitability by reference to the degree of inter-firm rivalry, the power and roles of customers and suppliers, new entrants and providers of substitute products and services. These factors have been shown to vary considerably across Western Europe (Roure et al., 1990) and in markets in transition such as Hungary, Poland and Slovakia, and may be expected to contain a mixture of positive and negative factors with the emphasis on the latter. Ooghe et al. (1991) and Murray (1991) argue that market development is likely to be associated with greater competition, reduced rates of return and a shift to later stage investments. In the three countries examined here, it may be expected that there is greater emphasis on earlier stage cases as well as projects specific to the country context, notably privatizations and turnarounds.

Firm level

Governance The power of suppliers of finance can be exerted through the governance mechanisms they introduce in their relationships with venture capital firms, notably in terms of the nature of the returns targets they set and the reporting requirements they impose. Though this has tended to be a neglected area in venture capital research it may be expected that as markets develop, more precise return targets and more detailed reporting requirements are formulated. In the Hungarian, Polish and Slovak situations at this stage in their transition, to the extent the market consists of more inexperienced domestic players and more experienced foreign players, differing requirements may be anticipated.

The key elements in the venture capital process given the current stage of the markets in Hungary, Poland and Slovakia would appear to relate to screening, valuation and monitoring, with later exit stages being as yet premature.

Screening

Venture capitalists face a general adverse selection problem in screening investment proposals. A considerable number of studies have now examined the criteria used by venture capitalists as a means of addressing this issue. Though there is some debate about the emphasis placed on market acceptance of products versus entrepreneurial characteristics, the viability of projects and timing of returns, and the trade-offs between these factors, venture capitalists typically place great emphasis on detailed scrutiny of all aspects of a business. Scrutiny of accounting and financial information, including sensitivity analysis, is of particular importance especially in later stage transactions where such information may be expected to be more robust (Wright and Robbie, 1996).

Venture capitalists, as with other investors, may be faced with serious adverse selection problems in investing in CEE since difficulties are posed in screening the capabilities of management who typically have not operated in a market environment before and information may be particularly subjective. In CEE there may also be concerns about the availability of appropriate managerial expertise, both in respect of the entrepreneurs making proposals and the executives who are to conduct investee monitoring, at least in the short to medium term. Venture capitalists may seek to hold positions in investee companies which give them effective control in order to address potential adverse selection issues.

Valuation and due diligence

Venture capital projects are typically valued by applying one or more valuation techniques to the financial and accounting information relating to the potential investee typically contained in the business plan submitted by management to the venture capitalist (Wright and Robbie, 1996). Forward looking information in the business plan may be subject to sensitivity analysis both by management and their advisers and by the venture capitalist according to the expected influence on future performance of other information. Evidence from the UK shows that most importance appears to be attached to price earnings multiples based valuation methods (Wright and Robbie, 1996), particularly among later stage investors. The process is likely to involve several iterations based on assumptions about the future trend in performance to test the robustness of the point at which the proposed venture meets an acceptable internal rate of return (IRR), the most common measure of performance used in the industry (Murray, 1991). Wright and Robbie (1996) indicate that by the early–mid-1990s venture capitalists were undertaking widespread assessment of risk. A variety of issues broadly categorised as time restrictions, cost constraints and situational factors, may directly impact the level of due diligence during the process of investee assessment and argue for an emphasis on own rather than third party analysis.

In Hungary, Poland and Slovakia, uncertain and developing market environments may be expected to pose particular problems for the valuation of enterprises. The absence of developed markets in corporate assets and the absence of historic records of businesses operating in a market environment pose potential problems for the use of mechanisms which rely on benchmarks against the prices of companies sold in similar sectors. Uncertain environments may pose problems for the use of discounted cash flow based methods of valuation or anticipated earnings, particularly because of difficulties in forecasting future performance, difficulties in enforcing contracts and the opening up of markets to new competition. Historically different accounting policies and vague ownership legislation, especially in relation to land and buildings, coupled with environmental uncertainty also raises potential difficulties for the use of mechanisms based on historic or replacement cost asset valuations. These issues have arisen throughout CEE in relation to the sale of state-owned assets, Hungarian experience being analysed in Valentiny et al. (1992) and Pasztor (1991), but are a general problem in transition economies. It may be expected that an important approach by venture capitalists towards dealing with these difficulties will be to use several methods in order to obtain a range of valuations[1] and, given the difficulties in obtaining information, to use their own due diligence.

Research from developed venture capital markets provides a number of important insights into the monitoring of investees. Sahlman (1990) shows that venture capitalists use various mechanisms to encourage entrepreneurs both to perform and to reveal accurate information. Lerner (1995) shows that the nature and intensity of monitoring activities varies as the need dictates and especially increases in early stage and problem cases. MacMillan et al. (1989) show that differing levels of involvement in venture capital investments was not related to the nature of the operating business but to the choice exercised by the venture capital firm itself as to the general style it wished to adopt. Mitchell et al. (1995) show that venture capitalists' accounting information demands are designed to deal with moral hazard and information asymmetry problems and provide safeguards through bonding arrangements. Accounting information flows are typically required on a more regular and more detailed basis than are statutory requirements for quoted companies.

An important aspect of monitoring concerns the relative roles of structural mechanisms and processes. Barney et al. (1989) examine the influences on the degree to which elaborate governance mechanisms are used by venture capitalists and found that high agency risks and business risks were associated with more elaborate governance structures. Sapienza and Gupta (1994) find that the frequency of interaction between the two parties depends on the extent of the CEO's new venture experience, the venture's stage of development, the degree of technological innovation being pursued and the extent of goal congruence between the CEO and the venture capitalist. Fried and Hisrich (1995) for the US also provide evidence of the importance of flexibility through personal relationships in the governance of venture capital and buy-out investments and that formal power needs to be used sparingly and almost only when things go wrong to be effective.

In the Hungarian, Polish and Slovak contexts, it may be expected that venture capital firms place great importance on offering strategic guidance to investees, and especially managing crises and problems figuring highly, though there may be differences between types of firms in their perceptions about these roles and their ability to undertake them, perhaps particularly in the case of public sector venture capitalists. Uncertain market conditions may be expected to be linked to the use of a wide range of monitoring devices, with close relationships being especially important. Moreover, the possibility for rapidly changing conditions in transition markets places considerable importance on the timely receipt of information concerning problems as well as effective and flexible responses.

The venture capital markets in Hungary, Poland and Slovakia

Hungary

The Hungarian venture capital market is one of the most developed in CEE, and using the elements of a market outlined in the previous section, this section analyses the factors influencing its growth. Estimates by the Hungarian Venture Capital Association suggest that in 1995 the value of amounts already invested and still available to be invested was in the region of US$400–500 million, excluding funds which may be invested in Hungary through European Bank for Reconstruction and Development (EBRD) funds and pan-CEE funds. By 1997 it was reported that the EBRD was contributing $8.5 million of the $40 million share capital of the new venture capital company to be established with the Hungarian–American Enterprise Fund and the British Foreign and Colonial Emerging Markets Fund. Precise figures are not available as many firms regard their investment activities as commercially secret, but estimates suggest that the US$250 million already invested has involved 350–400 investee firms, with an average size of investment of US$0.4–0.8 million. In the Czech Republic, per capita venture capital amounts already invested and still available were 44 per cent of the Hungarian figure, while the comparable figure for Poland was 53 per cent.

After an initial surge between 1989 and 1991, there was something of a hiatus in the development of the industry until 1994. Original expectations proved to be over-optimistic as the country's economic problems were deeper and longer lasting than anticipated (Adam, 1995), with a consequent impact on the availability of potentially attractive venture capital projects.

The Hungarian Venture Capital Association comprises 17 members, with there being other providers of venture capital who are not members. Providers of venture capital in Hungary can be divided into several broad groups, comprising: two state-owned venture capital firms financing innovation; internationally registered investment funds operating in Hungary as trust companies and which account for the major part of the industry, with investments generally in the range US$0.5–6 million; pan-CEE venture capital funds which include Hungary as part of their target market, including private sector firms, funds available from international agencies and the Hungarian–American Enterprise Fund, with investments generally in the range US$5–6 millions plus; the state-owned Hungarian Bank for Investment and Development (HBID), now renamed the Hungarian Development Bank (HBD); eight regional development companies, in which HBD owns a controlling interest and which are aimed at smaller regional investments (below US$0.5 million) within Hungary; commercial banks with venture capital interests; and private companies whose main interests encompass a range of consulting and financial services activities as well as venture capital. HBD has a unique legal status, being the only development bank regulated by a special chapter in the new Law on Financial Lending Institutions. HBD has contributed HUF 580 million as the main founder, with the National Technology Development Committee and the Ministry of Trade, Industry and Tourism, of the newly created HUF 1 billion state-owned venture capital company called Corvinus which aims to acquire minority stakes in foreign investments of Hungarian firms.

By 1996, the two state-owned innovation funds had essentially invested all their available funds and were constrained by a lack of profitable realizations from making further significant investments. The regional development funds are some of the most recent entrants into the market. Funds from outside Hungary generally have investment size limits significantly above those for venture capital firms based entirely within the country. Relatively new players in the venture capital market are compensation voucher utilisation companies such as HB Westminster and Arago, who invest their capital by managing and then selling off property acquired with the vouchers. Graboblast Holding, which represents the first manufacturing company to enter the venture capital market, has founded a venture capital company with HUF 0.5 billion in order to take part in privatisations of state-owned companies. Also Boeing Corporation and Advent International have introduced a $30–50 million private equity fund to be managed by Equinox a subsidiary of Creditanstalt.

Preferred industries for investment are primarily food processing, followed by electronics, telecommunication, pharmaceuticals, precision instruments, financial and information services and franchise networks. Few venture capital firms are involved in high risk innovation sectors, the two state-owned innovation companies being the primary exceptions, with other firms having a broader range of target sectors. Most firms focus on private companies with a comparatively short track record. Buy-outs arising on privatisation could benefit from preferential credit schemes which offered more attractive terms than venture capital, so that venture capital may only have a significant role when these firms begin to grow. Turnaround or liquidation cases also offer significant possibilities for venture capital firms.

Hungarian law as it currently stands involves a number of provisions which are not conducive to the development of venture capital firms. The law effectively prohibits the establishment of investment funds which aim to invest in venture capital since investment funds are able to purchase shares in unquoted companies to the value of ten per cent of their net capital worth. As a result the most common form of organisation for investment in venture capital is the corporation, with company law prescribing the rights of minority shareholders to convene general shareholders' meetings (10 per cent) or to have a veto (25 per cent). Under Hungarian company law, foreign investors are treated on an equal footing with domestic investors and have the right of free foreign exchange transfer. Venture capital companies are subject to the general provisions of corporate income tax law which make no provision for the special nature of venture capital investments. In addition, the taxation framework does not provide for the so-called portfolio concession in respect of losses or gains realised in portfolio companies.

Preparations for regulating Hungary's venture capital industry commenced in 1996 in the wake of a government decision to develop small and medium-sized enterprise. The architects of the bill began with the premise that venture capital is disadvantaged compared to other types of investment and with the objective that the new legislation would introduce concessions from the state which would offset this situation. The bill proposed enabling venture capital investments to be carried out through funds and through companies. Regulations on investment activity mean that venture capital investors wishing to benefit from the provisions of the law are prohibited from dealing with other kinds of activities, although exceptionally they may be permitted to engage in stock exchange deals and buy real estates. Free capital must be kept in government securities or bank deposits.

Investments in one company or group of companies cannot exceed 15 per cent of the equity capital of the venture capital investor. Venture capital investors are not allowed to give loans to their portfolio companies, unless their equity stake exceeds 25 per cent in a given investee. Loans and subordinated loan capital cannot exceed the volume of all invested capital in the investee company. The total of all loans plus subordinated loan capital plus invested share capital cannot exceed 20 per cent of the equity capital of the venture capital investor.

Investors wishing to use the possible concessions provided by the law would have to meet further requirements covering 'purposeful investment activity', that is venture capital firms and funds have to invest a given percentage of their available capital in other firms. The bill provided for two options. According to option 'A', during the first six years after foundation the average size of investment must reach at least 50 per cent of equity capital, 70 per cent of which must be invested within 3 years. Under option 'B', there is no need to meet these conditions as all tax exemptions are due only after venture capital investment income has been received.

The bill provided two options through which small investors willing to deposit their savings in venture capital funds can obtain tax concessions. Dividends coming from venture capital investment would receive preferential treatment with small investors paying only half of the usual tax rate. Under option 'A' small investors and corporations making qualifying investments receive a 50 per cent allowance on capital gains when investments are sold providing the appropriate investment obligations are met, while option 'B' applies general rules on the taxation of capital gains. Venture capital firms and funds would not be liable for corporation tax if they meet the requirements of option 'A'. Under option 'B', investors were required to pay corporation tax but were allowed to deduct the capital gain and dividend and yield from their taxable profits.

The bill also addressed the possible *role of the state* in venture capital financing. The state can play a direct role through buying shares in venture capital companies or funds. An important precondition for undertaking such kind of financing is to permit state funds to transfer their capital for venture financing purposes. Another proposed type of state involvement in venture capital activity concerns a provision to guarantee the return of the face value of invested capital (up to a maximum of 50 per cent of the whole investment). Special accounting rules are also planned for venture capital investors concerning write-off for losses and creating provisions. An amended version of the bill became law in March 1998.

Following a law introduced in 1991 and its subsequent amendments, the Hungarian accounting system follows closely international accounting standards. The 1995 amendment of the 1991 law permits firms to decide whether to record invested assets at book or market value. However, from the point of view of venture capitalist evaluation, the effect of taxation regulations on the presentation of financial reports may provide a misleading picture of the operating position of a company unless appropriate adjustments are made. Moreover, even though the accounting framework has been amended, there is still scope for distortions both as a result of the considerable discretion allowed by the rules and the persisting effects of the earlier regime (Valentiny et al., 1992).

The Budapest Stock Exchange is one of the most developed in CEE and in 1995/6 was one of the fastest growing stock exchanges in the world. Turnover in the 42 companies whose shares were listed on the market amounted in 1995 to US$634 million. Turnover in 1996 was higher than in the five previous years combined. The Budapest Stock Exchange Index rose 2.6 times in 1996 and in the first five months of 1997 rose by nearly 43 per cent. The average price–earnings (PE) ratio rose from 10.9 in 1995 to 16.5 in 1996. The number of listed companies rose to 45 in 1996 as a result of six new entrants and three exits. As a result of the new Securities Act, companies with publicly issued shares totalling more than HUF 200 million must be listed on the Budapest Stock Exchange by 1998.

Though foreign investors are active there are few domestic ones, with there being a general view that there is a further need for more companies to become listed on the market if it is to become developed. According to estimates, 70–80 per cent of market turnover is accounted for by foreign investors. As interest rates continue to fall, domestic private investors have appeared on the stock market which although riskier offer higher yields. The role of institutional investors is not yet major, with approximately HUF 20 billion being invested in shares on the Budapest Stock Exchange by insurance companies, investment funds and voluntary mutual benefit funds in 1996. There is a relatively active OTC market, where costs are lower and regulations more lax. The takeover market is also developing, not least through the acquisition of companies in commercial banks' portfolios facing financial problems by other firms who have already made the transition.

Owing to the relative newness of the Hungarian venture capital market, there have been few exits from venture capital firms' portfolios and those which have occurred have tended to be precipitated by financial problems. Up to 1996, two venture-backed firms had achieved an IPO – Global TH and Pannonplast. In 1997, three further IPOs occurred: Euronet Services, financed by the Hungarian–American Enterprise Fund; and Biorex and Nabi belonging to the First Hungary Fund. Because of the liquidity problems on the Hungarian market there appears to be a preference among some investors to aim for an IPO on a more developed market outside the country. Indeed the first two cases above were listed on the New York and London Stock Exchanges, while the third was listed on the Budapest Stock Exchange.

There are some indications that trade sales to other financial investors, especially where specialist reorganisation skills are involved, are becoming a feature of the Hungarian venture capital market. However, the most common form of exit for smaller and more troubled companies appears to be sale of the venture capitalists' shares to the other owners of the business. Successful examples of trade sales include among others the Kanisza Brewery and the Ocsai Gasheater Factory, both sold by Bankar. Other examples include the sale of Viktoria Cereal Trading, financed by the Hungarian Development Bank and Recognita Software, financed by the Hungarian–American Investment Fund. The Csaba Canning Factory was sold after partial reorganisation by the Hungarian Development Fund to another venture capital investor, Advent International. While sale to other financial investors is also a feature of some Western European markets, buy-back is less common (Wright et al., 1993b). There is little evidence as yet about the returns achieved on these investments. Evidence on the returns sought is presented below.

Some 70 per cent of the funds for venture capital firms is sourced from the US and UK, with further moderate amounts from other European countries such as Holland. Domestic commercial banks investing in venture capital type transactions through holding company structures can have an important influence on the ability of investee companies to obtain further credits. Very few investment banks are present in the Hungarian capital market, not least because the law until 1996 did not permit such institutions on the Anglo-American model. Investment funds have a limited role partly because of legal constraints and partly because safer and higher returns can be earned by investing in government securities. Similarly, insurance companies while potentially being highly important also tend to invest in more secure and more rewarding bonds. Pension funds are at present just beginning to develop significantly. No information is available on corporate venture capital investors and often for tax reasons business angels such as they exist tend to maintain a low profile. The National Technical Development Committee provides a modest amount of seed capital often in the form of soft loans.

A number of preferential credit schemes can provide both a complement to but often competitors for formal venture capital firms. Some of these schemes are aimed specifically at small firms while others have a broader size scope. A second group are aimed at promoting the acquisition by incumbents of privatised firms (such as the so-called Existence Credit scheme which provides for loans at advantageous terms but which was not available to venture capitalists only private individuals) or at encouraging the development and reorganisation of troubled firms. A further classification is whether the schemes are aimed at individuals or companies. Finally schemes may be funded domestically or through international agencies (such as the EU-PHARE programme, the Hungarian–American Enterprise Fund's credit scheme for small entrepreneurs). The PHARE Capital Credit program launched by the Hungarian Foundation for Enterprise Development (MVA) has important implications for the development of venture capital as it provides for small growing innovative to obtain access to credit on favourable terms. There are also a number of foreign financed schemes to help entrepreneurs establishing businesses gain access to skills training and expertise. It is anticipated that there will be further new entry by domestic and foreign venture capital firms, including an extension and development of available funds based in Hungary's regions, the establishment of venture capital firms focused on restructuring and supported by the EBRD, as well as the establishment of investment banks by existing commercial banks.

Though there are clear supply-side developments, the concept of venture capital remains underdeveloped among Hungarian entrepreneurs, including a familiar resistance to ceding part of their equity to outsiders. Hungarian entrepreneurs are probably presently ahead of their counterparts in other CEE countries in being aware of the role of venture capital. There is a clear recognition of the existence of a problem of under-capitalisation in many smaller growth-oriented firms (Roman, 1991) which together with the expected completion of the privatisation of a significant number of state-owned SMEs in the medium term, suggests the potential for a strong deal flow for venture capitalists.

Poland

The Polish venture capital industry is like that in Hungary, showing significant signs of development although as yet it remains immature. In 1996 capital under management by the twelve active venture capital firms was estimated at over $750 million. Types of venture capital firms in Poland include private limited partnerships, registered abroad; foreign investment companies, which take the form of management companies registered in Poland by foreign investors; development agencies; domestic independent companies; and bank affiliated firms typically taking the form of joint initiatives by Polish bank and the British Know-How Fund. The EBRD also plays an important role as sponsor of many venture capital firms.

The above types of firm cover three clear sectors: traditional early and expansion stage venture capital though not seed capital, the main focus of development agencies; bank affiliated firms targeting the development of deeply restructured companies; and firms focusing on turnaround and bridge financing for mature companies. Target companies arising from privatisations are the most dominant category, with the funding of innovative companies typically focusing on the introduction of commercial organisational structures. Enterprise Investors, for example, has introduced the notion of management privatisations aimed at companies which have growth prospects under the current management but which need new equity finance to become more efficient and to acquire the shares held by the state. As in Hungary, foreign venture capital firms play a very strong role in the industry and have adopted investment size criteria which may be considered large in the context of Polish firms. Development agencies tend to focus on smaller deal sizes, often below $50 000, whilst purely commercial organisations set a minimum limit of around $0.5 million, though this may be waived for very good proposals. Investments have primarily been in the construction and trade sectors. These sectors are often considered to involve significant risk in Poland and offer opportunities to adapt existing technologies.

Given the immature nature of the market there have been few exits as yet from venture capital investments. For larger firms the most common form of exit strategy is stock market flotation, with Enterprise Investors, the largest venture capital firm in Poland set up by the Polish American Enterprise Fund and the EBRD), using both the flotation route as well as staggered sales to strategic partners as means of exiting investments. Other firms emphasise trade sale or buy back of shares, although the extent to which this has occurred so far has been affected by some notable bankruptcies in the portfolios of development agencies. The Warsaw Stock Exchange has grown significantly since being established in 1991 but remains somewhat underdeveloped. Less than a hundred companies were quoted on the market in 1996 and less than a third of these used the market to raise new capital. The capitalisation of the main market in late 1996 was $7300 million and that of the parallel market was $200 million; in total these markets account for 6 per cent of GDP. From August 1996 a new less restricted free market has been added to the two existing ones with lower size hurdles that need to be met before a listing can take place ($1.5 million capitalisation as opposed to $8.8 million for the main market and $4.4 million for the parallel market) and the requirement to submit only the last year's audited accounts. Even this level of regulation poses problems for many Polish firms, so that an over-the-counter (OTC) market has also been established by 43 securities houses.

Despite the rapid growth in the creation of new firms in recent years, the underdeveloped entrepreneurial tradition and difficulties in accessing reliable information tend to mean that while venture capital firms may wish to obtain greater control in investee companies they have had to adapt the control aspect of deal structures to be compatible with the supervisory board structure of Polish corporate law. One of the most significant constraints on the development of the Polish venture capital market is the slowdown in both primary and secondary privatisation. Other aspects of the Polish economy are receiving greater attention at present than venture capital, such as macroeconomic stabilisation, foreign direct investment (FDI) and the mass privatisation programme. As in Hungary, entrepreneurs' awareness of venture capital is limited. Further problems arise from the typical situation where entrepreneurs are unwilling to be fully open with venture capitalists concerning information about their businesses. Mixed equity and debt financing is often used as a means to invest larger amounts of funds without taking control from current management.

The venture capital industry is not regulated by a specific law as yet and the legal and fiscal environment contains a number of restricting factors which mean that all private funds are registered abroad. However, there is no need for foreign firms to apply for permission to buy shares in Polish companies, although permission is required for the establishment of joint ventures with state-owned companies. Private equity funds established outside Poland generally avoid double taxation, but this does not apply to venture capital investments by domestic funds whose capital gains are taxed as ordinary income. Tax-exemption is available on income from the sales of shares in companies created under the employee leasing privatisation scheme, shares received from conversion of participation certificates in the Mass Privatisation Programme, participation units in investment trusts and some other schemes. Dividends for shareholders are subject to withholding taxes, with the amount involved for foreign shareholders dependent on various tax treaties and the level of their ownership in the company concerned. There is a 2 per cent stamp duty on share trades. There are taxation disincentives to changing businesses into limited companies, notably the much higher corporation tax rate to be paid and the liability for VAT arising from the formal requirement to 'sell' inventory and assets in moving to limited liability status. The Polish Commercial Code is based on the German model, which includes a supervisory board and relatively weak protection for minority investors.

A bill has been introduced which aims to regulate investment funds including closed-end funds, which *inter alia* would address the problem of double taxation on venture capital investments. However, the proposed law is considered restrictive as regards its emphasis on the public limited company as the only permissible legal form.

The largest amount of funds for investment in venture capital currently come from outside the country, such as the International Finance Corporation (IFC) and EBRD. To late 1996, IFC had invested $67 million in nine projects (37 per cent of its total involvement in Poland) and supported the establishment of two venture capital funds (Polish Private Equity Fund and New Europe East Investment Fund) and the EBRD had invested $310 million in 17 projects (45 per cent of its total involvement in Poland) and supported eight venture capital funds. As in Hungary, the pension system, which is important in the UK in providing the most significant source of funds for independent venture capital firms as well as their own captive firms, is only beginning to develop. The weakness of the capital structure of banks limits their ability to invest in venture capital projects, together with a legacy of bad debts resulting from lax investment activity in the late 1980s. Development agencies are active at both national and regional levels. The Industrial Development Agency (IDA) makes direct equity for debt investments in companies (mainly the restructuring of state-owned enterprises) and participates in the establishment of regional development agencies. IDA can offer soft credit and guarantees, technical assistance and capital investment. One of the first regional investment funds is the Lower Silesian

Investment Company which aims to manage equity investments in companies owned by KGHM Polish Copper and to promote regional development initiatives in activities outside the copper industry.

Slovakia

The venture capital market in Slovakia is the most underdeveloped of the three countries covered by this study and is accompanied by a poorly developed entrepreneurial culture. Although venture capital firms exist, they are few in number and the stock market ranks well behind that of Hungary and Poland. In 1996 an estimated US$96 million was available for investment by venture capital firms active in Slovakia, with US$33 million having been invested. The five main active venture capital firms in 1996 were Povbazsky a Kysucky Fond, funded by the EU and the Office for Strategic Development of Technology and Science in Slovakia; Seed Capital Company, owned by the National Agency for the Development and Support of Small and Medium-Sized Entrepreneurship; Slovak American Enterprise Fund (SAEF), fully US owned; Slovak Post Privatisation Fund, funded by EBRD and Framlington; and Investment and Development Bank, funded by the National Property Fund, VSZ, and other Slovak banks. The minimum size of investment targeted by the funds ranges from $60 000 by the Seed Capital Company to $9 million by Investment and Development Bank. The largest portfolio is held by SAEF with approximately 30 investments totalling $18 million.

There are special taxation and other incentives available in certain sectors but the legal infrastructure to encourage the development of venture capital firms remains to be introduced, including developments in appropriate financial instruments, definition of the activities permitted by venture capital funds, and so on.

Data and methodology

The surveys were carried out between May 1996 and May 1997. They involved either face-to-face interviews and/or mail questionnaires administered to managers in the venture capital firms in the three countries. The study was based on a common questionnaire developed from research carried out in the US and the UK adapted to the circumstances in Hungary, Poland and Slovakia. The number of venture capitalists asked to participate in the survey and the numbers actually interviewed in each country are shown in Table 4.1. Given the small number of active firms in each country and hence the small number of participants in the study, the mean scores reported in the results section below need to be considered only as indicative of differences between countries.

In Hungary, face-to-face interviews were conducted with venture capital firms managers. These interviews on average lasted about an hour, and covered issues concerning the background to the firm, sources of funds, main areas of activity, investment policy, and so on. Following the interview, the detailed questionnaire was left with the manager for completion. It became clear during the interviews that managers were reluctant to provide information on required rates of return, because of commercial confidentiality, and in some cases information relating to investment stages was not available. Seven of the Hungarian participants are members of HVCA and their cumulated investment value represents nearly 70 per cent of that of the HVCA. The Pan-European regional development funds were not surveyed as their establishment was too recent. Among the nine venture capital firms surveyed, three are investment funds registered outside Hungary but investing only in Hungary. Two of these funds are the largest institutions in the Hungarian venture capital industry. The remaining seven firms are mainly concerned with investment in the SME sector. Of the nine, two funds were founded by the state, two others belong to the Hungarian Bank for Investment and Development and the remaining two funds are private firms for whom venture capital is only a part of their activities. Overwhelmingly, the Hungarian firms have funds available for investment from their own sources, with one of the foreign funds and the independent fund making significant use of finance from outside sources. On average the funds have been established 4.67 years, though there is a wide variation which reflects the initial and later waves of development in the industry noted earlier. The average number of executives is 6.8 though there is also a wide range. At the time of the survey the number of investments ranged from 3 to 20. The main investment stage focuses were early and expansion stage, with three firms also engaging in investments in privatisations.

Table 4.1 Sample sizes by country

	Hungary	Poland	Slovakia
No. of firms approached	12	12	13
No. of responding firms	9	6	3

In Poland the detailed questionnaire was sent to the twelve venture capital firms which could be identified as playing an active role in the market and responses were received in six cases. Three of the funds are foreign owned, one has majority bank ownership, one is an independent private firm and one independent public firm. In four cases funds are from outside sources, in one case all funds are from own sources and in the remaining case 5 per cent of funds are from own resources. The oldest firm was established in 1991 whilst three were created in 1995. The firms still have a majority of their funds available for investment and have 2–6 investment executives, except for one firm with 33 investments in 1996 which has 14 executives. The most common investment stage focuses of activity are early and expansion phases. At the time of the survey, the number of investments made ranged from 4 to 33. The detailed questionnaire was sent to the 13 members of the Slovak Venture Capital Association. However, as seen earlier, only five of these are active in venture capital. Three venture capital firms provided full information.

Results

Governance by funds providers

The principal data on governance by funds providers was obtained from the Hungarian and Polish samples. All venture capitalists interviewed in Hungary were set a performance target of some kind, with six out of the nine being set a performance target in terms of the earning of a specific rate of return. The exceptions were the two publicly-owned companies, who were set a target in terms of being required to direct their investments into specific activities or regions, and one of the two bank captives whose targets were set in terms of the amount of cash invested in a given period.

The extent of monitoring by funds providers was very much in line with expectations. The same six venture capitalists experienced multiple types of monitoring by their funds providers: three of the foreign-owned funds having the greatest number of individual elements of monitoring; all of them being required to provide a regular written report; four having board membership by funds providers (three of the four venture capital firms with foreign ownership and one of the bank captives); three having funds providers' involvement in final investment decision; and two where monitoring focused on whether investment guidelines were being met and on where there was local control. The two publicly-owned firms and the same bank-owned captives as above were subject to only one form of monitoring, either board membership or involvement in final investment decisions.

In Poland, all the venture capital firms surveyed were set specific targets by their funds providers. The three public sector funds were required to generate a specific cash amount in a given period, the private sector firm was set a total cash return target without a time period being specified, and the mixed public/private firms were set a specific rate of return target. The public sector funds were required to target specific activities or regions. Regular written reports are required by all funds providers. Venture capital board or advisory committee membership was required in all but one case where there was the right to have a say in final investment decisions and the monitoring that investment guidelines were being followed. The most stringent control was exercised by a foreign government provider which in two firms required the full range of regular written reports, board membership, final say in investment decisions and monitoring that investment guidelines were being followed. The only private venture capital firm surveyed had the lowest level of funds provider monitoring, regular reports and membership of the advisory committee. The public-sector-funded venture capital firms tended to face detailed bureaucratic monitoring. Public-sector-funded venture capital firms tended to have less flexibility over the size of investment target but the industry of targets was of less importance.

Screening proposals

Not surprisingly, greatest emphasis across all three countries was placed on the entrepreneurs' experience in the area of the proposed project in screening proposals (Table 4.2). There was great emphasis in the three countries, especially Hungary, on the ability of venture capitalists to obtain a particular ownership stake in a project. Hungarian venture capitalists also placed greatest emphasis on clearly defined exit timings and method, and that proposals met given financial ratio benchmarks. Polish and Hungarian venture capitalists placed greater emphasis than others on the need for the legal structure of the investment meeting mutual interest. The three countries also placed emphasis on proposals meeting strictly defined size criteria, but there was less on proposals being in a given investment stage.

Table 4.2 Evaluation of investment proposals

Factors	Hungary	Poland	Slovakia
The proposal must require funding above or below a strictly defined minimum or maximum size	4.1	4.0	4.0
The proposal must result in a given percentage of ownership for your firm/fund	4.4	3.6	4.0
The proposal must fall in a given industry	1.6	1.6	2.6
The proposal must be in a given investment stage	3.2	2.6	3.0
The exit time and method must be clear	4.6	3.8	4.0
The proposal must meet a given financial ratio benchmark	4.4	3.8	2.6
The knowledge and experience of your firm/fund also must be important	2.9	3.4	2.3
The managers (entrepreneurs) must have thorough grounding in the given field	4.6	4.6	4.0
The investment pattern (legal structure) must result in a mutual interest	4.0	4.6	2.6

Note: Figures are mean scores on the basis of 1 = not important through to 5 = very important.

There were some within country differences. In the independent fund surveyed in Hungary, entrepreneurs' experience and the need for the proposal to meet a given financial benchmark stood out as being scored very low. Similarly, for one of the public venture capitalists, exit timing and method was scored very low.

Valuation and due diligence

Overall, greatest emphasis was placed on carrying out own market evaluations, with Hungarian venture capital firms recording the highest average score (Table 4.3). While Polish venture capital firms also emphasised this aspect of due diligence, their highest average score and the highest score for all five countries concerned access to previous track records. Slovakian venture capital firms placed least emphasis on independent accountants' reports.

Table 4.3 Carrying out due diligence

Factors	Hungary	Poland	Slovakia
Ordering independent accountant's report	3.0	3.8	2.0
Involving of independent financial adviser	–	2.4	2.0
Access to previous track records	3.7	4.6	4.0
Obtaining independent market report	3.9	3.8	3.0
Carrying out own market evaluation	4.7	4.4.	4.3
Personal references	4.2	3.8	3.6

Note: Figures are mean scores on the basis of 1 = not important through to 5 = very important.

In Hungary, the emphasis given to independent accountant reports varied, with the two publicly-owned venture capitalists, one of the bank captives and one of the foreign firms placing little emphasis on this source of information. These findings are similar to those for the UK (Wright and Robbie, 1996), except in the UK independent accountants' reports are accorded more importance than in Hungary.

In assessing projects, venture capital firms may use a variety of benchmark returns against which to compare individual investment opportunities. These benchmarks may be defined in standard terms or may attempt to take into account the characteristics of each proposal. The survey results suggest some differences between countries in respect of the type of benchmark which is used (Table 4.4). The developed UK market places little emphasis on standard benchmark required rates of return, as shown in Chapter 11. The three Central European countries fall between these extremes, though considerable emphasis is placed on meeting a standard required rate of return in Hungary in particular. There is less difference between the countries in respect of the average scores relating to the meeting of standard returns according to the risk band of an investment or to meeting specific returns according to the characteristics of each investment. However, Slovakian venture capital firms place greatest emphasis on the latter type of benchmark, as do UK firms (Wright and Robbie, 1996, and Chapter 11). Slovakian firms have the highest average score among the three countries surveyed. Least emphasis in general, and among Slovakian venture capital firms in particular, is given to the meeting of total cash return targets.

Table 4.4 Assessment of the targeted rate of return

Factors	Hungary	Poland	Slovakia
We require the investment to meet a standard required rate of return on equity (internal rate of return, IRR)	4.0	3.6	3.3
We require the investment to meet a standard required rate of return on equity (IRR), according to the risk band of the investment	3.4	3.8	3.6
We require the investment to meet a specific required rate of return on equity (IRR), according to the characteristics of each investment	3.1	3.4	4.3
We require a rate of return which yields a total cash return commensurate with amount invested	3.3	3.2	2.0

Note: Figures are mean scores on the basis of 1 = not important through to 5 = very important.

These results are in some contrast to those for the UK, where the order of importance was exactly reversed (Wright and Robbie, 1996). Interestingly, the independent fund in Hungary scored a requirement to meet a target IRR according to the characteristics of a particular investment highest and the meeting of a general benchmark lowest, while the foreign-owned funds gave strongest emphasis to the meeting of a general benchmark IRR.

The actual target rate of return which is sought may be varied according to a number of factors (Table 4.5). There are some noticeable variations in the relative importance of these factors between the three countries studied.

Hungarian venture capital firms place markedly greater emphasis than firms in the other countries on the expected length of investment time in a particular proposal and the actual amount of cash they invest in a proposal. Perhaps reflecting the particular problems faced by these countries, all three Central European firms place a higher emphasis than suggested by evidence from the UK on the market conditions relating to a particular proposal. General economic conditions are important in Hungary and Poland.

Interestingly, for Hungarian venture capital firms, one of the highest average scores also relates to whether they hold a majority of the equity in an investment. This finding reflects the emphasis placed by Hungarian venture capital firms on the share of the equity they own at the time of deal screening. Hungarian venture capital firms also place considerably greater emphasis among the firms in all three countries studied on the actual cash amount they receive from an investment and the industrial/product sector of the investment.

Table 4.5 Influencing factors of targeted return

Factors	Hungary	Poland	Slovakia
The expected length of investment in a particular proposal	4.7	2.8	4.0
The actual cash amount invested in a particular proposal	4.4	3.2	3.0
Market conditions relating to particular proposal	4.4	3.8	4.0
General economic conditions	3.7	3.6	2.6
Changes in returns for quoted equities	3.0	1.8	2.5
Changes in returns of long-term treasure bonds and bills	3.0	2.6	1.3
Changes in base rates	3.0	2.2	3.0
The actual cash amount you seek to receive from an investment	3.8	2.4	2.6
The industrial/product sector of the investment	4.0	3.2	2.0
The geographical region of the investment	3.0	3.2	2.0
The expected gearing ratio when the finance is structured	3.0	3.2	2.3
Whether you have a majority of the equity	4.3	2.2	2.6

Note: Figures are mean scores on the basis of 1 = not important through to 5 = very important.

As a reflection of the importance attached to the role of management at the deal screening phase, the contribution by management in terms of their managerial skills rated as a highly important factor in assessing the riskiness of a proposal in all three countries (Table 4.6). The nature of the product market of an investment proposal is also important across countries, but especially in Poland.

The financial contribution made by management is of some importance across all three countries, but especially in Slovakia. Slovakian venture capital firms also distinguish themselves from their counterparts in the other two countries because of the emphasis they place on the nature of the capital market and the expected participating dividend yield they expect to earn. Hungarian and Polish venture capital firms place considerably more emphasis on the expected time horizon to exiting their investment than do their counterparts in Slovakia.

Within the Hungarian market, the nature of the product market of the company was irrelevant for one of the publicly-owned companies and the financial contribution by management was not important for the independent venture capital firm. Some differences in objectives were reflected in assessment of riskiness, with notably one of the bank captives attaching greatest importance to the expected participating dividend yield. The expected time horizon to the redemption of preference shares was the least important factor on average, but two of the foreign-owned firms score this as important.

Table 4.6 Assessment of the riskiness of a proposal

Factors	Hungary	Poland	Slovakia
Nature of product market of the company	4.3	4.6	3.5
Nature of the capital market	3.1	2.8	4.0
Contribution by management in terms of their managerial skills	4.9	4.2	4.3
Financial contribution by management	3.8	3.8	4.5
Expected time horizon to exit of company	4.2	4.0	2.0
Expected time horizon to redemption of preference shares	2.2	3.0	2.5
Expected participating dividend yield	2.3	3.0	4.0
Legal deficiencies	3.4	3.6	3.5

Note: Figures are mean scores on the basis of 1 = not important through to 5 = very important.

Across all three countries studied, venture capital firms clearly make use of multiple sources of information in preparing their valuations of investments (Table 4.7). Apart from Slovakia, greatest importance is attached to own due diligence reports and also accounting/consulting firms' reports. Business plan financial data also figure highly, especially in Poland and Hungary. Venture capital firms in these two countries also place greater emphasis than their counterparts elsewhere on sales and marketing information, product information, and production capacity/technology information. Polish, followed by Hungarian venture capital firms, also place greater emphasis on the proposed exit timing and method. It is noticeable that information relating to or provided by entrepreneurs is of some importance in preparing valuations in Hungary and Poland, but less so in Slovakia.

Table 4.7 Sources of information in preparing valuation

Sources	Hungary	Poland	Slovakia
Financial and trade journals	–	3.6	2.6
Information provided by entrepreneurs	–	4.6	3.7
Information provided by the personnel of the given company	4.1	4.2	3.0
CSO statistics	2.3	3.4	2.3
Other statistical and information services	3.2	3.6	2.0
Other venture capitalists	3.3	3.2	3.0
Own due diligence report	5.0	4.8	3.3
Accounting/consulting firms' reports	4.0	4.4	3.3
Business plan data (e.g. balance sheet, income statement, planned data)	4.3	4.6	4.0
Proposed exit timing and method	3.9	4.4	2.5
Sales and marketing information	4.8	4.4	3. 6
Product information	4.3	4.4	3.0
Production capacity/technology information	4.0	4.2	3.3
Curriculum vitae of management	4.1	4.6	3.3

Note: Figures are mean scores on the basis of 1 = not important through to 5 = very important.

Venture capital firms in the three Central European countries place noticeably more importance on discounted cash flow (DCF) based valuation methods than do their counterparts in the UK (Table 4.8 and Wright and Robbie, 1996). Although strongly theoretically grounded, the weight of importance attached to these methods in Central European countries raises questions concerning reliability of forecasts in relatively uncertain emerging markets, as well as the extent to which sensitivity analyses are undertaken. The absence of developed capital and asset markets and concerns about the reliability of past trading records may help explain the importance of DCF-based valuation methods in these countries.

Reflecting the more developed nature of capital and asset markets in the UK, greater emphasis is placed here than in the three Central European countries on valuation methods relating to price/earnings multiples and recent transaction prices for acquisitions in comparable sectors to the investment proposals being considered. However, in Hungary EBIT multiple valuation methods score more highly than in either Poland or Slovakia.

Asset-based valuation methods are suspect theoretically and also may be particularly unreliable in emerging markets. These methods generally received low scores in all three countries surveyed, although some importance was attached to them in Poland and Slovakia.

Table 4.8 Methods used to value investments

Methods	Hungary	Poland	Slovakia
Historic cost book value	2.1	3.0	3.3
Replacement cost asset value	2.0	3.0	3.0
Liquidation value of assets	2.3	3.2	3.3
Discounted future cash flows	4.7	4.4	4.0
Dividend yield basis	3.4	3.2	4.3
Capitalised maintainable earning (price/earning multiple) (historic basis)	3.4	3.0	2.3
Capitalised maintainable earning (price/earning multiple) (prospective basis)	3.7	3.8	3.0
Capitalised maintainable earning (EBIT multiple)	4.4	3.0	2.7
Recent PE ratio of the parent company's shares	–	1.6	2.0
Recent transaction prices for acquisition in the sector	3.0	2.2	1.6
Responses to attempts to solicit bids for the potential investee	2.2	2.2	1.6
Industry-specific usual pricing ratios	2.4	3.0	2.3

Note: Figures are mean scores on the basis of 1 = not important through to 5 = very important.

There was some variation in practice within the Polish market, where DCF-based methods of valuation are only used sometimes by the private venture capital firm but almost always by the others. The publicly-owned venture capital firms usually used replacement and liquidation cost valuations of assets as well as dividend yield bases, whilst this was never the case with the private firm and the mixed private/public firm. In contrast, the private sector firm almost always used EBIT and price/earnings multiples, recent transactions prices in the sector and industry-specific pricing ratios.

Nature of services

Venture capital firms provide a wide range of services to their investee companies, but the relative importance of these services varies considerably between countries (Table 4.9). There appears to be somewhat greater involvement in the monitoring of investee firms by venture capitalists in Hungary in particular, and to a lesser extent Poland, than is the case in the less developed Slovak market. The control of portfolio management and the monitoring of financial performance is given particular emphasis in Hungary and reflects the importance venture capital firms in that country place on obtaining significant if not majority ownership stakes. Hungarian and Polish venture capital firms also place greater importance on resolving remuneration issues and motivating personnel than do their counterparts in Slovakia.

Venture capital firms in the three countries score acting as a sounding board for new ideas, seeking additional equity finance and evaluating acquisitions as of relatively low importance. However, they place greater importance on their roles in making introductions to potential customers and suppliers and in assisting with marketing plans. There is also a slightly greater importance attached to the provision of assistance in managing crises and problems. Venture capital firms in Hungary and Slovakia place very great importance on helping to form and manage the board.

Table 4.9 Services provided by venture capitalists

Services	Hungary	Poland	Slovakia
Control of portfolio management	4.3	3.8	3.3
Make introductions to potential customers and suppliers	3.9	3.8	3.7
Make introductions to potential service providers	2.9	3.0	2.7
Monitor financial performance	4.9	4.6	3.7
Monitor operational performance	3.9	4.2	3.7
Seek additional equity financing	3.0	4.0	3.7
Seek debt financing	–	3.8	3.7
Serve as sounding board for new ideas	3.9	4.0	3.7
Search/recruit management	3.4	2.6	3.3
Resolve remuneration issues	3.8	3.8	2.7
Assist with strategic planning	4.1	4.2	3.7
Assist in operational planning	2.7	3.2	2.0
Assist with marketing plans	4.1	3.6	3.7
Help form and manage the board	4.6	2.6	4.5
Monitor investments of the portfolio firm	4.2	3.6	4.2
Evaluate acquisitions	2.7	3.4	4.0
Development of new strategy to meet changing circumstances	4.6	3.8	4.5
Manage crises and problems	4.2	3.8	4.2
Motivate personnel	3.4	3.2	1.7

Note: Figures are mean scores on the basis of 1 = not important through to 5 = very important.

Within the Hungarian market, the independent firm surveyed attached importance to a narrower range of services, focusing greatest importance on monitoring financial performance, helping to form and manage the board and managing crises and problems; the two publicly-owned firms had the next lowest range. In contrast, the foreign firm surveyed attached importance to the broad range of operational and strategic services. Within the Polish market, public sector firms tend to assist portfolio companies with marketing plans and operational planning, whilst the private and mixed private/public firms surveyed have little involvement at this level.

Monitoring mechanisms

As with the general range of services which are provided to investees, venture capital firms generally utilise a number of methods of monitoring their investees (Table 4.10). Across the three countries considerable importance is attached to the provision of monthly management accounts by investees, commentaries on the accounts, board membership by the venture capital firm, limits to managerial discretion on investment expenditure, and restrictions on additional borrowings, on asset disposals and mergers, and on changes in ownership. The main areas of differences between countries concern the greater emphasis placed on the requirement for direct access to investees' accounting systems and for regular meetings with venture capitalists in Hungary, the greater emphasis on audited annual accounts in Slovakia and Poland, and the greater emphasis on the requirement to use a particular auditing firm in Hungary and Poland. In Slovakia there is less emphasis on the right of venture capitalists to make a board appointment.

Within the Hungarian venture capital industry, one of the two bank captives surveyed stood out as placing little importance on the requirement for regular meetings with the venture capitalist and board membership by the venture capitalist. Both bank captives gave lowest importance to monthly management accounts and commentaries on them. The publicly-owned venture capital firms tended to place less emphasis than others on requirements for investees to use certain accounting policies, restrictions on directors' remuneration, requirements to use a particular accounting firm and the frequency of full board meetings.

Notwithstanding the similar importance attached to the main monitoring mechanisms used by venture capital firms in the different countries, there are some noticeable differences between the countries with respect to the means by which impending performance changes are first identified (Table 4.11). Investee management does not appear likely to take the initiative in contacting the venture capital firm in advance of problems occurring, either by telephone or in writing. In Hungary and Poland, the initiative appears more likely to come from the venture capital firm directly communicating with the investee. One of the Hungarian bank captives did not rate highly own direct communication with management or monthly accounts as the mechanisms by which they were most likely to first hear of problems; rather they were the only venture capitalist to rate failure to pay dividend on the due date, annual accounts and notification from other financial institutions as the most important avenues for such information.

Table 4.10 Means of monitoring investees

Means	Hungary	Poland	Slovakia
Provision of monthly management accounts	4.3	4.2	4.3
Provision of commentary (evaluation) of monthly performance	4.2	4.2	4.2
Board membership of venture capitalist at the investee company	4.3	4.6	4.0
Industry specialist's board membership	2.4	2.4	2.3
Right of board appointment	4.2	4.4	2.7
Frequency of full board meetings	3.7	4.2	2.3
Restrictions on additional borrowings	4.3	4.0	4.0
Restrictions on asset disposals	4.6	4.0	4.3
Restrictions on mergers/acquisitions	4.4	3.2	4.4
Restrictions on changes in ownership	4.2	4.0	4.3
Audited annual accounts	3.8	3.4	4.3
Requirement to use a particular auditing firm	3.6	3.6	2.3
Requirement for venture capitalist to be a member of investee's audit committee	–	2.0	2.7
Requirement for direct access to investee's accounting system	4.2	2.8	2.7
Requirement for certain accounting policies	3.7	3.2	2.7
Requirement for regular meetings with venture capitalist	4.7	3.8	3.0
No capital expenditure beyond certain limits without approval	–	4.6	4.0
Restrictions on director's remuneration	3.8	3.6	3.0
Restrictions on senior management's remuneration	–	3.6	3.0

Note: Figures are mean scores on the basis of 1 = not important through to 5 = very important.

Indications are that venture capital firms in Slovakia have less strong mechanisms for identifying impending performance changes. This point is supported by the evidence concerning the timescale involved in learning of problems (Table 4.12). Venture capital firms in Hungary score learning of problems immediately or within one week as the most important. In Hungary, the publicly owned and bank captive venture capitalists tended to be the slowest to hear of investee problems. Polish venture capital firms generally appear to take a little longer on average to hear of problems. In Slovakia the highest score is attributed to learning of problems three to six months after they occur.

Table 4.11 First indicator of impending performance changes

Indicator	Hungary	Poland	Slovakia
Telephone communication from portfolio management	3.8	3.8	2.7
Written communication from portfolio management	3.7	2.6	2.7
Notification from lead banking institution	1.7	2.2	2.0
Monthly management accounts report	4.0	3.2	3.3
Audited annual results (income statements)	2.3	3.0	3.7
Failure to pay dividend on due date	1.8	2.0	3.0
Regular board meeting	3.0	4.0	3.0
Your own analysis of management reports	3.9	4.0	4.0
Your own direct communication to management	4.2	4.8	3.3

Note: Figures are mean scores on the basis of 1 = not important through to 5 = very important.

Table 4.12 Timescale of learning about problems

Time	Hungary	Poland	Slovakia
On warning given before	2.2	2.0	2.0
Immediately	3.7	3.0	2.0
Up to one week afterwards	3.7	3.0	2.0
One week to one month afterwards	–	3.4	3.0
One and up to three months afterwards	2.2	1.8	2.0
Three and up to six months afterwards	1.3	1.4	3.5
More than six months afterwards	–	1.0	1.0

Note: Figures are mean scores on the basis of 1 = not important through to 5 = very important.

Ineffective senior management is commonly the major cause of problems with investees in all countries (Table 4.13). However, whilst ineffective functional management is scored as an important cause of problems in two of the three countries, this is noticeably less true of Hungary. The independent company surveyed in Hungary did not consider that ineffective senior management was a sufficient cause of problems. Disputes between venture capital firms and investee management appear not to be a major cause of problems.

As might be expected in the Central European countries examined, problems with markets and investees' abilities to compete in them are of considerable importance. These problems are given particular emphasis by venture capital firms in Hungary.

Table 4.13 Causes of problems

Causes	Hungary	Poland	Slovakia
Ineffective senior management	4.4	4.6	4.3
Ineffective functional management	3.4	4.4	4.0
Disputes within management team	3.7	3.2	2.3
End user market fails to develop as expected	3.8	3.2	3.7
Failure to meet assumptions about post-deal efficiency improvements	3.9	3.4	2.7
Company fails to capture market share	4.3	3.4	3.3
Competitors take advantage of financially weakened state of investee company	4.1	2.6	3.3
Product problems	3.6	3.4	2.7
Limited exit potential	3.6	3.8	2.7
Inappropriate financial structure	–	3.3	2.7
Raw material cost escalation	3.0	3.0	2.3
Divergence in goals with venture capital investors	–	2.6	3.0

Note: Figures are mean scores on the basis of 1 = not important through to 5 = very important.

In response to problems, there are different emphases attached to the available actions between the countries studied (Table 4.14). Venture capital firms in the three countries place emphasis on keeping closer scrutiny on the investees' position and requesting more in-depth information from management. Hungarian and Polish venture capital firms also place greater emphasis on taking steps to change the management team as a course of action to improve investee performance. Renegotiation of dividends and seeking new financial partners were considered to be very important actions by one of the bank captives and one of the public sector firms.

Discussion and conclusions

This chapter has provided a preliminary analysis of the development of venture capital markets in transition using the cases of Hungary, Poland and Slovakia. There are marked differences in the current stage of development of the venture capital markets in Hungary and Poland compared with that in Slovakia. The first two have experienced marked growth whilst the Slovakian market remains somewhat underdeveloped. However, in all three countries there continue to be major infrastructure impediments to the development of venture capital including specific legislation to permit venture capital firms, the development of reliable sources of information on potential investees, and the development of stock and corporate asset markets.

Table 4.14 Courses of action to improve investee performance

Actions	Hungary	Poland	Slovakia
Keep the position under review more strictly	4.8	4.8	4.3
Request management to provide more in-depth information	4.9	4.8	4.3
Negotiate with management to take the necessary steps	4.8	4.6	4.3
Take steps to change the management team	4.2	3.8	3.0
Seek to renegotiate distribution of yields (concerning dividend and share price)	2.4	2.4	2.7
Seek to renegotiate financial issues (find additional financial partners)	2.6	3.4	2.3
Seek to find a buyer for the company	3.8	2.6	2.3
Force receivership/liquidation of investee	1.6	1.8	1.6

Note: Figures are mean scores on the basis of 1 = not important through to 5 = very important.

In Hungary, it is aimed to bring legislation to establish venture capital firms before parliament in October 1997. In Poland the passing of the law which regulates investment funds, including closed-end funds, and which would address problems relating to the double taxation of venture capital investments is still awaited. In Slovakia special taxation and other incentives are available in certain sectors but the legal infrastructure to encourage the development of venture capital firms remains to be introduced, including developments in appropriate financial instruments and definitions of the activities permitted by venture capital funds.

Foreign-owned venture capital firms are playing some role in Central Europe and besides providing funds appear to offer examples to domestic players of best practice investment screening and monitoring approaches. The monitoring of venture capital firms by their funds providers is somewhat underdeveloped in all three countries surveyed. Public sector fund providers generally tend to make greater use of cash amount targets whilst in the private sector greater use is made of rate of return targets. Unlike in the developed UK market, little use is made of rate of return targets set in excess of returns on other asset classes, reflecting the newness of such classes.

The importance attached to venture capital firms obtaining controlling equity stakes in the three countries, especially Hungary, emphasises the need for venture capitalists to exert control in highly uncertain environments. Hungary and Poland as the more developed markets in Central Europe placed greater emphasis on conducting their own due diligence in assessing investment projects.

There appears to be some lack of sophistication in the markets examined here compared with that in the UK with respect to the use of standard benchmark rate of return targets for investees rather than specific targets which reflect the characteristics of individual projects. As might be expected, market conditions have a greater influence in the three Central European countries than in the UK on the rate of return sought from investment projects. Product market factors are also more important in the former countries in assessing riskiness of projects. In Hungary especially, obtaining a majority equity stake has an important influence on the target rate of return which is sought. In Hungary and Poland, but not in Slovakia, there is an emphasis on the importance of own due diligence in preparing valuations. There appear to be important differences between Slovakia and the more developed Polish and Hungarian markets with respect to the importance attached to the business plan and the timing of exits in preparing valuations.

Venture capitalists in the three Central European countries make greater use of discounted cash flow methods of valuation than is the case in the UK. This may seem somewhat surprising given the difficulties involved in making forecasts in the uncertain environment of transitional economies but also reflects the difficulties in the use of other methods. In the UK PE ratio methods are preferred whilst asset based methods are given more emphasis in Poland and Slovakia than is the case elsewhere.

Venture capital firms in Hungary and Poland have in general greater involvement in the monitoring of their investees than is the case in Slovakia. There is, however, less involvement in strategic decisions and more involvement in operational decisions by venture capital firms in all three countries. The emphasis on the use of monthly reports is widespread across all three countries surveyed, but Polish and Slovak venture capital firms make more use of annual reports than their counterparts elsewhere and Hungarian venture capital firms make greater use of regular meetings. Investee management does not appear to be proactive in informing venture capital firms of problems in the three Central European countries; venture capital firms are more proactive in identifying problems in Hungary and Poland than is the case in Slovakia. There are differences in the speed with which venture capital firms learn of problems, with

Slovak firms being particularly slow. However, there are also within country differences with, for example, publicly-owned venture capital firms in Hungary being slower to learn of problems than their private sector counterparts. The quality of management and problems in competing in markets are common important causes of problems across all three countries. Although discussions and negotiations with management are approaches to dealing with problems which are common to all countries, Hungarian and Polish venture capital firms appear more ready to change management in order to resolve problems.

The analysis presented in this chapter also suggests a number of policy implications.

Perhaps the greatest requirement is to develop specific legislation conducive to the establishment of domestic venture capital firms, and especially limited partnerships, in Hungary, Poland and Slovakia along the lines available in the developed UK and US markets. It needs to be borne in mind that even in the UK limited partnership legislation continues to be less flexible than that in the US with respect to important issues of relevance to venture capital firms such as the timing of gains on taxes. Given the role already of foreign-based venture capital firms in the Central European markets there is a need to ensure that such investors are not discouraged by disadvantageous taxation arrangements.

There is a need to develop greater recognition of the broad scope of investment possibilities, beyond early stage projects, to which venture capital funding is applicable. There is a continuing general need to educate entrepreneurs about the attributes and roles of venture capital.

Public sector funds providers in the three countries examined here need to consider the use of rate of return and not simply cash amount targets for the venture capital firms in which they invest. It would also appear to be appropriate for venture capital firms in the three countries to develop closer relationships with their funds providers and also to develop strategic monitoring and assistance skills among venture capital firms in Hungary, Poland and Slovakia. While there are cases of best practice by venture capital firms in all three Central European countries, there is a need in particular to develop the investing and monitoring skills of public sector venture capital firms to enable these firms to play the role expected of them in the development of commercially successful enterprises. In the less developed Slovak venture capital market there is a need to develop greater involvement by venture capital firms in their investee companies.

The difference in the behaviour of private sector and public sector funds in the three countries examined here is greater than is generally the case in developed market economies. Much of this difference arises because of the not-for-profit nature of public sector funds. Rather, such funds are often required to represent regional development interests or to promote privatisation, innovation and small business development. Increasingly, public sector venture funds in developed markets have generally become more profit-oriented because of the problems of limited budgets and concerns about accountability (Lovejoy, 1988). For the future, it may become necessary for public sector funds in Central European countries to also follow this shift.

These findings from the study emphasise the need for practitioners seeking to enter the Central European markets to assess carefully how they are to enter and, if it is to be an important element of their strategy, to select carefully their domestic partner. As regards the screening, valuation and monitoring of investments, particular issues are raised which concern the need to be aware of appropriate valuation methods and of the importance of obtaining larger equity stakes than might be expected in domestic markets in order to achieve control which may otherwise be problematical. The evidence of problems with management and with firms failing to develop as expected emphasises the importance of careful screening and of undertaking sensitivity analysis using wide parameters around a base case.

Note

1. For an illustration of the use of this approach in the similar context of a Polish privatization see the case of B&C in Wright et al. (1993a).

References

Adam, J. (1995), 'The transition to a market economy', *Europe–Asia Studies*, **47** (6), 989–1006.

Barney, J., L. Busenitz, J. Fiet and D. Moesel (1989), 'The structure of venture capital governance: an organisational economic analysis of relations between venture capital firms and new ventures', *Academy of Management Proceedings*, 64–8.

Beecroft, A. (1994), 'The role of the venture capital industry in the UK', in N. Dinsdale and M. Prevezer (eds), *Capital Markets and Corporate Governance*, Oxford: Oxford University Press, 195–208.

Boycko, M., A. Shleifer and R. Vishny (1993), 'Privatizing Russia', *Brookings Papers on Economic Activity*, **2**, 139–92.

Bruno, A. (1986), 'A structural analysis of the venture capital industry', in D. Sexton and R Smilor (eds), *The Art and Science of Entrepreneurship*, Cambridge: Ballinger.

Estrin, S., P. Hare and M. Suranyi (1992), 'Banking in transition: development and current problems in Hungary', *Soviet Studies*, **44** (5), 785–808.

Filatotchev, I., I. Grosfeld, J. Karsai, M. Wright and T. Buck (1996a), 'Buy-outs in Hungary, Poland and Russia: governance and finance issues', *Economics of Transition*, **4** (l), 67–88.

Filatotchev, I., R. Hoskisson, T. Buck and M. Wright (1996b), 'Corporate restructuring in Russian privatizations: implications for US investors', *California Management Review*, **38** (2), 87–105.

Fried, V. and R. Hisrich (1994), 'Towards a model of venture capital investment decision making', *Financial Management*, **23** (3), 28–37.

Fried, V. and R. Hisrich (1995), 'The venture capitalist: a relationship investor', *California Management Review*, **37** (2), 101–13.

Frydman, R., A. Rapaczynski, E. Phelps and A. Shleifer (1993), 'Needed mechanisms of corporate governance and finance in Eastern Europe', *Economics of Transition*, **1** (2), 171–207.

Gibb, A. (1993), 'Small business development in Central and Eastern Europe – opportunity for a rethink', *Journal of Business Venturing*, **8** (6), 461–86.

Grosfeld, I. and P. Hare (1991), 'Privatisation in Hungary, Poland and Czechoslovakia', *European Economy*, July.

Karsai, J. and M. Wright (1994), 'Accountability, governance and finance in Hungarian buy-outs', *Europe–Asia Studies* (formerly Soviet Studies), **46** (6), 997–1016.

Lane, S. (1995), 'Business start-ups during the transition in Hungary', *Journal of Business Venturing*, **10** (3), 181–94.
Lerner, J. (1995), 'Venture capitalists and the oversight of private firms', *Journal of Finance*, **50** (l), 301–18.
Lovejoy, P. (1988), 'Management buy-outs and policy responses: the West Midlands', *Regional Studies*, **22**, 344–7.
MacMillan I., D. Kulow and R. Khoylian (1989), 'Venture capitalists involvement in their investments: extent and performance', *Journal of Business Venturing*, **4** (l), 27–47.
Mitchell, F., G. Reid and N. Terry (1995), 'Post investment demand for accounting information by venture capitalists', *Accounting and Business Research*, **25** (99), 186–96.
Murray, G. (1991), *Change and Maturity in the UK Venture Capital Industry 1991–95*, London: BVCA.
Ooghe, H., S. Manigart and Y. Fassin (1991), 'Growth patterns in the European venture capital industry', *Journal of Business Venturing*, **6**, 381–404.
Pasztor, S. (1991), 'Being hidden – the privatisation of Apisz', *Acta Oeconomica*, **43** (3), 297–314.
Porter, M. (1980), *The Competitive Strategy: Techniques for Analyzing Industries and Competitors*, New York: Free Press
Roman, Z. (1991), Entrepreneurship and small business: the Hungarian trajectory', *Journal of Business Venturing*, **6** (6), 447–65.
Roure, J., R. Keeley and T. van der Heyden (1990), 'European venture capital: strategies and challenges in the 90s', *European Management, Journal*, **8** (2), 243–52.
Sahlman W.A. (1990), 'The structure and governance of venture-capital organizations', *Journal of Financial Economics*, **27**, 473–521.
Sapienza, H. and A. Gupta (1994), 'Impact of agency risks and task uncertainty on venture capitalist–CEO interaction', *Academy of Management Journal*, **37** (6), 1618–32.
Valentiny, P., T. Buck and M. Wright (1992), 'The pricing and valuation of public assets: experiences in the UK and Hungary', *Annals of Public and Cooperative Economics*, **63** (4), 601–20.
Wright, M. and K. Robbie (1996), 'Venture capitalists and unquoted equity investment appraisal', *Accounting and Business Research*, **26** (2), 153–70.
Wright M., S. Thompson and K. Robbie (1992), 'Venture capital and management-led leveraged buy-outs: a European perspective', *Journal of Business Venturing*, **7**, 47–71.
Wright, M., K. Robbie, S. Thompson, Y. Romanet, R. Joachimsson, J. Bruining and A. Herst (1993b), 'Harvesting and the life-cycle of management buy-outs and buy-ins: a four country study', *Entrepreneurship: Theory and Practice*, **18** (2), 89–110.
Wright, M., I. Filatotchev, T. Buck and K. Robbie (eds) (1993a), *Management and Employee Buyouts in Central and Eastern Europe*, London: European Bank/CEEPN.

5. The role of trust in the informal investor's investment decision: an exploratory analysis

Mark Dibben, Richard Harrison and Colin Mason

Introduction

Research into the role of informal venture capital in financing the development of entrepreneurial ventures has grown significantly in North America and, more recently, Europe (Freear et al., 1996; Harrison and Mason, 1996a; Mason and Harrison, 1995a, 1995b, 1996a). This research can be characterised in three ways. First, it has been and remains primarily empirical in nature, reflecting the continuing need to 'put boundaries on our ignorance' (Wetzel, 1986, p. 132) of what is still largely an invisible and secretive marketplace (Freear et al., 1996; Harrison and Mason, 1996a; 1996b). Second, it has had a very strong public policy and prescriptive emphasis, focused on understanding how the market operates and identifying mechanisms by which it could be made to work more efficiently and effectively (Wetzel, 1986; Harrison and Mason, 1996a, 1996b; Suomi and Lumme, 1994; Mason, 1996). Third, and partly as a consequence of these two trends, research on informal venture capital has not been characterised to date by a high level of theoretical sophistication, although recent research has considered the applicability of the pecking order hypothesis (Harrison and Mason, 1991), decision theory (Landstrom, 1995; Riding et al., 1995), the economic analysis of altruism (Sullivan and Miller, 1990), and agency theory (Landstrom, 1993; Fiet, 1995a; 1995b).

In this chapter we extend this third strand of enquiry to explore the relevance of the concept of trust to the analysis of the informal venture capital market. Trust as a key constituent of economic relations is now receiving increased attention in both the general literature (Gambetta, 1990; Fukuyama, 1995; Kramer et al., 1996) and within entrepreneurship itself (Low and Srivatsan, 1993; Dibben et al., 1996). In the entrepreneurial context, under conditions of uncertainty in dyadic relations (Larson, 1992), trust has been identified as a major lubricant which is essential for cooperation to arise (Low and Srivatsan, 1993). Within the research canon on informal venture capital, the issue of trust has been explored as part of a wider study of information sources, networks and reliance structures (Fiet, 1991): for the informal venture capital market, Fiet's results suggest that the degree of reliance on others in the personal contact network (which was lower in any case for informal investors compared to venture capitalists) was a function of the amount of network experience; in other words, 'experience generated trust which controlled opportunism' (Freear et al., 1996, p. 16).

Trust in this context can be construed as a means of speeding decision making and negotiations by reducing transaction costs between individuals in organisations under conditions of risk (Creed and Miles, 1996, pp. 16–35; Mishra, 1996, pp. 276–8). As such, the detailed exploration of the trust construct and its application to the informal venture capital market as a community characterised by informality and personal contact and referral (Mason and Harrison, 1994) represents a potentially fruitful opportunity to provide a theoretically robust basis for continued research in this field. However, much of the interest in trust to date has focused on monitoring relationships post-investment, and there has been relatively little interest in the role of trust at earlier stages in the process: this represents the key focus of this chapter. In the following section we develop a model of the informal investment decision-making process based on the identification of five situational domains, or discrete stages in the process, within which we would expect to find evidence of trust relationships; following a theoretical discussion of the concepts of swift trust and swift cooperation and their relevance to the investment opportunity identification and appraisal process, we outline the methodology and data analysis procedures used to explore the applicability of this model of trust. The chapter concludes with a discussion of the implications of the analysis for the development of research in this field.

Characteristics of the informal investment decision situation

The investment process undertaken by both venture capitalists and informal venture capitalists has been subject to growing scrutiny since the first substantive analysis by Tyebjee and Bruno (1984). Based on their work, and subsequent refinements by Sandberg et al. (1988), Hall and Hofer (1993), Fried and Hisrich (1994), Riding et al. (1995) and Mason and Rogers (1996), it is possible to identify four basic stages in the investment process based on the fundamental activities of screening, evaluation, negotiation and post-investment involvement. In addition, as there is evidence to suggest that referred deals may be better able to survive the initial screening process if the investor has confidence in the referrer (Fried and Hisrich, 1994, p. 31), there is a fifth element in the decision process which should be separately identified, not by the phase or activity involved but by the institution or individual(s) involved – the intermediary or network providing access to or information on opportunities. This suggests that, from the perspective of an exploration of the role of trust and cooperation, we can identify five distinct *situational domains* in the informal investment decision-making process within which the role, development and influence of trust relations can be understood (see Table 5.1).

Table 5.1 Situational domains in the informal investment decision-making process

Domain		Description
Domain 1	Screening	Decision to pursue initial awareness of opportunity Review/examination of business plan or outline Decision on rejection or follow up with entrepreneur Multiple criteria used to reject opportunities Initial reaction to the opportunity
Domain 2	Assessment	Evaluation of the merits/worth of the information source Degree of confidence in the referrer of opportunities Quality of the information is key to the reject/proceed decision Issue of trust in the medium of information dissemination
Domain 3	Evaluation	Reaction to entrepreneur/management team Decision to reject or enter negotiations Management team and financial return factors increase Due diligence (if any) through network of personal contacts
Domain 4	Negotiation	To make the invest/not invest decision Issues of personal chemistry grow in importance Issues of deal structure and pricing grow in importance One major factor likely to lead to rejection by the investor
Domain 5	Involvement	Decision to become involved or remain hands-off Decisions on level of involvement

In the conceptualisation and analysis of trust there is a general assumption that it is something which emerges over time – indeed the understanding and definition of general trust, as 'the expectation that arises, within a community, of regular honest and cooperative behaviour, based on commonly shared norms, on the part of other members of that community' (Fukuyama 1995, p. 26), is based specifically on this assumption. This has direct applicability to the informal investment process in those cases where an opportunity is pursued through to investment (where the emphasis of much of the trust literature on the role and development of trust in existing organisational settings will directly apply to domain 5 as defined in Table 5.1). However, it is apparently less immediately relevant to the other domains identified, where organisational relationships cannot yet be said to exist and where there is much less time available over which to see trust relationships developing. This is particularly true in the case of the first two domains as the length of time required to develop trust is not present in the initial screening domain or in the opportunity identification and recommendation process. In order to permit the inclusion of these domains within a trust framework it is necessary to address the issue of how trust is established in the absence of significant lapsed time, and it is in this context that the concept of 'swift trust' becomes relevant as the basis for cooperative behaviour.

Swift trust

Temporary systems and swift trust

The concept of 'swift trust' has been developed by Meyerson et al. (1996) to account for the emergence of trust relations in situations where the individuals have a limited history of working together, have limited prospects of working together in the future, and are involved in tasks which are 'often complex and involve independent work . . ., have a deadline . . ., are non-routine and not well-understood . . . [and] are consequential . . . [requiring] continuous interrelating [with others in the group] to produce an outcome' (Meyerson et al., 1996, p. 169).

Such temporary systems (Goodman and Goodman, 1974) come about as a result of the coordinator bringing individuals together, and therefore do not have an 'existing structure to handle what has become a significant but non-routine issue' (Meyerson et al., 1996, p. 179). In them, in order to function, 'trust must be conferred *ex ante* of experience telling an individual that another is trustworthy' (Meyerson et al., 1996, p. 170). By extension, therefore, the group of individuals involved in an investment decision often complies with many of the characteristics of such temporary systems, requiring a swift trust based on faith in one's own ability and the expected ability of the other members. Such swift trust would be expected to only be strong or resilient enough to survive the life of the temporary group, since 'there is, quite literally, neither enough time or opportunity in a temporary group for the sort of experience necessary for thicker [i.e. stronger] forms of trust to emerge' (Meyerson et al., 1996, 181).

The swift trust that exists in temporary group situations, therefore, is made possible by the presence of the contractor (or coordinator, for example, the film director, the entrepreneur the go-between), whose reputation is also at stake because he is responsible for assembling the group in the first place (Meyerson et al., 1996, p. 171). As such, it is expected that, with the possible exception of the presence of 'friends of friends', the coordinator will know any of the other individuals within the group and will consequently have already formed a trusting relationship with each of them, prior to the present temporary group situation. Such heavy reliance on networks makes trust requirements high

(Creed and Miles, 1996, p. 26), since network members are obliged to 'forego the right to pursue self interest at the expense of others' (Powell, 1990, p. 303).

The decision to be a part of the temporary group, and hence the conferring of swift trust, *ex ante*, by one individual on another in the temporary group, will come about as a result of an assessment of the trustworthiness of the *coordinator*, in terms of his/her integrity, benevolence and ability to select appropriately able group members, combined with consideration of the risk involved and the potential outcomes (Mayer et al., 1995) from membership of the temporary group. The trusts that exist between the coordinator and each of the individuals in the group and between each of the individuals and the coordinator will not, on the other hand, be based on swift trust but will (depending on the nature of the relationships) be one of three other trust types which can be identified.

The relation between swift trust and other trust types

The relationship between the coordinator and each of the individuals is therefore of particular importance. This is because (a) they are (probably) the only non situation-specific link between the individuals in the group, and (b) the trust that exists between the coordinator and each of the other individuals is of a different nature, and therefore stronger, than the comparatively weak swift trust that exists among the other individuals. Trust between the co-ordinator and each of the other individuals comes about through the development of relationships over time, allowing trust to develop between the course of a number of separate social interactions. Thus, swift trust may be regarded as a special sub-type of other more commonly acknowledged types of situational trust. It is therefore necessary to briefly review a number of other trust types, in order to come to a deeper understanding of the theoretical development of swift trust. This in turn will enable an exploration of a number of trust determinants, including co-operation, and, consequently, the development of a protocol for the analysis of the role of trust in the informal investment domain.

Previous studies of trust have, for the most part, failed to illustrate adequately the role of trust in interpersonal business relationships. This is because they have concentrated, for the most part, on 'what generates, maintains, substitutes or collapses trusting relations' (Gambetta, 1990, p. xi), whereas the real impact of trust in interpersonal relationships is not seen in what determines trust itself but in how trust develops, and how it influences relationships. A recent attempt to propose a typology of trust in professional relationships has, however, been made by Lewicki and Bunker (1995; 1996). Acknowledging the notion of trust as residing within the individual, Lewicki and Bunker (1996, p. 118) argue trust development to be an iterative process that 'takes on a different character in the early, developing and mature stages of a relationship', as knowledge of the other person grows. They identify three categories of situational trust which are linked in a sequential iteration in which the achievement of trust at one level enables the development of trust at the next level. This development is described in Figure 5.1. The three trust types are briefly defined as follows. *Calculus-based trust* is the trust which exists between individuals in the early stage of a relationship, and 'is an ongoing, market-oriented, economic calculation whose value is derived by determining the outcomes resulting from creating and sustaining the relationship, relative to the costs of maintaining or severing it' (Lewicki and Bunker, 1996, p. 120). *Knowledge-based trust* is the trust which exists between two individuals who know each other well enough for the parties to have a history of interaction which allows each to make predictions about the other. In contrast with calculus-based trust, it is more often founded on 'the identification of similarities and commonalities' (Lewicki and Bunker, 1996, p. 157). *Identification-based trust* is the trust which exists 'because the parties effectively understand and appreciate the other's wants to such an extent that each can effectively act for the other . . . and substitute for the other in interpersonal interactions' (Lewicki and Bunker, 1996, p. 157).

Co-operation and trusting behaviour

A weakness of the Lewicki and Bunker trust model is that it takes no account of a number of other factors identified as influencing trusting behaviour. Other recent studies by, for example, Currall and Judge (1995) and Mayer et al.

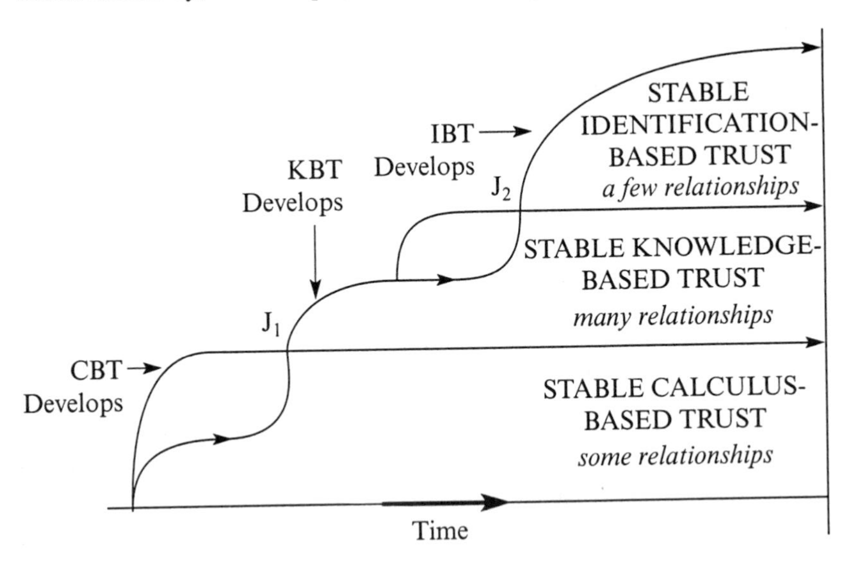

Notes:
J_1 At this point, some calculus-based trust relationships became knowledge-based trust relationships.
J_2 At this juncture, a few knowledge-based trust relationships, where positive affect is present, go on to become identification-based trust relationships.

Source: Lewicki and Bunker (1996).

Figure 5.1 The stages of trust development

(1995) have highlighted the importance of a number of trusting behaviour determinants, including the perceived ability, benevolence, and integrity of the trusted individual, the perceived risk of the situation and the trustor's propensity to trust. In any given situation, the central indication of (mutual) trusting behaviour may be seen in a willingness to cooperate (Powell, 1990, p. 326; Volery, 1995), which reduces 'the need for monitoring behaviour and [provides] greater speed in making decisions' (Shapiro et al., 1992, p. 365). It follows, conversely, that 'cooperation breeds trust' (Putnam, 1992, p. 171, in Meyerson et al., 1996). Based on both time-dependent and time independent criteria, the threshold for cooperation will not only vary subjectively but also in accordance with objective circumstances. A comparison of situational trust and cooperation threshold, therefore, will enable a prediction of co-operative behaviour in a given situation, since where trust is deemed to be greater than the cooperation threshold for both individuals, cooperation should ensue, and vice-versa (Marsh, 1995). Where trust is higher than the cooperation threshold for one of the individuals but not the other, then the relationship would be expected to undergo a period of stress during which the cooperating individual's trust is likely to be felt to be being violated by the uncooperating individual (Dibben et al., 1996). Such comparisons of situational trust and cooperation threshold may therefore also provide an indication of how trust might influence individual behaviour.

Furthermore, the Lewicki and Bunker framework explicitly deals with the development of trust over time; the development of concepts of swift trust, and their application to opportunity evaluation decision-making domains as in the present discussion, involves an a priori recognition that calculus-based trust will dominate in these time-compressed domains.

In an effort to simplify the trust concept for use in artificial intelligence, Marsh (1992, 1995) structured a limited number of key determinants of trust and co-operation as a computational trust formalism. This is less complex than other formalisms (for example, Kramer et al., 1996), but has proved effective in the analysis of trust in entrepreneurship contexts: for example an exploratory application of the computational trust formalism to entrepreneurship was made by Dibben et al. (1996), in an attempt to elucidate the trusting, cooperative behaviour of individuals in new venture crises. In addition to situational trust, this study found that accurate predictions of trusting cooperation could be made by taking into account the following four determinants: perceived risk, importance and utility of the situation for the trusting individual, and the trusting individual's perceived competence of the trusted individual. Adapting the work of Marsh (1995) and Dibben et al. (1996), we define each of these four determinants and identify propositionally the expected relationship with trust and cooperation as follows.

Utility is defined here as an individual's perception of the potential economic value of a situation, and may be seen most clearly in, for example, expected return on investment. Given its positive connotation, we propose:

Proposition 1 *the greater the perception of utility, the greater the possibility of trusting, cooperative behaviour.*

Importance is an individual's perception of the potential non-economic value of a situation. This is determined by issues which the individual concerned may hold dear, such as conservation or helping the disabled, but which utility, being based more on economic considerations (Simon, 1955) does not allow for. Given its positive connotation, we propose:

Proposition 2 *the greater the perception of importance, the greater the possibility of trusting, cooperative behaviour.*

Risk is an individual's perception of the potential loss (economic or otherwise) from a situation. The link between risk and trust is long established but difficult to clarify (Marsh, 1995, p. 32). Nevertheless, there is a wide acceptance of perceptions of risk in determining trusting, cooperative behaviour (Moesel et al., 1996). Given its negative connotation, we propose:

Proposition 3 *the greater the perception of risk, the less the possibility of trusting, cooperative behaviour.*

Competence is an individual's perception of the professional ability of another individual. Individuals have a 'fiduciary responsibility' to those they deal with (Barber, 1983 (in Marsh, 1995)). The impact of perceived competence on a professional relationship is therefore of importance in a consideration of whether to trust an individual, and it has been noted as a key trust determinant in a number of studies (for example, Clark, 1993; Kee and Knox, 1970; Mishra, 1996; and Tyler and Degoey, 1996). Given its positive connotation, we propose:

Proposition 4 *the greater the perception of competence, the greater the possibility of trusting, cooperative behaviour.*

A protocol for identifying trust and cooperation

Based on this discussion it is now possible to summarise the protocol developed for the analysis of trust in the informal investment domain and indicate how trust concepts have been operationalised in the empirical analysis which follows (Table 5.2). This protocol covers both of the key elements in the understanding of trust relations developed above: trust criteria, including calculus-based trust (characterised by intimations of difference between individuals), knowledge-based trust (characterised by intimations of agreement between individuals), and identification-based trust (based on intimations of the mutual sharing of values); and cooperation criteria, which are consistent with the factors identified as important in the informal investment decision-making process, including utility (potential economic value), importance (potential non-economic value), risk (potential loss), competence (professional ability of another individual), and coordinator judgement (the coordinating partner's ability to select potential investment opportunities). In addition, a residual 'other' category was included to cover any aspects of the proposal or opportunity which were not otherwise codeable.

The data used in this chapter were collected as part of a wider study of the decision-making process of business angels (Mason and Rogers, 1997). The focus of this study was on the initial screening stage when business angels first become aware of an investment opportunity and decide whether it is worth considering in detail. The study used verbal protocol analysis, a methodology which captures decision making in real time which has been used successfully to examine the decision-making processes of venture capitalists (Sandberg et al., 1988; Hall and Hofer, 1993; Zacharakis and Meyer, 1995). This methodology involves asking respondents to 'think out loud' while they perform a particular task, and is based on the assumption that the vocalisation of thoughts has the form of inner speech (Ericsson and Simon, 1980, 1993). Previous applications of the technique confirm that although the decision-making context is artificially constructed for research purposes, the results are no less reliable or valid than those obtained from 'recall' survey methods, such as questionnaire surveys or interview schedules (Hall and Hofer, 1993; Zacharakis and Meyer, 1995).

Respondents in this study were shown an investment opportunity featured in a recent issue of *Venture Capital Report* (VCR), the leading national business angel introduction service in the UK, which they were seeing for the first time (Cary, 1995). This opportunity featured a company seeking £100 000 in exchange for 20 per cent of the equity to finance the marketing of a rowing training machine using a patented water flywheel to simulate resistance during the rowing stroke (see Mason and Rogers, 1997). The entrepreneur had negotiated exclusive selling rights throughout Europe for the product which was manufactured in the USA by the company which had developed it. However, he believed that the machines were expensive and supply was unpredictable, and so decided to begin to manufacture the product in the UK, incorporating some of his own design improvements. Start-up finance was raised from two external investors. The company pays a royalty to the US company, which owns the patent for the machine, for every machine that it sells. The new funding was sought to significantly increase marketing expenditure.

Table 5.2 Classification of thought segments in the protocols: evaluation criteria

Criteria	Description
'Swift trust' (cf. Lewicki and Bunker, 1995)	
1. Calculus-based trust	Trust which is formed between individuals on the basis of what each sees s/he can get out of the relationship. Characterised by intimation of *difference* between individuals, and a lack of shared knowledge of the product/market situation.
2. Knowledge-based trust	Trust which is formed between individuals with shared knowledge of the product/market situation. Characterised by intimations of *agreement* between individuals, leading to perceptions of predictability and thus reductions of uncertainty.
3. Identification-based trust	Trust which is formed between individuals with a high degree of identification with the wishes/intentions of the other party. Characterised by strong agreement between the individuals, and intimations of the *mutual sharing of values*.
'Swift Cooperation' (cf. Marsh, 1995)	
1. Utility	An individual's perception of the *potential economic value* of a situation.
2. Importance	An individual's perception of the *potential non-economic value* of a situation.
3. Risk	An individual's perception of the *potential loss* from a situation.
4. Competence	An individual's perception of the *professional ability* of another individual. Characterised by comments regarding (for example) market analysis, data availability, quality and so on.
5. Coordinator judgement	An individual's perception of the *coordinating party's ability* to select potentially successful opportunities for investment.
6. Other	Comments on any other aspects of the business which cannot be coded in any other category.

As part of a wider study of the decision-making processes of business angels (Mason and Rogers, 1996) a total of 19 business angels, drawn from respondents to previous surveys (Mason and Harrison, 1994) or identified by business angel or other contacts, were asked to review three such business opportunity profiles. Ten investors, all of whom were active investors (with an average of 6.4 investments made over the past five years), reviewed this particular proposal. A separate analysis of investor reaction to the design elements of the product has been undertaken (Mason and Rogers, 1997. In the analysis which follows, we concentrate on more general issues concerning the decision-making process of these investors, and on the evidence for trust and cooperation which their accounts provide. They were asked to read the opportunity in the same way that they would normally read an investment proposal, but to verbalise their thoughts as they did so. The instruction was to say out loud whatever thoughts came into their mind. Respondents were not required to provide explanations or verbal description (Ericsson and Simon, 1993). Producing such verbalised reports is found not to change the course and structure of the cognitive process (Ericsson and Simon, 1980). The verbalisations were tape recorded and later transcribed and content analysed using a coding system devised for the study.

The verbatim transcriptions of each protocol were broken down into independent units to permit analysis. These thought units were firstly coded according to statement type, using a modified version of the classification used by Zacharakis and Meyer (1995), to indicate the investors' underlying cognitive processes (Table 5.3). The protocol was then coded according to the evaluation criteria established in Table 5.2, to indicate which factors are most important in determining the likelihood of cooperative behaviour (that is, a decision to investigate an investment opportunity in more detail).

Table 5.3 Classification of thought segments in the protocols: statement type

Description	Non-evaluative statement consisting of verbatim or paraphrased quotation of information presented in the plan
Recall	Non-evaluative information based on the past experience of the respondent
Preconception	Judgemental statement based on previous experience/ background knowledge
Inference	Statement which involves a judgement on some part of the plan
Question	Statement which seeks further information
Action	Statement of intention or action to be performed (e.g. to search for a source of information)
Comment	Uncodable or irrelevant statement

Source: Mason and Rogers (1996), modified from Zacharakis and Meyer (1995).

Given the provenance of the data, this empirical exploration of the role of trust in the business angel's investment decision is restricted primarily to domain 1, the opportunity screening stage, and this chapter will not therefore comment on the development of trust relationships and their impact in other situational domains. In view of the importance of the coordinator role, both in the establishment of swift trust and in the investment process, however, it is possible to include in the present analysis some evidence on the potential significance of trust in domain 2, the assessment stage. As most opportunities are rejected by informal investors at the initial screening stage this restriction of the present analysis is unproblematic. The discussion of trust and cooperation in these domains however, represents an extension of the existing research on swift trust (for example, Meyerson et al., 1996) in two respects: first, it includes specific assessment of the role of trust and cooperation as separately distinguishable elements important for the conduct of business relationships; second, it deals with the application of trust and cooperation criteria over very compressed timescales in the absence of direct interpersonal involvement. Using the results of the verbal protocol analysis (on the basis of the frameworks set out in Tables 5.2 and 5.3) we demonstrate that it is possible to apply concepts of swift trust and cooperation in the analysis of these investment decision-making situational domains. On the basis of this, we can then derive a number of propositions to guide more extensive and systematic research to test the theoretical framework we are proposing.

The results of this preliminary exploration of the role of trust in the business angel's investment decision-making process will be summarised in two stages. In the first stage, the results of the verbal protocol analysis will be presented in summary form using the framework developed (Table 5.4). This is in order to throw light on the first situational domain – the pursuit of initial awareness of an investment opportunity – identified above. In the second stage, additional evidence will be provided from the tape transcripts and from additional comments made by the respondents on the second situational domain – the pursuit of opportunities through an intermediary or network. This is in order to throw light on the model of swift trust development in a temporary group mediated by a coordinator.

Trust and the investment decision

Nine of the ten investors in the study rejected the proposal as an investment opportunity, and one indicated he might be prepared to consider the proposal further, to meet the entrepreneur involved. While this limits the interpretation of the analysis (discussed further below), it is consistent with other research which has established that between 93 per cent and 97 per cent of investment proposals received by business angels are rejected (Mason and Harrison, 1994; Riding et al., 1993). These decisions were based on time spent reviewing the proposal of

Table 5.4 Verbal protocol frequency analysis

	Description	Recall	Preconception	Inference	Question	Action	Comment	Total No.	Total %
CBT	–	–	22	23	1	–	2	48	22.5
KBT	–	1	2	1	–	–	–	4	1.9
IBT	–	–	–	–	–	–	–	–	0.0
U Low	–	–	13	6	–	–	–	19	8.9
U Med	–	–	5	1	–	–	–	6	2.8
U High	–	–	–	–	–	–	–	–	0.0
I Low	–	–	3	1	–	–	2	6	2.8
I Med	–	–	1	1	–	–	–	2	0.9
I High	–	–	–	–	–	–	–	–	0.0
R Low	–	–	1	1	–	–	–	2	0.9
R Med	–	–	7	2	–	–	1	10	4.7
R High	–	1	10	6	1	–	1	19	8.9
C Low	1	1	7	25	11	1	5	51	23.9
C Med	–	–	1	5	–	–	–	6	2.8
C High	–	–	–	–	–	–	–	–	0.0
CJ Low	–	2	3	3	7	1	5	21	9.9
CJ Med	–	–	–	–	–	–	1	1	0.5
CJ High	–	–	2	1	–	–	2	5	2.3
Other	–	–	2	5	1	4	1	13	6.1
Total	1	5	79	81	21	6	20	213	
(%)	0.5	2.3	37.1	38.0	9.9	2.8	9.4		

between 30 seconds and 26 minutes, with an average time spent of 11.25 minutes. Overall, as Table 5.4 summarises, some 213 thought units were coded from the verbatim transcripts. Five investors account for 71 per cent of the coded thought units: however, no individual investor represents more than around 16 per cent of coded thought units, and the results discussed here can therefore be taken as representative of the sample as a whole. The frequency matrix (Table 5.4) gives an indication of the information types most frequently used in the investor's decision and a sense, therefore, of the cognitive processes the investor is going through. As Mason and Rogers (1996, 1997) point out, the frequency of mention is not an exact measure of importance, merely a useful proxy. The results of this verbal protocol analysis can be summarised under three headings: evidence of trust; evidence of cooperation; and nature of the statement type.

Evidence of trust

It is clear from the first three lines of Table 5.4 that almost all the references to trust issues by the investors in this sample refer to calculus-based trust: some 92 per cent of the trust references (that is, 22.5 per cent of all thought units coded) fall into this category. Given that we are dealing with a swift trust situation in which investors are being asked to express an evaluative opinion and reach a decision on an investment opportunity which they are seeing for the first time, this is what would be expected. It confirms the work of Lewicki and Bunker (1995) which identifies calculus-based trust as the most common form of trust in business relationships and concludes that it is characterised as being partial and quite fragile since there is little motivation for continuing the relationship (in this case, making a positive decision in domain 1 to proceed with an evaluation of the opportunity). Mason and Rogers (1996, 1997) conclude that in this domain investors look for reasons to reject an opportunity; the dominance of calculus-based trust helps explain this finding. What the present research does not tell us, however, because we do not have enough investors in the sample who make a positive decision to explore the opportunity further, is whether a positive decision will be made by investors who give evidence of relying more on knowledge-based trust which, in the swift trust situation, will be reflected in the identification of similarities and commonalities with the entrepreneur even in the absence of personal knowledge and a history of interaction. This remains a fruitful area for further research.

Evidence of cooperation

Three-quarters of the thought segments coded in this analysis relate to the five dimensions of swift cooperation identified earlier in this paper – utility, importance, risk, competence, and coordinator judgement. For each of these criteria, the thought segments were classified into three categories – high, medium and low – to reflect the specific context of the investors' comments.

Based on the results in Table 5.4, a number of conclusions can be drawn. First, investor thoughts are dominated by comments about the low perceived competence of the entrepreneur/management team, characterised by comments about market analysis, data availability and the quality of the proposal among others. These represent 24 per cent of all thought segments coded, and almost one third of the comments on swift cooperation threshold. This is consistent with the role of ability and expertise as determinants of trust and cooperative behaviour (Good, 1990; Mayer et al., 1995) and with the importance attached to entrepreneur/management team issues in the informal investment literature (Mason and Harrison, 1996b).

Second, comments about risk account for almost 15 per cent of the thought segments coded, and for 20 per cent of the swift cooperation comments in particular. The importance of an investor's perception of the potential loss from a situation (rather than the assessment of the potential gain to be realised in the form of utility) is consistent with the view that at the initial screening stage investors are looking more for reasons to reject an opportunity without investing significant time and effort. Third, the issue of coordinator judgement is of considerable importance in the initial screening situational domain, accounting for almost 17 per cent of the swift cooperation statements, and suggesting that there may be a complex interpenetration of situational domains one and two as defined in Table 5.1 above: the issue of investor trust in domain 2 is discussed briefly in the following section, but the strong expression of low coordinator judgement in this case analysis of a situational domain 1 decision process confirms the suggestions from other studies (Fried and Hisrich, 1994; Mason and Harrison, 1996c) that the level of trust which an investor has in the referral source is a key influence on his/her attitude to the investment opportunity.

Fourth, the utility of the opportunity, in terms of the investor's perception of the economic value of the situation, ranks relatively low in this analysis, being cited in only 12 per cent of thought segments. This would suggest that, in the screening situational domain where the investor is concerned to make a very rapid decision to reject or consider further the opportunity, descriptions of the upside potential of the investment opportunity are rather less important than assurances about the competence of the entrepreneur, reassurance about the potential risk of the situation and confidence in the referral mechanism. Table 5.4 suggests that the importance criterion, that is the investor's perception of the potential non-economic value of the situation is of almost no importance at this stage of the process.

Nature of statement type

Based on the analysis of statement types (as defined in Table 5.3 above) informal investors make their decisions in this situational domain primarily on the basis of preconception and inference; there is relatively little use made of recall (non-evaluative information based on past experience), action statements (statements of intention or actions to be performed), and of question statement types (seeking further information). This is consistent with the very low levels of knowledge-based trust identified, and suggests that informal investors are not systematically or commonly seeking out additional information to assist in coming to a decision at this stage.

There is no doubt from this analysis that informal investors bring their preconceptions to bear on their investment decisions in this early domain, and these preconceptions are more likely to be negative than positive at this stage. While some preconceptions arise from a lack of information in the proposal itself, and can therefore in principle be rectified by the entrepreneur, most reflect strongly-held investor preconceptions which have been formed before the proposal has been read. Equally, as they read the information provided on the situation, investors make a series of inferences and draw conclusions which may well be inaccurate and arise from a lack of clarity in the expression and description of the proposal itself. Unlike investor preconceptions, which are essentially outside the scope of the entrepreneur to influence, inferences do arise at least in part from the proposal itself and are therefore capable of modification by the entrepreneur.

The importance of this point can be gauged from a more detailed examination of the relationship between statement type and swift trust category and swift cooperation criteria (Table 5.4). Both statement types are equally involved in the forming of calculus-based trust. However, investor preconceptions are particularly significant in the development or a perception of high risk and low utility for the situation: as Mason and Rogers (1996) have already pointed out, investor perceptions of market related factors may play a particular role in this process. By contrast, investor inferences, which are driven by the information which is provided – or more specifically not provided – in the proposal, are dominant in the formation of low competence assessments: as Table 5.4 shows, half of the statements coded to indicate low competence are inference statements. Furthermore, a further 20 per cent (11 statements) of the low competence thought segments are question statements (representing half of the incidence of that statement type), which are also driven by problems with or incompleteness in the proposal document itself.

In other words, based on this analysis it would appear that the most significant barrier to the development of trust and cooperation in the first situational domain – the screening of the opportunity – is the low perceived competence of the entrepreneur, and this judgement is made on the basis of inference and questioning based on the proposal document itself. This judgement is reinforced by the perception of high risk and low utility for the investor based largely on investor preconceptions which arise not from the proposal itself but from the prior knowledge, experience and prejudices of the investor. More specifically, with reference to the framework outlined earlier in this chapter, the combination of low competence, high risk, low coordinator judgement, low importance and low utility generate a high cooperation threshold. When combined with low (calculus-based) trust, as here, it is unsurprising that only one investor in the sample would consider the opportunity further.

Swift trust and the role of the coordinator

From Table 5.4 it has already been shown that coordinator judgement is an important element in the informal investor's investment decision-making process at the initial screening stage. More detailed scrutiny of the results suggests that the importance of coordinator judgement arises from a wider range of statement types than is the case for the other swift cooperation criteria. In particular, preconception and inference are relatively less important, and questions and comments are more prevalent. Given that the focus of this study has been on the first situational domain identified in Table 5.1 above, rather than on domain 2 which deals with the assessment of the referral source itself, this is not perhaps surprising. However, additional comments were made by respondents before and after the interviews which do include coordinator judgement issues. In this section we include an analysis of these additional data to illustrate the trust issues which arise in this context. Because of the nature of the data, we draw on responses from all 19 business angels in the full study, as the focus of attention here is on the intermediary providing the information on the opportunity (VCR) and not on the specific opportunity itself. As part of the wider study from which this analysis has been extracted (Mason and Rogers, 1996), a total of 19 investors were asked to respond to one or more of three investment opportunities drawn from the same source – *Venture Capital Report.* The analysis presented so far for domain 1 has been based on the responses only of the ten investors who were asked to comment on that specific opportunity. The analysis of domain 2 – coordinator judgement – is based on comments on the source itself made by all 19 investors in the study. As with the first set of results, this discussion is exploratory only, and serves to illustrate the potential applicability of the swift trust/swift cooperation framework to the analysis of informal investment decision making.

In general, some two-thirds of these business angels derive information on investment opportunities through personal networking with friends and associates, confirming previous research that personal networks are the most important source of investment opportunities for business angels (Mason and Harrison, 1994). Business angels were split on whether the source of referral affects their attitude to the investment proposal. Eight investors stated that it did, suggesting that 'it makes a difference if they come through people I can trust and have an investment and/or entrepreneurial record' (investor B3), 'knowing the reference is vital for reliability and credibility' (investor F), and 'it's a form of informal screening' (investor R). A further four investors indicated that the source of the referral may have some effect. For example, investor S commented that the only situation was 'if I have a high regard for the person'. The remaining seven angels stated that the source of the referral made no difference. Investor C commented that 'I am more interested in the key players than the referral'.

Opinion of the actual activities of business introduction services such as *Venture Capital Report*, amongst those investors who had either used them, or knew of how they operated, was varied. Two investors had insufficient knowledge of such services and did not comment; ten of the remaining 17 investors are or have been members of business introduction services. Three investors had positive views, and another three investors recognised that some business introduction services were better than others, so it was impossible to generalise. The remaining 11 were critical, one commenting that they are 'frightful' (investor B5) and another stating that 'they're all rubbish' (investor M1). The criticisms can be grouped under five headings.

First, the opportunities provided are of poor quality and the people running the business-seeking investment are not screened. Second, the staff running such services are perceived as being of poor quality with little business or investment experience. Third, the information provided on opportunities is of poor quality and fragmented. Fourth, business introduction services often act only as forwarding agents for the information and there is, therefore, a lack of value added to that information. Fifth, there is a low level of sophistication in the matching process, and effective targeting of the right investor with the right opportunity is absent.

Investors were also suspicious about entrepreneurs who had to resort to business introduction services in order to raise finance:

> This magazine does worry me though, in that if [an investment proposal] reaches this magazine it surprises me. Because one assumes that they've all got friends, relatives, uncles and aunties and God knows what. It's not much they're looking for – and their local network of accountants, lawyers, solicitors, 3i [a venture capital firm], you name it – if it's any good there's no shortage of people to finance it. It may be my perception is quite wrong but this particular magazine is more for one's last resort or it's so way out of the back of a garage and that sort of thing. (investor L)

It is therefore clear that for many of the business angels in this study the source of referral influences their view of the investment opportunity. Furthermore, the majority have a low opinion of the quality of opportunities provided by business introduction services, although a few make a differentiation between services, considering that some offer a better quality of opportunities than others. Even more significantly, some investors are suspicious that if a business has to seek an investor through a business introduction service rather than finding one through the entrepreneur's own contacts, then it is likely to be of poor quality. In other words, the negative judgement of (or lack or trust in) the coordinator itself leads to a perception of low entrepreneurial competence: while this does not necessarily lead investors to automatically reject opportunities identified in this way (VCR and other such networks have proved successful in facilitating investment matches – see Cary, 1995; Harrison and Mason, 1996a, 1996b), it does raise an additional barrier to be overcome by entrepreneurs seeking capital.

Overall, therefore, this preliminary evidence does suggest that investors or prospective investors do place considerable reliance on the coordinator providing them with information of a kind and in a way which enables them to form judgements of trust and identify cooperation thresholds. This discussion emphasises the importance of understanding trust issues in coming to a full appreciation of the role and potential of business introduction services in stimulating the flow of informal investment (Harrison and Mason, 1996a). This discussion also indicates, however, that the degree of trust in and willingness to cooperate with a coordinator body or organisation (which does not necessarily have to be a business angel network, but could be an archangel, lead investor in a syndicate or other intermediary) has in turn an influence on how the merits and attractiveness of the investment opportunity itself is perceived. As the analysis in Table 5.4 above confirms, low coordinator judgement issues were the third most frequently cited issues in the verbal protocol analysis of the rowing machine case. The role of the coordinator in the informal investment decision therefore requires the development of trust in two sets of actors: trust in the promoters of the investment, and trust in the source of information on that opportunity, with the realisation that the latter will itself influence the former.

Implications for further research

The exploratory research discussed in this chapter does suggest that it is possible to extend the current conceptualisation of swift trust to incorporate three advances: the formal distinction between trust and cooperation as separately identifiable influences on business behaviour; the identification of swift trust and swift cooperation bases for decision making in time-constrained and only indirectly interpersonal contexts; and identification of the specific role of coordinator judgement in shaping trust and cooperation thresholds in these investment decision-making domains.

Based on this initial exploration of the application of swift trust concepts to informal investment decision-making domains, we can identify a number of key propositions around which to structure further more extensive research:

Proposition 1 *calculus-based trust will dominate investor–investee relationships in all decision-making domains.*

Proposition 2 *knowledge-based trust and identification-based trust will become relatively more important in later situational domains of the decision-making process as investor–entrepreneur relationships develop.*

Proposition 3 *the relative importance of each of the three trust types in investor–coordinator relationships will vary according to the type of coordinator: informal referral sources, such as family, friends and business associates, will be relatively more likely to depend on knowledge or identification based trust than formal referral sources such as business angel networks.*

Proposition 4 *calculus-based trust will be relatively less important than knowledge- or identification-based trust in situations where an investment opportunity is being considered than where it is rejected.*

Proposition 5 *even in situational domain 1, where calculus-based swift trust dominates, the decision to proceed with an opportunity to the next domain will be relatively more reliant on knowledge-based trust.*

Proposition 6 *measures of utility (upside potential) will become relatively more important than measures of risk (downside potential) as the investment opportunity moves from early to later situational domains.*

Proposition 7 *while coordinator judgement is important in early situational domains, its importance will fall once the initial reject/proceed decision has been made by the investor.*

Proposition 8 *investor preconceptions and inferences which dominate in early situational domains will be replaced in relative importance by questioning and action statement types in later situational domains.*

Conclusion

The building of trust relationships between the entrepreneur and the informal investor appears to be essential for successful capital investments on the part of the investor to take place. Based on the initial analysis presented, the business angel's trust in the entrepreneur is determined in the first instance by an assessment of the proposal, with the type of trust formed (be it calculus-based trust, knowledge-based trust or identification-based trust in the entrepreneur) depending on the judgement made from that assessment. However, numerous factors are taken into account by business angels, regarding perceived risk, utility and importance of the opportunity, as well as the perceived competence of the entrepreneur, when assessing investment opportunities. Furthermore, as swift trust may (or may not) develop in a context mediated by a coordinator, perceptions of the judgement and ability of the coordinator itself may affect investment decisions. Overall, therefore, the swift trust framework proposed here appears to allow the accurate identification of different trust types, and appears to provide the basis for uncovering the interplay between cooperation and trust in the informal investment decision-making process. By providing a means for assessing and studying the processes that go towards the formation of business relationships at the level of entrepreneur, trust theory also provides a means by which to access the wider social and political processes (in addition to more specific business, product and market issues) that have remained relatively untouched by previous studies restricted to firm level analysis (Scott and Rosa, 1996).

Nevertheless, a number of limitations remain. Although this study has included some analysis of investor trust in the coordinator, there are two domain restrictions which restrict our ability to draw general conclusions on the development of a trust framework for the analysis of the business angel's informal investment decision-making process. First, the study has been primarily restricted to one situational domain – the initial screening process – and our conclusions, therefore, on the nature of trust relations (and on the dominance of calculus-based trust and entrepreneur competence issues in particular) in this domain will not necessarily transfer to other domains. While acknowledging that most informal investment opportunities are rejected at this stage on the basis of no more detailed examination than the experimental design employed in this project, it remains important to extend this initial research to other situational domains in the decision-making process. Second, within this, the present study is restricted to analysis of trust and cooperation in the context of an investment opportunity which all but one investor in the sample would have rejected at this stage. Before concluding on the trust and cooperation factors which come to bear on the investment decision-making process it will be necessary to extend the analysis to investigate the propositions developed above, to cover situations where there is a positive outcome in this domain and the investor decides to pursue the opportunity to the evaluation stage and a meeting with the principals. Until these extensions of the research are undertaken, this study, as with others in a similar vein, provides evidence on the relative importance of the trust-based factors which lead an investor to reject an opportunity, but not on those which lead him/her to accept and pursue an interest in that opportunity.

Acknowledgements

The data reported on in this chapter were collected as part of a study funded by the Design Council. The authors wish to thank Amy Rogers for assistance in undertaking the fieldwork and data analysis in connection with that project. They would also like to thank Stephen Marsh of the National Research Council for Canada, Ottawa, Bob Hamilton (University of Canterbury) and Mike Wright

(University of Nottingham) for their comments on earlier versions of the chapter.

References

Barber, B. (1983), *Logic and Limits of Trust*, New Jersey: Rutgers University Press.

Cary, L. (1995), 'Venture Capital Report', in L. Cary (ed.), *The Venture Capital Report Guide to Venture Capital in the UK and Europe*, Henley on Thames: VCR, 7th edition, pp. 79–86.

Clark, M. (1993), *Interpersonal Trust in the Coal Mining Industry*, PhD Thesis: University of Manchester.

Creed, D. and E.E. Miles (1996), 'Trust in organizations: a conceptual framework linking organizational forms, managerial philosophies, and the opportunity costs of controls', in *Trust in Organizations: Frontiers of Theory and Research*, R.M. Kramer and T.R. Tyler (eds), Thousand Oaks, CA: Sage Publications, pp. 16–38

Currall, S. and T. Judge (1995), 'Measuring trust between organization boundary role persons', *Organizational Behaviour and Human Decision Processes*, **64**, 151–70.

Dibben, M.R., S. Marsh and M.G. Scott (1996), 'Exploring interpersonal trust in the new venture: qualitative applications of a computational trust formalism', Working Paper, University of Stirling.

Ericsson, K.A. and H.A. Simon (1980), 'Verbal reports as data', *Psychological Review*, **87**, 215–51.

Ericsson K.A. and H.A. Simon (1993), *Protocol Analysis*, Cambridge, MA: MIT Press, 2nd edition.

Fiet, J.O. (1991), 'Network reliance by venture capital firms, and business angels: an empirical and theoretical test', in N. Churchill et al. (eds), *Frontiers of Entrepreneurship Research*, Wellesley, MA: Babson College, pp. 445–55.

Fiet J.O. (1995a), 'Reliance upon informants in the venture capital industry', *Journal of Business Venturing*, **10**, 195–223.

Fiet J.O. (1995b), 'Risk avoidance strategies in venture capital markets', *Journal of Management Studies*, **32**, 551–74.

Freear, J., J. Sohl and W. Wetzel (1996), 'The informal venture capital market: milestones passed and the road ahead', Paper to 4th State of the Art in Entrepreneurship Research Conference, Center for Entrepreneurial Leadership, Kansas City, MO.

Fried, V.H. and R.D. Hisrich (1994), 'Toward a model of venture capital investment decision-making', *Financial Management*, **23**, 28–37

Fukuyama, F. (1995), *Trust: The Social Virtues and the Creation of Prosperity*, London: Hamish Hamilton.

Gambetta, D. (1990), *Trust: Making and Breaking Co-operative Relations*, Oxford: Blackwell.

Good, D. (1990), 'Individuals, interpersonal relations and trust', in D. Gambetta (ed.), *Trust: Making and Breaking Co-operative Relations*, Oxford: Blackwell.

Goodman, R.A. and L.P. Goodman (1974), 'Some management issues in temporary systems: a study of professional development and manpower – the theatre case', *Administrative Science Quarterly*, **21**, 494–501.

Hall, J. and C.W. Hofer (1993), 'Venture capitalists' decisions in new venture evaluation', *Journal of Business Venturing*, **8**, 25–42.

Harrison, R.T. and C.M. Mason (1991), 'Informal investor networks: a case study from the United Kingdom', *Entrepreneurship and Regional Development*, **3**, 269–79.

Harrison, R.T. and C.M. Mason (1996a), *Informal Venture Capital: Evaluating the Impact of Business Introduction Services*, Hemel Hempstead: Woodhead Faulkner.

Harrison, R.T. and C.M. Mason (1996b), 'Developing the informal venture capital market: a review of DTI's informal investment demonstration projects', *Regional Studies*, **30** (8), 765–71.

Kee, H. and R.T. Knox (1970), 'Conceptual and methodological considerations in the study of trust and suspicion', *Journal of Conflict Resolution*, **14**, 357–65.

Kramer, R.M., M.B. Brewer and B.A. Hanna (1996), Collective Trust and Collective Action: The Decision to Trust as a Social Decision. In *Trust in Organizations: Frontiers of Theory and Research*, R.M. Kramer and T.R. Tyler (eds), Thousand Oaks, CA: Sage Publications, pp. 357–89.

Landstrom, H. (1993), 'Agency theory and its application to small firms: evidence from the Swedish venture capital market', *The Journal of Small Business Finance*, **2**, 203–18.
Landstrom, H. (1995), 'A pilot study on the investment decision-making of informal investors in Sweden', *Journal of Small Business Management*, **10** (4), 67–76.
Larson, A. (1992), 'Network dyads in entrepreneurial settings', *Administrative Science Quarterly*, **37**, 76–104.
Lewicki, R.J. and B.B. Bunker (1995), 'Trust in relationships: a model of trust development and decline', in B.B. Bunker and J.Z. Rubin (eds), *Conflict and Justice*, San-Francisco: Jossey-Bass, pp. 133–73.
Lewicki, R.J. and B.B. Bunker (1996), 'Developing and maintaining trust in work relationships', in R.M. Kramer and T.R. Tyler (eds), *Trust in Organizations: Frontiers of Theory and Research*, Thousand Oaks, CA: Sage Publications, pp. 114–39.
Low, M. and V. Srivatsan (1993), 'What does it mean to trust an entrepreneur?', Paper to Third Global Entrepreneurship Research Conference, Groupe ESC, Lyon.
Marsh, S. (1992), 'Trust and reliance in multi-agent systems: a preliminary report', in MAAMAW' 92: 4th European Workshop Autonomous Agents in a Multi-Agent World, Rome, Italy.
Marsh, S. (1995), 'Formalising trust as a computational concept', Technical Report CSM133, Stirling: Department of Computing Science and Mathematics, Stirling University.
Mason, C.M. (1996), 'Informal venture capital; is policy running ahead of knowledge?', *International Journal of Entrepreneurial Behaviour and Research* **2**, 4–14.
Mason, C.M. and R.T. Harrison (1994), 'The informal venture capital market in the UK', in A. Hughes and D.J. Storey (eds), *Financing Small Firms*, London: Routledge, pp. 64–111.
Mason, C.M. and R.T. Harrison (1995a), 'Closing the regional equity gap: the role of informal venture capital', *Small Business Economics*, **7**, 153–72.
Mason, C.M. and R.T. Harrison (1995b), 'Informal venture capital and the financing of small and medium-sized enterprises', *Small Enterprise Research*, **3**, 33–56.
Mason, C.M. and R.T. Harrison (1996a), 'Informal venture capital: a study of the investment process, the post-investment experience and investment performance', *Entrepreneurship and Regional Development*, **8**, 105–26.
Mason, C.M. and R.T. Harrison (1996b), 'Why business angels say no: a case study of opportunities rejected by an informal investment syndicate', *International Small Business Journal*, **14** (2), 35–51.
Mason, C.M. and R.T. Harrison (1996c), 'Information, networks and informal venture capital: the role of business introduction services', in R.T. Harrison and C.M. Mason (eds), *Informal Venture Capital: Evaluating the Impact of Business Introduction Services*, Hemel Hempstead: Woodhead Faulkner, pp. 27–58.
Mason, C.M. and A. Rogers (1996), 'Understanding the business angel's investment decision' Working Paper No. 11, Venture Finance Research Project Dept. of Geography, University of Southampton, April.
Mason, C.M. and A. Rogers (1997), 'The business angel's investment decision: an exploratory analysis', in D. Deacons, P. Jennings and C. Mason (eds), *Entrepreneurship in the 1990s*, London: Paul Chapman, forthcoming.
Mayer, R.C., J.H. Davis and F.D. Schorman (1995), 'An integrative model of organizational trust', *Academy of Management Journal*, **20**, 709–34.
Meyerson, D., K.E. Weick and R.M. Kramer (1996), 'Swift Trust and Temporary Groups', in R. M. Kramer and T.R. Tyler (eds), *Trust in Organizations: Frontiers to Theory and Research*, Thousand Oaks, CA: Sage Publications, pp. 166–95.
Mishra, A.K. (1996), 'Organizational responses to crisis: the centrality of trust', in R.M. Kramer and T.R. Tyler (eds), *Trust in Organizations: Frontiers of Theory and Research*, Thousand Oaks, CA: Sage Publications, pp. 261–87.
Moesel, D., J. Fiet, L. Busenitz and J. Barney (1996), 'Factors underlying change in risk perceptions of new ventures by venture capitalists', in P.D. Reynolds et al. (eds), *Frontiers of Entrepreneurship Research 1996*, Wellesley, MA: Babson College, pp. 377–91.
Powell, W.W. (1990), 'Neither market nor hierarchy: network forms of organization', in B.M. Staw and L.L. Cummings (eds), *Research in Organizational Behaviour*, Vol. 12, Connecticut: JAI Press, pp. 295–336.
Putnam, R. (1992), *Making Democracy Work*, Princeton, NJ: Princeton University Press.

Riding, A., P. Dal Cin, L. Duxbury, G. Haines and R. Safrata (1993), *Informal Investors in Canada: the Identification of Salient Characteristics*, Ottawa: Carlton University.

Riding, A., L. Duxbury and G. Haines (1995), 'Financing enterprise development: decision-making by Canadian angels', Unpublished paper, Carleton University, Ottawa.

Sandberg, W.R., D.M. Schweiger and C.W. Hofer (1988), 'The use of verbal protocols in determining venture capitalists' decision processes', *Entrepreneurship Theory and Practice*, **13**, 8–20.

Scott, M.G. and P.J. Rosa (1996), 'Opinion: has firm level analysis reached its limits? Time for a rethink', *International Small Business Journal*, **14** (4), 81–9.

Shapiro, D., B.H. Sheppard and L. Cheraskin (1992), 'Business on a handshake', *Negotiation Journal*, **8**, 365–77.

Simon, H.A. (1955), 'A behavioural model of rational choice', *Quarterly Journal of Economics*, **69**, 99–108.

Sullivan, M.K. and A. Miller (1990), 'Applying theory of finance to informal risk capital research: promises and problem', in N. Churchill et al. (eds), *Frontiers of Entrepreneurship Research 1990*, Wellesley, MA: Babson College, pp. 296–310.

Suomi, M. and A. Lumme (1994), *Yksityishenkilot Paaoma-Sijoittajina Suomessa* (Informal Private Investors in Finland), Helsinki: SITRA (English summary).

Tyejbee, T. and A. Bruno (1984), 'A model of venture capitalist investment activity', *Management Science*, **30**, 1051–66.

Tyler, T.R. and P. Degoey (1996), 'Trust in organizational authorities: the influence of motive attributions on willingness to accept decisions', in *Trust in Organizations: Frontiers of Theory and Research*, R.M. Kramer and T.R. Tyler (eds), Thousand Oaks, CA: Sage Publications, pp. 331–56.

Volery, T. (1995), 'Co-operative strategies for small and medium-sized enterprises', Paper presented at the 40th World Conference of the International Council for Small Enterprises, Sydney, June.

Wetzel, W. (1986), 'Entrepreneurs, angels and economic renaissance', in R.D. Hisrich (ed.), *Entrepreneurship, Intrapreneurship and Venture Capital*, Lexington, MA: Lexington Books, pp. 119–39.

Zacharakis, A.L. and G.D. Meyer (1995), 'The venture capitalist decision: understanding process versus outcome', Paper to 15th Babson College–Kauffman Foundation Entrepreneurship Research Conference, London Business School.

6. Relationship participation: the case of banks and smaller businesses[1]

Martin Binks and Christine Ennew

1 Introduction

Until recently, much of the research relating to the financing of entrepreneurial activity has focused on issues relating to equity funding in general and the role of the venture capital industry in particular, as will be apparent from other chapters in this volume. While venture capital is clearly important, particularly in some of the high-risk/high-return areas of activity, the majority of businesses continue to rely heavily on the banking sector for external finance. This is particularly so in the case of smaller businesses, and while not all smaller businesses are entrepreneurial a significant amount of entrepreneurial activity is manifest among these organisations. For the beneficial potential of entrepreneurial activity to be realised, it is important that such businesses are not constrained by imperfections in either output markets (Mayes and Moir, 1989) or input markets (Binks and Vale, 1990). On the input side, access to finance in general and credit rationing in particular are often identified as factors constraining the development of the more entrepreneurial smaller business; indeed in a recent survey of smaller businesses in England, both micro and small businesses identified finance as the major barrier to future growth (ICAEW, 1996).

Problems with respect to the provision of external finance typically arise as a consequence of information asymmetries which impact on the lending decision. The relative costs and benefits of information collection means that it is unlikely that any financing transaction would be conducted under conditions of perfect information. When information is less than perfect some firms may suffer from restricted access to finance because of the difficulties experienced by lenders in evaluating and monitoring proposals. However, the more limited the information available, the greater potential for misallocation of funds and the greater the constraints on growth. The theoretical basis for credit rationing is well established (Stiglitz and Weiss, 1981) although its empirical significance has been subject to rather more debate. To the extent that credit rationing exists, the provision of collateral can be seen as a device to mitigate the effects of the information asymmetries which are its cause. However, collateral is not the only mechanism for addressing the problem of information asymmetries; while perfect information may be an unobtainable goal, information flows between a business and a bank can be improved by the development of a closer working relationship. Such relationships are, by definition, two way, and a truly effective relationship is likely to require the active commitment and participation of both parties. As such, there are clearly costs to the development and maintenance of such relationships, but equally both parties should expect to receive benefits as a consequence of improved information flows and greater understanding.

This chapter examines the banking relationship in detail with a particular focus on the impact of participative behaviour on both banks and businesses using data from a survey of over 3000 smaller businesses in Britain. Section 2 provides an overview of factors governing the provision of finance to UK small businesses and Section 3 discusses the problems of asymmetric information and examines the extent to which the banking relationship can, in principle, ameliorate these problems. The results of an empirical analysis of these issues are presented in Section 4 and the conclusions from the study are discussed in Section 5.

2 The provision of finance to small businesses

The efficient and effective provision of finance to small firms has long been recognised as a key factor in ensuring that those firms with genuine growth potential can expand and compete and a number of studies have noted a positive association between external finance, particularly bank finance, and business performance (Keasey and McGuiness, 1990; Keasey and Watson, 1992). In the UK, successive government sponsored enquiries, including the Macmillan, Radcliffe, Bolton and Wilson Committees, have all highlighted the problems experienced by small businesses in gaining access to debt and equity finance. It is generally accepted that size may preclude firms from access to certain sectors of the capital markets, particularly where equity finance is concerned. The development of the venture capital market and the introduction of the Business Expansion Scheme have improved the supply of equity finance to small businesses in the UK, although recent evidence suggests that the equity gap has not been eliminated (Harrison and Mason, 1990). Arguably, however, it is in relation to debt that the problem of access to finance may be more pressing, since debt is generally identified as the most common type of external finance used by small businesses in both the UK (Keasey and Watson, 1992) and the US (Scherr, Sugrue and Ward, 1993). In the UK, access to external equity from venture and development capital firms is typically restricted to projects requiring in excess of £250 000 while informal sources from Business Angels are still embryonic (Mason, Harrison and Chaloner, 1992). Even in cases where projects are large enough to justify venture capital, there is evidence to suggest that a large number of small businesses are resistant to external equity participation (Binks, Ennew and Reed, 1992; Cowling, Samuels and Sugden, 1991; Dow, 1992). Consequently, small businesses in the UK rely primarily on debt finance from the banking sector either in the form of fixed term loans, or more commonly, overdraft finance (lines of credit). Where such businesses experience difficulties in obtaining debt finance, potential viable growth may be foregone. If such difficulties occur with any regularity then they may inhibit the positive economic contribution which would be expected from the small firms sector.

Difficulties in obtaining debt finance do not refer simply to the fact that some firms cannot obtain funds through the banking system. Indeed, we should not expect that all projects would automatically be financed. Genuine difficulties occur first, in situations in which a project which is viable and profitable at prevailing interest rates is not undertaken because the firm is unable to obtain appropriate funding, and second, in situations in which viable projects can only obtain funding on apparently disadvantageous terms. Restricted access to finance is not necessarily attributable directly to size, but is instead a result of the problems associated with the availability of information on which projects are evaluated (Berger and Udell, 1993; Constand, Osteryoung and Nast, 1991; Keasey and Watson, 1992). Such information problems are not unique to the small firms sector, but are considerably more prevalent there because of the anticipated higher costs of information collection.

3 Asymmetric information and the banking relationship

Information asymmetry poses two problems for the provision of debt finance. First, the lender (the bank) cannot observe *ex ante* certain information which is relevant to the decision to enter into the contract, typically the actual abilities of the individuals applying for finance and the qualities of the project (the problem of adverse selection). Second, the risk that the small business will not perform in a manner consistent with the contract necessitates some form of *ex post* monitoring procedure (to address the moral hazard problem). In principle, information could be collected with respect to the abilities of the entrepreneur, the nature of the industry and market, and the behaviour of the business once finance has been made available. In practice, the cost of gathering such information at a single point in time is likely to be high, and in most cases prohibitively high relative to the risk and return associated with any given project. Even if a comprehensive information set were available (and this is unlikely), the lender (the bank) is likely to encounter difficulties in processing that information, thus limiting its practical usefulness. However, during the lifetime of a firm's relationship with its bank, there exists considerable potential gradually to accumulate information (Berger and Udell, 1993; Sharpe, 1989) which might be expected to ease the problems of adverse selection and moral hazard.

The issue of information asymmetry and its implications for the provision of bank finance has been the subject of extensive discussion. From a theoretical perspective, it is commonly accepted that information asymmetry results in credit rationing (Stiglitz and Weiss, 1981) although an alternative perspective suggests that the true problem may be an oversupply of credit (de Meza and Webb, 1987). Empirically, the evidence is ambiguous. Evans and Jovanovic (1989) and

Holtz-Eakin, Joulfaian and Rosen (1994) present evidence to indicate that there is a capital constraint with respect to start-ups which does not appear to be reduced through the provision of bank finance. However, UK evidence (Cressy, 1996) suggests that this type of constraint is not significant and that bank lending decisions reflect evaluations of human capital rather than any implicit, information based credit rationing.

While there is a need for further work to reconcile these views, there is evidence to suggest that they may not be mutually exclusive. Berger and Udell (1992) argue that while the macro effects of credit rationing may be small, there is evidence to suggest that when credit is rationed to some firms it may be more readily available to others. In particular, this result may be related to the role of collateral in bonding debt finance. Indeed, from a theoretical perspective it has been shown that the availability of sufficient collateral can counteract these problems; the low-risk borrowers who leave the market in the Stiglitz–Weiss model can signal their status by a willingness to offer appropriate levels of collateral, and the taking of collateral by the banks can provide an incentive to ensure that the firm will perform to the best of its abilities in undertaking the project (Bester, 1987). However, if collateral is in limited supply, debt gaps may still exist. In effect, the information costs associated with the evaluation and monitoring of a project may prohibit an income-gearing or prospects-based approach to project evaluation, thus causing the lender to default to a capital-gearing approach which is contingent upon the availability of sufficient collateral. This collateral may be in the form of either personal or business assets. Securitizing loans against appropriate assets (preferably personal) represents a rational approach for banks in the face of high project evaluation costs because it allows good projects to self-select. The downside of such approaches may be that valuable projects may be lost in instances in which the proposer has inadequate personal collateral. In addition, the provision of personal collateral in the form of a guarantee or house deeds effectively erodes limited liability status and the protection it provides. This may be expected to discourage investment at the margin, given the additional personal risk it implies.

Small firms may also experience a debt gap because they have insufficient business collateral. With a capital-gearing approach, a debt gap may be more frequent in the case of small firms because asset-backed collateral must be valued at 'carcass value' prices to ensure that the loan is covered realistically in the event of default and immediate realisation. Loans for specific items of plant and equipment will require more than the current resale price of the equipment for full collateral since the depreciation rate of the machinery will often be assumed by the bank to surpass that of the decline in loan values outstanding in the early periods of repayment.

Thus information problems can produce financial constraints either because debt finance is not provided or is only provided on disadvantageous terms.

Although perfect information is an unobtainable goal, the quantity and quality of information available to a bank will be influenced by the nature of the relationship with each business (Berger and Udell, 1993). A close relationship has the potential to provide the bank with a better understanding of the operating environment facing a particular business; a clearer picture of the managerial attributes of the owner and a more accurate overview of the prospects for the business. Thus, from the perspective of the bank, the relationship provides the basis for understanding customer needs and resources and identifying the most appropriate ways of meeting those needs. This relationship is not simply a one way process. An effective banking relationship requires a positive contribution from both parties. The ability of the bank to meet customer needs requires that the owner/manager provides the bank with appropriate and timely information and is receptive to suggestions and advice provided by the bank. The development of close working relationships between banks and small businesses has often been identified as a weakness of traditional Anglo-Saxon banking systems (Yao-Su Hu, 1984; Edwards, 1987) and a comparative analysis of medium-sized enterprises in Germany, France and the UK lends some support to this hypothesis (Binks, Ennew and Reed, 1992). Nevertheless, many of the recent developments in the provision of banking services to small businesses in the UK have attempted to deal with this weakness, particularly through the introduction of specialist small business account managers (Binks and Ennew, 1991).

The nature and consequences of the banking relationship have been relatively under-researched, despite their potential importance. The current study looks to identify relationship types based upon the degree of involvement or participation described above and establish the extent to which there is variation in the experiences of firms according to the type of relationship they have with their bank. The basic proposition underlying the research is that there will be identifiable benefits to firms and banks involved in more participative relationships and particularly so with respect to financing terms and conditions.

The empirical setting is the relationship between banks and small businesses in the UK. As is the case in most parts of the world, small firms in the UK rely heavily on the banking sector for external finance. The UK banking sector is dominated by a small number of large banks providing retail and corporate services both nationally and internationally. From the perspective of the banks, the small business segment is arguably of particular importance because of the profit and revenue opportunities it presents (Bannock and Doran, 1991). The value of developing good working relationships with business customers in general and small business customers in particular has been highlighted in a number of studies (Turnbull and Gibbs, 1987; Watson, 1986). However the small business segment has not been an easy one for the main banks to target and a number of studies have highlighted imperfections in service provision and problems regarding service quality (Ennew, Reed and Binks, 1993). Although the range and variety of products available to small businesses has expanded, the management of the banking relationship continues to be problematic. In part this may reflect failures on the part of the banks, such problems may also arise as a consequence of some customers' reluctance to participate in the banking relationship.

4 Empirical analysis

Data used for the empirical analysis were obtained from a survey conducted among its members by the Forum of Private Business (FPB) in January/February 1996. This is a biennial survey which provides one of the most comprehensive sets of data relating to the bank–small business relationship in the UK. Approximately 14 000 questionnaires were distributed in a single mailing to a random sample of the membership. This resulted in 3843 usable responses which represents a response rate of around 27 per cent. A follow-up telephone survey of non-respondents was used to check for non-response bias. A comparison of responses suggested that there was little evidence of significant bias. However, the sample itself was not truly representative of the national population of small businesses. Specifically, respondents tended to be larger (whether measured by sales revenue or number of employees); the sample had a significantly higher proportion of manufacturing firms (and a lower proportion of agricultural businesses) and a significantly higher proportion of firms located in the south-east. None of these problems was considered to be sufficiently substantial to threaten the generalizability of the subsequent findings.

The questionnaire collected a wide range of information including basic details of the business itself, the financing terms and conditions, measures of service quality, the banking relationship and overall satisfaction. Ideally, data for such a study would be collected independently from both parties to a relationship as was the case in a study of venture capital relationships by Sapienza and Gupta (1994). In the case of banking relationships, the number of smaller clients handled by any given account manager may be well in excess of 100 making account manager evaluations difficult, irrespective of issues which may arise relating to confidentiality. Thus, for largely practical purposes, the banking relationship was measured from two angles using business perspectives only. First, respondents were asked to assess their behaviour towards their bank in terms of willingness to share various types of information, monitoring of charges and account and the nature of personal contact with their bank manager. Second, respondents were also asked to provide their assessment of how their bank manager behaved towards them in terms of the provision of advice and support, awareness and understanding, and implementation of bank policies. These two sets of scale items provided a measure of the two sides of the relationship and while, admittedly, the use of the firms perception of the banks behaviour rather than an objective measure is a crude proxy, it was considered to be an acceptable indicator given the difficulty of directly measuring both sides of a given relationship.[2]

A single measure of the degree of participation was constructed by averaging across the scales and this provided the input to a cluster analysis which sought to identify distinct types of relationship. An iterative partitioning algorithm was used and 3, 4 and 5 cluster solutions were generated; discriminant analysis and one-way ANOVA suggested that the four-cluster solution was marginally superior and given the ease of interpretation, this solution was the one adopted. This solution produced a simple 2 × 2 classification of relationship types according to whether each party was participative or non-participative. Details of the solution are provided in Table 6.1.

Table 6.1 The cluster solution

Firms' behaviour	Banks' behaviour	Relationship type	Number
2.96	2.28	Non-participative firm/non-participative bank	545
3.33	3.43	Non-participative firm/participative bank	755
4.01	2.83	Participative firm/non-participative bank	934
4.36	3.99	Participative firm/participative bank	1281

The first cluster has the lowest score on both measures of participation and was described as 'non-participative firm/non-participative bank'. In contrast, the fourth cluster displayed the highest scores on both measures and these cases were described as 'participative firm/participative bank'. For the in-between cases, the mean scores seemed to indicate that one part was relatively participative and that the other was not. These clusters were labelled accordingly.

Having identified these four relationship types, the analysis proceeded to examine the extent to which there were identifiable differences between the clusters in terms of financing, quality of service and attitudinal outcomes including customer satisfaction and value for money. ANCOVA was used to test for differences while controlling for the impact of other relevant variables. In general, the analysis sought to control for the effect of relevant aspects of financing terms, size of business, self perceived risk associated with business and finally whether the respondent's bank was English or Scottish (to accommodate the impact of potential variability arising from differences in the banking systems). In all cases a hierarchical decomposition was used with covariates entering first and relationship type entering last.

As shown in Table 6.2, four aspects of financing terms and conditions were examined, namely interest rate margin over base for an overdraft (line of credit), the collateral ratio for overdraft limit, the size of the overdraft limit and the extent to which the overdraft was being used (limit/amount overdrawn). Although some loan data were available, the more extensive use of overdraft funding suggested that this would be the more appropriate subject for analysis.

Table 6.2 ANCOVA for financing terms and conditions

Source of variation	Mean square	Sig. of F
Margin over base		
Covariates	28.12	0.00
Size of overdraft	83.76	0.00
Collateral ratio	0.38	0.52
Business risk	0.43	0.50
Main effects	14.20	0.00
Turnover	20.24	0.00
English/Scottish banks	7.95	0.00
Relationship type	10.27	0.00
Collateral ratio		
Covariates	135.30	0.00
Margin over base on OD	2.91	0.60
Size of overdraft	224.48	0.00
Business risk	178.50	0.00
Main effects	60.46	0.00
Turnover	79.48	0.00
English/Scottish banks	62.41	0.02
Relationship type	40.78	0.01
Size of overdraft limit		
Covariates	1 181 561.27	0.00
Margin over base rate on OD	2 858 455.84	0.00
Collateral on OD limit	674 328.65	0.00
Business risk	11 899.32	0.52
Main effects	793 061.82	0.00
Turnover	1 810 774.34	0.00
English/Scottish banks	60 800.94	0.15
Relationship type	19 436.27	0.57
Overdraft use		
Covariates	0.34	0.00
Margin over base on OD	0.89	0.00
Size of overdraft	0.27	0.06
Collateral ratio	0.17	0.13
Business risk	0.00	0.10
Main effects	0.15	0.05
Turnover	0.10	0.26
English/Scottish banks	0.20	0.10
Relationship type	0.19	0.06

Table 6.3 ANCOVA for dimensions of quality

Source of variation	Mean square	Sig. of F
Price		
Covariates	23.03	0.00
Margin over base on OD	81.66	0.00
Size of overdraft	2.72	0.60
Collateral ratio	7.70	0.00
Age of business	0.04	0.81
Main effects	28.62	0.00
Turnover	4.10	0.00
Profitability	0.60	0.37
English/Scottish banks	2.51	0.07
Relationship type	71.19	0.00
Core product		
Covariates	6.41	0.00
Margin over base on OD	21.76	0.00
Size of overdraft	0.02	0.85
Collateral ratio	1.81	0.03
Age of business	2.07	0.02
Main effects	39.46	0.00
Turnover	0.55	0.23
Profit group	0.40	0.75
English/Scottish banks	0.70	0.68
Relationship type	104.62	0.00
Knowledge		
Covariates	7.96	0.00
Margin over base on OD	20.50	0.00
Size of overdraft	6.46	0.00
Collateral ratio	3.77	0.01
Age of business	1.11	0.16
Main effects	52.76	0.00
Turnover	0.33	0.62
Profit group	0.42	0.39
English/Scottish banks	1.56	0.10
Relationship type	139.69	0.00

Table 6.3 (continued)

Source of variation	Mean square	Sig. of F
Operations		
Covariates	3.94	0.00
Margin over base on OD	14.05	0.00
Size of overdraft	0.31	0.42
Collateral ratio	1.37	0.94
Age of business	0.04	0.77
Main effects	26.18	0.00
Turnover	0.30	0.60
Profit group	0.37	0.38
English/Scottish banks	26.2	0.02
Relationship type	68.52	0.00
Access		
Covariates	2.41	0.00
Margin over base on OD	4.69	0.00
Size of overdraft	0.64	0.27
Collateral ratio	2.20	0.04
Age of business	2.13	0.04
Main effects	7.84	0.00
Turnover	1.26	0.07
Profit group	0.26	0.48
English/Scottish banks	1.62	0.08
Relationship type	19.02	0.00

The results demonstrate that relationship type has a significant impact on interest rate (margin over base), and collateral ratio and a marginal impact on extent of overdraft use. In all cases the evidence suggests that where both parties are participative, interest rates, collateral ratios and the extent of overdraft use are all lower even after controlling for the effects of other relevant financing variables, size of business and degree of business risk.

Similar findings are in evidence when considering the quality of service more generally. Five dimensions of quality were used for the analysis: namely, price, core product, knowledge, operations and access. Each of these measures was constructed as an average of ratings across a set of specific quality-related scale items. Results of ANCOVAs, controlling for relevant business and financial measures are presented in Table 6.3.

Again, it is evident that the clusters representing the different categories of relationship are strongly significant, indicating considerable variation in perceptions of service quality across relationship types. As might be expected, the more participative relationships are associated with higher levels of perceived quality.

So far, the variables examined focus essentially on outcomes for the firm; but the initial proposition anticipated benefits for both parties. Thus, for banks, two indirect measures of performance were used in the form of customer perceptions of value for money and levels of customer satisfaction. Both measures were scored on a five point scale and were subjected to the same form of ANCOVA. The results are contained in Table 6.4. Once again, it is apparent that participative relationships have a strongly significant effect and inspection of the mean values confirms that this effect is in the direction anticipated.

Table 6.4 ANCOVA for attitudinal outcomes

Source of variation	Mean square	Sig. of F
Value for money		
Covariates	9.60	0.00
Margin over base on OD	34.30	0.00
Size of overdraft	0.95	0.30
Collateral ratio	2.79	0.07
Age of business	0.37	0.52
Main effects	14.96	0.00
Turnover	5.49	0.00
Profit group	0.00	0.96
English/Scottish banks	3.26	0.05
Relationship type	33.32	0.00
Satisfaction		
Covariates	9.44	0.00
Margin over base on OD	32.39	0.00
Size of overdraft	1.11	0.15
Collateral ratio	4.22	0.01
Age of business	0.04	0.78
Main effects	64.91	0.00
Turnover	1.22	0.07
Profit group	0.30	0.45
English/Scottish banks	0.05	0.77
Relationship type	171.78	0.00

5 Conclusions

Information asymmetries and transactions costs inevitably mean that the bank/small business relationship will occur under conditions of imperfect information. Imperfect information is in turn one of the main reasons why firms face constraints in the market for finance. While collateral may be one mechanism for reducing the adverse effects of information asymmetries, the development of a close working relationship is an alternative. An effective banking relationship, by its nature, must involve two parties. For banks and businesses to invest time and effort in developing and maintaining such relationships requires that there are discernible benefits from so doing. Using measures of the behaviour of owner-managers and measures of perceptions of bank behaviour, four distinct clusters of relationship types can be identified based on the degree to which each party participates in the relationship. Further analysis suggests that more participative relationship types are associated with benefits to the firm in the form of better financing conditions and better quality of service and benefits to the bank in the form of more favourable customer assessments of bank service.

Clearly, these findings are preliminary and there are important issues relating to dimensions of the relationship which have not been considered in detail (for example, trust and commitment) and relating to the measurement of those aspects which have (participation). Nevertheless, the strength of the findings and the size of the data set on which they were based would suggest that this is an area which would warrant further investigation and analysis. Indeed the whole issue of managing relationships is likely to be of growing importance in the banking sector; faced with cost and competitive pressures, banks may need to consider carefully what types of relationship they wish to offer and how they might charge. Similarly, from the perspective of firms, there is clearly a strong case for more active information sharing and also perhaps a need to consider what type of relationship is most appropriate for a given business. In some cases, the 'hands-off' style of relationship which characterises the non-participative firm/non-participative bank category may be entirely appropriate if the business concerned is stable and mature with no obvious growth aspirations. However, for the entrepreneurial young firm with ambitions to grow fast, the more participative style of relationship may be desirable and even essential if growth opportunities are to be realised.

Notes

1. The authors acknowledge the help of the Forum of Private Business in the provision of the data used in this chapter.
2. Given the advances in relationship research which have occurred in relation to venture capital (Sapienza and Gupta, 1994) and the results of preliminary studies in banking by Perrien and Ferguson (1996) there is a strong case for further research to examine the development of relationships from the perspective of both parties simultaneously.

References

Bannock, Graham and A. Doran (1991), *Business Banking in the 1990s: A New Era of Competition*, Dublin: Lafferty Group.

Berger, A.N. and G.F. Udell (1992), 'Some evidence on the empirical significance of credit rationing', *Journal of Political Economy*, **100** (5), 1047–77.

Berger, A.N. and G.F. Udell (1993), 'Lines of credit, collateral and relationship lending in small firm finance', Working Paper (S-93/17), Salomon Brothers Center for the Study of Financial Institutions, New York University.

Bester, H. (1987), 'The role of collateral in credit markets with imperfect information', *European Economic Review*, **31**, 887–99.

Binks, M.R. and C.T. Ennew (1991), 'Bank finance to small business', in J. Curran (ed.), *Bolton 20 Years On*, London: PCP, pp. 50–74.

Binks, M.R. and P.A. Vale (1990), *Entrepreneurship and Economic Change*, London: McGraw Hill.

Binks, M.R., C.T. Ennew and G.V. Reed (1992), *Small Business and their Banks: An International Perspective*, London: National Westminster Bank.

Constand, R.L., J.S. Osteryoung and D.A. Nast (1991), 'Revolving asset backed lending contracts and the resolution of debt-related agency problems', *Journal of Small Business Finance*, **1** (1), 15–28.

Cowling, M., J. Samuels and R. Sugden (1991), 'Small firms and clearing banks', Report Prepared for the Association of British Chambers of Commerce.

Cressy, R. (1996), 'Are business start-ups debt rationed?', *Economic Journal*, **106** (September), 1253–70.

de Meza, D. and D.C. Webb (1987), 'Too much investment: a problem of asymmetric information', *Quarterly Journal of Economics*, **102**, 281–92

Dow, S. (1992), 'The regional financial sector: A Scottish case study', *Regional Studies*, **26** (7), 619–63.

Edwards, G. (1987), *The Role of Banks in Economic Development*, London: Macmillan.

Ennew, C.T., G.V. Reed and M.R. Binks (1993), 'Importance performance analysis and the measurement of service quality', *European Journal of Marketing*, **27** (2), 59–70.

Evans, D.S. and B. Jovanovic (1989), 'An estimated model of entrepreneurial choice under liquidity constraints', *Journal of Political Economy*, **97** (4), 808–27.

Harrison, R.T. and C.M. Mason (1990), 'The role of the business expansion scheme in the UK', *Omega*, **17** (2), 147–57.

Holtz-Eakin, D., D. Joulfaian and H.S. Rosen (1994), 'Sticking it out: entrepreneurial survival and liquidity constraints', *Journal of Political Economy*, **102** (1), 53–75.

ICAEW (1996), *Barriers to Growth: A Report by the Enterprise Group of the ICAEW*, Milton Keynes: Institute of Chartered Accountants of England and Wales.

Keasey, K. and P. McGuiness (1990), 'Small new firms and the return to alternative sources of finance', *Small Business Economics*, **2**, 213–22.

Keasey, K. and R. Watson (1992), 'Investment and financing decisions and the performance of small firms', London: National Westminster Bank.

Mason, C.M., R.T. Harrison and J. Chaloner (1992), 'Informal risk capital in the UK: a study of investor characteristics, preferences and decision making', in M. Robertson, E. Chell and C. Mason (eds), *Towards the Twenty First Century: The Challenge for Small Business*, Cheshire: Nadamal pp. 141–61.

Mayes, D.G and L.B. Moir (1989), 'Small firms in the UK economy', *Royal Bank of Scotland Review*, December, 15–33.

Perrien, P.M. and R.J. Ferguson (1996), 'Relational contract norms and the effectiveness of commercial banking relationships', Paper presented at Frontiers in Services Marketing Conference, Owen Graduate School of Management, Nashville (October).

Sapienza, H. and A. Gupta (1994), 'Impact of agency risk and task uncertainty on venture capitalist–CEO Interaction', *Academy of Management Journal*, **37** (6), 1618–32.

Scherr, F.C. T.F. Sugrue and J.B. Ward (1993), 'Financing the small firm start-up: determinants of debt use', *Journal of Small Business Finance*, **3** (l), 17–36.

Sharpe, S.A. (1989), 'Asymmetric information, bank lending and implicit contracts: a stylized model of customer relationships', *Finance and Economics Discussion Series*, no. 70, Washington: Federal Reserve Board, May.

Stiglitz, J. and A. Weiss (1981), 'Credit rationing in markets with imperfect information', *American Economic Review*, **71**, 393–410.

Turnbull, P.W. and M.L. Gibbs (1987), 'Marketing bank services to corporate clients: the importance of relationships', *International Journal of Bank Marketing*, **5** (1), 19–26.

Watson, I. (1986) 'Managing the relationship with corporate clients', *International Journal of Bank Marketing*, **4** (1), 19–34.

Yao-Su Hu (1984), *Industrial Banking and Special Credit Institutions*, London: Policy Studies Institute.

7. Loan covenants, relationship banking and management buy-outs in default: a comparative study of the UK and Holland

David Citron, Ken Robbie, Mike Wright, Hans Bruining and Arthur Herst

Introduction

Jensen (1986) and Wruck (1990) argue that leveraged buyout firms achieve operating efficiencies due to the discipline and monitoring imposed by high leverage. Furthermore, if such firms become distressed, timely loan default should ensure that they are more likely to be rescued before their going concern value dissipates. Beneish and Press (1995a), however, find for non-LBOs in default that the cost of additional constraints imposed by lenders outweighs the benefits of increased monitoring.

Furthermore, studies of firms breaching covenants have focused on those firms that have violated accounting-based covenants alone (see for example Beneish and Press, 1993, and Chen and Wei, 1993, on the costs of breach; DeFond and Jiambalvo, 1994, and Sweeney, 1994, on accounting responses to breaches). However, lenders often require a range of both accounting-based and non-accounting-based covenants and it is possible that these interact as firms approach default. In this spirit Smith (1993) suggests that research into technical default needs to be integrated into a broader view of the lending process (p. 301). Similarly Singh (1993) makes a plea for introducing more institutional detail into studies of corporate restructuring, by which he means 'a precise understanding of the actual mechanics of decision making' (p. 164).

This chapter focuses on the role of both accounting-based covenants and other sources of information in signalling financial distress in UK and Dutch MBOs. Its main contribution is that, taking up the challenge of Smith and Singh, it does this in the wider context of how impending default is communicated to the lender and how the lender responds.

A further important issue concerns the role of relationships in the operation of covenants. Although there has been extensive attention to the nature and extent of relationships in the venture capital industry (for example, Barry, 1994; Elango et al., 1995; Hatherly et al., 1994; Lerner, 1995; and Robbie and Wright, 1995, it is becoming increasingly clear that relationships are an important feature of bank lending. Mayer (1988) sees the chief characteristics of close bank–client relationships as comprising 'procedures for evaluating prospective borrowers, monitoring the performance of borrowers and, most crucially of all, reacting to instances of financial distress' (pp. 1180–81). Similarly Holland's case studies lead him to the view that 'close relationships generally involve rich information flows . . . high loyalty and commitment between parties and expectations of fair dealing and longevity of relationship' (Holland, 1994, p. 372). In the context of covenants there may, for example, be a range of actions available to lenders which may draw heavily on the development of a relationship rather than being a mechanistic reaction to covenant breaches. Hence the chapter also draws on certain features of relationship banking, as a means of addressing agency cost problems, to place the insights of Jensen and Wruck into a broader view of the lending process. This study investigates the extent to which the use of covenants in MBO lending reflects banking relationships of these sorts.

Previous research, in investigating different types of debt, has focused on the distinction between public and private lending. However lender/borrower relationships are also likely to be affected by whether the lender is a sole lender or syndicate leader as compared to being merely a syndicate member (see Smith, 1993, p. 298). This chapter adds to previous research by exploring the implications of this distinction for MBOs in loan default.

A further issue is whether the role and operation of debt covenants vary in different environments. To address this issue the study compares the operation of debt covenants in buy-outs in the UK and Holland. These two countries are selected because while being, respectively, the first and third most developed buy-out markets in Europe,[1] there are marked differences in their respective sizes and operations of banks (see below).

The remainder of the chapter consists of four sections. The theoretical framework for the research is contained in the next section and is followed by a description of the data and research methodology. The fourth section contains the findings and the chapter concludes with a summary and discussion of implications for future research.

Theoretical framework

There is a well-known agency cost involved in the general provision of debt which arises from the potential conflict of interest between equity holders and debt providers (Smith and Warner, 1979). Debt covenants provide a means of controlling the moral hazard problems which may arise in monitoring management. For debt covenants to be effective in addressing moral hazard problems there is a need for them to be set at appropriate levels, for there to be an associated regular flow of (unbiased) information from the borrower to the lender, and for there to be timely and appropriate action by lenders when such covenants are breached.

Much of the covenants literature to date examines three main issues: (i) the incidence and nature of various debt covenants; (ii) how accounting-based covenants affect management's accounting policy choices (for example, DeFond and Jiambalvo, 1994; Sweeney, 1994); and (iii) the costs to the borrower of violating covenants (for example, Beneish and Press, 1993).

However, in a recent review of research into accounting-based covenant violations, Smith argues that 'further progress requires the integration of technical default into a broader view of the lending process' (1993, p. 301). This is because accounting-based covenants are merely a subset of the undertakings that characterise the borrower/lender relationship. One aspect of research which has addressed this dimension is that of Rajan and Winton (1995) who examine the role of covenants as a contractual device to increase lender's incentives to monitor, that is they provide incentives for lenders to take action and obtain information on which to base action. A proper understanding of their role, therefore, requires an understanding of the wider context within which they operate.

One particularly important feature of this wider context is that, as in the venture capital industry (Sapienza and Gupta, 1994), the borrower/lender relationship rests on informal as well as formal contracts (Holland, 1994). Accounting-based covenants are clearly an integral part of the formal contractual structure. It is likely, however, that their use will interact with both other formal and informal flows of information. This paper seeks to provide evidence on the functioning of accounting-based covenants in the wider setting of the formal and informal loan monitoring process.

MBO lending has been selected as a particularly appropriate context for this investigation for a number of reasons. First, MBO lenders can be expected to make greater use of a wider variety of both accounting-based and non-accounting-based covenants in their loan agreements than are found in general lending agreements. This is because the problems of both moral hazard and adverse selection are likely to be more acute in MBOs than in general corporate lending situations. Research into the agency costs of debt generally makes the assumption that the interests of management and shareholders coincide. Garvey and Swan (1994), however, summarising recent literature on management turnover in distressed firms, question the assumption that managers are always willing to act against the interests of lenders even when it means courting financial distress.

Though managers as significant equity holders in buy-outs are undiversed investors, there are strong arguments to suggest that share ownership provides an increased incentive to invest in risky projects, so increasing the probability of failure. Emerging evidence on post-transaction performance across the full range of buy-out types indicates that managers engage in both cost cutting as well as innovative, more risky activities, such as new product development (Wright et al., 1992; Phan and Hill, 1995; Zahra, 1995).[2]

The moral hazard problems associated with monitoring managers in buy-out companies may be particularly acute because incumbent management's relative information advantage may persist for some time after the MBO has been effected. Finally, competition for lending to a buy-out within a short timescale to deal completion also raises adverse selection problems in that such pressures may mean that management's assumptions about future performance are inadequately scrutinised.[3] Moreover, because MBO lending is typically lending by new bankers to a firm with changed ownership, the bankers may use covenants as a means of circumventing costly information gathering about the new borrower. For all these reasons, therefore, there may be greater incentives to emphasise the monitoring role of debt covenants in MBOs than in other forms of corporate lending. In addition, these incentives may be greater where there is greater use of vertical strip financing, which mitigates many of the agency problems discussed above.[4] Vertical strip financing tends to be more common in US buy-outs than in those taking place in the UK. In Holland also the banks tend to be involved directly in more layers of the finance structure (equity, mezzanine or subordinated debt, and senior debt) and there tends to be closer links between the banks and the private equity providers.

Second, MBO lending is likely to provide a particularly fruitful context for studying the loan monitoring process since lenders to MBOs are expected to place a strong emphasis on monitoring borrowers through close relationships. Smith and Warner (1979) argue that because contract renegotiation is less costly in private debt issues covenant constraints will be set with less slack, so that technical defaults are more likely in private than public debt cases. This suggests that in the case of buy-outs which go private and move from using public debt, there will be greater emphasis on the role of tight covenants. Close lender/borrower relationships will therefore be important if the presence of a large number of relatively tight covenants are not to result in frequent and costly loan renegotiations. Moreover the high degree of leverage in buy-outs and the typical links between the timing of predicated asset sales and exit and repayment of debt emphasises the importance of close relationships between borrowers and lenders in order to ensure that such targets are met.

While the empirical literature to date has focused on the private/public debt dichotomy referred to above, Smith (1993) hypothesises that private syndicated debt will be more costly to renegotiate than a private bilateral agreement. This chapter provides initial evidence on this issue by examining the views of syndicate members in contrast to those of sole lenders.

Differences in the environments in which bank lending takes place may also affect the operation of covenants. The nature of the relationship between equity and debt providers has already been identified above as a difference between the UK and Dutch buy-out markets. In the larger and more developed UK market there are also significantly more banks involved in lending to buy-outs and a greater number of private equity institutions investing in this kind of transaction. In their lending practices, UK banks typically insist at the time of negotiating a loan on the exclusive pledging of collateral to the lending bank whereas Dutch banks are less likely to insist on this condition, preferring to negotiate agreements that management will not pledge their shares to other lenders or sell them without gaining advance permission from the bank. At the same time Dutch banks preserve the right to withdraw the loan at any moment. In addition, there are important differences between the UK and Holland with respect to the giving of *financial assistance* which affects the ability to obtain security for borrowings in buy-outs.[5]

The main objective of this research, therefore, is to extend our understanding of the process of monitoring MBO lending, with especial reference to the role played by loan covenants. It aims to achieve this overall objective by examining in particular MBO lenders' perceptions of:

1. The extent of use of covenants (both accounting and non-accounting-based) in MBO loan agreements and in comparison with their use in general lending agreements;
2. The process whereby they monitor their lending arrangements, in particular as borrowers enter financial difficulties;
3. The effectiveness of accounting-based covenants as signals of impending distress;
4. Alternative responses to breaches of covenant and how the choice of response is influenced by the nature of the borrower/lender relationship.[6] Different types of borrower/lender relationship are characterised firstly by the presence or absence of a specialist MBO lending unit and, secondly, by comparing the views of sole lenders/syndicate leaders with those of syndicate members.

Data and methodology

The aim of the research is to elucidate key aspects of the borrower/lender relationship, focusing on how MBO lenders monitor their customers as they enter financial distress and how they react once a customer is in breach of covenant. In order to gain an understanding of both the formal and informal dimensions of this relationship it was decided to use a survey questionnaire as being the most appropriate research tool for examining the perceptions of one of the parties in this relationship, the MBO lender, drawn from as large a population of lending institutions as possible.[7] This approach follows closely the methodology used by Citron (1992a) in relation to the attitudes of lending bankers to the use of accounting ratios in loan contracts. The advantages of this approach were seen to be important in overcoming major difficulties relating to obtaining access to highly sensitive information, especially that relating to the actual operation of covenants. Given also that the respondents to the survey (see below) were senior executives in organisations which were generally involved in small numbers of transactions per year the potential problems of relying on perceptions rather than actual documents should be minimised.

The questionnaire was predominantly structured, but also included open-ended sections to permit a freer expression of respondents' views. The questions were drafted with a view to investigating MBO lenders' perceptions of the issues set out at the end of the previous section. It is recognised, therefore, that the results do not provide direct evidence on actual cases of MBOs in default.

In the UK, the questionnaire was mailed to 62 bank departments representing 58 bank groups which the Centre for Management Buy-Out Research (CMBOR) database had shown as having participated in at least one buy-out debt financing in the period 1989 to 1994. Mailing of the questionnaires was undertaken in late November 1994 with a follow-up letter sent in late December 1994.

The questionnaire was addressed to the heads of the relevant departments or other senior colleagues with whom CMBOR has regular contact through its buy-out and buy-in surveys in order to obtain organisation-wide perceptions of the process.[8] Discussions with senior executives involved in this form of lending indicated that banks had clear organisational policies on the approach to be adopted so that the discretion of individual executives with respect to lending decisions would be extremely limited. Moreover, such specialised lending departments tend to be small (in our sample, more than three quarters had less than ten executives) who would typically interact closely on a relatively small number of transactions per year. Hence it appeared appropriate to address the questionnaire to only one person in the organisation. This point is emphasised in respect of four cases where it was known that banks had two units devoted to buy-out lendings. In each case one of the units responded indicating that another unit in the bank was the appropriate respondent, with these other units providing completed questionnaires.

A total of 29 complete and usable replies were received for the UK, representing a response rate of 50 per cent of the bank groups surveyed. A further six incomplete replies were received. Reasons for non response concerned the paucity of new advances made over the previous three years or problems in providing information in the required format.

Analysis of the job titles of respondents showed that they held senior positions of responsibility. Bearing in mind that terminology for the same job may differ between banks, the distribution of job titles was: seven directors, six heads of structured/acquisition finance, four senior managers, three assistant directors, two assistant general managers, one assistant vice president and six managers. Analysis of the responding banks revealed that they covered a substantial proportion of the buy-out senior debt market with most of the principal and longest established buy-out debt providers included. Face to face interviews were held with those banks who were unwilling to respond to the questionnaire but who were willing to discuss general issues relating to debt covenants; two of these were considered to be important participants in the buy-out senior debt market. Banks responding to the survey or participating in the face-to-face interviews accounted for 82.7 per cent of the total number of senior debt buy-out financings identified by CMBOR in the period 1989 to 1994.

The banks in which the questionnaire respondents worked had made an average £101 million of advances over the previous three years and extended gross facilities totalling £3.7 billion. They had at the time of the survey a total of about £2.0 billion outstanding on their buy-out loan books.

The Dutch questionnaire was mailed to all the banks registered as a bank in Holland. Analysis of the banks involved in MBO/MBI lending shows that only a limited number of approximately eight Dutch banks are active in this field. From our database most of these participated in at least one buy-out debt financing in the period 1989–94. This rather small population indicates the concentration in debt provision to MBOs/MBIs in Holland. These included foreign banks, all the general banks (including their network of locally operating bank offices), specialised subsidiaries of them, investment banks set up after the Second World War and a mortgage bank. Mailing was undertaken to all these in late December 1995 with a follow-up letter sent in February 1996. A total of six complete and usable replies were received. Some of the non-response reasons regard problems in providing information in the required format because of the absence of a centrally organised unit.

Half of the respondents refused to supply information or were not able to supply information about the number of MBOs/MBIs the banks provided advances to in the last three years. The same is true for the questions about the numbers currently in their loan book, the current value of advances made to Dutch MBOs/MBIs and the net value of advances made over the previous three years. The net value of advances over the previous three years fluctuated enormously and ranged from *f*1 billion in one case to *f*40 million and *f*80 million in other cases. Current values outstanding in their loanbook at the time of the survey ranged between *f*30 million to *f*50 million and numbers of MBOs and MBIs currently in the loanbook varied from 25 to 60.

Results for the UK

Covenants used in MBO lending agreements

Accounting-based covenants Consistent with the expectation that MBO lenders exert a relatively high degree of control and monitoring over their customers, the great majority of respondents indicate a greater use of accounting-based covenants in MBOs as compared with their general lending. However the contrast is greater when compared with plcs (93 per cent of respondents making greater use in MBOs) than with private companies (61 per cent making greater use).

This general result is confirmed by the following specific findings regarding the use of covenants in MBO lending agreements as compared with other types of loan agreements. Previous research (Citron, 1992a) finds that in general bank lending there is a significant increase in the use of accounting-based covenants as loan size increases; also there is some evidence of a lesser use in secured as compared with unsecured loans, suggesting that covenants and security are substitutes for one another.

In the view of respondents to this survey MBO lending, in contrast, is universally both secured and covenanted for all sizes of loan. Thus for MBOs security and covenants are used to reinforce one another.

Citron (1995) also finds that term to maturity is strongly positively associated with the use of accounting-based covenants in the high credit quality UK public debt market, where the chief risk is that creditworthiness may deteriorate at some future date. A sizable minority (25 per cent) of general bank lenders indicated the same positive relationship with term (Citron, 1992a). However, virtually all MBO lenders (97 per cent) indicate that term of loan is irrelevant, consistent with the universal covenanting of MBO loan agreements.

Table 7.1 Frequency with which respondents use various accounting-based covenants in MBO/MBI lending agreements

Covenant	Frequency (%)
Cash flow to total debt service	92
Dividend restriction	89
Minimum net worth	86
Profit before interest and tax (PBIT)-based interest cover	83
Gearing	82
Cash-flow-based interest cover	62
Other interest cover	44
Net current assets/borrowings	29
Proportion of good debtors below certain days outstanding	29
Current ratio	20
Quick asset ratio	17
Industry average margins	15

Note: Percentages are calculated by reference to the mid-points of the various response categories (0–5%, 6–35%, 36–65%, 66–95%, 96–100%). $n = 29$ respondents.

MBO lending agreements contain on average both more and a greater variety of accounting-based covenants than do general bank lending agreements. As shown in Table 7.1, respondents cited five accounting-based covenants that are each used in over 80 per cent of lending agreements as finally negotiated. Three of these five are also widely used in general lending agreements – minimum net worth, profit-based interest cover and gearing (Citron, 1992b). However, MBO agreements generally contain two additional covenants not commonly found in other UK loan contracts – cash flow to total debt service and dividend restrictions. This appears to reflect the premium that lenders to MBOs place on short-term cash generation for reinvestment in the business and for the servicing of debt.

Sweeney (1994) suggests that 'tighter constraints in private bank agreements are expected if bankers have a comparative advantage in dealing with and helping managers deal with financial difficulties . . .' (p. 290). Similarly our findings regarding the number of accounting-based covenants are consistent with MBO lenders having a closer relationship than the general bank lender.

Non-accounting-based covenants Previous research contains no systematic evidence on use of non-accounting covenants. This paper shows non-accounting covenants to be of major importance in MBO lending (see Table 7.2). We show that, in the view of respondents, as many as ten non-accounting covenants are used almost universally (90 per cent of the time or more on average).

Smith and Warner (1979) classify covenants into four categories: production/investment; financing; dividend; and bonding. The first three groups seek to control management behaviour while the purpose of bonding covenants is to reduce monitoring costs. Most of the non-accounting covenants found in MBO agreements fall into three of these categories (dividends are restricted by an accounting-based covenant). Two key bonding covenants requiring the supply of information are ranked first (audited accounts within a specified period) and fourth (monthly management accounts within specified period). Almost universally used controls over production/investment policy are charges over assets and restrictions on mergers, asset disposals and capital spending. Restrictions on additional borrowings is a widely used covenant seeking to control financial policy.

Thus non-accounting covenants play a vital role in MBO loan agreements, and central to these are covenants requiring the supply of accounting information. The large number of covenants seeking to control production and investment policy reflects the inherent difficulty of directly controlling this class of behaviour (Smith and Warner, 1979).

In summary, our findings confirm that MBO loan agreements contain a large number of both accounting-based and non-accounting-based covenants, including an emphasis on cash flow-based covenants.

Table 7.2 Frequency with which respondents use various non-accounting-based covenants in MBO/MBI lending agreements

Covenants	Frequency (%)
First charge over specified assets	98
Audited annual accounts within specified period	98
Cross default clauses	98
Monthly management accounts within specified period	97
Restrictions on changes in ownership	96
Restrictions on additional borrowings (from other sources)	96
Maintenance of adequate fire, theft and other insurances	96
Restrictions in mergers/acquisitions	92
Restrictions on asset disposals	91
No capital expenditure beyond certain limits without approval	90
Compliance with environmental laws and regulations	87
Compliance with other laws and regulations	84
No redemption of preference shares whilst loans outstanding	81
No undisclosed tax liabilities	78
Charges over Keyman insurance	74
Keyman critical illness policy	49
Requirements for certain accounting policies	48
All banking to be transferred to bank within specified period	38
Restrictions on directors' remuneration	34
Restrictions on senior management's remuneration	28

Note: Percentages are calculated by reference to the mid-points of the various response categories (0–5%, 6–35%, 36–65%, 66–95%, 96–100%). $n = 29$ respondents.

Monitoring MBO loan agreements

As seen above, great reliance is placed on the buy-out company supplying the bank with up-to-date accounting information and in particular monthly management accounts. The vast majority of buyout companies (85.5 per cent on average) submit monthly accounts within 30 days of the end of the month. The importance placed on the information contained in the audited annual accounts was seen in almost nine-tenths (89.2 per cent) of the respondents sometimes asking for covenants to be certified by the client's auditor each year. Of those banks requesting such information over three-fifths (61.0 per cent) of buy-out covenants were certified in this way.

A critical issue in the identification of potential covenant breach is the frequency with which covenant monitoring is carried out and whether it mirrors the submission by buy-out management of their monthly accounts. Responses indicate somewhat surprising differences in attitudes between banks (see Table 7.3). Only about two-fifths (39.3 per cent) of respondents appear to monitor covenants on a monthly basis, that is, in line with the submission of management accounts. Almost a half (46.3 per cent) do so on a quarterly or less frequent basis.[9]

Table 7.3 Frequency of monitoring covenants

Average frequency with which covenants are monitored	% of respondents monitoring with stated frequency ($n = 28$)
Monthly	39.3
Every second month	14.3
Every third month	32.1
Less frequently	14.3
Total	100.0

First indicators of financial distress

The way in which MBO lenders first become aware of impending problems was investigated by asking respondents to state how frequently a wide range of alternative information flows provided this first indication. This extends previous research which has focused predominantly on which accounting-based covenants are the first to be breached (Beneish and Press, 1993; Sweeney, 1994).[10]

Table 7.4 First indicators of impending difficulties when sole lender or syndicate leader

Indicator	Average frequency with which item is indicator (%)
Monthly management accounts	69
Telephone communication from management	68
Breach of accounting covenants	43
Written communication from management	41
Overdraft levels	36
Notification from lead equity institution	28
Breach of non-accounting covenants	25
Failure to pay interest on due date	13
Failure to pay scheduled capital repayment	13
Audited annual accounts	13

Note: Percentages are calculated by reference to the mid-points of the various response categories. The banks were asked to report for each item the distribution of the frequency with which it was the first indicator (in the ranges 0–5%, 6–35%, 36–65%, 66–95%, 96–100%). There is also the possibility that several factors may simultaneously be the initial indicators of distress and as such the sum of percentages for all the items is greater than 100. $n = 25$ respondents.

As shown in Table 7.4, respondents rank accounting covenant breach only 3rd in importance among initial indicators of distress (43 per cent average likelihood). The two most important sources are based not on contractual default but on good banker/borrower communications – monthly management accounts (69 per cent) and telephone communication from management (68 per cent), as is the fourth, written communication from management (41 per cent).

This result is confirmed by responses to the question: On average how soon after a covenant is breached do you learn about the breach? to which the most frequent response was 'on warning given before'. While 62 per cent of respondents acting as sole lenders or syndicate leaders (n = 26) reported that they were given such prior warning 'almost always' or 'very frequently', only 15 per cent said they received it only 'occasionally' or 'almost never'. The issue of whether bankers who are non-lead syndicate members receive less timely information than sole lenders/syndicate leaders was explored by asking for responses to the same question when acting as a syndicate member ($n = 21$). As expected there was some evidence that in this situation there was likely to be somewhat greater delay in detecting problems, with 29 per cent indicating that they were given prior warning 'occasionally' or 'almost never' and only 48 per cent receiving it 'almost always' or 'very frequently'. Using the Wilcoxon matched-pairs signed-ranks test to compare the responses of the 19 respondents who responded to both questions, they were found to be significantly different with $z = -1.69$ (p = 0.045, one-tailed).

Non-accounting covenant breaches rank low as first indicators of difficulties (seventh; 25 per cent) as expected since these are predominantly negative covenants, that is, covenants that proscribe certain actions, violation of which is relatively easily avoided simply by avoiding the proscribed actions (see Healy and Palepu's study on dividend restrictions, 1990). Beneish and Press (1993) provide some confirmation of this in a general lending context. In their US study of 74 firms in first-time violation of accounting-based covenants, they find 126 occurrences of accounting covenant breaches but only four of non-accounting covenant breaches. Sweeney (1994, Table 2) reports very similar results.

Role of accounting-based covenants in signalling distress

This section examines lenders' views on the effectiveness of covenants at signalling difficulties and the relative frequency with which the various accounting-based covenants are breached.

Although communication from management is a more frequent first indicator of difficulties than actual covenant breach, it is possible that anticipated covenant breaches stimulate timely management communication. This issue is raised by Beneish and Press (1995b) who study cases of debt service default and bankruptcy that are not preceded by accounting-based covenant breaches. They conclude, however, that accounting-based covenants may not always provide warnings of future difficulties. The implications of this finding were explored further here by asking respondents open-ended questions about (a) their perceptions of the effectiveness of covenant breaches at signalling financial difficulties and (b) circumstances in which borrowers may have entered financial difficulties without any accounting-based covenant breach.

Of the 25 responses regarding the effectiveness of covenants, 11 banks considered that they were extremely effective, a further 13 that they were good indicators subject to certain qualifications and only one respondent that they were not good indicators.

While covenants are thus perceived as effective in signalling financial problems, many respondents emphasised the importance of the relationship between the bank and the buy-out customer in this process. Generally financial information received for covenant monitoring could be seen as acting as a catalyst for discussions with management. Indeed, while monthly financial data should have already shown any danger signs, management may have differing perceptions about the significance of any deterioration. Financial covenants in particular provide the discipline to force management to address issues which they might otherwise be inclined to avoid.

However, a number of banks stressed that with good regular monthly financial reporting, bankers should anyway be in a position to anticipate breaches of covenants. Thus the actual reporting process may be just as important if not more so than the covenants themselves. The most effective signal of impending financial problems may thus be gained from a frank and open working relationship between bank and customer, covenants themselves being more important as a trigger event and as a negotiation or pressure tool. If banks have a close relationship with the customer and understanding of the business with regular dialogue, impending problems may be solved before covenants are themselves breached.[11] Covenants to trigger actions by the bank may only have to be used where this relationship is not as strong as it should be or where management and their backers are running out of solutions. Indeed one respondent stressed that they do not seek to use covenants to trip borrowers up but as a means to provide input into the process by which financial performance deterioration is corrected.[12]

A further qualification on the effectiveness of covenants is their appropriateness at the time of the buy-out and the influence of the passage of time since buy-out. Covenants need to be set at a realistic level against the original management plan for the first few years of the buy-out. If assumptions in the original buy-out proposal are unrealistic, or cashflow generation is inconsistent or soft, then problems are likely to arise. Additionally the process of winning the bank mandate may have resulted in the negotiating out of certain covenants which will decrease their overall effectiveness. While the lender's ideal position is to provide effective signalling of financial distress through covenants, this may have been eroded through competition from other banks and the influence of the equity institution.

Furthermore with covenants sometimes originally being set on financial models looking forward five to ten years, breaches may in fact be occasioned by changes in business which are planned and agreed by all parties some time after buy-out. Banks need to take account of such changing circumstances.

Regarding the issue of borrowers entering financial difficulties without breaching accounting-based covenants, 14 banks (almost half of all respondents) described such breaches, covering a wide variety of situations. Responses covered several main types of situations including managerial issues, problems of both an operational and market nature encountered by the buy-out company, and the nature of the original covenants which may not have covered certain financial eventualities.

Among managerial issues there was one case of 'managerial misbehaviour' and another where management resignations had taken place at short notice without detailed explanation. Another bank had encountered problems following the death/incapacity of management even though covered by Keyman policies. In a further case management had allegedly engaged in false accounting and in another there had been unauthorised pension transfers.

Several buy-out companies had encountered market problems. Regulatory changes and environmental problems were causes of difficulties.[13] Protracted disputes with customers such as price adjustments as well as the loss of a major contract may have subsequently caused liquidity problems. Of course the actual loss of a major customer or contract may be because of external reasons effectively beyond the control of buy-out management. Circumstances may suddenly alter, causing the prospects for an industry to change overnight thereby creating additional risk. Higher investment by competition may bring problems. Other operational reasons contributing to financial difficulties concerned production and supply problems.

There was also some evidence that covenants may not have been set up appropriately. One respondent noted problems where covenants had been too lax and another noted a case where a working capital covenant had not been set, allowing an excessive stock build up to take place. Other financial issues concerned trade creditor liabilities, third party claims, off balance sheet agreements and a trade credit flight causing loss of liquidity.

Respondents were also asked to what extent breaches were avoided by creative accounting on the part of management. Reassuringly only 3.8 per cent felt that this usually happens and none that it was almost always the case. Nevertheless almost three-fifths (57.7 per cent) felt that breaches were sometimes avoided by creative accounting on the part of management. Quite apart from the possibility that MBO management may avoid such actions because of fear of the consequences of being caught, this finding also suggests the importance of informal monitoring relationships in reducing the incentive for managers to take such actions.

Given the central role of accounting-based covenants in signalling distress, which of these covenants are the most likely to be breached? As shown in Table 7.5, profit and cash flow based covenants are, in the view of respondents, the most likely to be breached. The two balance sheet ratios (gearing and minimum net worth) rank fourth and fifth respectively.

Table 7.5 Frequency of breaching various accounting-based covenants by firms that are in breach

Covenant	Likelihood of breach[1] %	Likelihood of breach[3] Rank	Average likelihood of inclusion[2] %	Average likelihood of inclusion[3] Rank
PBIT-based interest cover	47	1	83	4
Cash flow to total debt service	44	2	92	1
Cash-flow-based interest cover	42	3	62	6
Gearing	30	4	82	5
Minimum net worth	26	5	86	3
Other interest cover	18	6	44	7
Proportion of good debtors below certain days outstanding	7	7	29	8 =
Net current assets to borrowings	5	8	29	8 =
Quick ratio	5	9	17	11
Current ratio	5	10	20	10
Dividend restriction	3	11	89	2

Notes:

1 Means of actual percentages stated by respondents; $n = 25$, 26 or 27.

2 See Table 7.1.

3 The Spearman rank correlation coefficient is 0.88 (significant at the 0.01 level one-tailed) when dividend restrictions are excluded, but only 0.49 (not quite significant at the 0.05 level) when they are included.

Comparing the frequency with which a particular covenant is used with the likelihood of its being breached, the main discrepancy occurs with dividend restrictions which are almost universally present but rarely breached (see Table 7.5). This is in line with evidence that negative covenants, such as dividend restrictions, are unlikely to be breached (Beneish and Press, 1993; Smith, 1993). Once dividend restrictions are ignored, however, there is a highly significant positive correlation between respondents' rankings for inclusion in contracts and the rankings for likelihood of being breached. The implications of this finding require further investigation, however. It could be that certain covenants are used frequently because they are effective indicators of distress. Alternatively it may be that certain covenants are frequently breached simply because they are used more frequently.

Variety and speed of banker reactions to breaches of covenant

It is expected that close banker/customer relationships result in attempts to preserve a distressed borrower's long-term going concern value. This is because close monitoring and open lines of communication provide timely signals of impending problems, and possibly also because of the loyalty and commitment between the parties involved in relationship banking (Holland, 1994). This expectation was tested by asking respondents about the average likelihood of their adopting each of four progressively severe courses of action once they had learned about a breach of covenant – discussion with borrower/equity investor group; waiver of covenant breach; renegotiation of loan document; and recall of loan. In recognition of the fact that the negotiation process is often drawn out, respondents were asked what actions they would take both within six months and within two years of the breach. Finally, in order to explore the relationship issue further, the results were partitioned according to whether or not the respondent's bank had a specialist unit for MBO/MBI lending. The presence of a specialist unit is used here as a proxy for a closer customer relationship as it is indicative of a commitment to MBO lending and of the availability of resources to monitor such loans. The 22 banks with specialist units had made significantly more UK MBO/MBI advances in the last three years than the seven without such units (an average of 15.0 advances compared with 4.6; t-value = 3.26, $p = 0.003$ two-tailed) and the total net value of these advances was significantly higher (£128.1 million versus £20.9 million; t-value = 3.82, $p = 0.001$ two-tailed).

The evidence as shown in Table 7.6 suggests that, in the view of respondents, many breaches are relatively minor and can be dealt with through discussions with management rather than the more drastic measure of recalling the loan. In over four-fifths (83.9 per cent)[14] of cases there would be discussions with the borrower and equity investor groups within a six-month period and in over three-fifths (61.2 per cent) of cases overall there would be a relatively quick waiver of the covenant breach. Moreover, a significantly higher percentage of cases dealt with by specialist units (66.2 per cent) are likely to have their breach waived within six months than those without specialist units (only 47.1 per cent) ($z = -1.93$ ($p = 0.027$, one-tailed) using the Mann–Whitney U test). This difference becomes more pronounced by the time two years have elapsed, by which time the percentage of waivers among specialist units is stated to increase to 70.2 per cent while that among bankers without specialist units has not changed ($z = -2.21$; $p = 0.014$, one-tailed).

Table 7.6 *Time taken for various actions by banker after learning about breach of covenant*

Actions	Within 6 months Specialist unit ($n = 20$) (%)	Within 6 months No specialist unit ($n = 7$) (%)	Within 6 months Total ($n = 27$) (%)	Within 2 yrs Specialist unit ($n = 20$) (%)	Within 2 yrs No specialist unit ($n = 7$) (%)	Within 2 yrs Total ($n = 27$) (%)
Discussion with borrower/ equity investor group	82	89.3	83.9	84.0	90.7	85.7
Waiver of covenant breach	66.2	47.1	61.2*	70.2	47.1	64.2*
Renegotiation of loan document	32.7	35.0	33.3	44.7	50.7	46.2
Recall of loan	3.9	5.7	4.4	10.7	24.3	14.2**

Notes:
The percentages are means of actual percentages stated by respondents.
* = difference significant at 5% level (one-tailed).
** = difference significant at 1% level (one-tailed).

Respondents perceive more detailed renegotiation of the loan document to take longer to achieve, being completed in one-third (33.2 per cent) of cases within six months although in only a half (46.2 per cent) of cases is this course of action achieved within two years. Actual recall of the loan is stated to be very unlikely in the short term and even in the two year time framework only 14.2 per cent of loans are likely to be recalled. However, the likelihood of recall within two years is perceived to be significantly higher among banks without specialist units (24.3 per cent) than among those with specialist units (10.7 per cent) ($z = -2.45$; $p = 0.007$, one-tailed, using the Mann–Whitney U test).

Finally, the perceptions of the 22 respondents who act as non-lead syndicate members were explored. They were asked about the differences which they perceived in the use of covenants between the position when they acted as a non-lead syndicate member compared to being the deal leader or sole debt provider. Respondents indicated, on average, a 47 per cent[15] expectation that there would be a longer delay in implementing action in response to covenant breach for non-lead syndicate members and only a 12 per cent likelihood that action would be implemented sooner. Applying the Wilcoxon matched-pairs signed-ranks test to the entire range of responses to these questions, the difference in responses is found to be significant with $z = -3.06$ ($p = 0.001$, one-tailed). Regarding the effectiveness of action once taken, there was a 55 per cent expectation that such action was less effective from the syndicate member's perspective and only a significantly lower 14 per cent likelihood that it would be more effective ($z = -3.29$ ($p = 0.001$, one-tailed).

In summary, therefore, the timing of responses to covenant breaches appears to indicate that banks take a flexible and perhaps pragmatic approach to the breach of covenants. Clearly in some cases covenant breach may be relatively minor and discussions will clarify the extent of financial problems and determine whether they are of a relatively temporary nature. In more problematical cases it takes longer to arrive at a decision to renegotiate the loan arrangements and documentation, or possibly to recall the loan.

There is also evidence that banks with specialist MBO units are more likely to waive covenant breaches and less likely to recall loans. To the extent that the presence of a specialist unit is a valid proxy for relationship banking, these findings confirm expectations that close relationships are conducive to preserving the going concern value of borrowers in distress. Moreover syndicate members, who have a less close relationship with borrowers than either sole lenders or syndicate leaders, indicate that responses to covenant breaches are slower and less effective.

Renegotiation of loan agreement subsequent to covenant breach

Virtually one-half of MBO covenant breaches result in the loan agreement being renegotiated within two years of the breach (Table 7.6). As shown in Table 7.7, the most frequent modifications cited by respondents are dividend and capital spending restrictions. These are aimed at preserving the borrower's asset levels and, in the case of dividend restrictions, at enhancing the bank's position *vis-à-vis* that of the equity providers, who in MBOs are typically likely to use various quasi-equity instruments with cumulative dividend rights.

MBO lenders tended not to rate the taking of additional security highly, which contrasts with findings on contract renegotiations in a general lending context where additional security is the most frequently cited modification (Citron, 1992a). This probably reflects the high degree of security taken in MBO lending when the loan is first made and hence there may be little scope for taking more.

Banks appeared to be reluctant to enter into major restructuring options through reclassification of the debt. Thus the conversion of some debt into equity and the replacement of all or part of secured debt by mezzanine type debt was not scored highly.[16] It was also very unlikely that share options would be issued to enhance the bank's potential position. Surprisingly the injection of new equity has a less than 50 per cent likelihood of occurrence.

Table 7.7 Frequency of modifications to loan agreements in response to breach of accounting-based covenants – MBOs vs general private lending

Modification	MBO lending (*n* = 28) mean %	General private lending (*n* = 33) mean %
Dividend restrictions	75	63
Capital spending restrictions	65	61
Increased interest rate margin	54	47
Injection of new equity	46	–
Relaxation of accounting-based covenants	46	42
Merger and acquisition restrictions	39	–
Additional security	38	67
Issue of share options	25	–
Replacement of all or part of secured debt by mezzanine-type debt	22	–
Conversion of some debt into equity	20	–

Note: The mean percentages have been calculated by reference to the mid-points of the various response categories (0–5%, 6–35%, 36–65%, 66–95%, 96–100%). The results for general private lending have been derived from the data used to construct Table 4 in Citron (199122a).

Results for Holland

Given the smaller number of respondents to the Dutch survey, these results are presented in more qualitative form with comparisons being made with the UK findings.

Covenants used in MBO lending agreements

Accounting-based covenants In Holland a majority of the respondents, including most of the general banks and a prominent international investment bank, indicate a greater use of accounting-based covenants in MBOs as compared with their general lending. The number of respondents is too small to differentiate further whether the contrast is greater between buy-outs and plcs' lending or between buy-out and private companies.

Most of the banks report that the term of loan is not a factor affecting the decision to include accounting-based covenants in MBO lending. Virtually all size categories of loans are both secured and covenanted. However, two banks gave opposite views. One bank argued that they consider that they can make advances up to a maximum of 3–5 years' free cash flow. The second stressed the importance of the change in value of the legal charge as a reason why accounting-based covenants are more likely to be included in buy-outs and buy-ins. As in the UK, dividend restrictions (91 per cent Dutch; 89 per cent UK) and minimum net worth (85 per cent Dutch; 86 per cent UK) rank among the three most widely used accounting-based covenants in Dutch MBO lending agreements.

However, in the Dutch MBO lending agreements the following accounting-based covenants are less important than in the UK: gearing ratios (66 per cent Dutch; 82 per cent UK), cash flow to total debt (49 per cent Dutch; 92 per cent UK) and PBIT-based interest cover (49 per cent Dutch; 83 per cent UK). During negotiations the Dutch MBO lenders would drop, in order to secure the business, such covenants as current ratio, quick asset ratio, net current assets vs borrowings. No general rules can be identified; precisely what is dropped depends on the circumstances.

Non-accounting-based covenants While the Dutch banks also rank audited accounts within a specified period in 88 per cent of the cases as number one, the monthly management accounts within a specified period are used only occasionally (23 per cent) in Dutch MBO agreements. This may be an indication that Dutch banks have not yet developed as close a monitoring relationship with the MBO company as English banks. Furthermore this finding may be due to the fact that the use of non-accounting covenants may vary between small MBOs/MBIs and bigger ones. Locally operating offices of general banks indicate that non-accounting-based covenants are used to a similar extent as in public and private companies; this is in contrast to UK experience. However, these banks normally service smaller buy-outs and buy-ins and this may explain why there may be no differences between buy-out and other corporate lending. For other respondents it depends strongly on specific cases.

Another remarkable difference between the UK and the Dutch banks can be found in respect of requirements regarding the transfer of all banking within a specified period to the lending bank. In 77 per cent of the cases, Dutch respondents use this covenant in MBO/MBI lending agreements. British banks are less (38 per cent) inclined to require all the banking of their client to be conducted through them as a condition of the loan. Foreign banks operating in the Dutch market behave as their UK colleagues. In respect of controls over production and financial policy, the Dutch general banks use the same covenants as their UK counterparts. Dutch banks are more likely to use requirements for certain accounting policies than are their UK counterparts, but slightly less likely to have requirements for non-redemption of preference shares while loans are outstanding. Occasionally, UK banks use restrictions on directors (34 per cent) and senior management remunerations (28 per cent). The Dutch banks use these approximately 20 per cent less frequently in their lending agreements. Restrictions on mergers/acquisitions and on asset disposal are in more than 90 per cent of UK MBO/MBI lending covenants, whereas the Dutch banks use them in about 50 per cent of cases.

Monitoring MBO loan agreements

Dutch banks do not monitor covenants on a monthly basis, but do so quarterly or even less frequently. This finding is consistent with the suggestion that they have not developed a close monitoring relationship with their clients in contrast to most of the UK banks, and may also indicate that Dutch banks do not fully identify buy-outs as a different risk category but treat them as with other corporate lending.

First indicators of financial distress

In contrast to what the general banks observe as an important indicator of impending difficulties, telephone and written communications from management rank very low in the case of the mortgage bank. Experiences of the Dutch general banks are in line with the finding in Table 7.4, except with regard to the monthly management accounts. However, as stated before there is an absence of a close monitoring relationship with the directors of MBO companies. Therefore it is not too surprising why they rank the audited annual results as one of the most important first indicators of impending difficulties (third rank, 77 per cent of Dutch cases, compared with 13 per cent in the UK). Consistent with the view on close monitoring is the response of a UK-based bank active in Holland which expects that this information has virtually no monitoring role. Given this finding, it might be too late for banks using this information to prevent failure to pay interest on due date and failures to repay capital on schedule.

One of the Dutch respondents could not give very precise answers concerning how it behaved in cases of impending difficulties. This arose because the monitoring of these companies was transferred to a department within the bank specialising in giving assistance to financially troubled companies.

When acting as sole lender or syndicate leader Dutch general banks were most of the time given prior warning of problems. When acting as a syndicate member, Dutch general banks very frequently receive less timely information, as in the case for their UK counterparts; delays of a week to one month are not unusual. A mortgage bank and a locally operating general bank reported learning about the breach in a broad range varying from one week to six months afterwards. Both, whenever acting as a sole lender or syndicate member, were almost never given a warning before or informed immediately. Long delays were not unusual for this type of bank.

Dutch respondents rank breaches of non-accounting covenants as an indicator of financial trouble somewhat higher than was found in the UK survey, and higher than evidence from the US would suggest. Such covenants are an indication of problems with a frequency varying from about half of the time to very frequently.

Most British banks monitor more intensively than the Dutch lenders and this seems to be true for those respondents which do not use a specialist unit for MBO/MBI lending. Monthly management accounts, which are seen as the number one indicator of impending difficulties in the UK are given less importance by the Dutch general banks. They perceive monthly management accounts as only effective about half of the time, while the mortgage bank almost never perceives them to be a dominant signal of financial distress.

Role of accounting-based covenants in signalling distress

One of the respondents reported that a package of accounting and non-accounting covenants coupled with a request for regular contact with management and management information, such as updated cashflow projections generally ensures the banks' position is protected as far as possible. The mortgage bank reported that breaches of covenants vary from being non-effective due to the amount of time which elapses, to somewhat effective in the case where management provides appropriate information. This bank monitors covenants much less frequently than the other respondents, approximately 12 months where others monitor every three months. No monthly accounts of clients are submitted within 30 days of the end of the month, while the other Dutch banks approximately receive 50 per cent and the British banks 75 per cent. The other answers were also in line with the remarkably passive attitude towards MBO lending in this bank. For example, the person who negotiates the covenants does not look after them once the advance has been made and notification from the lead equity institution is almost never received. This contrasts sharply with the experiences of other Dutch general banks.

Regarding the issue of entering financial difficulties without any accounting-based covenant breach, some banks describe situations such as sudden market swing; former parents abruptly ending sponsoring and the government imposing very high environmental protection costs. Avoiding breaches by creative accounting on the part of management happens according to the Dutch banks usually or sometimes.

As in the UK, profit and cash-flow-based covenants are one of the most likely to be breached by Dutch MBOs, according to the general banks. The minimum net worth ranks as the accounting-based covenant most frequently breached, and perhaps reflects the stronger bookkeeping tradition in the Netherlands compared to the UK. Dividend restrictions are likely to be violated more frequently by the management of Dutch MBOs as compared to UK MBOs. The locally operating offices of the general banks report this in 70 per cent of cases. This may reflect the particular situation of the smaller sized Dutch MBOs which are not monitored as closely as MBOs in the UK, and thus are placed in a more favourable situation where these dividend restriction breaches may occur more frequently.

It is interesting to compare these results with US evidence from covenant breaches not specifically in LBO situations (Beneish and Press, 1993; Sweeney, 1994). In common with the Dutch study but in contrast with the UK one, the two US studies both find net worth and working capital to be breached most frequently.[17] In contrast UK MBOs appear most likely to breach three entirely different covenants – profit-based interest cover, cash flow to total debt service and/or cash flow-based interest cover. Working capital covenants are used rarely in the UK so it is not surprising that they are rarely breached. However the net worth covenant is widely used and it may underperform as an indicator of trouble, since three ratios which are used less frequently (cash-flow-based interest cover, PBIT-based interest cover and gearing) trigger breaches more frequently. Dividend restrictions rank very low in both the US and the UK but not in Holland.

Because of the small numbers in the Dutch sample there is a need for caution in making comparisons but it appears to be the case that Dutch banks (mortgage banks as well as locally operating general banks) adhere more strictly to net worth as an indicator of impending troubles than their British counterparts.

Variety and speed of banker reactions to breaches of covenant

Because of the small number of Dutch banks involved in MBO/MBI lending it is not possible to generalise about the relationships between having a specialist unit for monitoring MBO/MBI lending and the likely behaviour of banks in dealing with covenant breaches. But there are indications that speed of renegotiation and waivers of covenant breaches occur earlier if banks possess such a specialist unit.

Actual recall of the loan is reported to be very unlikely in the short term, but is nevertheless a realistic option in the opinion of banks without specialist units and the locally operating offices of general banks. This happens in cases when there are non-technical breaches. The common reaction followed by all banks is reserving rights to recall the loan at any time, but this action is more likely to be taken by banks without a special lending unit. Waiving the breach and allowing a limited time for improvement to occur is also commonly used, as is the waive with renegotiations of the term of the loan document. Banks without a special lending unit strongly expressed the view that there was a need for tighter monitoring by equity institutions and by management in comparison to those which have this facility. This is consistent with the expectation that close relationship banking is conducive to preservation of going concern value.

Renegotiation of loan agreement subsequent to covenant breach

With respect to renegotiation, the most frequent top three changes cited by Dutch respondents are the same as reported by the UK banks. There is, however, an indication that Dutch banks, especially those without a special unit and the bank offices operating locally, attach more importance to modifications such as restrictions of mergers and acquisitions and to more additional security than the other respondents. Perhaps this reflects the higher degree of bank loan financed smaller sized Dutch MBO/MBIs in Holland.

This last finding comes close to general private lending policy and contrasts sharply with the MBO/MBI lending policy of British banks and that of Dutch banks when the supply of equity is involved in the MBO/MBI deal. Conversion of debt into equity and issuance of share options happens occasionally while the injection of new equity takes place about half of the time, except in the case of the mortgage bank.

Summary and conclusions

This chapter examines MBO lenders' perceptions of the role and effectiveness of covenants in the wider context of the loan monitoring process and, in particular, as their customers enter financial difficulties. The findings are based on lenders' views expressed via a questionnaire survey and therefore do not necessarily reflect how they actually do react in particular cases in practice. However, the process of negotiating a loan agreement, monitoring subsequent performance and dealing with breaches of covenant are an integral part of the lender/borrower relationship, and the findings of this study are of value as reflecting the views of one of the partners in this relationship. The study has also highlighted similarities and important differences between the UK and Holland.

A key group of findings relates to the nature of relationships between MBO lenders and their customers as evidenced by the use of both accounting-based and non-accounting-based covenants and the timing of communication of distress. In the UK there is evidence of the existence of close relationships between MBO lenders and MBOs. Not only is there extensive use of both accounting- and non-accounting-based covenants but impending distress is frequently communicated early, in advance of actual loan default. Once covenants are breached, discussions are stated to ensue quickly and virtually universally. Waiver, which occurs in almost two-thirds of cases in the UK, is also perceived to occur relatively quickly, but loan renegotiation or (less frequently) recall take longer to resolve. As expected, in the UK lenders with specialist units state that they are both more likely to waive covenant breaches and less likely to recall loans in default.

The development of close relationships between MBO lenders and their customers appears to be less common in Holland. Banks specialising in mortgages have no special MBO lending unit and seem to lack this kind of relationship. Monitoring happens most of the time once a year, and although they waive breaches, recalling the loan remains a realistic option in their opinion. However, they stress the importance of becoming more frequently informed in the near future, instead of being dependent upon the willingness of management to be proactive in supplying information. This is also the case for locally operating bank offices of the general banks. The activity of the Dutch general banks seems to be closer to UK practice, especially where they have specialist lending units or have strong connections with investment banks. Dutch general banks, like their UK counterparts, appear to place higher emphasis on links with management through telephone and written communications than do other Dutch banks.

If equity is not provided by the bank, MBO lending is not centrally registered and the local operating banks deploy their monitoring in line with the bank's general lending policy. This indicates that a large part of Dutch MBO deals consist of small-sized and bank-loan-financed companies. Covenants used in MBO/MBIs do not differ from those used in other credit facilities. Financial risks are generally much lower than is usually the case when the equity base needs to be enlarged to restart a company.

Despite very frequent communication when financial problems arise, Dutch general banks give great weight to the audited annual results as the first indicator of impending difficulties. This is in contrast to the finding for the British sample and may reflect close organisational relationships between Dutch banks and Dutch venture capitalists. Dutch general banks have major equity stakes in these venture capital institutions, which may undertake the actual monitoring for them. This strip financing appears to be closer to US practice rather than that generally found in the UK.

In both the UK and Holland syndicate members, as compared with sole lenders or syndicate leaders, indicate that they are less likely to be informed of covenant breaches prior to their occurring, and that subsequent corrective action is likely to both take longer to implement and be less effective. These findings confirm expectations that, from a syndicate member's perspective, resolving default may have more in common with public debt than one-to-one private debt. However, in Holland it also appears that the general banks were better placed than other banks in the timing of the receipt of information.

While MBO lenders proclaim the effectiveness of accounting-based covenants, initial evidence was obtained on the important issue of instances in which such covenants have failed to signal distress. These included either cases where distress was caused by factors not encompassed by accounting measures (for example, management problems) or poorly set covenants. Only in a very few cases covenants failed to signal distress.

This investigation of the process of monitoring MBOs and resolving loan default raises important issues for further research. The finding that the frequency with which accounting-based covenants are breached is positively related to their use leaves open the question as to how effective covenants are at signalling distress on a timely basis. This question is reinforced by the preliminary findings reported here of cases where financial difficulties have occurred without covenants being breached.

In addition it would be of interest to develop more powerful measures of banking relationships than those used here, to better investigate their costs and benefits. The finding that management accounts are often monitored less frequently than they are submitted requires further investigation, in particular regarding the actual role of accounting-based covenants and periodical accounting reports to bankers. For example, do bankers see the regular provision of accounts as an important discipline on management, is the frequency of detailed scrutiny related to the age of the relationship and the establishment of a sound track record, and so on?

In providing both new evidence from the UK and Holland and comparisons with previous studies in the US, the paper has suggested that there are differences in covenant use not just between different types of lending but in the same type of lending in different countries.

Finally, this research has examined the operation of covenants and the relationships involved from the point of view of the banks. Further work might usefully examine experience from the position of the managers involved in the MBOs.

Notes

1. According to monitoring by the Centre for Management Buy-out Research and the Dutch Management Buy-out Research Unit, there were 3361 buy-outs and buy-ins completed in the UK between 1990 and 1995 for a total transaction value in current prices of £21 291 million and 279 buy-outs and buy-ins in Holland in the same period for a total transaction value equivalent to £2384 million. Only France and Germany saw more transactions in this period than Holland, though their economies are substantially larger. For further details see Initiative Europe/CMBOR, *Europe Buy-out Review*, Initiative Europe, London, Seventh Edition, 1996.
2. Evidence relating to the motivations of management in undertaking a buy-out also emphasises their desires to control and develop their own business (for example, Wright et al., 1992).
3. It is also possible that MBO managers and advisors collude against the debt supplier to complete a transaction because advisors are typically remunerated largely through completion fees. However, countering this point is the argument concerning reputation effects, such that behaviour of this kind may result in the banks being reluctant to deal subsequently with the advisor.
4. See, for example, Thompson et al. (1992). It may be argued close relationships between venture capitalists and a network of banks established to effect transactions, as is often the case, may go some way to mitigating agency cost problems. However, the point remains that ultimately there are potential conflicts of interest between venture capitalists and banks.
5. Financial assistance refers to the giving of securities on the assets of the company for the purchase by third parties of shares in its own capital. In the UK there are exceptions to this general prohibition so that in a buy-out subject to certain substantive and procedural safeguards relating to the solvency of the company financial assistance may be given. The giving of financial assistance in Holland is absolutely prohibited, except for certain specific exceptions involving smaller companies with distributable reserves and for the transfer of shares to employees, both for the company in which shares are acquired and for that company's subsidiaries. For further elaboration of these legal issues in the UK and Holland see O'Neill (1995).

6. This extends previous research in this area which investigates how the lender's decision varies either according to the cause of the breach (Citron, 1992a) or according to the financial health of the borrower and the characteristics of the debt instrument (Chen and Wei, 1993).
7. A copy of the questionnaire is available from the authors on request.
8. The covering letter to the questionnaire specifically asked for an overall view. The letter said 'In order to obtain an overall view of the monitoring, operation and triggering of covenants, . . . [T]he enclosed questionnaire asks for senior debt providers' perceptions on key elements of their covenant writing and monitoring as well as on the circumstances most likely to surround a breach and the type of action taken when this occurs . . .'.
9. Banks may view the requirement to supply monthly accounts as imposing an important discipline on management to produce information.
10. The Beneish and Press (1993) and Sweeney (1994) studies analyse instances of firms that actually breached accounting-based covenants in the 1980s.
11. This point might suggest that trust is an important aspect of the relationship between bankers and MBO management. Detailed discussion of this point is beyond the scope of this chapter, but fuller understanding of this issue would need to include analysis of the incentives to maintain or not maintain a situation of trust and the explicit and implicit contracts put in place in anticipation of breakdown in trust.
12. This of course only represents the bank's perspective and further research, which is beyond the scope of the present chapter, might usefully be directed to ascertaining management's views on this issue.
13. For instance one bank reported problems resulting from the deregulation of the dairy industry, which led to a general increase in milk prices and gave supermarket retailers the option to contract directly with producers rather than being obliged, as formerly, to purchase through the Milk Marketing Board.
14. The percentages in Table 7.6 are the means of the actual percentages cited by respondents.
15. Calculated by reference to the mid-points of the various response categories (0–5%, 6–35%, 36–65%, 66–95%, 96–100%).
16. There is some incidence of this kind of restructuring, notably in the case of Isosceles (Gateway Stores) the largest buy-out in the UK where in 1993 £923 million of debt was restructured into £256 million bank loans, £400 million deep discount bonds and £267 million preference shares (Wright et al., 1995).
17. It is possible that differences between these results and those for the US may be influenced by the differing time periods of the studies, but the focus here is not on how frequently firms enter distress (which is influenced by macroeconomic factors at different times) but on the relative importance of different accounting covenant breaches.

References

Barry, C. (1994), 'New directions in research on venture capital finance', *Financial Management*, **23** (3), 3–15.

Beneish, M.D. and E. Press (1993), 'Costs of technical violation of accounting-based covenants', *The Accounting Review*, **68** (2), April, 233–57.

Beneish, M.D. and E. Press (1995a), 'The resolution of technical default', *The Accounting Review*, **70** (2), April, 337–53.

Beneish, M.D. and E. Press (1995b), 'Interrelation among events of default', *Contemporary Accounting Research*, **12** (3), 57–84.

Chen, K.C.W. and K.C.J. Wei (1993), 'Creditors' decisions to waive violations of accounting-based debt covenants', *The Accounting Review*, **68** (2), April, 218–32.

Citron, D.B. (1992a), 'Financial ratio covenants in UK bank loan contracts and accounting policy choice', *Accounting and Business Research*, **22** (88), Autumn, 322–35.

Citron, D.B. (1992b), 'Accounting measurement rules in UK Bank loan contracts', *Accounting and Business Research*, **23** (89), Winter, 21–30.

Citron, D.B. (1995), 'The incidence of accounting-based covenants in UK public debt contracts: an empirical analysis', *Accounting and Business Research*, **25** (99), Summer, 139–50.

DeFond, M.L. and J. Jiambalvo (1994), 'Debt covenant violation and manipulation of accruals', *Journal of Accounting and Economics*, **17** 145–76.

Elango, B., V. Fried, R. Hisrich and A. Polonchek (1995), 'How venture capital firms differ', *Journal of Business Venturing*, **10** (2), 157–79.

Garvey, G.T. and P.L. Swan (1994), 'The economics of corporate governance: beyond the Marshallian firm', *Journal of Corporate Finance: Contracting, Governance and Organization*, **1** (2), 139–74.

Hatherly, D., F. Mitchell and J. Innes (1994), 'An exploration of the MBO–financier relationship', *Corporate Governance*, **2** (1), 20–29.

Healy, P. and K. Palepu (1990), 'The effectiveness of accounting-based dividend covenants', *Journal of Accounting and Economics*, **12**, 97–123.

Holland, J. (1994), 'Bank lending relationships and the complex nature of bank–corporate relations', *Journal of Business Finance and Accounting*, **21** (3), April, 367–93.

Jensen, M.C. (1986), 'Agency costs of free cash flow, corporate finance, and takeovers', *American Economic Review*, **76** (2), May, 323–9.

Lerner, J. (1995), 'Venture capitalists and the oversight of private firms', *Journal of Finance*, **50** (1), 301–18.

Mayer, C. (1988), 'New issues in corporate finance', *European Economic Review*, **32**, 1167–89.

O'Neill, D. (1995), *Buy-outs in Europe*, London: Clifford Chance.

Phan, P. and C. Hill (1995), 'Organisational restructuring and economic performance in leveraged buy-outs: an ex post study', *Academy of Management Journal*, **38** (3), 704–39.

Rajan, R. and A. Winton (1995), 'Covenants and collateral as incentives to monitor', *Journal of Finance*, **L** (4), 1113–46.

Robbie, K. and M. Wright (1995), 'Corporate restructuring and managerial and ownership succession: the case of management buy-ins', *Journal of Management Studies*, **32** (4), 527–50.

Sapienza, H. and A. Gupta (1994), 'Impact of agency risks and task uncertainty on venture capitalist–CEO interaction', *Academy of Management Journal*, **37** (6), 1618–32.

Singh, H. (1990), 'Management buyouts and shareholder value', *Strategic Management Journal*, **11** (5), 111–29.

Smith, C.W. (1993), 'A perspective on accounting-based covenant violations', *The Accounting Review*, **68** (2), April, 289–303.

Smith, C.W. and J.B. Warner (1979), 'On financial contracting: an analysis of bond covenants', *Journal of Financial Economics*, **7** (2), June, 117–61.

Sweeney, P.A. (1994), 'Debt–covenant violations and managers' accounting responses', *Journal of Accounting and Economics*, **17**, 281–308.

Thompson, S., M. Wright and K. Robbie (1992), 'Management equity ownership, debt and performance: some evidence from UK management buy-outs', *Scottish Journal of Political Economy*, **39** (4), 413–31.

Wright, M., S. Thompson and K. Robbie (1992), 'Venture capital and management-led, leveraged buy-outs: a European perspective', *Journal of Business Venturing*, **7** (1), 47–71.

Wright, M., N. Wilson, K. Robbie and C. Ennew (1995), 'Restructuring and failure in buy-outs and buy-ins', *Business Strategy Review*, **5** (2), 21–40.

Wruck, K.H. (1990), 'Financial distress, reorganization, and organizational efficiency', *Journal of Financial Economics*, **27**, 419–44.

Zahra, S. (1995), 'Corporate entrepreneurship and financial performance: the case of management leveraged buy-outs', *Journal of Business Venturing*, **10** (3), 225–47.

8. Small business demand for trade credit, credit rationing and the late payment of commercial debt: an empirical study*

Nicholas Wilson, Carole Singleton and Barbara Summers

Introduction

In recent years a considerable amount of research has been devoted to understanding the functioning of credit markets, credit market imperfections, the phenomenon of credit rationing and the role of asymmetric information (Stiglitz and Weiss, 1981; de Meza and Webb, 1987). One strand of this debate has focused on the impact of finance (debt)-gaps, under asymmetric information, on the dynamics of small firm survival and growth (Black, de Meza and Jeffreys, 1996; Cressy, 1996). The provision of debt to small firms is widely recognised as a key factor in enabling (potentially) successful small firms to start-up and grow and *inter alia* in improving the dynamic efficiency of the economy. Indeed concerns about a 'finance-gap' and the terms on which debt finance is available to smaller companies have led successive policy makers in the UK and abroad to launch many initiatives in an attempt to alleviate the perceived problem. Yet survey evidence suggests that small companies are often under-capitalised and consequently highly reliant on short-term finance (for example, bank overdraft), a factor that has been widely cited as a main contributor to constraining growth, cash-flow problems and premature business failure (see Bickers, 1994).

Trade credit, sellers accepting payment after the delivery of goods and services, plays an important role as a component of net working capital and a source of short-term finance for business.[1] Indeed, some researchers (see Petersen and Rajan, 1995), have argued that firms that are rationed on credit by the banks are more likely to take trade credit loans (often at a premium implicit interest rate) in order to satisfy a financing demand. Recently, however, the problem of the late payment of commercial debt, that is, when actual payment periods exceed the stated terms of trade credit loans, has been cited as a major

* The authors are grateful to the Department of Trade and Industry and the Institute of Credit Management for part funding this research. The views expressed are the authors only. We would like to thank seminar participants at Nottingham University, the CMBOR and the DTI for helpful comments.

problem facing small business[2] and has precipitated much political debate (in the UK and at EC level) on whether legislation for a 'statutory right to interest' on late payments would be desirable.[3]

There has been relatively little work, theoretical and/or empirical, on the reasons why businesses extend and use trade credit (and how much), given its importance, and on understanding the payment behaviours of companies. Empirical research that examines the demand for trade credit and the use of extended trade credit (late payment) will have a particular bearing on the late payment policy issue and may help to inform the debate on credit rationing.

The chapter has the following structure. In the next section we discuss, briefly, issues surrounding the question of small firm financing. The following section discusses the nature and role of trade credit. We then focus on trade credit from the perspective of the lender, that is, the motivations for extending credit with a particular emphasis on the role of asymmetric information. The next section sets out the basic theory that can be used to explain demand-side issues and specifies a simple demand model based on work by Chant and Walker (1988) and Elliehausen and Wolken (1993). The chapter goes on to estimate various trade credit demand models using a rich firm-level database. The final section draws some conclusion.

Small firm financing

The financing of new, small and growing businesses is the subject of enduring academic and political debate. A number of studies and government enquiries have pointed to the problems small firms have in raising external equity and more recently to the availability and cost of debt finance. Indeed, at the time of writing, it is exactly 20 years since the 'Wilson Committee' under a Labour government was set up to 'review the functioning of financial institutions' (Wilson Committee, 1979) with reference to the financing of industry and more particularly small business finance. Some would argue that the impediments that affect the flow of finance to the smaller business sector still remain. For instance, the presence of informational asymmetries between borrower and lender create the potential for credit rationing. The problems and costs involved in assessing and setting appropriate premiums for risk, and the relatively high transaction and monitoring costs, hinder the flow of loan capital to certain small business sectors. The difficulties new and growing firms face, particularly technological-based firms, in raising collateral affect the firms' ability to counteract the effects of informational asymmetries (Binks and Ennew, 1996).

The difficulties that small businesses have in obtaining institutional finance and in the conditions attached to it by banks in the UK have been explored in Ennew and Binks (1996), Binks and Ennew (1996) and Storey (1994). Indeed, the banking sector in the UK has come under a fair amount of criticism in relation to small firm financing. In consequence, small firms are often over-reliant on overdrafts to finance their business and secure funding on the back of property prices; banks allegedly charge too high an interest premium and place too much emphasis on security or collateral. As Black, de Meza and Jeffreys (1996, p. 61) argue: '. . . the role of banks in the provision of small business finance seems to be closer to that of pawnbrokers than of venture capitalists'.

In the age of information technology, new intermediaries are beginning to play a role in small firm financing. For instance, as information technology progresses the boundaries between companies engaged in financial services, other credit and the credit services industries (for example, credit insurance, credit reference provision, factoring) and are becoming increasingly blurred as each develops new products which cut across these various interrelated services. Technological developments are changing the economics of information management and the management of corporate and consumer lending. Summers and Wilson (1997) argue that the rapid growth of factoring in the UK, for instance, is primarily explained by the factors' ability to extend finance.

Empirical verification of credit rationing at the macroeconomic level generally show it to be of inconsequential magnitudes (Fair and Jafee, 1972; Berger and Udell, 1992). The widespread use of an alternative source of finance, trade credit, has been suggested as a basic explanation for this. In the context of this chapter it is a puzzle, then, why firms can lend on trade credit to (customers) firms that are rationed on bank credit. We turn to this issue next.

The nature and role of trade credit

Trade credit is a particularly important source of funding for smaller companies. For instance, the stocks and flows of trade credit are typically twice the size of bank credit in both the UK and US (Wilner, 1996; Elliehausen and Wolken, 1993). Trade credit thus represents a substantial component of both corporate liabilities and assets, especially in the case of intermediate companies. In the UK corporate sector it is estimated that more than 80 per cent of daily business transactions are on credit terms. The data drawn from a recent survey of UK manufacturing companies (Wilson, Summers and Watson, 1995) shows that 96 per cent of sales (by value) are on invoice and on average just less than 50 per cent of invoices are actually paid on time, that is, in accordance with stated terms. Consequently trade debtors is one of the main assets on most corporate balance sheets, representing up to 35 per cent of total assets for all companies. From the suppliers' point of view the management of trade credit (debtors) is, thus, an important facet of short-term financial management and supplier–customer relations.

Any discussion of the demand for trade credit must begin with definitions as the use of the terms in academic articles varies, and differs again from common usage. In common speech buying on trade credit often means simply that goods and services are paid for after they are obtained, with payment often being sent in response to an invoice or statement from the supplier, that is, deferred payment. The time between obtaining the goods or services and making payment will vary depending on the terms offered and some suppliers will offer discounts for early payment, for example terms of 2/10 net 30 mean a 2 per cent discount is available if invoices are paid in ten days or less with full payment being required in 30 days or less. Although the percentage discount offered may often seem small it is, for regular buyers, equivalent to a very high rate of interest being charged for the additional extension of credit to net terms – in the above case, for example, the equivalent annual interest rate is 40 per cent. Some writers only class customers as using trade credit if they forego a discount and therefore incur the higher cost for trade credit. In this chapter purchasing on credit is used in the common usage sense, with the situation where a discount is foregone being described as such, and as one proxy for the price of trade credit.

Credit terms refer to the written or stated policies given to a customer with regard to the timing of payments; discounts for early settlements; the methods of payment; ownership of goods prior to payment (for example, retention of title); and (if applicable) interest or penalties for late payment. The terms of payment on business to business sales can take many forms and a wide variety of possible payment terms can be offered. Cash on or before delivery (CoD, CBD) obviously does not involve trade credit. Progress or 'stage payment' terms usually involve an upfront deposit or downpayment with the outstanding invoice value being spread in payments over a set period. The majority of trade credit sales, however, are offered on a net period or net period with cash discount for earlier settlement. In the UK, predominantly, the payment period specified is 30 days (net 30 or 30 EOM, that is, 30 days from the end of month) but can vary from 7 days up to 120 days. Typically credit periods offered on export contracts are slightly longer than those for domestic sales but this varies according to both the destination country and the industry sector of the buyer.

Thus, in practice, we observe much variation in both credit terms and the extent to which payment to terms *is* or *can be* enforced. For instance, the net periods on offer vary around 30 days or a calendar month, but quoted payment terms can be as long as 120 days or as short as 7 days. Firms can vary discount periods and/or discount rates on early settlement; they can write provisions for interest penalties on payments received after the agreed period. Firms may allow certain customers to take unearned discounts or waive interest penalties on late payments. On the other hand firms may not be able to (cost-effectively) enforce their payment terms in the face of recalcitrant customer behaviour. The effective price of trade credit is somewhat difficult to determine and varies greatly across firms and industries. It may be reflected in the discount rates/periods and/or built into product prices. Generally it is thought that trade credit loans carry a higher interest rate than the going bank rate but it is feasible that some agreements may carry a zero rate (a simple net term) and others a very high implicit rate. Wilner (1995) argues that late payment behaviour may be either a function of firms with a strong market position leveraging their cash flow, or cash-constrained firms attempting to reduce the high implicit interest rate in trade credit contracts.

Theories of trade credit: supply-side

Understanding the fundamental reasons for the differences in the extent to which firms extend trade credit (supply credit) and their motivations for so doing is not the focus of this chapter (see Wilson and Summers, 1997). Nonetheless it is useful to provide a brief overview of the main motives that (non-financial) firms have for extending credit, not least because this may help us to understand why firms may extend trade credit to firms that appear to have difficulty raising other forms of (institutional) credit or are adjudged to be uncreditworthy by the financial institutions.

The core argument put forward for explaining the existence of trade credit is that product and capital (financial) markets are not perfectly competitive and perfectly informed. If perfectly competitive and informed financial and product markets existed there would be nothing to choose between bank and trade credit. The imperfections referred to revolve around the provision of information or 'informational asymmetries'. For instance, in some product markets buyers may be uncertain, or have insufficient information, to be able to fully assess product quality prior to purchase (that is, the lemons problem, Akerlof, 1970) and therefore require an 'inspection period' via deferred payment. Firms may extend trade credit in an attempt to differentiate their own product/finance offering from competitors and/or use trade credit periods as a signal to the market of high and consistent product quality and/or long-term presence in the market. Extending credit generates information on customers and reduces search costs which may facilitate some price discrimination (Crawford, 1992). Suppliers may use trade credit as a means of competing in markets and generating sales and customer loyalty. Trade credit as a competitive tool is many faceted and can be used to respond to customers' sensitivities to total effective price (goods plus finance); their needs or demand for short-term finance; their focus on product quality and after-sales service; and their requirements for continuity and reliability in the timing and quality of supplies. There will be certain market situations where suppliers can pass on the full cost of the credit to the customer and others where the firm will wish to trade-off the short-term profitability of individual customers with the increased volume of sales or market share and, of course, the potential for generating repeat purchase behaviour and market or customer information. Some firms will add a premium on to product price in order to cover the costs of extending credit, others may offer credit at a loss to illiquid buyers but offset this against a surplus from cash buyers. Trade credit may be used to discriminate between different classes of risk in the customer base. Moreover, survey evidence suggests that firms often vary credit terms proactively as part of the marketing mix or as a means of building stable and long-term relationships with customers, that is, goodwill and a future income stream. Trade credit extension may be used to smooth the pattern of customer demand. For instance trade creditors may relax credit terms in order to stimulate demand in lean periods and recover the costs of this policy in more buoyant times. Thus, whereas the seller may regard the bundling of products and finance from a marketing point of view the buyer may view it from a credit point of view. As Crawford points out, 'it is precisely because the supplier has different motives from the buyer that trade credit is a potential substitute for those rationed in the market for bank credit . . .' (1992, p. 7)

In financial markets banks may have insufficient information, compared to other lenders, to be able to assess the credit risk of lending to particular organisations engaged in the manufacture and distribution of goods and services. The asymmetries in information are likely to be related to a difference in the costs of collecting and managing information facing producers and lenders. Moreover, trade creditors, who are primarily concerned with selling products, may generate more customer information via the selling process and have more collateral (that is, recover the product) in the event of debtor default.

Of course, the nature and way in which credit can be used as a tool for gaining competitive advantages and reducing demand uncertainties will depend on the competitive structure of the markets facing the supplier and the customer, their relative bargaining strengths and the conditions affecting the supply of alternative sources of corporate finance.

Thus, a number of key factors have been suggested in theoretical studies that may help us to understand the observed variations in credit terms and credit periods. In these writings, for instance, it is suggested that industry structures and characteristics (for example, the nature of competition and bargaining relationships); product characteristics (quality, standardisation, customisation); firm-specific characteristics (for example, size, position in the value chain, competitive strategy); the nature of customer–supplier relationships (frequency of purchase, repeat purchase, geography) and the selling process (and the information generated); the availability (and rationing) of institutional or bank credit and the prevailing economic conditions or stage in the business cycle; all affect credit offerings.

The demand for trade credit

In this section we will attempt to explain and understand the firm's decision making with regard to the use of trade credit (that is, the demand-side). A number of theories have been put forward in order to address this issue (Schwartz, 1974; Ferris, 1981). At the heart of these theories, again, lies an assertion that imperfections in product and capital markets and asymmetries of information between lenders and borrowers drive these choices.

The decision to take credit and the total amount of trade credit loans a company uses will depend on the availability and relative prices of alternative financing arrangements. The credit rationing hypothesis posits that firms will take trade credit loans only when they are denied credit by other providers. If imperfections in credit markets result in some buyers having an unsatisfied demand for finance[4] then the firm is likely to possess both bank and trade credit loans even when trade credit rates exceed comparable bank rates, perhaps due to foregone discounts or late payment penalties. The implication is that credit rationed firms use trade credit, and other firms only do so when it is relatively cheap or when it is being offered as part of a total marketing package of product and finance which is attractive relative to alternative offerings.[5] This motive for trade credit demand implies that firms who are higher credit risks would have a higher demand for trade credit and would be more likely to display cheating behaviour that may attract penalties (that is, late payment). Wilner (1995) suggests that credit-rationed firms may attempt to stretch the payment periods on their trade debts (that is, pay late) in attempt to reduce the trade credit interest rate. Suppliers may, to some extent, tolerate this behaviour because the firms have more in common than the financial transaction; the supplier benefits in the longer term by helping a customer in short-term difficulty to stay in business and therefore make future sales. The supplier may be able to generate information for making credit decisions via the selling process. Further, a number of authors have argued that the banking sector often has difficulty making lending decisions to growing and/or high tech businesses due to informational problems. As Binks and Ennew (1996, p. 19) point out, 'in the case of growing businesses there is the potential for information gathering and processing on the part of the bank to be more difficult because of the pace of change within the business' and that 'banks default to a capital rather than income-gearing approach for the evaluation of loans'. The data used in the analysis for this chapter provides some support for this assertion.

The second line of theoretical argument that attempts to explain why firms use trade credit centres around the notion of *transaction costs*. The transaction cost motive posits that firms use trade credit in order to obtain efficiencies in cash management (Ferris, 1981). In the absence of trade credit, firms would have to hold large cash balances in order to pay for supplies. If the firm faces variable and uncertain delivery schedules, and converting liquid assets to cash at short notice is costly, then firms would have to hold precautionary balances of cash. Trade credit allows the firm to accumulate invoices and anticipate its cash requirements with more certainty and therefore hold smaller cash balances. This argument in fact gives rise to two motives: the buyer can plan the management of cash versus liquid assets, more effectively optimising returns on assets, and also potentially reduce the number of transactions on the bank account thereby reducing charges. Ferris (1981) demonstrated how uncertainty in, for example, delivery schedules can lead to a need for increased precautionary balances. We might, therefore, expect that uncertain deliveries schedules or reliance on supplier timings (for example, just in time) would be associated with more use of trade credit.

Moreover, the transaction costs of obtaining credit from a bank in order to purchase from suppliers may make institutional credit more expensive than trade credit. For instance, a firm making small but regular purchases from a supplier would have to arrange credit with a bank each time. Obtaining a credit limit from the supplier may be a less expensive option of financing working capital. This will be the case when the supplier market is very competitive and/or the buyer has a wide choice of suppliers.

It is clear from the arguments above that some firms use trade credit because they achieve a package involving goods, finance, reliability in the timing of supplies, and perhaps after-sales service that is cost-effective overall. Linked to this is the issue of product quality. Trade credit can be a tool for buyers, providing information (signals) on seller performance and to some extent protecting the buyer from non-compliance. The idea that credit terms might provide signals of confidence in product quality by allowing the buyer an inspection period before payment is due (and hence some protection from non-compliance) is often put forward as a motivation for sellers to extend credit (see Ackerlof, 1970; Smith, 1987). This motivation would apply to services as well as goods. Smith suggests that longer credit periods would therefore be expected where buyers cannot identify high quality sellers in advance, where a particular seller does not have sufficient reputation to make buyers feel guaranteed of their performance, and where the supplier has the possibility to behave opportunistically against the buyers' interest. Uncertainty about the quality of goods or services or about the likelihood of opportunistic behaviour by the seller may motivate buyers to take net terms rather than pay cash or take early payment discounts. Lee and Stowe (1993) develop a model which relates the size of early payment discount to product quality, with lower quality producers offering higher discounts to induce buyers to share the quality risk.

A simple demand function for trade credit

This section explores, via a simple model, the determinants of trade credit demand. In the earlier section it was posited that the demand for trade credit or trade credit usage could be broken down into a 'financing demand' and a 'transaction demand'. In summary, it was suggested that the use of trade credit should be related to: the relative price of trade versus bank credit (P_{TC}; P_{BC}); the availability of alternative institutional credit and 'creditworthiness'; the structure of supplier markets; relationships with suppliers (that is, the volume and variability of transactions with suppliers); the timing and uncertainty of the operating cycle and cash-flow; the costs of holding cash balances and converting liquid assets.

There are varying degrees of trade credit usage amongst the sample under investigation including a proportion of firms who do not use trade credit. Moreover, understanding the factors affecting the demand for trade credit is crucial if we are to understand the factors precipitating late payment (that is, taking extended trade credit).

Based on work undertaken by Chant and Walker (1988) and more recently Elliehausen and Wolken (1993), for the US small firm sector, we are able to derive a simple demand function for trade credit. The model, based on Elliehausen and Wolken (1993), enables the specification of an empirical formulation that can be modelled using our questionnaire and financial data. The transaction demand component (TD) can be modelled as a function of: the volume of purchases with suppliers (S); the variability in the timing of delivery of purchases (VS); the return on liquid assets (RLA) and the cost of converting liquid assets into cash (BC). The theory suggests that firms will use trade credit if it helps to manage cash-flow so that the firm does not have to hold cash balances and/or can reduce the costs of converting assets to cash in order to pay different suppliers at different times. Trade credit demand for an individual firm will increase as the volume of purchases increases and when the timing of delivery is difficult to accurately anticipate. The cost of holding cash balances is related to the return on liquid assets and the brokerage costs of converting assets to cash. The financing demand component (FD) is a function of financial and business risk (R_F, R_B). Firms with high default risk may be unable to obtain bank credit but suppliers of trade credit, who perhaps have more information on the buyer and/or assess risks differently, may feel able to extend finance. Financing demand will be related to the relative prices of trade and institutional credit. The issue of whether bank and trade credit are substitute or complements is an empirical question and the results will be relevant to the credit rationing debate.

An equation for trade credit demand can be derived as in Elliehausen and Wolken (1993) with the exogenous variables defined as above.

$$\begin{aligned} QD^{*}_{TC} = Td + Fd = (b0 + b1S + b2VS + b3RLA + b4BC) \\ + [c0 + c1R_F + c2R_B + c3P_{TC} + c4P_{BC}) \end{aligned} \tag{8.1}$$

Elliehausen and Wolken assume that in equilibrium trade credit demand equates to supply. QD^{*}_{TC} is the anticipated (ex-ante) trade credit demand. The amount of trade credit used by a buyer is assumed equal to the amount of trade creditors (accounts payable, AP). 'The above arguments suggest that it is possible that a firm's demand for trade credit is not fully satisfied. We assume that excess demand would be a function of credit risk – riskier firms are less likely to have their full demand for trade credit satisfied. Thus excess demand for trade credit is assumed to be a linear function of business and financial risk. Moreover, the demand for bank credit is a linear function of its price and firms are assumed to be price-takers. Thus,

$$QD^{*}_{TC} = AP + el\ R_F + e2\ R_B \tag{8.2}$$

$$QD_{BC} = a0 + al\ P_{BC} \text{ where } al < 0 \tag{8.3}$$

and we substitute quantity rather than the price of bank credit into the empirical model.

A reduced-form model of trade credit use can be specified by substituting (8.2) and (8.3) into (8.1) as:

$$\begin{aligned} QD_{TC} = AP = Td + Fd + \mathscr{E} = {} & [b0 + c0 - c4\ (a0/al)] \\ & + (b1S + b2VS + b3RLA + b4BC) + [(cl - el)R_F \\ & + (c2 - e2)R_B + c3P_{TC} + (c4/a1)\ QD_{BC}] + \mathscr{E} \end{aligned}$$

Empirically,

$$QD_{TC} = f\,(S;\ VS;\ RLA;\ BC;\ R_F;\ R_B;\ P_{TC};\ QD_{BC}) \tag{8.4}$$

The data

A detailed postal questionnaire was administered in October 1995. The survey collected detailed data on the firm itself; its ownership and organisational structure, products, markets, product characteristics, supplier relationships, credit policy, credit terms and credit and financial management practices, financing and bank relationships. The target group was small businesses, in particular those with a turnover less than £2.5 million. The origin of the sample frame was One Source, a comprehensive small company database (One Source, Dos CD Oct 95). A filtered sample was extracted on the basis of turnover and number of employees. The sample frame was selected from a broad range of industry sectors in manufacturing, services and construction, and firms were located throughout the United Kingdom.

In order to capture data on the granting and acceptance of trade credit and credit management practices, the survey aimed to sample companies engaged in inter-firm trade and with only one predominant product line. The number of usable completed questionnaires returned was 343, representing a response rate of 20 per cent.[6] The questionnaire data was supplemented by detailed financial and behavioural data provided by Dun & Bradstreet Ltd. This included the profit and loss account data which coincided with the year of the postal survey and information on payment behaviour in that year.

The section below describes the variables used in the multivariate analysis of trade credit demand. A reduced sample of 321 firms was used in the estimation as a result of missing variables.

Variables affecting demand

The theory has suggested that certain variables affect the transaction or financing demand for trade credit. The full list of variables used in the demand models along with descriptive statistics are reported in Table 8.1. The empirical definitions used to proxy the above model are briefly as follows.

Table 8.1 Demand model descriptive statistics

		Mean	(S.D.)
Transaction variables			
STOCKTA	Ratio of stocks to total assets	0.131	(0.18)
STOCKTU	Ratio of stocks to sales	0.095	(0.20)
SUPPLTA	Number of suppliers/total assets	0.358	(0.56)
CHOICE	Choice of suppliers (speed; lead time)	–0.011	(1.03)
Financing risk and price variables			
CSCORE	Credit score (Financial Risk)	51.27	(22.42)
AGE	Age of firm	19.97	(26.37)
OWN	Proportion of company owned by directors	92.14	(18.41)
STLTA	Short term loans/total assets	0.39	(0.20)
STFIN	Factor score (short term finance)	2.49	(1.05)
DFIN	Factor score (difficulty raising financing)	–0.020	(0.99)
NODISC	1 = not offered cash discounts, 0 = otherwise	0.49	(0.50)
TAKEDISC	Take cash discounts when offered (1,0)	0.72	(0.44)
PINT	Pay interest on late payments (0,1)	0.14	(0.35)
SIZE	Size (log of sales)	11.88	(0.63)
Other variables			
EXPORT	Export sale (0,1)	0.29	(0.45)
SEASON	Seasonality of demand (1 = not, 5 = highly)	2.12	(1.13)
Dependent variables			
APTA	Accounts payable/total Assets	0.22	(0.19)
TC	Used trade credit (0,1)	0.88	(0.32)
PAYLATE	Made late payments (0 = never, 5 = frequent)	1.76	(1.21)
PLATE	Made late payments (0 = no, 1 = yes)	0.56	(0.49)

Financing variables Financial risk was measured by the businesses credit score (CSCORE) taken from a credit reference agency. The score could take on values 0–100 with the lower score indicating higher risk. Such scores are usually based on a linear combination of financial ratios reflecting liquidity – gearing, profitability and activity – and calculated using multivariate techniques such as logistic regression and/or discriminant analysis.

Business risk was proxied by ownership concentration (OWN), the proportion of equity owned by current directors, on the premise that owner–managers prefer riskier projects than hired managers and the age of the firm (AGE). Age was expected to be negatively related to trade credit demand. The price of trade credit was represented by two proxy variables. NODISC indicated whether the firm was offered discounts for early payment or not. The existence of a discount implies a higher price of trade credit. Thus, being offered a discount is expected to be negatively related to demand.[7] A further variable, TAKEDIS, was constructed in order to isolate those firms who do or do not take cash discounts on credit sales when they are offered, that is, firms not taking a discount are paying a premium price for trade credit. Making late payments (PLATE) reveals a preference for using trade credit for finance and will be positively related to trade credit demand. Firms incurring interest charges (PINT) on late payments will also be indicating a preference for trade credit but are, again, paying a relatively high price for it.

The price of institutional credit is proxied by the quantity of short-term bank loans in relation to total assets (STLTA) or variables proxying the usage of short term finance (STFIN). The latter was constructed from principal component analysis of answers to Likert scale-type questions concerning the usage (never too often) of various sources of finance. Thus high factor scores on STFIN reflected firms with a relatively heavy reliance on short-term institutional finance. The expected signs on these variables are ambiguous. In order to proxy credit rationing a variable measuring the firms perceived difficulty in raising bank finance, using factor analysis, was constructed (DFIN). This reflected a perceived difficulty in raising bank finance for day-to-day working capital and for growth. A positive relationship was expected with the latter variable and the demand for trade credit.

Transaction variables The ratio of stocks to total assets (STOCKTA) was used to indicate the volume of transactions with suppliers. Greater levels of stocks suggests greater volumes of purchases from suppliers and greater demand for trade credit. Stock turnover, proxied by the ratio of stocks to sales (STOCKTU), and the number of firms supplying stocks relative to firm size (SUPPLTA) were used as proxies for the variability or uncertainty in transactions with suppliers. A further variable constructed by factor analysis (CHOICE) identified those firms that chose their suppliers primarily for 'speed of response' and 'lead time'.

Thus firms with low stock turnover ratio may have more frequent purchases and more uncertainty in transactions. This was expected to be negatively related to demand whereas CHOICE was expected to be positive. Firms that conduct business with a large number of suppliers face additional uncertainty from variations in the timing of deliveries because of differences in the behaviour and location of suppliers. SUPPLTA should attract a positive sign. Other variables reflecting the concentration of supplier markets were collected: SIZE, as a proxy for brokerage costs, that is, larger firms are more likely to face costs of converting liquid assets to cash; market competitiveness (MKTCOMP); export orientation (EXPORT) that is, firms typically allow longer credit periods on export sales so that this variable is expected to be positively related to trade credit demand; and seasonality of demand (SEASON); were included in various model specifications.

The set of financing and transaction demand component variables were related to accounts payable adjusted for size (APTA) and whether the firm used trade credit or not (TC). Two further models determining the probability that the firm made late payments (PAYLATE, PLATE) were estimated. The discussion of the factors affecting the demand for trade credit has some utility in helping us to understand the reasons why firms pay late. It is clear that a number of factors can be related to a firm's propensity to pay its suppliers beyond the invoice due date. These relate to poor financial and credit management practice, or inadequate capital base and credit rationing and/or abusing a dominant position. Two multivariate models were estimated in order to model the probability that firms make some payments after the due date. The question, 'do you ever pay your suppliers late?' was scaled from 0 (never) to 6 (frequently) forming the variable PAYLATE and further split into a binary variable with the category 1, paid late relatively frequently, and the category 0, paid late never or very occasionally (PLATE). This outcome was then modelled in relation to the transaction cost and financing theory variables. It is expected that making payments on trade credit after the due date will reflect a financing motive for using trade credit.

Empirical results

Models determining trade credit usage

Two equations were estimated based on equation (8.4) reported above. A model explaining whether a firm used trade credit was estimated using a probit model. In this case the dependent variable was specified as 1 for firms that used trade credit regularly and 0 for those that predominantly do not. The probability of using trade credit was modelled in relation to the set of financing and transaction variables excluding the price variables since we can only infer price effects from firms that use credit. The amount of trade credit used by the firm was modelled in relation to the transaction and financing demand variables with proxies for the prices of bank and trade credit included in the model. The dependent variable here was the ratio of accounts payable to total assets (APTA) and the equation was estimated using classical linear regression with the errors corrected for heteroscedasticity (Limdep, 1988). The results are reported in Tables 8.2 and 8.3. Two specifications are reported for each equation with alternative variables reflecting the use of short-term bank finance (STLTA, STFIN).

The probit estimates predict the probability that a firm in the sample uses trade credit (for example, in 1994/5) and are reported in Table 8.2. The model produces strongly significant equations that are generally consistent with the theoretical expectations. Two of the transaction variables are significant in the model and give some support for a transactions demand for trade credit. The probability of trade credit use increases with the volume of transactions with suppliers (STOCKTA). The variability of transactions (STOCKTU) is not quite significant at 5 per cent but attracts the correct sign. However, firms appear to use trade credit to reduce the uncertainty in the timing of delivery (CHOICE). Further, SIZE, the proxy for brokerage costs of converting liquid assets is positive and strongly significant. Thus the larger the firm in terms of sales turnover the higher the probability of trade credit usage.

Table 8.2 Demand model 2: TC (0,1). Model determining the probability of using trade credit: probit estimates (use trade credit 0 = no, 1 = yes)

Variable	Equation 1	Equation 2
STOCKTA	4.423**	4.422**
STOCKTU	–0.574	–0.573
CHOICE	0.178*	0.178*
SUPPLTA	0.248	0.248
SEASON	0.0001	–0.002
SIZE	0.472**	0.471**
AGE	0.005	0.005
OWN	0.009*	0.009*
CSCORE	–0.007*	-0.007*
STFIN	–0.003	n.a.
STLTA	n.a.	0.003
DFIN	0.015	0.015
EXPORT	–0.019	–0.019
Constant	–5.27*	–5.272*
Chi-squared	42.53	42.53
Log-likelihood	–95.47	–95.47

Notes:
* significant at 5%.
** significant at 1%.

There is some support for the financing demand hypothesis. Two of the five financing/business risk variables are statistically significant in the model. The credit score variable (CSCORE) attracts the correct sign, that is, the greater the degree of financial risk the higher the trade credit demand. Firms with a higher perceived financial risk are unlikely to attract institutional finance. However, the variables proxying the usage of short-term institutional finance (STLTA, STFIN are not significant in this model, neither is the variable measuring finance constraints (DFIN). OWN, the proxy for business risk, is positive and significant, as predicted by the theory.

Table 8.3 Demand model 1: AP/TA. Estimated regression model for trade credit demand: accounts payable/total assets

Variable	Equation 1	Equation 2
STOCKTA	0.025	0.040
STOCKTU	–0.133**	–0.115**
CHOICE	0.009	0.010
SUPPLTA	0.017	0.024
SEASON	0.018*	0.006
EXPORT	–0.022	–0.026
SIZE	0.035*	0.025*
AGE	–0.0003	–0.0007**
OWN	0.001**	0.001**
CSCORE	–0.003**	–0.004**
STFIN	–0.029**	n.a.
STLTA	n.a.	–0.397**
DFIN	–0.01	–0.02
NODISC	0.036	0.016
TAKEDIS	0.004	0.0001
PLATE	0.019	0.009
Constant	–0.121	0.164
R^2	0.19**	0.31**

Notes:
* significant at 5% or better.
** significant at 1% or better.
Nb: Heteroscedasticity corrected standard errors.

The accounts payable model as defined in equation (8.4) proxies the factors affecting the *total amount of trade credit demanded* as opposed to whether or not the firm uses trade credit. The dependent variable is specified as the total accounts payable relative to the size of the firm (that is, total assets). The independent variables were the full sets of transaction and financing demand variables and the proxies for relative price responsiveness between bank and trade credit. The results are reported in Table 8.3. Again two equations are estimated where we substitute the alternative measures of the usage of short-term institutional credit.

Both of the estimated equations are significant and explain up to 31 per cent of the variance in APTA. The positive and negative signs on STOCKTA and STOCKTU respectively give support for the transactions demand theory but in these equations only the latter is significant. Thus the greater the variability of transactions with suppliers the greater the usage of trade credit. Moreover, there is some evidence that seasonality of demand affects the usage of trade credit as a tool for smoothing cashflow. The size variable, hypothesised to pick up the higher return on liquid assets and brokerage costs of larger firms is positive and highly significant and therefore consistent with the transactions demand motive.

The set of financing and price variables explain a greater proportion of the total demand for trade credit. The financing motive for trade credit usage is given considerable support from these results. The estimated coefficient on CSCORE, a proxy for financial risk, is highly significant. Thus firms with a higher risk (lower score) have a greater demand for trade credit. The implication is that high risk firms use trade credit because institutional credit is rationed by the banks. Rationing takes place because of credit market imperfections, that is, lack of information and/or insufficient collateral. The variable proxying business risk, OWN, is also significant. OWN is positive, that is, owner-managed firms take greater risks than those with a higher external ownership stake and greater business risk is associated with a higher demand for trade credit. AGE, another proxy for business risk, is negative and significant in equation 2 suggesting that firms with more experience and trading history are less reliant on trade credit to finance their activities .

The variables reflecting the usage of short-term institutional finance (short to medium term loans and overdraft) are both negative and significant. The signs suggest that short-term bank finance is, on the whole, a substitute for trade credit finance. The price variables NODISC, TAKEDIS, PLATE are not significant factors affecting the total demand for trade credit in these firms.

In summary, the decision to use trade credit and the level of trade credit usage is influenced by both the transaction and financing demand motives. The decision to use trade credit appears to be influenced by the transactions demand variables but the extent of the usage is clearly affected more by the financing motives.

Models determining the probability of paying late

Ordered probit estimates of the propensity to pay commercial debts late are reported in Table 8.4. The probability that a business will pay late is related to

Table 8.4 Late payment models. Estimated model for probability of paying late on trade credit: ordered probit estimates (0 = never, 5 = frequently)

Variable	Equation 1	Equation 2
STOCKTA	0.283*	0.327*
STOCKTU	–0.215	–0.286
CHOICE	0.216**	0.209**
SUPPLTA	0.105	0.098
EXPORT	–0.037	–0.054
SEASON	0.145**	0.140**
SIZE	0.238*	0.258**
AGE	–0.0005	–0.0004
OWN	0.005	0.005
CSCORE	–0.009**	–0.010**
STFIN	0.128*	n.a.
STLTA	n.a.	–0.390
DFIN	0.255**	0.290**
NODISC	0.485**	0.484**
TAKEDIS	–0.764**	–0.768**
PLINT	0.430*	0.442*
Constant	–2.009*	–1.703*
Chi-squared	122.3**	119.2**
Log-likelihood	–438.5	–497.3

Notes:
* significant at 5%.
** significant at 1%.

many of the factors predicted by theory and much support is given to the financing theory of trade credit demand. The transactions demand variables retain the signs and significance of the previous demand equations (Tables 8.2 and 8.3) but seasonality of demand appears to have a stronger impact on late payment behaviour. Firms paying late are more likely to choose suppliers for speed of response and lead time or for availability of credit (CHOICE). There is some support for the transactions theory in that CHOICE, choosing suppliers for speed of response, is significant, and STOCKTA, the ratio of stocks to total assets is weakly significant in both equations. Thus they are tied in to certain suppliers in order to ensure continuity of production and speed of response and face seasonal demands for their final products. Firms who pay late regularly appear to forego cash discounts when they are offered (TAKEDIS) and are more likely to incur interest payments (PLINT). This lack of responsiveness to the price of trade credit may provide more support for the credit rationing hypothesis.

Thus, the loss of cash discounts and the added cost of interest may not discourage firms with relatively high costs for institutional credit, especially rationed firms, from delaying payment on trade credit beyond the due date. The coefficient on DFIN, that is, experience difficulty raising bank finance, is statistically significant and positive. This suggests that businesses paying late are constrained from raising further short-term finance from the banks. Moreover, these firms regard themselves as *growing firms*. The sign on CSCORE is negative and statistically significant. Thus the firms paying late are perceived to have a higher financial risk and are attempting to satisfy their demand for finance by using trade credit above their level of bank credit; again supporting a credit rationing argument. Interestingly the sign on STFIN turns positive and significant in these equations suggesting bank and (extended) trade credit are complementary. The probit estimates on the binary dependent variable (Table 8.5) provide a similar profile of results giving a great deal of support for a financing motive for taking extended trade credit.

Table 8.5 Late payment models. Estimated model for probability of paying late on trade credit: probit estimates (0 = never, 1 = yes)

Variable	Equation 1	Equation 2
STOCKTA	0.241	0.327
STOCKTU	–0.758	–0.857
CHOICE	0.221**	0.207**
SUPPLTA	0.053	0.047
SEASON	0.213**	0.215**
SIZE	0.138	0.167
AGE	0.002	0.003
OWN	0.001	0.002
CSCORE	–0.009**	–0.010**
STFIN	0.212**	n.a.
STLTA	n.a.	–0.041
DFIN	0.278**	0.319**
NODISC	0.517**	0.533**
TAKEDIS	–0.982**	–0.963**
PLINT	0.946**	0.974**
EXPORT	0.211	0.192
Constant	–2.006*	–1.673*
Chi-squared	116.6**	101.2**
Log-likelihood	–169.2	–169.5

Notes:
* significant at 5%.
** significant at 1%.

Conclusions

In summary, taking the multivariate and other evidence into consideration, the profile of smaller firms who pay late suggests that these are firms trading in competitive markets, who are having difficulty in raising external finance from the banking sector. They appear to have reached a credit limit from the banking sector, based on perceived business and financial risk, and are having difficulty managing short-term finance. Their cash flow is further affected by customer demands for long credit periods; liquidity is relatively low and they choose to finance their operations via extended trade credit at a premium rate of interest (foregone discounts and interest penalties).

The chapter has attempted to test a simple model of trade credit demand using firm-level data. There is support for the extant theory, in that demand is determined by transaction costs and financing reasons. The chapter suggests, indirectly, support for a credit-rationing hypothesis in relation to small firm financing. Further, there are implications for any proposed government policy in respect of legislation introducing a 'statutory right to interest' on commercial debt. The results from this analysis would indicate that measures designed to affect the price of trade credit would be ineffective against late payment behaviour and may in fact further damage a dynamic but finance-constrained small firm sector.

Notes

1. Trade credit, of course, is not new and has been around as long as trade itself. For example, Bennett (1989) in a study of fifteenth century Britain, suggests that sales on credit (that is, trade credit) '. . . accounted for more than half of all credit transactions' and notes that, '. . .many firms had more of their assets tied up in credit than in capital'. Interestingly, the latter was not always deliberate '. . . in many cases the creditor never intended to extend credit to the debtor; these debts originated when debtors failed to pay for goods on delivery . . .' (p. 236).
2. Indeed, in a recent survey, the CMRG found that over 50 per cent of 655 manufacturing companies regarded late payment as an important problem affecting their business and that typically a firm which extends 30 days credit can be expected to be paid in 57 days. Moreover, 84 per cent of small businesses indicated that they paid their suppliers late 'often' or 'frequently'. Recent evidence (*Trade Indemnity Quarterly Financial Trends Survey*, 1997) suggests that payment periods on commercial debt continue to lengthen.
3. The departing Conservative government ruled out legislation to enforce a statutory right to interest on late payments in favour of voluntary measures (for example, British standard BS7890, a voluntary but enforceable prompt payment code), education and training in financial and credit management and legislation to enforce the disclosure of payment policies and practice in company accounts. The incoming Labour government, however, have included a commitment to legislation in their manifesto. Moreover, the EC remains committed to the imposition of a statutory right to interest across member states.
4. Stiglitz and Weiss (1981) demonstrated that credit rationing can exist in a loan market in equilibrium. De Meza and Webb (1987) suggest that credit rationing arises in markets where the ability of lenders to offer equity finance is constrained for example, the small firm sector.
5. Even if a firm does not suffer credit rationing trade credit may be an economic option compared to other finance because suppliers are in a position to save on information costs in assessing a buyers creditworthiness and in collection and monitoring costs, particularly with regular customers. The lack of the fixed costs associated with arranging a loan or line of credit and the

administrative costs to the borrower may also make trade credit more attractive (for example, lower transactions costs, see below).

6. Most (94 per cent) of the respondents are private limited companies. Four per cent are partnerships or sole proprietors and 1 per cent are plcs. In 73 per cent of the sample (251 companies) the current directors own 100 per cent of the company. In only 4 per cent of the companies do the current directors have a minority (50 per cent or less) stake. Thus the sample consists almost entirely of owner-managed businesses. The oldest company was founded in 1762 with a further 7 companies founded before 1900. Twenty-eight per cent of companies are less than 5 years old having been founded in 1990 or later. The mean number of employees was 9. The majority (81 per cent) of respondents had 10 employees or less.
7. If firms are not offered a discount but a net period only, then it is difficult to draw any conclusions about the price that they are paying for trade credit. We cannot necessarily assume that the rate of interest is zero since a premium may have been built into product price.

References

Akerlof, G. (1970), 'The market for lemons: quality, uncertainty and the market mechanism', *Quarterly Journal of Economics*, **84**, 488–500.

Bennett, E.Z. (1989), 'Debt and credit in the urban economy: London 1380–1460', Phd Thesis, University of Yale.

Berger, A.N. and G.F. Udell (1992), 'Some evidence on the empirical significance of credit rationing', *Journal of Political Economy*, **100** (5), 1047–77.

Bickers, M. (1994), 'Factoring: an industry of last resort', *Director*, **47**, (6), 43–8.

Binks, M.R. and C.T. Ennew (1996), 'Growing firms and credit constraint', *Small Business Economics*, **8**, 17–25.

Black, J., D. de Meza and D. Jeffreys (1996), 'House prices, the supply of collateral and the enterprise economy', *Economic Journal*, **106**, 60–75.

Chant, E. and D.A. Walker (1988), 'Small business demand for trade credit', *Applied Economics*, **20**, 861–76.

Crawford, P. (1992), 'Trade credit and credit rationing', University of Bristol Discussion Paper No. 92/323.

Cressy, R. (1996), 'Small business failure: failure to fund or failure to learn', paper presented at the ESRC Workshop in Industrial Economics at Durham.

De Meza, D. and D.C. Webb (1987), 'Too much investment: a problem of asymmetric information', *Quarterly Journal of Economics*, **102**, 281–92.

Elliehausen, G.E. and J.D. Wolken (1993), 'The demand for trade credit: an investigation of motives for trade credit use by small businesses', *Federal Reserve Bulletin*, Paper 165.

Ennew, C.T. and M.R. Binks (1996), 'The provision of finance to small businesses: does the banking relationship constrain performance', *Journal of Small Business Finance*, **4** (1), 57–73.

Fair R. and D. Jafee (1972), 'Methods of estimation for markets in disequilibrium, *Econometrica*, **40** (3), 497–514.

Ferris, S.J. (1981), 'A transactions theory of trade credit use', *Quarterly Journal of Economics*, pp. 243–70.

Lee, Y.W. and J.D. Stowe (1993), 'Product risk, asymmetric information and trade credit', *Journal of Finance and Quantitative Analysis*, **28** (2), 285–300.

Limdep (1988), William H. Greene, Econometric Software, V7.0.

Petersen, M.A. and R.G. Rajan (1995), 'The effects of credit market competition on lending relationships', *Quarterly Journal of Economics*, **110**, 407–44.

Schwartz, R.A. (1974), 'An economic model of trade credit', *Journal of Financial and Quantitative Analysis*, **9**, 643–57.

Smith, J.K. (1987), 'Trade credit and informational asymmetry', *Journal of Finance*, **62**, (4), 863–72.

Stiglitz, J.E. and A. Weiss (1981), 'Credit rationing in markets with imperfect information', *American Economic Review*, **71** (3), 393–410.

Storey, D.J. (1994), *Understanding the Small Business Sector*, New York: Routledge.

Summers, B. and N. Wilson (1997), 'Trade credit management and the decision to use factoring: an empirical study', Working Paper 9701, University of Bradford Management Centre.

Wilner B.S. (1995), 'Trade credit versus bank credit', Working Paper, University of Michigan, Ann Arbor.

Wilner, B.S. (1996), 'Paying your bills: an empirical study of trade credit, Working Paper, University of Michigan, Ann Arbor.

Wilson Committee (1979), *The Financing of Small Firms*, HMSO: Cmnd 7503.

Wilson, N. and B. Summers (1997), 'Trade credit terms and the motives for trade credit extension: theory and evidence', Working Paper 9708, University of Bradford Management Centre.

Wilson, N., B. Summers and K. Watson (1995), 'Trading relationships, credit management and corporate performance: a survey', Credit Management Research Group, University of Bradford Management Centre.

9. Funds providers' role in venture capital firm monitoring

Ken Robbie, Mike Wright and Brian Chiplin

Introduction

The venture capital process can be characterised as involving two sets of key relationships, those between venture capital firms and the entrepreneurs in whom they invest and those between venture capital firms and their funds providers. As shown in Chapter 1, there is a substantial literature on the relationship between the venture capital firm and its investees. However, the monitoring relationship between venture capital firms and their funds providers has been relatively neglected. This omission raises a number of important issues for both academic researchers and practitioners. For academic researchers questions are raised concerning the extent and nature of the monitoring by funds providers of venture capital firms, the information required and the implications for the performance of the industry. For practitioners, examination of the operation of funds providers may provide insights into their objectives and information needs and may also be important given indications (see below) that their approaches may be changing.

This chapter examines these issues as follows. The first section briefly reviews previous literature. The second section considers the implications for funds providers of the current competitive position of the UK venture capital market as reviewed in Chapter 3. The third section describes the data and methodology used and the fourth section presents the results. The final section presents conclusions and implications of the research.

Existing literature

Previous literature which helps in formulating expectations about the nature of monitoring relationships between venture capitalists and their funds providers is sparse. An agency theory perspective has been used to examine the issues in a pioneering study by Sahlman (1990) which analysed the nature of the relationship between funds providers and venture capital firms, and identified the mechanisms used to help minimise these agency problems. These mechanisms included incentives for mutual gain, the specific prohibition of certain acts on the part of the venture capital firm which would cause conflicts of interest, limited life agreements, mechanisms to ensure gains are distributed to investors, expenditure of resources on monitoring the venture capital firm and the regular provision of specific information to the funds providers by the venture capital firm. Venture capital firms' remuneration is typically based on an annual management fee plus some percentage of the realised profits from the fund. Sahlman points out that good venture capital firms by accepting a finite funding life and performance dependent compensation are signalling their quality in relation to weak ones, but that the funds provider has to invest in intensive screening in order to guard against false signalling. More recently, an empirical study by Gompers and Lerner (1996) finds evidence that the use of covenants in the contracts between funds providers and venture capital firms is both a means of dealing with agency problems but also a reflection of supply and demand conditions in the industry.

A significant agency problem may also arise in the valuation of investments for the purposes of reporting to providers of funds. It is venture capital firms as agents who are responsible for such valuations and on which their performance will be judged (Fried and Hisrich, 1994). However, since it may take many years for a venture capital investment to come to fruition, considerable subjectivity surrounds the valuation of investments in any particular year before the investment is realised. In the absence of clear and complete rules, management may have the scope and incentive to report biased interim investment values. The adoption of different valuation practices also makes it difficult to compare the performance of individual venture capital firms. In the UK, the British Venture Capital Association (BVCA) has introduced guidelines which recommend four appropriate valuation methods for its members. Evidence from UK venture capital firms shows that almost nine-tenths of BVCA members have adopted these guidelines and that the most popular of the valuation methods available is cost (less provision) (57 per cent of cases), followed by price earnings multiples (25 per cent), third party valuations (14 per cent) and net assets (4 per cent) (Wright and Robbie, 1996a).

Notwithstanding these points, there are reasons for questioning the extent of funds providers' monitoring of their investments in venture capital firms. The extent and nature of monitoring by funds providers may be influenced by the effort–cost–return trade-offs. If, as is typically the case, venture capital forms a very small percentage of pension funds' and other institutions' asset portfolios, a *de minimis* approach to monitoring may be adopted. Possible changes to regulations concerning the ability of institutions to treat venture capital investments as an asset class may to some extent change this position. However, requirements to maintain particular levels of liquidity could offset such a change. A second issue concerns the nature of the monitoring of executives in institutions providing funds to venture capitalists. Lax monitoring by pension fund trustees and executive remuneration which is not significantly influenced by the performance of investments in venture capital firms may also mean that the monitoring of such firms is at best passive. Changes in corporate accountability regimes in pension funds, whereby trustees focus greater attention on the use executives make of funds may be expected to lead to closer monitoring of investments in venture capital firms. This may take the form of more regular meetings, more detailed requirements for information, and tighter contractual arrangements in terms of the balance between fund management fees and performance-related returns. It may also be expected to be associated with some increase in the role of intermediaries ('gatekeepers') in identifying appropriate venture capital funds in which pension funds, and so on may invest. Increasing pressure from institutional investors for more frequent reporting could mean that funds providers begin to take a more short-term view of investment.

A further monitoring problem facing providers of funds to venture capital firms is access to comparator information resulting from the private nature of venture capital investments and of many venture capital firms themselves. Bygrave (1994), for example, noted that until the late 1980s in the US there was an astonishing paucity of reliable information to support venture capitalists' high expectations. Recent developments which, as seen in Chapter 3, involve the publication of mean and upper quartile returns on various stages of investment by a number of national venture capital associations in Europe (UK, France and Holland) go some way to alleviating these informational problems, which may be expected to influence the setting of target rates of return by funds providers. However, evidence also suggests that these actual returns are some way below expected returns (Manigart et al., 1997). This is particularly a problem for early stage investments, whereas actual returns for later stage and buy-out investments are close to expectations. Increasing information availability may be expected to have an impact on the setting of benchmark rates of return by funds providers, perhaps in terms of industry upper quartiles rather than means, and of returns to venture capitalists being structured such that they are required to earn above these levels for their investors before being able to achieve higher returns themselves (so-called 'hurdle rates of return').

The nature of the monitoring of venture capitalists may also vary between independent and captive types of firm. The former typically involve funding from limited-life funds, whereas the latter may typically be funded on a more open-ended basis. It is well-known that, in general, subsidiaries and divisions of large groups are required to conform to group monitoring systems even though their particular market circumstances may be different (Jones, Rickwood and Greenfield, 1993). Captive venture capital firms which are subsidiaries of banks and insurance companies, for example, may thus be required to provide at least monthly management accounting information. To the extent that other activities in the institution operate on an open-ended basis, this information may be more likely to be required to be presented in terms of returns on assets rather than internal rates of return which may be more appropriate for limited-life funds. Where funds providers to venture capitalists also invest in listed securities, where it is more feasible to undertake regular valuations, venture capital firms may also be expected to provide more frequent valuations of their portfolios. This may be expected to be more likely in independent venture capital firms.

The monitoring of venture capital firms

The competitive position of the UK venture capital industry as reviewed in Chapter 3 introduces a number of pressures for increased monitoring of venture capital firms by their funds providers. These pressures can be identified as emanating from both the side of funds providers and venture capital firms themselves. For funds providers the pressures can be identified as follows. First, increasing transparency of returns provides a greater opportunity for benchmarking venture capital firms. Second, the increasing trend towards venture capital investments being recognised as an asset class suggests a growing need for closer scrutiny of performance. Third, increasing pressure on funds providers' trustees in respect of corporate accountability has a clear feed-through effect on the monitoring of venture capital firms in whom investments are being made. Fourth, the increasing trend towards focusing on a smaller number of key relationships involving larger amounts of investment in any one venture capital firm emphasises the need to monitor more closely because of the potential for problems arising from reduced diversification. Moreover, there may be expected to be scale benefits from monitoring fewer larger investments. Fifth, the need for funds providers to develop their investment strategies has introduced a need for a greater degree of non-standard information. Sixth, the increasing role of gatekeepers also implies a greater pressure for monitoring.

From the point of view of venture capital firms the pressures for increased monitoring may be identified as follows. First, a developing perception by venture capital firms of the need to demonstrate performance in the top quartile for the industry if they are to receive funding brings with it an increased acceptance of the monitoring role of funds providers. Increasing transparency about the performance of individual venture capital firms in relation to industry averages is likely to increase rationalisation but would mean that good performers would have little difficulty in raising funds. Established funds providers may increasingly concentrate their investments on fewer key relationships with well-known venture capital firms in whom they had previously invested successfully. Moreover, in cases of good performance, institutional investors may be more likely to commit a larger amount to a particular venture capital fund. There may be some residual inertia whereby funds providers maintain relationships with venture capital firms with acceptable rather than outstanding performance. The pressure on venture capital firms of greater scrutiny by funds providers of the rates of return being earned contributes to a more proactive search for new forms of transaction, such as investor-led buy-outs, where the venture capital firms perceive that greater added value can be achieved (Wright and

Robbie, 1996b). These developments pose particular issues about the ability of venture capital firms to obtain such gains, especially where they are required to enter into an auction process to obtain the deal.

Second, rationalisation of funds providers may reduce the alternative sources available to venture capital firms. There may be fewer providers of domestic funds as some with poor returns exit the market and as mergers in the corporate and financial services sectors reduce the numbers of major UK pension funds and the number of major insurance companies interested in venture capital. This may be offset were venture capital to become an accepted asset class in institutional investors' portfolios, which could lead to increased allocations to venture capital funds, though liquidity requirements could offset such a shift.

Third, pressure from funds providers on management fees and carried interest produces an increased emphasis for venture capital firms to demonstrate that a high level of service is being provided. Fourth, and following from the previous point, there is an increased need for venture capital firms to differentiate themselves from their competitors to help their fundraising ability and this is an extra means of doing so. Actions could include being proactive in providing greater information on performance and developments in funds, maintaining personal contacts throughout the life of a fund rather than simply at the time of raising funds, and generally being more imaginative in identifying and satisfying the requirements of funds' providers. Of course, not all funds are likely to have the resources to provide such services, which may mean that smaller funds in particular may be placed at a competitive disadvantage. Fifth, there are at present few new domestic funds providers entering the UK market, with likely new foreign entrants, especially US state pension funds, coming from an environment where greater monitoring is increasingly expected.

The changing conditions in the market reviewed above raises the expectation that funds providers will become more proactive in their monitoring of venture capital firms. As part of this change it is also expected that in the light of information availability on performance, venture capital funds providers will increasingly set specific target returns and these returns will incorporate benchmark comparisons with alternative investment sources.

However, what is not clear is the nature of the reporting mechanisms and monitoring relationships within which information on valuations is provided. If expectations of a more proactive monitoring stance and greater focus on target returns hold, it may also be expected that more regular and systematic reporting requirements will be introduced.

In the light of this discussion, the survey reported below was designed to provide an answer to the following questions:

(a) Competition for funds

- What is the relative perceived importance of the factors influencing venture capital firms' ability to access funds in the future?

(b) Monitoring policies

- What is the current approach of funds providers to the monitoring of venture capital firms?
- Is the general approach likely to change over the next five years?
- Given the agency problems involved is there a difference between the policies of funds providers to independent venture capital firms as compared with captives or semi-captives?

(c) Performance targets

- What performance targets do funds providers set for the venture capital firms in which they invest?
- Are these targets likely to change over the next five years?
- Is there a difference between independent and other types of venture capital firm?

(d) Monitoring information

- What type of information is required by funds providers for the monitoring of venture capital firms?
- Is the type of information required likely to change over the next five years?
- Are there any differences between independent and other types of venture capital firms?

(e) Monitoring actions

- Do funds providers take any actions in respect of the venture capital firms in which they invest?
- Are any changes anticipated over the next five years?
- Is the position different between independent and other types of venture capital firm?

Data and methodology

The study involved a questionnaire survey of UK venture capital firms. Face-to-face interviews were conducted with 22 leading individuals involved in venture capital, principally chief executives of venture capital firms, identified with the assistance of the BVCA. Mailed questionnaires were sent to remaining venture capital firm members of the BVCA.

The in-depth face-to-face interviews sought additional information on developments in venture capital beyond those reported on here and which are reported in Chapter 3 and in Wright and Robbie (1996c). The questionnaire checklist for the in-depth interviews was devised by the researchers on the basis partly of past studies and recent developments which appeared to be occurring in the industry. The checklist was piloted with members of the BVCA and others, with several new questions being added at this stage. It was stressed to the interviewees that the study sought their views on market developments as individuals rather than as representatives of their particular firm. These interviews were conducted in June and July of 1996. Interviews lasted between one and two-and-a-quarter hours and were all tape recorded. Undertakings were given that the tape recordings would remain with researchers and that material from the interviews would be used to provide a general overview of developments.

The second stage of the study involved the development of a mail questionnaire which focused on the monitoring issues addressed here. The items included in the questionnaire were derived in the same way as for the in-depth interviews. The questionnaire survey was conducted in August to mid-September 1996, with a reminder letter being sent in early September.

The results from the two stages were integrated to provide an overall perspective. In total 77 responses from a total of 108 BVCA members were obtained, representing a response rate of 71.3 per cent. Respondents were overwhelmingly senior people in the industry: 60 per cent were CEOs or equivalent; 23 per cent were directors/partners; and 17 per cent were assistant directors/investment managers or equivalent.

A standard Chi^2 test of independence is used to analyse the difference between independent and non-independent (captive, semi-captive and other) venture capital firms. To analyse the changes between now (1996) and 2001 the null hypothesis of inertia (that is, each firm expects the same in 2001 as occurs now) is tested using the Chi^2 distribution with the 1996 figures generating the expected values for 2001 which can be compared to the actual responses supplied by the firms for 2001.

Results

Competition for funds

The respondents to the mail questionnaire were asked to rank the ways in which they expected competition for funds to change over the next five years on a range from 1 being the most important change, 2 being the next most important, and so on (Table 9.1).

Respondents clearly saw an increasing emphasis on previous performance to be the most important factor affecting competition for funds in the future. The second most important factor was the increasing difficulty likely to be faced for smaller venture capital firms in raising new funds. This reflects the third most important item which was expected to be an increasing focus of funds providers on investing in a few large funds, which in turn is also linked to performance issues. The fourth most important item concerned an expected increasing emphasis on differentiation of venture capitalists through added value relationships.

Table 9.1 *Changes in competition for funds over the next five years (avg. ranking)*

	Independent	Semi-captive	Captive	Other	Total
Increasing importance of co-investment rights	6.4	5.8	5.4	6.8	6.2
Increasing role of 'gatekeepers'	5.0	5.4	5.4	6.0	5.2
Increasing emphasis on previous performance	2.6	2.0	1.8	3.3	2.5
Increasing emphasis on differentiation of venture capitalists through added value relationships	4.8	3.4	5.1	3.8	4.6
Increasing competition from funds providers' own in-house venture capital products	5.8	6.8	6.6	5.8	6.0
Increasing focus of funds providers' on investing in a few larger funds	3.6	2.4	3.3	5.3	3.5
Increasingly difficult for smaller venture capitalists to raise funds	3.5	4.0	3. 6	1.8	3.4
Fewer institutions willing to provide funds for venture capital	5.6	6.8	6.9	5.0	5.9
Increasing reluctance of overseas funds to invest in UK-only opportunities	7.4	7.2	7.2	7.5	7.4

Note: Averages of rank made in order of descending importance (where 1 = most important, 2 = next most important, etc.).

Source: CMBOR/BVCA.

A number of other issues were ranked as less important, notably expectations about the reluctance of overseas funds to invest in the UK market and about the possibility that fewer institutions would be willing to provide funds for venture capital.

Some variation of views was evident between different types of venture capital firm. Venture capital firms in the 'Other' category, who are based primarily in the public sector, were most concerned about the expected increasing difficulties for smaller venture capital firms to raise funds. Semi-captives ranked the increasing focus of funds providers on investing in a few large funds as their second most important concern, and also placed more emphasis than independents or captives on the issue of increasing emphasis on differentiation of venture capital firms through added value relationships.

Funds providers' monitoring policies

Most venture capital firms (75 per cent) see their funds providers currently having a passive or reactive monitoring policy (Table 9.2). Using a Chi^2 test the hypothesis that independent and non-independent firms are the same is strongly supported. Although the numbers are small it does seem, however, that captive venture capitalists are a little more likely to view their funds providers, that is their parent companies, as more proactive than for other types.

Table 9.2 Funds providers' monitoring policy

	All		Independent		Non-independent	
	1996	2001	1996	2001	1996	2001
Passive	43.2	17.8	47.7	18.6	36.7	16.7
Reactive	32.4	41.1	29.5	41.9	36.7	40.0
Proactive	18.9	32.9	15.9	32.6	23.4	33.3
Highly proactive	5.4	8.2	6.8	7.0	3.3	10.0

Source: CMBOR/BVCA.

Overall, there is an expectation that over the next five years, there will be a shift away from passive monitoring policies. The Chi^2 test shows that these changes are significant at the 1 per cent level (value 21.5). Of the 74 firms in the sample, some 31 see themselves moving into a more active category, with 42 staying the same and only one firm expecting a decrease. While the single most likely approach is expected to be reactive, almost a third of venture capital firms expect funds providers to become proactive compared to around a fifth currently (Table 9.2). The changes are not statistically significant at the 10 per cent level.

Performance targets set by funds providers

Whilst venture capital firms may be set multiple performance targets, it is clear from Table 9.3 that a single one is the most common (62 per cent of responses). Less than 12 per cent are set two targets and 14.5 per cent are given no specific target. Overall there is no statistically significant difference between the types of venture capital firm. However, it is worth noting that a fifth of independent companies in the sample are given no specific target whilst that position applies to only one of the captive or semi-captive firms. For these latter, 70 and 80 per cent respectively are set a single target.

Table 9.3 *Number of performance targets set by funds providers (%)*

	All		Independent		Non-independent	
	1996	2001	1996	2001	1996	2001
0	14.5	6.6	20.0	8.9	6.5	3.2
1	61.8	64.5	53.3	60.0	74.2	71.0
2	11.8	15.8	11.1	15.6	12.9	16.1
3	6.6	7.9	6.7	8.9	6.5	6.5
4	3.9	3.9	6.7	4.4		3.2
5	1.3	1.3	2.2	2.2		

Source: CMBOR/BVCA.

In five years' time a much lower percentage are expected to be set no specific target. whilst there is some increase in the proportions set two or more, the most marked change occurring for the independent companies. However, these changes are not statistically significant at the 10 per cent level.

Table 9.4 *Performance targets set by funds providers*

	1996						2001					
	All		Independent		Non-independent		All		Independent		Non-independent	
	A	B	A	B	A	B	A	B	A	B	A	B
Specific raw IRR	21.3	30.3	21.7	33.3	20.5	25.8	16.7	25.0	14.1	22.2	20.9	29.0
IRR > return on other assets by given %	24.1	34.2	21.7	33.3	28.2	35.5	26.3	39.5	26.8	42.2	25.6	35.5
IRR adjusted for life of fund	4.6	6.6	5.8	8.9	2.6	3.2	3.5	5.3	5.6	8.9		
Cash amount generated over given period	14.8	21.1	17.4	26.7	10.3	12.9	14.9	22.4	16.9	26.7	11.6	16.1
IRR + cash	13.9	19.7	15.9	24.4	10.3	12.9	19.3	28.9	21.1	33.3	16.3	22.6
Annual return on capital*	5.6	7.9	1.4	2.2	12.8	16.1	7.9	11.8	4.2	6.7	14.0	19.4
No specific target	10.2	14.5	13.0	20.0	5.1	6.5	5.3	7.9	7.0	11.1	2.3	3.2
Other	5.6	7.9	2.9	4.4	10.3	12.9	6.1	9.2	4.2	6.7	9.3	12.9

Notes:
A: % responses.
B: % companies.
* hypothesis of independence rejected at 3% level.

Source: CMBOR/BVCA.

The most common target currently is an IRR which exceeds the rate of return on other asset classes by a given percentage (24 per cent of responses: 34 per cent of companies – Table 9.4) closely followed by a specific IRR (21 per cent and 30 per cent, respectively). The difference in responses between independent venture capital companies and others are not statistically significant at the 10 per cent level for all the targets except an annual return on capital. In that case the hypothesis of independence can be rejected at the 3 per cent level: captives, in particular, are more likely to be set such a target.

There is relatively little change in the distribution of these targets in five years time. For only one of the variables (combination of IRR and cash amount generated) is the difference significant at the 5 per cent level and even here only 7 of the 76 firms show a change adding 50 per cent to the number of firms using this target. The difference in responses between the two types of firm for 2001 are not statistically significantly different at the 10 per cent level for all targets.

Monitoring information required by funds providers

As Table 9.5 reveals, venture capital firms are typically required to provide between four and six pieces of information to allow the funds providers to monitor their performance with the modal figure being four (24 per cent of companies).

Table 9.5 Amount of monitoring information required

	All		Independent		Non-independent	
No.	1996	2001	1996	2001	1996	2001
0	1.3	2.7	2.2	2.2		3.3
1	6.7	6.7	4.4	4.4	10.0	10.0
2	10.7	12.0	6.7	6.7	16.7	20.0
3	12.0	6.7	13.3	4.4	10.0	10.0
4	24.0	18.7	22.2	24.4	26.7	10.0
5	16.0	21.3	20.0	20.0	10.0	23.3
6	13.3	8.0	13.3	8.9	13.3	6.7
7	8.0	10.7	11.1	11.1	3.3	10.0
8+	8.0	13.2	6.6	17.8	10.0	6.6

Source: CMBOR/BVCA.

As Table 9.6 shows, the most common information required (10–12 per cent of responses in each case) are annual reports, semi-annual reports, quarterly reports, semi-annual portfolio valuations and an annual presentation/visit. Each of these is required from over half of the companies. Thirty-seven per cent of the companies are required to provide detailed information on each deal (8 per cent of the responses), but in only 28 per cent of the cases does the funds provider have a seat on the Board of the venture capital company.

Table 9.6 Monitoring information required by funds providers

	1996						2001					
	All		Independent		Non-independent		All		Independent		Non-independent	
	A	B	A	B	A	B	A	B	A	B	A	B
Annual reports	12.1	55.4	12.0	56.8	12.3	53.3	10.7	52.1	10.4	54.5	11.5	46.7
Semi-annual reports*	12.4	56.8	14.9	70.5	8.5	36.7	10.7	52.1	12.6	65.9	7.4	30.0
Quarterly reports	11.2	51.4	9.1	43.2	14.6	63.3	11.5	56.2	10.0	52.3	14.8	60.0
Monthly/more frequent reports*	3.6	16.2	1.0	4.5	7.7	33.3	3.4	16.4	1.3	6.8	7.4	30.0
Annual portfolio valuations	8.0	36.5	8.7	40.9	6.9	30.0	6.5	31.5	6.9	36.4	5.7	23.3
Semi-annual portfolio valuations	10.4	47.3	10.1	47.7	10.8	46.7	10.1	49.3	10.0	52.3	10.7	43.3
More frequent portfolio valuations	4.1	18.9	3.8	18.2	4.6	20.0	5.9	28.8	5.2	27.3	7.4	30.0
Annual presentation/visit	10.9	50.0	11.5	54.5	10.0	43.3	8.4	41.1	8.2	43.2	9.0	36.7
Semi-annual presentation/visit	3.6	16.2	3.8	18.2	3.1	13.3	3.9	19.2	4.3	22.7	3.3	13.3
More frequent presentation/visit	2.1	9.5	1.4	6.8	3.1	13.3	3.9	19.2	4.3	22.7	3.3	13.3
Detailed information on each deal	8.3	33 7	8.7	40.9	7.7	33.3	8.7	42.5	9.5	50.0	8.2	33.3
Investor has seat on board	6.2	28.4	6.7	31.8	5.4	23. 3	6.7	32.9	7.4	38.6	5.7	23.3
Access to investor relations executives as required	4.1	18.9	4.8	22.7	3.1	13.3	5.1	24.7	6.1	31.8	3.3	13.3
Regular access to investee companies	1.2	5.4	1.4	6.8	0.8	3.3	2.2	11.0	2.2	11.4	0.8	3.3
Other	1.8	8.1	1.9	9.1	1.5	6.7	2.2	11.0	1.7	9.1	1.6	6.7

Notes:
A: % responses.
B (%) companies.
* hypothesis of independence rejected at 1% level.

Source: CMBOR/BVCA.

The differences in reporting requirements between independent companies and the others are not statistically significantly different for all the measures except semi-annual reports and monthly or more frequent reports where the hypothesis of independence can be rejected at the 1 per cent level. At an individual level, the following are worth noting: independents and semi-captives are more likely to be required to provide semi-annual reports; requirements for captives are more likely to involve quarterly reports with approaching 40 per cent also required to produce monthly reports; there is less emphasis on reporting valuations and on an annual presentation among the providers of funds to captives than is the case for independents and semi-captives; however, captives are more likely to be required to provide detailed information on each deal.

There is quite a variety in the combinations of information required across the companies and there is no combination which is used by a majority. Forty per cent of the sample supply both annual and semi-annual reports, whilst 30 per cent have an annual presentation or visit as well. The most common combination of four items (20 per cent of the sample) is annual and semi-annual reports, an annual presentation or visit and semi-annual portfolio valuations.

By the millennium there is expected to be an overall increase in the amount of information required with the model number being 5 items with 72 per cent of the sample expecting to provide four or more pieces of information. There is expected to be some decline in the emphasis on annual and semi-annual reports and on annual presentations or visits. There is also expected to be something of a shift away from annual and semi-annual portfolio valuations to more frequent ones. There are very slight indications of a shift towards the provision of information on individual deals and funds providers having a seat on the Board and almost a quarter expect there to be a requirement for access to investor relations executives on demand.

The same statistically significant differences between independents and others are observed as is the case for the 1996 data, but the general pattern is that the hypothesis of independence cannot be rejected at the 10 per cent level. In respect of individual types of venture capitalist, there are a number of notable departures from the overall position and for both captives and independents there is evidence of an expected shift to more frequent reporting, typically towards a quarterly emphasis. Captives are more likely to see a shift towards more frequent valuations than twice a year. Independents, in particular, expect to see a shift away from annual presentations and visits towards more frequent interactions with the providers of their funds: there is also an expectation that they will be more likely to be required to provide detailed information on each deal. Independents also envisage a more noticeable increase in requirements to have investors on their Boards and to allow access to investor relations executives as required, but still only in around a third of cases. Some increase is expected in allowing funds providers access to investee companies, but in very few cases. However, the only two variables for which the changes are statistically significant at the 5 per cent level are more frequent portfolio valuation and regular access by funds providers to investee companies.

As regards combinations of information, some 41 per cent are expecting to provide annual and semi-annual reports; 32 per cent are, in addition, expecting an annual presentation or visit; and 24 per cent are expecting to include semi-annual portfolio valuations as well.

Monitoring actions by funds providers

Despite their extensive reporting requirements and even though such requirements are expected to increase, funds providers are unlikely to take monitoring actions (Table 9.7). In two-thirds of cases funds providers do not currently take any monitoring actions and by the millennium over half still expect that position to remain. In 19 per cent of cases only one monitoring action is currently taken and, thus, two or more actions only applies to 14 per cent of the sample. By the millennium, 25 per cent of cases are expected to involve one monitoring action, and 19 per cent two or more. These changes are not, however, statistically significant at the 10 per cent level.

Table 9.7 Monitoring actions required by funds providers

	All		Independent		Non-independent	
	1996	2001	1996	2001	1996	2001
0	66.2	55.2	67.4	54.8	64.3	56.0
1	19.7	25.4	18.6	21.4	21.4	32.0
2	11.3	13.4	11.6	19.0	10.7	4.0
3		3.0		2.4		4.0
4	2.8	3.0	2.3	2.4	3.6	4.0

Source: CMBOR/BVCA.

The most common action currently taken is an increased amount and/or frequency of reporting followed by the introduction of Board representation (Table 9.8). In five years' time an increased amount and/or frequency of reporting remains the most likely if any action is taken, but it is expected to be closely followed by renegotiation of fees towards the end of the fund life (Table 9.8). For all the actions listed it is not possible to reject the hypothesis of independence at the 10 per cent level and hence that there are no significant differences between the responses of independents and other types of venture capital firm. Further, for none of the actions is it possible to reject the hypothesis that there is no change in response between 1996 and 2001 at this level of significance.

Table 9.8 Monitoring actions by funds providers

	1996						2001					
	All		Independent		Non-independent		All		Independent		Non-independent	
	A	B	A	B	A	B	A	B	A	B	A	B
Increased amount and/or frequency of reporting	12.9	15.5	13.7	16.3	11.8	14.3	12.8	16.4	12.7	16.7	12.9	16.0
Introduction of Board representation	8.2	9.9	9.8	11.6	5.9	7.1	9.3	11.9	10.9	14.3	6.5	8.0
Establishment of divestment policy after investee flotation	4.7	5.6	3.9	4.7	5.9	7.1	5.8	7.5	7.3	9.5	3.2	4.0
Suspension of new investment funds	4.7	5.6	3.9	4.7	5.9	7.1	2.3	3.0	1.8	2.4	3.2	4.0
Suspension of payment of management fees	1.2	1.4			2.9	3.6	3.5	4.5	3.6	4.8	3.2	4.0
Pressure to remove executives	3.5	4.2	2.0	2.3	5.9	7.1	4.7	6.0	3.6	4.8	6.5	8.0
Renegotiation of fees towards end of fund life	8.2	9.9	9.8	11.6	5.9	7.1	11.6	14.9	12.7	16.7	9.7	12.0
Other	1.2	1.4			2.9	3.6	7.0	9.0	5.5	7.1	9.7	12.0
No actions	55.3	66.2	56.9	67.4	52.9	64.3	43.0	55.2	41.8	54.8	45.2	56.0

Source: CMBOR/BVCA.

Conclusions and implications

This chapter has examined developments in funds providers' monitoring of venture capital firms in the context of recent developments in the venture capital market. The main findings can be summarised as follows.

Venture capital firms clearly see an increasing emphasis on previous performance to be the most important factor affecting competition for funds in the future. An increasing focus by funds providers on investing in a few large funds and an expected increasing emphasis on differentiation of venture capital firms through added value relationships were also seen as highly important. These changing conditions may be expected to be directly linked to changes in the monitoring of venture capital firms by funds providers.

There is a clear expectation of a shift away from passive approaches to the monitoring of venture capital firms, although new approaches may be as much reactive as proactive. The relatively minor share of venture capital in institutional investors' portfolios may be an important influence on this more reactive approach to monitoring, but as this share increases the cost–benefit trade-offs of closer monitoring may be expected to change.

There are statistically significant differences between the monitoring requirements for independent venture capital companies and all other types. There is some expectation of a shift towards target IRRs set in relation to the returns on other asset classes and/or returns for the better performers in the venture capital sector, within the context of the use of multiple performance targets. However, this shift is not expected to be strong. Similarly, there is some evidence of an expected increased use of targets set in the form of a combination between IRRs and cash amounts generated.

Between now and the next millennium it was expected that the proportion of venture capital firms not set specific target rates of return would halve. Reporting requirements are multi-layered, but there was an anticipated shift towards the greater use of quarterly reporting and portfolio valuation as well as more frequent direct contact between venture capital firms and their funds providers. In a significant minority of cases it was anticipated that there would be an increased requirement to provide regular access to investor relations executives as well as seats on boards for fund providers. Funds providers typically engage in few monitoring actions and this was generally expected to continue. The most notable change was expected to be some increased use of renegotiations of management fees towards the end of a fund's life. However, good performers may continue to be in a strong position to maintain their remuneration structures.

The monitoring of venture capital firms seems set to become an increasingly important issue for both practitioners and academic researchers and the findings of this study suggest a number of specific observations.

The findings emphasise the importance for venture capital firms of developing relationships with funds providers: first, through more frequent direct personal communication which continues over the life of a fund, and second through identifying their information needs. The development of relationships appears to have an important influence on the nature of the return target which may be set. The development of relationships is also likely to involve a growing need for venture capital firms to be proactive in providing early warning signals about impending problems. If increased monitoring and reporting is to develop, there is a need to strike an appropriate balance between the provision of specific information to meet funds providers needs and standardised information. If the role of gatekeepers increases, however, this may affect the development of relationships between venture capital firms and funds providers.

There also appears to be a continuing need to educate funds providers about the nature and timing of the returns to be earned from venture capital, especially given pressures for more frequent reporting. The development of relationships is one means of addressing this issue. However, such developments raise major cost–benefit trade-offs and resource issues.

For academic researchers, as noted in Chapter 1, there would appear to be considerable scope for researching governance issues. In contrast to the vast amount of research concerning venture capital firm–investee relationships, examination of funds providers–venture capital firm relationships has been neglected. This chapter has provided some initial insights from the perspective of venture capital firms. In the same way that recent research on investor–investee relationships has focused on the entrepreneurs' side and on dyads involving the two parties, similar possibilities would appear to present themselves in respect of funds providers and venture capital firms. Also drawing parallels with venture capital investor–investee research, there would appear to be scope for further research concerning funds providers–venture capital firm relationships which adopts a multi-theoretic perspective embracing principal–agent theory, procedural justice theory, power theory and game theory in particular.

References

Bygrave, W. (1994), 'Rates of return from venture capital', ch. 1 in W. Bygrave, M. Hay and J. Peeters (eds), *Realizing Investment Value*, London: FT-Pitman.

Fried, V. and R. Hisrich (1994), 'Towards a model of venture capital investment decision-making', *Financial Management*, **23** (3), 28–37.

Gompers, P. and J. Lerner (1996), 'The use of covenants: an empirical analysis of venture partnership agreements', *Journal of Law and Economics*, **39**, 463–98.

Jones, S., C. Rickwood and S. Greenfield (1993), *Accounting Control and Management Philosophies*, London: ICAEW Research Board.

Manigart, S., M. Wright, K. Robbie, P. Desbrieres and K. de Waele (1997),'Venture capitalists' appraisal of investment projects: an empirical European study', *Entrepreneurship: Theory and Practice*, Summer, **21** (4), 29–43.

Sahlman, W.A. (1990), 'The structure and governance of venture-capital organizations', *Journal of Financial Economics*, **27**, 473–521.

Wright, M. and K. Robbie (1996a), 'Venture capital firms and unquoted equity investment appraisal', *Accounting and Business Research*, **26**, 153–68.

Wright, M. and K. Robbie (1996b), 'The investor-led buy-out: a new strategic option', *Long Range Planning*, October, **29**, 691–702.

Wright, M. and K. Robbie (1996c), *Venture Capital into the Next Millennium*, London: BVCA.

10. Sources of venture capital deals: MBOs, IBOs and corporate refocusing

Michelle Haynes, Steve Thompson and Mike Wright

I. Introduction

Management buy-outs comprise one of the most important sectors of the UK venture capital industry. In 1995 they accounted for 31 per cent of the number of investments made by venture capitalists and 73 per cent in terms of value (BVCA, 1996). Both of these were a record share of the market. Moreover, a significant proportion of institutions focus exclusively on investing funds in later stage transactions in which buy-outs form a major part (Wright and Robbie, 1996a). Within the broad scope of buy-out activities, the largest single source of transactions is divestment of subsidiaries and divisions of larger groups, accounting for half of buy-outs in 1995 (CMBOR, 1996). In terms of the overall pattern of corporate restructuring, divestments to other organisations and management teams account for 71 per cent of the volume and 33 per cent of the value of all mergers and acquisitions in the UK in 1995.

The divestment process is typically part of corporate refocusing programmes involving a reduction in the scope of often unrelated activities by a firm, enabling it to concentrate on its core business. According to a number of authors, refocusing can be understood as an attempt to correct the problems of unsuccessful diversification, most of which occurred in the late 1960s and 1970s (Shleifer and Vishny, 1991). Unlike previous eras in corporate restructuring, the latest emphasis on focus is argued to be driven to a large extent by the desire to maximise firm value.

MBOs arising on divestment developed as attractive investments for venture capitalists as they provided risk–return trade-offs that were often better than could be obtained from investing in earlier stage transactions. This position subsequently changed as growing competitive pressures on venture capitalists led them to seek alternative means of earning attractive rates of return at a time when divestors came under increasing pressure to maximise the sales proceeds from sell-offs. Venture capitalists experiencing greater competition from both trade buyers and other private equity providers from the mid-1980s looked to MBIs as an investment route as they offered the possibility of adding value to turnaround situations. However, these too proved problematic; evidence that failure rates were significantly above those for buy-outs suggested that institutional investors had underestimated the risks involved (Wright et al., 1995). The conditions of the mid-1990s produced further pressure on venture capitalists to find investments which can generate attractive enough returns, particularly as the ending of the recession dramatically reduced the prospects for investing in buy-outs from receivership. These problems have been accentuated by intense competition between venture capitalists and a high availability of funds, producing greater pressure to identify novel investment opportunities.

One major aspect of venture capitalists' strategic response has been to become proactive in identifying potential divestment candidates, rather than reacting to proposals brought to them from divisional management or intermediaries. Venture capitalists may take the initiative in leading the acquisition themselves before bringing in incumbent management and outside managers as direct equity holders in the new entity (Wright and Robbie, 1996b). These so-called investor-led buy-outs (IBOs) attempts may increasingly face competition in the divestment process from existing corporations seeking to make strategic acquisitions. There thus becomes an important need for venture capitalists to more fully understand the divestment process.

This chapter represents one step in this direction as it examines the characteristics of refocusing firms. It uses a sample of 45 UK companies covering the period 1985–89 to analyse the prior determinants of the divestment decision. The remainder of the chapter is structured as follows. Section II provides a brief review of the empirical evidence on corporate refocusing and divestment. Section III examines the theoretical arguments for refocusing and constructs testable hypotheses. Section IV describes the data on the 45 firms to be analysed and develops statistical models based on the Poisson distribution. Section V presents the estimation results. Section VI provides a discussion of the results and conclusions are drawn in the final section.

II. Empirical evidence

In reviewing the available empirical evidence it is necessary to note the paucity of systematic research on the long-run performance consequences of a refocusing strategy to vendor companies. Most published work takes a relatively short-term measure of performance by adopting an efficient markets methodology to examine the share price effect around the time of a divestment announcement (see Wright et al., 1993, for a review of the literature). The results indicate that sellers earn significant positive excess returns, which have been shown to be related to the sale of a division to a more synergistic acquirer. Evidence shows that abnormal returns are greater for divestment announcements linked explicitly to business level strategies (Montgomery et al. 1984) or to focus-increasing transactions (John and Ofek, 1995).

Whilst both buyers and sellers earn abnormal returns from divestments, the excess returns earned by the buyer are smaller than the gains realised by the seller (Jain, 1985). This can be explained by the effects of asymmetric information between the buyer and seller on the valuation of the traded unit. Generally, this approach has not sought to distinguish the real efficiency gains from transfers from other stakeholders within the firm to equity holders. Shleifer and Summers (1988), in the context of hostile takeovers, have pointed out that shareholders' gains result, at least in part, from a breach of implicit contracts with stakeholders by the acquiring firm. For example, the acquiring management may aim to cut employment and wage levels to the disadvantage of employees. There is also evidence to suggest that existing bond (Marais et al., 1989) and pension holders (Ippolito and James, 1992) may account for some of the increased value in leveraged buy-outs if the market considers that new debt issues increase the default risk on existing debt securities or if there is a post-LBO termination of a defined benefit pension plan. Similarly, the tax savings from highly leveraged transactions represent a redistribution from the government.

An examination of the motives preceding divestment decisions indicates that poor profitability, high leverage (for example, Hoskisson et al., 1994), weak governance mechanisms (for example, Hoskisson and Turk, 1990; Thompson and Wright, 1987) and excessive diversification (for example, Markides, 1992) are among the reasons for refocusing. Wright and Robbie (1996b) also provide initial evidence that divestment programmes in the 1990s are unwinding what have turned out to be under-performing and ill-fitting subsidiaries acquired in the 1980s as part of a claimed value-enhancing strategy. In addition, a unit's relationship to other units within the firm (Duhaime and Grant, 1984) and units brought into the firm through acquisition (Ravenscraft and Scherer, 1987) are important determinants of the divestment process, suggesting that unrelated and ill-fitting operations are more likely to be divested. Findings from US divestments (Markides, 1995a) show that about 60 per cent were unrelated to the firm's core business. There is also evidence that subsidiaries which have a trading relationship with the parent may be divested if a managed market relationship improves efficiency (Wright, 1986). These findings help to explain the occurrence of related divestments. Ravenscraft and Scherer (1987) also find that a recent change in top management increases the probability of divestment.

Studies on management buy-outs (MBOs), summarised by Wright et al. (1995) have demonstrated that divestment of a unit may enable the profitability of the disposed unit to increase, partly due to the change in incentives structure post restructuring (Kaplan, 1989; Smart and Waldfogel, 1994). Thompson et al. (1992) demonstrate that managements' equity share is the dominant determinant of performance improvements, supporting the view that value gains from corporate restructuring result primarily from increasing managerial motivations (Jensen, 1989). Longer-term performance effects of MBOs are ambiguous, although there are censoring problems associated with the reversion to quoted status or the sale to a third party of the more successful firms (Kaplan, 1991).

Ex post evidence on the operating profit consequences of refocusing to vendor firms is limited, but research indicates that refocusing is associated with profitability improvements (Markides, 1995b). In addition, evidence shows that asset sales lead to an increase in the operating performance of a seller's remaining assets following divestment. Performance improvements are greater for firms that increase focus by concentrating on their core business (John and Ofek, 1995) and for firms that divest unrelated business units (Bergh, 1995).

A number of studies have started to examine whether the increase in corporate focus during the 1980s resulted in a growth in aggregate industry specialisation. Experience with refocusing in the US indicates that the increase in firms' focus has had little effect on average concentration levels in the economy as a whole (for example, Liebeskind et al., 1996). Whether this is the case in the UK remains to be established.

III. Theoretical considerations

According to a number of authors, refocusing can be understood as an attempt to correct excessive diversification, most of which occurred in the late 1960s and early 1970s. Transaction costs theory and the resource-based view of the firm (Wernerfelt, 1984) emphasise the benefits that arise when a firm diversifies to exploit its excess firm-specific assets. The issue of externalising transactions through divestment will be addressed when the costs of internalisation exceed the benefits. The optimal position of an operation may be breached when economies of scope become exhausted or when there is opportunity for capital gains by divestment to a more synergistic or related acquirer than the vendor. If this is the case, externalising the transaction by divestment to form an independent entity (for example, MBO) or to another organisation becomes worthwhile (Wright and Thompson, 1987).

This line of reasoning implies there is an optimal limit to diversification and that some firms diversified beyond their profit-maximising level in the 1960s and 1970s. As a result, a significant proportion of corporations restructured their diversified businesses during the 1980s in search of maximising shareholder value. This explanation of refocusing suggests the following testable hypotheses:

Hypothesis 1: *firm diversification will be positively correlated with corporate refocusing in the 1980s.*

Hypothesis 2: *firm profitability will be negatively correlated with corporate refocusing in the 1980s.*

One interpretation as to why firms diversified beyond their optimum level is provided by agency theory.[1] An agency relationship is 'a contract under which one or more persons (the principal(s)) engage another person (the agent) to perform some service on their behalf which involves delegating some decision making authority to the agent' (Jensen and Meckling, 1976). An agency conflict derives from the agent's tendency to pursue private objectives that are inconsistent with the interest of the principal. For example, managers have an incentive to expand and diversify operations beyond the point that optimises shareholder value, since their personal wealth and employment risk is linked more to firm size than performance. According to Jensen (1986), the conditions for such behaviour are ripe for firms in mature industries which generate greater cash flows than can be profitably reinvested.

Agency theory proposes various means by which shareholders can attempt to solve some of the agency problems created by diversification, including share option schemes and board of directors. Managers with little or no equity interest in their firm have the incentive to engage in opportunistic and ineffective behaviour to the detriment of shareholders. By increasing managers' equity ownership, managers' interests become realigned with those of other shareholders. Management equity interests discipline entrenched management to overturn complacency and inefficiency, and engage in value-maximising behaviour. As a result, we would expect to see firms with a high level of insider share ownership to divest unrelated activities to increase shareholder value. Therefore, agency theory implies the following:

Hypothesis 3: *the level of insider share ownership at the outset of the 1980s will be positively correlated with corporate refocusing during the 1980s.*

The board of directors serves as a mechanism to realign interests when ownership of a firm's stock is diffuse and free-rider problems prevent shareholders from taking a direct interest in monitoring managers. The board of directors is composed of inside directors (that is, current and former members of top management) and outsiders (that is, directors with no personal relationship with a firm other than as the position of director). If outsiders represent shareholders' interests, the higher the proportion of outside directors on a board, the greater the likelihood of board involvement in restructuring decisions that increase shareholder value (Johnson et al., 1993). Therefore, agency theory predicts that the proportion of outsiders on the board of directors at the outset of the 1980s will be positively correlated with subsequent refocusing activity:

Hypothesis 4: *the ratio of outside board members to insiders at the outset of the 1980s will be positively correlated with corporate refocusing during the 1980s.*

An additional disciplinary device on management is a high level of debt. A high debt burden implies that managers have little discretion in the allocation of free cash flow of a company (Jensen, 1986). The incentive effects associated with highly leveraged firms foster better asset utilisation and the divestment of unrelated activities as a source of liquidity to service repayments. If a high level of debt forces managers to operate efficiently, then firms with a high debt level at the outset of the 1980s should have undertaken more refocusing than other firms:

Hypothesis 5: *the level of debt at the outset of the 1980s will be positively correlated with refocusing during the 1980s.*

In addition to the above explanations of refocusing, a number of authors have suggested that restructuring may be initiated with the arrival of new top management (for example, Ravenscraft and Scherer, 1987; Gabarro, 1985). Lacking the emotional commitment of incumbent managers, a new management team is more likely to initiate the disposal of unrelated activities in an attempt to maximise market value. Therefore, we also test the following hypothesis:

Hypothesis 6: *a change in top management at the outset or during the 1980s is positively correlated with refocusing in the 1980s.*

Finally, firm size was introduced as a cross-sectional control variable in the regression analysis. Firm size has been shown to be related to governance (Aron, 1988), the level of diversification (Montgomery, 1982) and is hypothesised to be positively correlated with divestment activity. In the following section we describe the data and methodological approach on which the analysis is based.

IV. Data and methodology

Sample description and data sources

The sample comprises 45 publicly quoted companies randomly selected from the 1985 FT200 list. Companies were excluded if they were foreign-owned, if they were trading companies or if they were in the financial services sector. Information regarding acquisitions and parent-to-parent divestments was compiled from *Acquisitions Monthly* and the popular business press for the years 1985 through to 1989. Information on divestment to management buy-outs was supplied by 'The Centre for Management Buy-out Research' at the University of Nottingham. Divestments had to take place in the context of voluntary restructuring[2] to be included in the sample. Information about the sample firms was collected from various sources. Data on accounting performance, firm leverage and firm size were constructed from Datastream. SIC codes were collected from FAME and Datastream. Data on governance characteristics and diversification level were taken from company annual reports and extel cards.

Table 10.1 presents some descriptive information about the sample. The average firm studied divested 19 per cent of sales through 14.2 divestments between 1985 and 1989. Thus, the average firm made 2.71 divestments per year for prices representing 3.8 per cent of its sales in the previous year. Table 10.1 panel (B) classifies acquisitions and divestments as related or unrelated to the firm's core business. A transaction was classified as related if it belonged to the same 2-digit SIC code as the firm's core activity. Overall, there were 641 divestments and 764 acquisitions. Of these, 52 per cent of divestments were unrelated in nature, while 61 per cent of acquisitions were related. The 'refocusing ratio' (defined as related acquisitions plus unrelated divestments as a percentage of unrelated acquisitions plus related divestments) equals 1.30, which implies that firms were refocusing by the logic described in Section I.

Table 10.1 Sample characteristics

(A) Seller characteristics		Mean	s.d.
Total number of divestments over period		14.200	11.929
Selling price of divestments over period (£m's)[a]		586.073	1051.148
Ratio of sales price to total sales over period		0.189	0.229
(B) Methods of refocusing	**Total**	**Related[b]**	**Unrelated**
Divestments by all firms	641	309	322
Acquisitions by all firms	764	464	300

Notes:

a In the absence of a selling price, the lowest observed value of a divestment by a firm was assigned. This method implicitly assumes that unreported values represent the lowest priced divestments. In this respect, the figure in the table is a lower bound estimate of divestment value over the period.

b Any transaction belonging to the same 2-digit SIC as the firm's core, defined as the 2-digit SIC in which the company has the largest percentage of its sales (information from Datastream). Related acquisitions + Unrelated divestments/Unrelated acquisitions + Related divestments = 1.30.

To measure the extent of refocusing, each firm's diversification level was calculated for the years 1984 and 1989 using the Berry–Herfindahl and entropy measures of diversification (see Appendix). Firms were classified as refocused if their level of diversification decreased over the period. Employing this method, approximately 52 per cent of firms reversed their previous trend towards conglomeration and narrowed the scope of their activities. This figure dominates the number of firms (45 per cent) who diversified further during the period.

Model specification and description of variables

Consideration of the hypotheses lead to the following model specification:

$$y_i = f(\mathbf{X}_i), \text{ where}$$
$$\mathbf{X}_i = (\text{PERF}_i, \text{GEAR}_i, \text{BOARD}_i, \text{INSIDER}_i, \text{SIZE}_i, \text{DIVERS}_i, \text{CEO})$$
$$i = 1, 2, \ldots, n$$

where y_i denotes the number of divestments by the ith firm, PERF is firm performance, GEAR is financial gearing, BOARD is board composition, INSIDER is insider share ownership, SIZE is firm size, DIVERS is diversification level and CEO is change in top management. Each variable is defined in Table 10.2.

Since the observations on divestment are count data, we estimate the above model based on the Poisson distribution.[3] The Poisson distribution is widely used in analysing count data where the dependent variable has a non-negligible probability of zero and is defined for non-negative integers corresponding to the number of events occurring in a given interval. The Poisson probability model captures the discrete and non-negative nature of count data, and allows inference to be drawn on the probability of the event occurring. In comparison, the usual normal probability model for which OLS is the maximum likelihood estimator, admits of fractional as well as negative integers, and does not represent the true data generating process underlying non-negative counts. Application of the normal distribution to analyse non-negative counts will produce inefficient parameter estimates and biased inference.

We model the number of divestments as being generated by the following Poisson process:

$$\text{Prob}(y_i) = \lambda_i^{y_i} e^{-\lambda_i} / y_i! \qquad y_i = 0,1,\ldots \qquad i = 1,2,\ldots,n$$

where λ_i is the conditional mean and variance of the Poisson distribution. The most common formulation for λ_i is to assume that λ_i is log-linearly dependent on the explanatory variables:

$$\ln\lambda_i = \mathbf{X}_i\beta$$

where $\mathbf{X}_i$ is a vector of regressors. This parameterisation ensures the non-negativity of λ. The log-likelihood function for the sample of n firms can be written as:

Table 10.2 Definition of variables

Variable	Definition/measurement
Divestment	A count of the total number of divestments undertaken by each firm during 1985–89.
Firm performance	Accounting-based performance was measured using three indicators: (1) return on capital employed (ROCE); (2) return on equity (ROE); and (3) return on sales (ROS). All values were calculated one year prior to divestment and as an average over the three years preceding the divestment programme.
Financial gearing	Financial gearing was measured using two variables: (1) the ratio of debt to total assets; and (2) the ratio of debt to equity, both measured as book values. Both values were calculated one year prior to divestment and as an average over the three years preceding the divestment programme.
Board composition	Representation of outsiders on a board was calculated as the ratio of the number of outside directors to inside directors.
Insider share ownership	The equity interest of directors is calculated as the ratio of ordinary shares held by directors to the total number of issued and fully paid ordinary shares of the company.
Firm size	The book value of total assets (ASSETS), total sales (SALES) and the number of employees (EMP) were used as proxies for firm size.
Diversification level	The level of firm diversification was measured using two indices: (1) the Berry–Herfindahl index (HERF); and (2) the entropy index (ENTROP).
CEO	Dummy variable = 1 if the chief executive or managing director of a firm changed immediately prior or during the sample period; 0 otherwise.

$$\ln L = \Sigma (y_i \mathbf{X}_i \beta - \lambda_i - \ln y_i!)$$

Parameter estimates are obtained by solving the first order condition using Newton's iterative techniques:

$$\partial L / \partial \beta = \Sigma (y_i - \lambda_i) \mathbf{X}_i = 0$$

Global concavity of the log-likelihood function ensures rapid convergence to a unique solution. This property follows from the negative–definite Hessian matrix of the likelihood function:

$$\partial L/\partial\beta\partial\beta' = -\Sigma(\mathbf{X}_i'\mathbf{X}_i\lambda_i)$$

In our application, convergence to unique maximum likelihood (ML) estimates was always rapid. Estimates of the asymptotic variances of the ML estimates, which are needed to compute *t*-statistics, are obtained from the negative inverse of the above matrix.

One restriction of the basic Poisson model is the imposition of an equal conditional mean and variance. In many economic applications, it is not uncommon to find that the variance of y_i exceeds the mean, implying 'overdispersion' in the data. Overdispersion, or extra-Poisson variation, occurs if there is unobserved heterogeneity or interdependence between events, for instance, prior events influence the probability of future occurrences of the same event. The latter cause of overdispersion is to be suspected in many economic phenomena. An important consequence of fitting overdispersed data to the Poisson model, is that the estimated covariance matrix will be biased downwards, producing spuriously small estimated standard errors of the parameter estimates and overstated *t*-statistics. The presence of overdispersion has consequences similar to those for heteroscedasticity in the classical linear regression model, that is, the estimated standard errors are inefficient and invalidate hypothesis testing.

A solution to the problem of overdispersion is to use a distribution that allows for a less restricted variance function. Within these generalisations the negative binomial model has been proposed as a useful alternative to the Poisson model (for example, Cameron and Trivedi, 1986). The negative binomial model allows for unobserved heterogeneity in the mean function by introducing an additional stochastic component to λ_i:

$$\ln \lambda_i = \mathbf{X}_i\beta + \varepsilon_i$$

where ε_i captures unobserved heterogeneity and is uncorrelated with the explanatory variables. The model can be derived by assuming λ_i to be distributed randomly and follow a gamma distribution of the form:[4]

$$f(\lambda_i) = 1/\Gamma(1/\alpha)^{1/\alpha} e^{-\lambda_i/\alpha} \lambda_i^{1/\alpha-1}$$

By choosing the particular form of gamma distribution given above, one obtains a model which has the same conditional mean as the Poisson model but admits of overdispersion since:

$$\text{var}\,(y_i|\mathbf{X}_i\beta) = \lambda_i(1 + \alpha\lambda_i) > \text{var}\,(y_i|\mathbf{X}_i\beta) = \lambda_i$$

Since the mean equals the variance when y_i is Poisson distributed, the natural basis for testing the adequacy of the Poisson model is to propose tests of the form $\alpha = 0$.

In the following sections we present the estimation results of the above models and discuss their fit to the divestment data.

V. Results

Table 10.3 presents the descriptive statistics and correlations among the dependent and explanatory variables. Some of the variables in the model use several measures to capture the same phenomenon and are highly correlated. By introducing them separately into the regression model and given that the inter-correlations among the remaining variables are sufficiently low, the problem of multicollinearity is minimised. The information presented on the number of divestments suggests the importance of testing the validity of the Poisson specification since the variance of the dependent variable is appreciably greater than the mean.

The estimation results for three different models are presented in Table 10.4. Throughout the dependent variable is a count corresponding to the number of divestments during 1985–89. The OLS estimates in column (1) have been included for comparison purposes. Although the regression is statistically significant at the 99 per cent level, it shows a negligible role for a majority of the explanatory variables.

The results from the Poisson model are given in column (2). Since we suspect that overdispersion is a feature of our data, we tested the moment restrictions implied by the Poisson model. Rejection of the mean–variance equality lead us to re-estimate the regression using the negative binomial model. The negative binomial estimates are reported in column (3). The Wald statistic for testing the Poisson model against the negative binomial model equals 2.687. The corresponding likelihood ratio statistic is 80.46 (that is, –2[–142.145 – (– 182.376)]). Both tests are significant at the 99 per cent level and again lead to a rejection of the Poisson model. Although this does not imply that the negative binomial model is an automatic alternative choice, it is favoured to the Poisson specification for this data set.

Turning to a comparison of the parameter estimates in columns (1)–(3), we notice that whilst there are some similarities in the results, there are also noticeable differences. In particular, the estimated variances of the Poisson model are considerably smaller than those of the negative binomial estimates, reflecting the consequences of imposing the mean–variance equality on the data. The signs of the coefficients generally come out as predicted from the discussion in Section III and are largely unchanged by a change in model specification.

Table 10.3 Means, standard deviations and intercorrelations

Variables	Mean	s.d.	1	2	3	4	5	6	7	8	9	10	11	12	13	14	15	16	17	18	19
1 No. of divestments	14.20	11.92	1.00																		
2 ROCE	0.18	0.04	–0.36	1.00																	
3 ROCE (av.)	0.17	0.04	–0.29	0.90	1.00																
4 ROE	0.15	0.05	–0.04	0.73	0.72	1.00															
5 ROE (av.)	0.14	0.05	–0.17	0.74	0.84	0.93	1.00														
6 ROS	0.07	0.02	–0.04	0.17	0.22	0.15	0.15	1.00													
7 ROS (av.)	0.07	0.02	–0.04	0.16	0.26	0.17	0.21	0.95	1.00												
8 Debt to total assets	0.31	0.12	0.36	–0.23	–0.21	0.25	0.15	–0.21	–0.17	1.00											
9 Debt to total assets (av.)	0.30	0.12	0.38	–0.27	–0.28	0.15	0.03	–0.18	–0.14	0.93	1.00										
10 Debt to equity	0.57	0.36	0.05	–0.21	–0.16	0.31	0.18	–0.13	–0.11	0.91	0.83	1.00									
11 Debt to equity (av.)	0.53	0.29	0.48	–0.26	–0.25	0.20	0.07	–0.12	–0.09	0.89	0.93	0.93	1.00								
12 Board composition	0.57	0.43	0.06	–0.01	–0.05	–0.03	–0.05	–0.01	–0.05	–0.05	0.03	–0.08	0.04	1.00							
13 Insider share ownership	0.02	0.05	–0.17	0.04	0.06	0.05	0.06	–0.23	–0.22	0.06	0.03	0.05	0.06	–0.14	1.00						
14 Employees	49.94	53.12	0.34	–0.12	–0.07	–0.06	–0.11	0.01	0.01	0.01	0.02	–0.06	0.06	–0.23	–0.05	1.00					
15 Assets	1597.99	3673.08	0.21	–0.08	–0.10	–0.07	–0.13	0.08	0.08	–0.02	0.01	0.05	0.09	0.12	–0.10	0.56	1.00				
16 Sales	3262.71	6999.55	0.21	–0.05	–0.06	–0.03	–0.09	0.02	0.03	–0.01	0.04	0.05	0.08	0.08	–0.07	0.62	0.98	1.00			
17 Herfindahl index	0.57	0.22	0.36	–0.37	–0.34	–0.30	–0.37	0.04	0.01	0.15	0.23	0.18	0.25	0.15	–0.35	0.18	0.08	0.06	1.00		
18 Entropy index	1.10	0.48	0.42	–0.38	–0.34	–0.24	–0.34	0.02	–0.24	0.23	0.29	0.28	0.33	0.15	–0.29	0.20	0.12	0.10	0.97	1.00	
19 CEO	0.75	0.43	–0.24	0.16	0.11	–0.04	–0.19	0.01	–0.01	–0.24	–0.27	–0.27	–0.29	0.01	–0.16	–0.22	–0.28	–0.28	0.05	0.01	1.00

Financial gearing, firm size, board composition and the diversification level enter positively, and profitability enters negatively in all regressions. The coefficients on CEO and insider share ownership change from negative to positive in going from the Poisson to the negative binomial model, although they both remain highly insignificant.

Table 10.4 Characteristics of refocusing firms

Independent variables	(1)	(2)	(3)
Constant	–7.826	0.982	0.860
	(–0.549)	***(2.431)	(0.933)
ROCE	–8.117	–0.665	–0.652
	(–1.248)	***(–3.982)	*(–1.703)
Debt to total assets	6.086	0.557	0.476
	**(1.987)	***(4.937)	*(1.735)
Board composition	1.3092	0.105	0.113
	(1.077)	***(3.282)	(1.479)
Insider share ownership	–0.158	–0.006	0.012
	(–0.203)	(–0.303)	(0.337)
EMP	5.088	0.354	0.387
	***(2.335)	***(6.091)	**(2.302)
ENTROP	1.124	0.130	0.119
	(1.224)	***(3.390)	**(2.009)
CEO	–1.710	–0.065	0.015
	(–0.426)	(–0.699)	(0.059)
– ln L		–182.376	–142.145
Variance parameter α			0.205
			***(2.687)
R^2	0.37		

Notes:
$n = 44$.
t-statistics appear in parentheses.
* $p < 0.1$.
** $p < 0.05$.
*** $p < 0.01$.

Since we have argued that the negative binomial specification is the most appropriate, the remainder of the paper concentrates on the estimates from the negative binomial model. Turning to the tests of the hypotheses themselves, the negative binomial estimates provide support for some of the hypotheses in Section III. The coefficient on ROCE is negative and significant, implying that

Table 10.5 Regression results with different measures of profitability, firm size, financial gearing and diversification level

Independent variables	(1)	(2)	(3)	(4)	(5)
Constant	0.577	1.080	1.131	0.732	–0.541
	(0.705)	*(1.625)	(1.316)	(0.623)	(–0.466)
ROCE	–0.671				–0.819
	*(–1.816)				** (–2.037)
ROE		–0.336	–0.316		
		** (–1.982)	*(–1.784)		
ROS				–0.257	
				(–1.071)	
Debt to total assets			0.548	0.491	
			**(1.894)	*(1.609)	
Debt to equity	0.394	0.438			0.349
	***(2.362)	***(2.596)			**(2.073)
Board composition	0.112	0.107	0.071	0.076	0.091
	(1.512)	(1.367)	(1.001)	(0.959)	(1.318)
Insider ownership	0.003	0.016	0.002	–0.009	–0.008
	(0.086)	(0.408)	(0.041)	(–0.240)	(–0.202)
EMP	0.365	0.382			
	**(2.243)	**(2.262)			
ASSETS			0.263	0.285	
			***(2.353)	***(2.397)	
SALES					0.273
					**(2.308)
ENTROP		0.118		0.128	0.108
		**(1.923)		**(2.023)	*(1.847)
HERF	0.116		0.097		
	*(1.647)		*(1.659)		
CEO	0.051	–0.022	–0.128	–0.095	–0.031
	(0.199)	(–0.079)	(–0.467)	(–0.352)	(–0.129)
– ln L	141.334	141.646	144.940	145.504	142.760
Variance parameter	0.194	0.198	0.243	0.250	0.214
α	***(2.622)	***(2.720)	***(2.654)	***(2.830)	***(2.344)

Notes:
n = 44.
t-statistics appear in parentheses.
* $p < 0.1$.
** $p < 0.05$.
*** $p < 0.01$.

poor performance is an important influence on the divestment decision. In addition, high leverage at the outset of the 1980s is positively and significantly correlated with divestment activity during the 1980s. As we expect, large firms and more diversified firms have a higher propensity to divest. It is clear that the data provide little evidence of a change in top management, board composition and the level of insider share ownership as having an effect on the divestment decision.

Further sensitivity analysis

We also test the sensitivity of the results to the exact definition of our explanatory variables. The regression equation is calculated using different measures of profitability, capital gearing, firm size, and diversification level. The results from some of the regressions are reported in Table 10.5. The basic relationships uncovered above remain largely the same. We find similar results when profitability was measured using ROE but the regression equations have a statistically insignificant profitability variable when ROS is used. Financial gearing remains positive and significant throughout, regardless of the measurement. Again, we can take this as evidence in support of hypothesis 4. Similarly, the expected signs and statistical significance for the measures of firm size and diversification level, are representative of the results obtained above.

Table 10.6 Regression results with proportion of divestments as dependent variable

Independent variables	
Constant	–4.728 ***(–4.095)
ROCE	–1.118 **(–2.123)
Debt to total assets	0.799 ***(3.221)
Board composition	0.220 **(2.235)
Insider share ownership	0.059 (0.941)
EMP	0.208 (1.179)
ENTROP	0.139 *(1.868)
CEO	0.028 (0.087)
R^2	0.47

Notes:
n = 44.
t-statistics appear in parentheses.
* $p < 0.1$.
** $p < 0.05$.
*** $p < 0.01$.

In Table 10.6 we present the results from the OLS regression model in which divestment activity is measured as the percentage of sales divested. Percentage of sales divested was calculated as the sale price of a sold unit divided by the firm's total sales for the previous year, a similar measure to that used by Hoskisson et al. (1994). In the absence of a reported sales price, the lowest observed value of a divestment by a firm was assigned. This method implicitly assumes that the unreported values represent the lowest priced divestments. In this respect, the figure obtained is a lower bound estimate of the proportion of divestments. The signs of the coefficients are similar to those in column (3), Table 10.4, reinforcing the results obtained from the count data model. The only noticeable difference from the negative binomial regression results is the level of significance on firm size and board composition.

VI. Discussion

The main findings in this chapter are that profitability, leverage, firm size and firm strategy correlate significantly with divestment activity during the 1980s. These findings appear fairly robust and are not sensitive to the definition of the variables or the model specification. The results obtained from applying a methodological approach based on count data, corroborate findings from previous research on corporate restructuring.

Unlike previous research on corporate governance in determining restructuring, we fail to find a relationship of outside directors and management equity interests to restructuring activity. Our results provide no support for the benefits of internal governance mechanisms as a device for initiating structural change. The results may improve by including valuations of executive share options in the estimation of insider share ownership, to help capture the full extent to which managers directly bear the wealth consequences of their decisions. A recent study by Main et al. (1996) shows that the effect of including an options component in calculating executive pay is to produce a more performance-sensitive remuneration package, helping alleviate agency problems. Finally, our results provide no support for the view that a change in top management increases the probability of divestment.

Given the small sample size, it was not possible to obtain any significant results for the subset of firms who refocused over the period. Future research efforts intend to increase the sample size and develop the model in the context of panel data. Preliminary investigations indicate that a panel approach improves the results from applying the Poisson distribution to the data. In addition, the relationship between acquisitions and divestments needs to be explored further, in particular, whether acquisitions are correlated with divestments over time.

VII. Conclusions

Throughout much of the 1980s and into the 1990s, refocusing has been an important form of corporate restructuring in the UK. The desire to focus on a few core strengths is evident from the type of restructuring transactions prevalent during the period. We have shown that firms were refocusing by divesting unrelated assets and acquiring related businesses.

The aim of the chapter has been to enhance venture capitalists' understanding of the characteristics of refocusing firms by concentrating on the divestment process. Applying a count data model to observations on divestment, the results show that asset sales are correlated with high leverage and poor performance at the firm level. In addition, firm size and diversification strategy are positively related to divestment activity. Board composition, management equity interests and a change in top management have no effect on the divestment decision. The evidence provides support for previous studies on divestment and refocusing, and has shown that divestment is more than just a phenomenon associated with the sale of poorly performing operations.

The evidence in the chapter goes some way to explaining the nature of firms that are refocusing, however, there are still a number of questions about the specific strategy of refocusing firms which need to be explored. In particular, there is a paucity of systematic evidence on the long-run performance consequences of a refocusing strategy to UK vendor companies. This may be particularly of interest given recent case study evidence which suggests that a second wave of corporate restructuring is already in process as corporations undo acquisitions completed in the 1980s which have become under-performing or ill-fitting (Wright and Robbie, 1996b).

Appendix

The Berry–Herfindahl index of total diversification (DT) is calculated across n industry segments as 'one minus the sum of the squares of each segment i's sales, S_i, as a proportion of total sales':

$$DT = 1 - \Sigma (S_i/S)^2 \qquad i = 1,2, \ldots, n$$

The entropy components of diversification are defined as:

$$DT = \Sigma P_i \ln (1/P_i) \qquad i = 1,2 \ldots, n$$

where P_i is the share of the ith segment in the total sales of the firm and $\ln(1/P_i)$ is the weight for each segment i. Both are continuous measures and take into account the number of segments in which a firm operates and the relative importance of each of the segments in total sales. The closer DT is to zero, the more concentrated are a firm's sales within a few of its industry segments.

The diversification indices are computed treating SIC industries at the 3-digit level as the industry segments. Given the nature of disclosure in company accounts, it was not possible to disaggregate a firm's sales at the 4-digit level.

In the few cases where a unique SIC code was not assigned to a segment, an upper bound estimate of one product segment (or two segments in the case where sales were greater than in the smallest defined industry segment) was assumed. For both these reasons, the extent of diversification by a firm will tend to be underestimated.

Notes

1. Other explanations include mistaken stock market signals to diversifying acquisitions, managers' overoptimism about their ability to transfer assets across industries ('hubris' hypothesis; Roll, 1986) and tax savings considerations.
2. Voluntary restructuring refers to companies that freely initiate a programme of restructuring as opposed to restructuring in response to competition policy.
3. For an example of a methodological approach using count data see Hausman et al. (1984) who apply the Poisson distribution to count data on patent applications across firms.
4. This is only one of a number of possible parameterisations of the gamma distribution.

References

Aron, D.J. (1988), 'Ability, moral hazard, firm size and diversification', *Rand Journal of Economics*, **19**, 72–87.

Bergh, D.D. (1995), 'Size and relatedness of units sold: an agency theory and resource-based perspective', *Strategic Management Journal*, **16**, 221–39.

BVCA (1996), *Report on Investment Activity*, London: BVCA.

Cameron, A.C. and P.K. Trivedi (1986), 'Econometric models based on count data: comparisons and applications of some estimators and tests', *Journal of Applied Econometrics*, **1**, 29–53).

CMBOR (1996), 'Management buy-outs', Quarterly Review from CMBOR, University of Nottingham.

Duhaime, I. and J. Grant (1984), 'Factors influencing divestment decision-making: evidence from a field study', *Strategic Management Journal*, **5**, 301–18.

Gabarro, J.J. (1985), 'When a new manager takes charge', *Harvard Business Review*, **63** (3), 110–23.

Hausman, J., B.H. Hall and Z. Griliches (1984), 'Econometric models for count data with an application to the patents–R&D relationship', *Econometrica*, **52** (4), 909–38.

Hoskisson, R.E. and M.A. Hitt (1994), *Downscoping: How to Tame the Diversified Firm*, New York: Oxford University Press.

Hoskisson, R.E. and T.A. Turk (1990), 'Corporate restructuring: governance and control limits of the internal capital market', *Academy of Management Review*, **15** (3), 459–77.

Hoskisson, R.E., R.A. Johnson and D.D. Moesel (1994), 'Corporate divestiture intensity in restructuring firms: effects of governance, strategy and performance', *Academy of Management Journal*, **37** (5), 1207–51.

Ippolito, R.A. and W.H. James (1992), 'LBOs, reversions and implicit contracts', *The Journal of Finance*, **47** (1), 139–67.

Jain, P.C. (1985), 'The effect of voluntary sell-off announcements on shareholder wealth', *The Journal of Finance*, **40** (l), 209–24.

Jensen, M. (1986), 'Agency costs of free cash flow, corporate finance, and takeovers', *American Economic Review Papers and Proceedings*, **76** (2), 323–29.

Jensen, M. (1989), 'The eclipse of the public corporation', *Harvard Business Review*, **67** (5), 61–74.

Jensen, M. and W. Meckling (1976), 'The theory of the firm: managerial behaviour, agency costs and ownership structure', *Journal of Financial Economics*, **3**, 305–60.

John, K. and E. Ofek (1995), 'Asset sales and increase in focus', *Journal of Financial Economics*, **37**, 105–26.

Johnson, R.A., R.E. Hoskisson and M.A. Hitt (1993), 'Board of director involvement in restructuring: the effects of board versus managerial controls and characteristics', *Strategic Management Journal*, **14**, 33–50.

Kaplan, S. (1989), 'The effects of management buyouts on operating performance and value', *Journal of Financial Economics*, **24** (2), 217–54.
Kaplan, S. (1991), 'The staying power of leveraged buy-outs', *Journal of Financial Economics*, **29** (2), 287–314.
Liebeskind, J.P., T.C. Opler and D.E. Hatfield (1996), 'Corporate restructuring and the consolidation of US industry', *The Journal of Industrial Economics*, **XLIV** (1), 53–68.
Main, B.G., A. Bruce and T. Buck (1996), 'Total board remuneration and company performance', *The Economic Journal*, **106**, 1627–44.
Marais, L., K. Schipper and A. Smith (1989), 'Wealth effects of going private for senior securities', *Journal of Financial Economics*, **23** (l), 155–91.
Markides, C. (1992), 'Consequences of corporate refocusing: ex ante evidence', *Academy of Management Journal*, **35** (2), 398–412.
Markides, C. (1995a), *Diversification, Refocusing and Economic Performance*, Cambridge, MA: The MIT Press.
Markides, C. (1995b), 'Diversification, restructuring and economic performance', *Strategic Management Journal*, **16**, 101–18.
Montgomery, C.A. (1982), 'The measurement of firm diversification: some new evidence', *Academy of Management Journal*, **25**, 299–307.
Montgomery, C.A., A.R. Thomas and R. Kamath (1984), 'Divestiture, market valuation, and strategy', *Academy of Management Journal*, **27** (4), 830–40.
Ravenscraft, D.J. and F.M. Scherer (1987), *Mergers, Sell-offs and Economic Efficiency*, Washington, DC: The Brookings Institution.
Roll, R. (1986), 'The hubris hypothesis of corporate takeovers', *Journal of Business*, **59** (2), 197–216.
Shleifer, A. and L. Summers (1988), 'Breach of trust in hostile takeovers', in A. Anerbach (ed.), *Corporate Takeovers: Causes and Consequences*, Chicago: University of Chicago Press, pp. 33–67.
Shleifer, A. and R.W. Vishny (1991), 'Takeovers in the '60s and the '80s: evidence and implications', *Strategic Management Journal*, **12**, 51–9.
Smart, S.B. and J. Waldfogel (1994), 'Measuring the effect of restructuring on corporate performance: the case of management buyouts', *The Review of Economics and Statistics*, **76** (3), 503–11.
Thompson, S. and M. Wright (1987), 'Management buy-outs, debt finance and agency costs: a critical appraisal', CMBOR Occasional Paper 2.
Thompson, S., M. Wright and K. Robbie (1992), 'Buyouts, divestment and leverage: restructuring transactions and corporate governance', *Oxford Review of Economic Policy*, **8** (3), 58–69.
Wernerfelt, B. (1984). 'A resource-based view of the firm', *Strategic Management Journal*, **5**, 171–80.
Wright, M. (1986), 'The make–buy decision and managing markets: the case of management buy-outs', *Journal of Management Studies*, **23** (4), 443–65.
Wright, M. and K. Robbie (1996a), 'Venture capitalists, unquoted equity investment appraisal and the role of accounting information', *Accounting and Business Research*, **26** (2), 153–70.
Wright, M. and K. Robbie (1996b), 'The investor-led buy-out: a new strategic option', *Long Range Planning*, **29**, 691–702.
Wright, M. and S. Thompson (1987), 'Divestment and the control of divisionalised firms', *Accounting and Business Research*, **17**, 259–67.
Wright, M., B. Chiplin and S. Thompson (1993), 'The market for corporate control: divestments and buy-outs', in M. Bishop and J. Kay (eds), *European Mergers and Merger Policy*, Oxford: Oxford University Press, 96–133.
Wright, M., S. Thompson, K. Robbie and P. Wong (1995), 'MBOs in the short and long term', *Journal of Business and Financial Accounting*, **22**, 461–82.

11. Venture capitalists, investment appraisal and accounting information: a comparative study of the US, UK, France, Belgium and Holland

Sophie Manigart, Koen De Waele, Mike Wright, Ken Robbie, Philippe Desbrières, Harry Sapienza and Amy Beekman

Introduction

Evidence is now emerging of the contrasting approaches used by venture capitalists to appraise investments in unquoted firms (Wright and Robbie, 1996a). However, there is very limited evidence which compares approaches in different countries. This appears to be an important omission since it is increasingly recognised that culture plays a significant role in the conduct of business (Hofstede, 1984) such that important differences may be apparent between countries in the operation of similar activities. Further, Hampden-Turner and Trompenaars (1993) show that the values of managers vary between countries; on this basis they group managers in the US, UK and the Netherlands together in a separate group from those in France, Japan and Germany. There are also marked differences in governance systems between countries. The US and UK have been characterised as having market-based systems where the disciplinary role of capital markets and the market for corporate control are important. In continental Europe, governance systems can be viewed as network-oriented (Moerland, 1995). In respect of venture capital and related industries previous studies have highlighted the heterogeneity of such markets across differing countries (Wright et al., 1992; Manigart, 1994; Sapienza et al., 1996). Sapienza et al., who covered the same countries as in this study, find that in respect of monitoring roles, practices in the UK were most like those in the US, with those in France being least like the other countries. In the light of such general evidence, differences may also be expected in the approaches to the valuation of venture capital projects and the information used in the screening process.

This chapter seeks to fill the gap in research with respect to international comparisons, at least in part, by examining the activities of venture capitalists in relation to the appraisal of investment opportunities in unquoted firms in five different countries – the US, UK, France, Belgium and Holland – selected on the basis that their venture capital markets were sufficiently developed to permit meaningful quantitative surveys and afforded comparisons between different types of regime. The results of the study show that evidence on the due diligence and valuation stages of venture capital investment decisions and the relative importance of different types of accounting and financial information from the UK (Wright and Robbie, 1996a) cannot be generalised to other countries.

The chapter provides evidence relating to the general policies adopted by venture capitalists in each country in terms of approaches to due diligence, valuation methods, benchmark rates of return and adjustments for risk. The types of accounting and non-accounting information utilised in arriving at valuations and risk-adjusted rates of return are analysed. The chapter is structured as follows. The following section discusses the conceptual issues concerning the due diligence and valuation stages of venture capital investment decisions and the importance of accounting and financial information in the international context of the chapter. In particular, this section discusses structural differences between the markets, due diligence, valuation methods, information for valuation, required rates of return, assessment of the riskiness of proposals and differences between venture capitalists in terms of different investment stage focus and captive (dependent) versus independent venture capitalists. The third section describes the data and methodology utilised in the study and the fourth section presents the results. The final section discusses the implications of the results and suggests some conclusions.

Comparisons between the venture capital markets in the five countries

There is now extensive evidence concerning the stages of the venture capital investment process, with the general behaviour of venture capitalists in these stages being influenced at least to some extent by the structure of the industry, including the relative importance of different investment stages and captive versus independent venture capitalists (Elango et al., 1995; Wright and Robbie, 1998). It is thus necessary to have some understanding of the different structural composition of individual venture capital markets. Following the approach adopted by Wright and Robbie (1996a) for the UK, the empirical results in this chapter focus on the stage in the appraisal process after a proposal has passed through initial screens and has reached a stage where detailed valuation and assessment of potential returns takes place. During this stage there is a need for firm-wide policies as well as detailed accounting and financial information. These policies relate to due diligence and valuation methods, benchmark target returns, approaches to the assessment of returns from a potential investee and to the assessment of project riskiness. This section develops the analysis of Wright and

Robbie (1996a) by discussing the conceptual aspects relating to each of these aspects in turn in an international context.

Structural differences in venture capital markets

From major initial developments in the US, there has been a diffusion of venture capital market growth first to the UK and then throughout Europe and beyond. Tyebjee and Vickery (1988) note the variation in maturity of different venture capital markets in Europe, while Roure et al. (1990), Ooghe et al. (1991) and Murray (1995) argue that market development is likely to be associated with greater competition, reduced rates of return and a shift to later stage investments. Manigart (1994) finds support for a population ecology approach to the entry of firms into venture capital markets, with the major influences on the overall founding rate being the density of the industry. Interestingly, institutional changes were not found to be influential. Wright et al. (1992), in examining the management buy-out sector of the overall venture capital market, suggest that institutional changes are important at least in the initial stages of market development, but that subsequently new entrants are encouraged by evidence that attractive returns are being earned. Roure et al. (1990) also show that greater market maturity is associated with entry by a greater variety of funds providers, especially by pension funds and insurance companies. Ooghe et al. (1991) support this view and in addition find that public sector funds providers are more likely to exit. However, Ooghe, et al. also suggest that venture capital industries in different countries have unique characteristics which are associated with different behaviour between countries.

Table 11.1 shows some key characteristics of the venture capital industries in the five countries of our study. In absolute terms, the markets differ quite substantially, with the US market being larger than the other four markets combined, and the UK in turn being larger than the other three continental European markets combined. As seen in Chapter 3, the markets also vary considerably in relation to countries' GDP in 1995. The annual investments made by US venture capitalists in 1995 was 0.05 per cent of GDP In Europe, while the UK venture capital industry amounts to 0.33 per cent of that country's GDP, in France the comparable figure is only 0.07 per cent. The Dutch market figures as 0.19 per cent of GDP, while that in Belgium is 0.05 per cent.

The French, Dutch and Belgian venture capital industries have a much higher proportion of investors that are dependent on a financial institution or on an industrial parent company than their British and American counterparts. A specific feature of the Belgian venture capital industry is that government-backed venture capital companies play a very important role. European venture capitalists invest much less in early stage ventures than American ones, while expansion investments are more popular. However, there are also differences between the European countries examined in this study. Management buy-outs

Table 11.1 Overview of the venture capital industry in the five countries in 1994

Figures in million US$	USA	UK	France	Belgium	Netherlands
Total new funds for venture capital	4400 (1995)	2882	790	67	193
Total funds invested		1698	815	80	242
Distribution of investments by investor type					
Independent		65.4%	33.1%	23.4%	64.2%
Captive		21.4%	40.4%	34.9%[1]	28.5%
Semi-captive		12.5%	25.3%	n.a.	0.0%
Public sector		1.4%	1.0%	41.5%	7.1%
Distribution of investments by investment stage					
Seed	36%	0.1%	0.2%	1.1%	2.0%
Start-up	(early stage)	2.4%	2.0%	12.8%	11.0%
Expansion		28.6%	46.2%	35.9%	67.0%
Replacement	64%	3.9%	22.3%	38.5%	0.0%
Buy-out	(expansion)	64.7%	29.0%	11.4%	20.0%
Capital gains tax for venture capital		40%	19%	None if criteria apply	None if criteria apply

Note: 1 The proportion invested by bank related investors.

are very important in the UK, representing nearly 65 per cent of the amounts invested there. In the Netherlands and France, expansion capital forms the largest single investment stage.

The US and UK have been characterised as having market-based systems where the disciplinary role of capital markets and the market for corporate control are important. In continental Europe, governance systems can be viewed as network-oriented (Moerland, 1995). Within this broad dichotomy it is important to recognise that there are variations. Hence, for example, board structures and takeover mechanisms differ markedly between the US and the UK (Charkham, 1994). In continental Europe, countries such as France, Belgium and other Latinic countries can be characterised as having network or holding company governance systems, with the state also playing an important role. For example, in France, holding companies account for a third of quoted companies and in 21 per cent of cases are majority shareholders. There are also interlocking shareholdings which may take the form of direct cross-holdings, by which companies hold reciprocal shareholdings in each other, or more complex webs of holdings. In contrast, in countries such as the Netherlands, the banking sector plays a major governance role, there are two-tier rather than unitary boards and the stock market is typically less well developed (Pike et al., 1993; Cooke, 1988). Despite these differences, venture capitalists in France and the Netherlands are less involved in investee monitoring, whereas in the US and the UK there is generally a closer relationship (Sapienza et al., 1996).

Due diligence

Sapienza et al. (1996) have shown that France and Belgium, the relatively younger venture capital industries covered by this study, are more financially oriented in that the investors often have a financial or banking background and that an important part of the investment companies are subsidiaries of larger financial institutions. This means that investors in these countries provide much less added value to their investee companies. In the same vein, it may be that more financially oriented venture capitalists have more difficulties in assessing the market potential and, more generally, to do their own due diligence, because of their financial rather than managerial background.

The expertise of venture capital executives may be expected to develop over time. Such expertise means greater skills to evaluate proposals. As noted above, the US market was the first to emerge, followed in Europe by that in the UK and thence continental Europe, starting with the Netherlands (Manigart, 1994; Wright et al., 1992). Markets may develop both at different rates and with different emphases, one aspect of which is the role of due diligence. It may be expected that more experienced investors, as in the US and the UK, will be more comfortable relying on their own due diligence and evaluations, and, conversely, that less experienced investors will rely more upon reports from outsiders, such as auditors.

The valuation method

Valuation methods and information usage may be influenced by the dominant corporate culture in a particular country. As capital markets are more dominant in Anglo-American countries, it may be expected that the valuation process is both more developed and more likely to rely on standard corporate finance theory developed in an advanced capital market context. Evidence of differences in appraisal techniques used by investment analysts in the UK and Germany has been attributed to the relative importance of stock markets in the two countries. German analysts, for example, are found to place more emphasis on technical analysis than their UK counterparts who place more emphasis on net assets per share and dividend growth models (Pike et al., 1993). Efficient and developed capital markets may provide comparator valuations, either in terms of prices at which companies are traded (takeovers) or sector price/earnings ratios (even though this method does not have any real theoretical justification). This information may in practice be weighted more heavily than DCF-based methods which are influenced by the choice of discount rate and uncertainty over expected cash flows. In countries where holding and networking structures predominate, long-term relationships are important and the frequent valuation of companies may be less important.

Information for valuation

Venture capitalists place great emphasis on financial information, especially projections, in their assessment of potential investees, but such information may be subject to considerable error and variation. Besides financial information, venture capitalists considering start-ups may place great reliance on evidence concerning an entrepreneur's track record as a means of gauging the likelihood that performance will be delivered (MacMillan et al., 1987), notwithstanding evidence that previous experience carries liabilities as well as assets (Starr and MacMillan, 1991) and that it is typically difficult to identify an attractive venture the second time around (Wright et al., 1997a).

The role of financial information versus information relating to entrepreneurs may vary between countries. In countries characterised by market-based systems, publicly available financial information is crucial to the functioning of capital markets. However, even in market-based systems, the information relating to early stage ventures is likely to be limited and surrounded by considerable uncertainty. In network-based systems such as France and the Netherlands (Moerland, 1995), greater emphasis may be placed on information relating to the individual entrepreneur than in market-based systems such as the US and UK.

The required return

In theory, the required return from an investment is a function of its riskiness. Riskiness may be considered as deal-specific or in relation to the investment stage of a project. Hence early stage projects may be expected to be higher risk than later stage ones, with the changes involved in buy-outs and buy-ins suggesting that expected returns will be between these two extremes. In addition to the investment stage of a project, the target rate of return on an investment may be influenced by other factors. Standard finance theory would suggest that changes in the returns available on alternative investment projects, such as quoted equities, long term gilts or changes in base rates would affect the target rate of return (Brealey and Myers, 1996). The last may also reflect the effects of changing general economic conditions.

Differing target rates of return may be expected between differing countries. Required rates of return may be influenced by the legal and fiscal infrastructure in individual countries. In particular, differing capital gains tax regimes may influence the level of pre-tax rates of return which are sought. Where differing regimes specify minimum holding periods for investments to obtain taxation relief, this may also be associated with differences in the length of expected investment horizons. There is evidence of differential taxation regimes between countries (EVCA, 1996 – see summary in Table 11.1). In Belgium, realised capital gains are not taxed, while in Holland dividends and capital gains may be exempt from corporation tax for shareholdings above a certain level. Although in some respects the UK has one of the most favourable legal and fiscal environments for venture capital, capital gains tax rates are the highest in Europe. In France, venture capital firms are able to obtain some tax exemptions. Although the measurement of rates of return on a post-tax basis should mean that the effect on cross-country comparisons should be reduced, differences may still remain because of other market imperfections.

Expectations about the effects of experience are ambiguous. On the one hand, greater expertise at the venture capital task may mean that venture capital firms in more developed markets may expect to earn higher rates of return. On the other hand, more developed markets may be subject to greater competition for deals which results in the entry price being bid up and a consequent lowering of returns to more normal levels. Coupled with, perhaps less strong, arguments that it may become more difficult to identify good investments *per se*, then expected returns may be lower in more developed markets.

Evidence on the performance of venture capital funds is now available in the US and Europe (see Wright and Robbie, 1997 for a review), with the Dutch venture capital industry publishing systematic evidence on investment returns much sooner than its counterparts in the UK and France. To the extent that this information reveals lower actual returns than anticipated, future expectations may be revised downwards. However, there is also emerging evidence that providers of funds to venture capital firms in the UK and US are paying increasing attention to the setting of target rates of return *per se* (Wright et al. 1997b). With increasing transparency of investment returns, these targets are more likely to be set such that the venture capital firm is expected to perform in, say, the top quintile of the industry. These pressures feed through to the returns sought on venture capitalists' investments, but may not be felt evenly across countries.

Assessment of the riskiness of a proposal

The role of management (skills, experience, and so on) and the nature of the product market of a potential investee may be important indicators of the riskiness of a project as suggested by evidence on their importance in the venture screening process (for example, MacMillan et al., 1987). Highly skilled and experienced entrepreneurs may be perceived to be more likely to reduce the riskiness of a project as they are more capable of dealing with uncertain situations. These transaction-specific factors may be most important in assessing the riskiness of a proposal. It is also possible that the equity ownership by managers is an important factor in the reduction of risk for investors (for example, Leland and Pyle, 1977; Morck et al., 1988).

The riskiness of a proposal may also be assessed in terms of the timescale over which venture capitalists obtain their return; this may be in terms of both the expected time horizon to exit and the time taken to redeem preference stocks ahead of an exit for ordinary stocks. To some extent, differing investment time horizons may be linked to notions about the extent to which countries' corporate governance systems are 'short-termist'. This view is typically expressed in respect of market systems *vis-à-vis* network ones. In addition to specific factors, the riskiness of a proposal may be assessed in relation to the nature of the capital market. The importance of this factor may vary to the extent that the importance of the capital market varies across countries.

Differences between venture capitalists

Differences may arise between venture capitalists in respect of this detailed process of scrutiny both in respect of the investment stage and the distinction between captive and independent venture capitalists.

While information on individual entrepreneurs may be important for early stage investments, in buy-outs and buy-ins there are further issues. Where such investment stages involve private/family businesses there will be an independent track record available. Where they involve divested divisions, prior reporting requirements may mean that accurate historical information is difficult to construct *ex post* (Wright and Coyne, 1985). Further problems occur in respect of the entrepreneurs in that while buy-out managers have been running the enterprise they are not equity owners, and while buy-in entrepreneurs may have a track record this does not relate to the entity which they are acquiring (Robbie and Wright, 1996).

Depending on the focus of the venture capital industry in a particular country, executives within it may also have very different skills. The US venture capital market involves a substantially greater proportion of funds going to early stage ventures than is the case in Europe (see Table 11.1), which suggests a greater need to emphasise the skills of the entrepreneur and the market prospect of a new product. Sapienza et al. (1996) find, for example, that the European venture capital industry in general is more financially oriented than that in the US. Wright and Robbie (1996b) find that the skills required for the early and buy-out stages of a venture capital market are markedly different. While the latter requires predominantly financial skills, the former emphasises industry-specific knowledge and an ability to assess and work with entrepreneurs. However, growing recognition of the need to achieve returns in these kinds of investment from adding value rather than straightforward restructuring also suggests that entrepreneurial and product information skills are important.

Independent venture capitalists are typically funded through limited-life closed-end funds. Dependent (captive) firms are funded primarily by banks and insurance companies. Evidence suggests there may be important differences in investment time horizons for particular investment stages and harvesting methods between venture capital firms in differing countries (Bygrave and Muzyka, 1994; Wright et al., 1993; and Bleackley et al., 1996). To the extent that venture capital investments are funded by independent limited-life closed-end funds this may also influence the expected investment time horizon, since these funds more than dependents (captives) are more likely to be committed to generating a return for investors through realising a capital gain within a more clearly specified period of time (Wright et al., 1997b). In the UK and the Netherlands, independent venture capital firms account for a substantially greater share of investments than is the case in the other countries covered by this study (Table 11.1).

Data and research method

In order to empirically study the above issues, a draft postal questionnaire was developed in the UK and pre-tested with venture capitalists, advisors and academics (Wright and Robbie, 1996a). The questionnaires were translated into French and Dutch, in order to be used in France, Belgium and the Netherlands. They were sent to the full members of the British Venture Capital Association in early 1994 and to the full members of the 'Association Française des Investisseurs en Capital', the Belgian Venturing Association, the 'Nederlandse Vereniging voor Participatiemaatschapppijen' and to the French, Dutch and Belgian members of the European Venture Capital Association in late 1995–early 1996 and to a random sample of 299 US venture capitalists listed in *Pratt's Guide to Venture Capital Sources*, in late 1996. Follow-up reminders were sent after two to three months. The questionnaires were sent to senior investment managers. As for the UK study reported in Wright and Robbie (1996a), this chapter is concerned with the general policies adopted by venture capitalists. An organisation-wide response was sought, with the covering letter to senior investment managers specifically asking respondents to report institutions' perceptions rather than individual approaches. In framing the initial UK-based questionnaire, discussions with venture capitalists had suggested that during the stages with which this study is concerned, there is close adherence to firm-wide policies, and this practice is also evident in the other countries examined here.

The response rate was as follows: 66 completed and useable replies out of 114 questionnaires sent in the UK (58 per cent response rate); 73 out of 299 in the US (24 per cent response rate); 32 out of 133 in France (24 per cent response rate); 24 out of 58 in the Netherlands (41 per cent response rate) and 14 out of 28 in Belgium (50 per cent response rate). No significant differences were identified between respondents and non-respondents in terms of type of venture capitalists and amount of capital under management. The venture managers, who filled out the questionnaires, were very senior: the median number of years' work in the venture sector of the respondents varies between 9.5 years in Belgium and 14 years in the Netherlands. Sixty-one per cent of the responses come from independent venture firms and 20 per cent from venture firms, dependent on a financial institution or an industrial company (captive funds). The remainder are government agencies or semi-captive funds. The US and the Netherlands have the highest proportion of independent companies in the sample (82 per cent and 62 per cent respectively), while more French companies are dependent on financial institutions (44 per cent).

As there were few significant differences between the results for Belgium and the Netherlands, the data relating to these closely similar countries are combined for presentational purposes in the analysis which follows; significant differences are identified as appropriate.

Country differences relating to each of the issues identified above were analysed using Kruskal–Wallis ANOVA by ranks as this test relies on less stringent assumptions about the nature of the data than does one-way ANOVA. The former requires that data relating to variables are at least ordinal in nature whereas the latter requires interval level variables which satisfy normal distribution criteria. There is some debate about whether data from Likert scales can be regarded as interval level and in recognition of this the more conservative approach is used. However, in the absence of other suitable tests, examination of the interaction effects between countries, stage of venture capital investment and type of venture capital fund are analysed using three-way ANOVA.

Empirical results

Due diligence reports

Significant differences were identified between the countries in respect of the relative importance of carrying out own due diligence (Table 11.2). Belgium/the Netherlands gave the lowest score to this item, with the former being somewhat below the latter. Venture capitalists in the US and France placed greatest emphasis on personal references in their due diligence and were also more likely to terminate proposals where inadequate current performance is available.

Table 11.2 Due diligence

Mean (STD)	USA (N = 73)	UK (N = 66)	Belgium and Netherlands (N = 38)	France (N = 32)
Carry out own market evaluation****	4.74 (0.48)	4.14 (0.89)	3.95 (1.11)	4.25 (0.80)
Place great reliance on personal references****	4.58 (0.72)	3.94 (0.86)	3.97 (0.89)	4.74 (0.44)
Terminate proposals where inadequate current performance is available****	4.19 (0.84)	3.49 (1.15)	3.26 (1.27)	4.52 (0.77)
Always have independent accountant reports*	3.25 (1.18)	3.69 (1.44)	3.58 (1.27)	3.72 (1.46)
Always obtain independent market reports***	3.71 (0.92)	3.09 (1.18)	3.11 (1.03)	3.32 (1.11)
Never use same reporting accountant as management's accounting adviser****	3.18 (1.25)	3.14 (1.35)	1.89 (1.20)	2.44 (1.40)

Note: Significant differences between countries: Kruskall–Wallis Anova by ranks: * $p < 0.1$; ** $p < 0.05$; *** $p < 0.01$; **** $p < 0.001$.

French and UK-based venture capitalists were more likely than institutions in the other countries to always make use of an independent accountant's report, with the US firms being least likely to use such information in their due diligence. In contrast, US venture capitalists placed greatest emphasis amongst the countries examined on always obtaining independent market reports. Venture capitalists in both the US and the UK placed greater emphasis than those in the other countries on the importance of never using the same reporting accountant as management's accounting adviser.

The valuation method

There is a significant difference between the importance of textbook valuation techniques, such as PE multiples, dividend yield and payback, in the different countries (Table 11.3). Methods based on price earnings are more popular in the UK, in particular. The dividend yield method is least popular in the US, the UK and France. However, there are no significant differences between countries in respect of DCF-based methods, which rank, in general, as less important than PE, EBIT and 'recent transactions in the sector'-based approaches in relative importance in all countries.

Table 11.3 Methods used in valuing potential investments

Mean (STD)	USA (N = 73)	UK (N = 66)	Belgium and Netherlands (N = 38)	France (N = 32)
Capitalised maintainable earning (P/E multiple) (prospective basis)****	3.63 (1.06)	4.31 (0.87)	3.58 (1.08)	4.31 (0.82)
Capitalised maintainable earning (EBIT multiple)*	3.83 (1.06)	3.90 (1.23)	3.76 (1.13)	4.13 (0.94)
Recent transaction prices for acquisitions in the sector	3.78 (1.53)	3.63 (1.18)	3.61 (1.00)	4.19 (0.78)
Discounted value of free cash flows	3.62 (0.97)		3.89 (1.15)	3.69 (1.09)
Capitalised maintainable earning (P/E multiple) (historic basis)****	3.27 (0.98)	4.27 (0.86)	3.03 (1.12)	4.19 (0.74)
Payback period****	3.47 (1.14)		2.92 (1.08)	2.16 (1.22)
Industry's special 'rule of thumb' pricing ratios (e.g. turnover ratios)****	3.61 (1.01)	2.97 (1.13)	2.97 (0.92)	4.16 (0.77)
Discounted future cash flows	3.67 (1.26)	3.23 (1.37)	3.74 (1.18)	3.75 (1.16)
Responses to attempts to solicit bids for the potential investee	2.90 (0.96)	2.74 (1.20)	2.76 (1.03)	3.30 (1.20)
Historic cost book value*	2.12 (1.04)	2.42 (1.26)	2.63 (1.15)	2.06 (1.03)
Liquidation value of assets (orderly sale)***	2.79 (1.04)	2.05 (1.14)	2.26 (1.13)	2.35 (1.08)
Dividend yield basis***	2.14 (1.17)	2.22 (1.11)	3.03 (1.04)	2.51 (1.23)
Liquidation value of assets (forced sale)***	2.66 (1.28)	1.97 (1.06)	2.13 (1.02)	2.00 (0.88)
Recent PE ratio of the parent company's shares****	2.33 (0.88)	1.97 (1.01)		3.22 (1.22)
Replacement cost asset value	2.21 (1.04)	1.91 (1.10)	2.24 (0.94)	2.28 (1.14)

Note: Significant differences between countries: Kruskall–Wallis Anova by ranks: * $p < 0.1$; ** $p < 0.05$; *** $p < 0.01$; **** $p < 0.001$.

There are weakly significant differences between countries in the use of EBIT multiples or recent transaction prices of comparable takeovers. Relationship-based valuation techniques, for example, responses to soliciting bids for the potential investee or industry's rule of thumb ratios, are most popular in France, the most network-oriented country in our sample. They are, however, less popular in Belgium, the Netherlands and the UK than in the US.

Finally, accounting-based measures, such as book value or liquidation value, show significant differences between the countries, although they are generally less important than the above measures. Historic book value is relatively more important in Belgium/Netherlands and the UK. The liquidation value approach – either ordinary or forced – is relatively more popular in the US.

The subjectivity of valuations is an international phenomenon, with all countries scoring highest the placing of the greatest weight on one particular valuation method and using the others as a check (Table 11.4). The UK, in particular, appears to place greatest emphasis on this approach. The weighted average method was significantly more important in Belgium and the Netherlands.

Table 11.4 Selection of final/benchmark valuation

Mean (STD)	USA (N = 73)	UK (N = 66)	Belgium and Netherlands (N = 38)	France (N = 32)
Place greatest weight on one particular method and use others as a check***	3.44 (1.21)	4.15 (1.13)	3.47 (1.43)	3.77 (1.53)
Use the average valuation	3.05 (1.15)	2.61 (1.25)	2.77 (1.11)	2.79 (1.40)
Use the weighted average valuation**	2.54 (1.08)		3.31 (1.23)	2.81 (1.66)
Use the median value**	2.74 (1.08)	2.29 (1.08)	2.04 (1.04)	2.28 (1.28)
Use the lowest value*	2.47 (0.95)	2.33 (1.11)	1.88 (1.09)	2.26 (1.26)
Use the highest valuation*	2.05 (0.99)	1.65 (0.77)	1.69 (0.97)	1.58 (0.81)

Note: Significant differences between countries: Kruskall–Wallis Anova by ranks: * $p < 0.1$; ** $p < 0.05$; *** $p < 0.01$; **** $p < 0.001$.

Information for valuation

The respondents were asked to assign values from 1 ('irrelevant') to 5 ('extremely important') to 22 possible sources of information for valuation purposes or, more generally, for the overall due diligence process. The means, standard deviations and significant differences between the countries are reported in Table 11.5. Apart from in France, where it comes in second position, the most important source of information in each country is the own due diligence report, particularly in the US. In France, the overall coherence of the business plan receives the highest score, with unaudited management projections also being significantly more important than in the other countries.

Table 11.5 Sources of information in preparing a valuation

Mean (STD)	USA (N = 73)	UK (N = 66)	Belgium and Netherlands (N = 38)	France (N = 32)
Own due diligence report****	4.88 (0.37)	4.47 (0.75)	4.61 (0.64)	4.57 (0.63
Business plan: overall coherence of business plan***	4.19 (0.85)	4.06 (1.06)	4.47 (0.60)	4.77 (0.50)
Business plan: profit and loss account****	3.81 (0.97)	4.36 (0.92)	4.48 (0.60)	4.38 (0.94)
Curriculum vitae of management	4.19 (0.88)	3.91 (1.06)	4.34 (0.75)	4.41 (0.84)
Interviews with entrepreneurs****	4.22 (1.09)	3.65 (1.14)	4.47 (0.92)	4.25 (1.05)
Sales and marketing information**	3.89 (0.83)	3.80 (0.88)	4.24 (0.68)	4.25 (0.72)
Business plan: unaudited management projections (1 year ahead)****	3.40 (1.21)	4.03 (0.91)	4.08 (0.91)	4.57 (0.62)
Business plan: balance sheet****	3.42 (1.04)	4.00 (1.05)	4.26 (0.80)	4.31 (0.97)
Production capacity/technical information	3.71 (0.90)	3.42 (0.95)	3.71 (0.73)	4.19 (0.69)
Product information****	3.89 (0.83)	3.47 (1.00)	4.11 (0.76)	4.41 (0.67)
Due diligence by accounting/consulting firms	3.82 (0.70)	3.75 (1.17)	4.03 (0.92)	4.03 (0.98)
Business plan: qualified audit report****	3.41 (1.21)	3.70 (1.25)	4.21 (0.74)	4.44 (0.67)
Business plan: unaudited 'latest period' financial statements*	3.51 (1.14)	4.00 (0.99)	3.95 (0.90)	3.79 (1.15)
Business plan: unaudited management projections (more than 1 year ahead)****	3.27 (1.17)	3.63 (1.02)	4.03 (1.05)	4.36 (0.83)
Interviews with other company personnel	3.74 (0.99)	3.17 (1.30)	4.00 (0.96)	4.25 (0.95)
Proposed exit timing and method***	3.64 (0.91)	3.70 (1.08)	3.34 (1.17)	3.68 (1.05)
Business plan: unqualified audit report	3.25 (1.18)	3.45 (1.22)	3.61 (1.05)	3.61 (1.12)
Other venture capitalists**	3.32 (1.05)	2.82 (1.05)	3.00 (0.87)	3.06 (0.84)
Statistical and information services		2.77 (1.04)	2.63 (0.79)	2.83 (1.05)
Trade journals****	2.79 (1.00)	2.69 (1.09)	2.51 (0.99)	2.71 (0.86)
Financial press****	2.19 (0.94)	3.03 (1.19)	2.73 (1.07)	2.65 (0.84)
Government industry statistics	2.25 (0.87)	2.27 (1.00)	2.55 (0.95)	2.59 (0.95)

Note: Significant differences between countries: Kruskall–Wallis Anova by ranks: * $p < 0.1$; ** $p < 0.05$; *** $p < 0.01$; **** $p < 0.001$.

There are significant differences in the importance of the information sources in the different countries for the four information items relating to individuals, particularly in respect of interviews with entrepreneurs. British venture capitalists especially, followed by their American colleagues, place the least importance upon interviews with the entrepreneurs and other personnel, and upon the curriculum vitae of the management team. France and Belgium/Netherlands, place relatively higher emphasis on these information sources, perhaps reflecting notions of the greater importance of individuals in a network-type environment where the venture capitalist is less formally involved.

The required rate of return

Table 11.6 shows that the required return varies significantly between the countries according to the investment stage. British and American investors require a significantly higher return for expansion investments than their continental counterparts, while British investors require the highest returns for MBO-type of investments. The Belgian/Dutch investors require the lowest returns for all investment stages. The findings suggest that the expected return increases as the venture markets become more developed and provide more detailed return figures of the past. Increased competition in the older venture capital industries may be driving the expected returns up. These results seem somewhat paradoxical for Belgium/Holland which have the oldest established venture capital markets in Continental Europe.

Table 11.6 Required rate of return on equity

Mean (STD)	USA (N = 73)	UK (N = 66)	Belgium and Netherlands (N = 38)	France (N = 32)
IRR****	30% (33.3%)	30% (29.2%)	15% (18.5%)	25% (24.1%)
IRR early stage**	46–55% (42.8 %)	46–55% (49.4 %)	31–35% (31.1%)	36–45% (39.0%)
IRR expansion development****	31–35% (33.4%)	31–35% (28.9%)	21–25% (25.1%)	21–25% (23.8%)
IRR acquisition/ buy-out****	26–30% (23.2%)	31–35% (34.7%)	21–25% (20%)	26–30% (25.4%)

Note: Significant differences between countries: Kruskall–Wallis Anova by ranks: * $p < 0.1$; ** $p < 0.05$; *** $p < 0.01$; **** $p < 0.001$.

There were significant differences between countries in relation to venture capitalists' policies regarding influences on target rates of returns. Greatest emphasis was given in all countries to a target rate of return which reflected some measure of the characteristics of a particular investment (Table 11.7). French venture capitalists were significantly more likely to require an investment to meet a standard IRR both according to risk band (with a low standard deviation indicating a high degree of unanimity in the industry) and according to the

Table 11.7 Target rates of return

Mean (STD)	USA (N = 73)	UK (N = 66)	Belgium and Netherlands (N = 38)	France (N = 32)
We require the investment to meet a specific required rate of return on equity (IRR), according to the characteristics of each investment*	3.63 (1.39)	3.64 (1.22)	3.97 (1.12)	4.23 (1.10)
We require the investment to meet a standard required rate of return on equity (IRR) according to the risk band of the investment****	3.33 (1.43)	3.29 (1.25)	3.93 (1.06)	4.81 (0.40)
We require a rate of return which yields a total cash return commensurate with amount invested****	4.01 (1.13)	3.38 (1.32)	2.91 (1.15)	3.00 (1.48)
We require the funding structure to meet gearing ratios appropriate to each investment****	2.52 (1.36)	3.40 (0.98)	3.44 (1.21)	3.50 (1.33)
We require the investment to meet a standard required rate of return on equity (internal rate of return, IRR), regardless of the investee company's risk profile**	2.82 (1.36)	2.27 (1.31)	2.97 (1.31)	2.85 (1.46)
We require the funding structure to meet standard gearing ratio according to the risk band of the investment****	1.99 (1.19)	2.41 (1.07)	3.35 (1.03)	3.58 (1.23)
We require the funding structure to meet standard gearing ratios****	1.75 (0.97)	2.06 (0.98)	2.87 (1.25)	2.68 (1.28)

Note: Significant differences between countries: Kruskall–Wallis Anova by ranks:* $p < 0.1$; ** $p < 0.05$; *** $p < 0.01$; **** $p < 0.001$.

Table 11.8 Targeted return variations

Mean (STD)	USA (N = 73)	UK (N = 66)	Belgium and Netherlands (N = 38)	France (N = 32)
Degree of market innovation of the company	3.52 (1.11)		3.54 (0.77)	3.40 (1.13)
The expected length of investment in a particular proposal	3.61 (1.15)	3.52 (1.01)	3.31 (1.06)	3.53 (1.32)
Market conditions relating to a particular proposal	3.39 (1.09)	3.34 (0.97)	3.39 (0.87)	3.64 (1.11)
Whether the exit has been planned ex ante	3.35 (1.23)		3.22 (1.38)	3.28 (1.40)
Round of investment (first, follow-on)**	3.54 (1.13)		3.08 (0.97)	3.00 (1.14)
Degree of technological innovation of the company	3.49 (1.23)		3.46 (0.96)	3.46 (1.11)
The industrial/product sector of the investment**	3.06 (1.20)	3.11 (1.01)	3.38 (0.92)	3.81 (1.12)
The actual cash amount you seek to receive from an investment***	3.58 (1.24)	2.88 (1.16)	3.17 (1.11)	2.85 (1.32)
Whether the investment is solely in shares***			2.92 (0.97)	3.67 (1.40)
General economic conditions	2.96 (0.96)	3.16 (0.88)	2.94 (0.96)	3.30 (0.95)
The expected gearing ratio when the finance is structured*	2.60 (1.23)	2.94 (1.02)	3.11 (1.17)	3.40 (1.13)
The actual cash amount invested in a particular proposal (i.e. size of proposal)	3.04 (1.20)	2.81 (1.08)	2.92 (1.08)	3.09 (1.30)
Whether you (and the institutional syndicate where appropriate) have a majority of the equity****	3.28 (1.22)	2.40 (0.87)	2.67 (1.31)	2.74 (1.48)
Changes in returns for quoted equities*	2.76 (1.05)	2.48 (1.00)	2.17 (0.88)	2.63 (1.07)
Changes in base rates**		2.52 (0.98)	2.14 (0.90)	2.71 (1.18)
Geographical region of the investment****	2.62 (1.27)	2.06 (1.11)	2.19 (1.31)	3.47 (1.11)
Changes in returns for long term gilts****	1.68 (0.86)	2.14 (0.96)	2.69 (0.98)	2.54 (1.12)

Note: Significant differences between countries: Kruskall–Wallis Anova by ranks: * $p < 0.1$; ** $p < 0.05$; *** $p < 0.01$; **** $p < 0.001$.

characteristics of each investment. US investors were most likely to emphasise a requirement that the investment yielded a total cash return commensurate with the amount invested. European investors place more importance on financial structures than their US counterparts, particularly those in France who emphasise the importance of the level of gearing in relation to the risk category of the investment.

The main effects on targeted return variations across all countries related to the market conditions of a particular proposal, the expected length of investment, whether exit has been planned ex ante, and the degree of market innovation of the company (Table 11.8). A change in stock market returns has only a moderate effect on the required rates of return. Significantly greater emphasis was placed in the US compared to other countries on the effect of the round of investment and on the actual amount of cash expected to be received from the investment. In contrast, significantly greater emphasis in France was placed on the industrial/product sector of the investment, on whether the investment was solely in shares and on the expected gearing ratio when the finance was structured. In the US, in particular, greater emphasis was given to whether or not the venture capitalist had a majority of the equity than was the case in the other countries. In France, the geographical region of the investment was significantly more important than elsewhere.

Assessment of the riskiness of a proposal

Table 11.9 reports the responses to the answers to the questions concerning indicators of risk, reported on a 1 'irrelevant' to 5 'extremely important' Likert scale. The quality of management is a very to extremely important indicator of the riskiness of a proposal in each of the countries in this study; there is no significant difference between countries. The financial contribution by the management, however, is significantly more important in the US than in Europe, including the UK which is often seen as very similar to the US. French investors display behaviour which is closest to those in the US in this area.

The nature of capital markets is a much less important indicator of risk than the management-related issues in all the countries. The nature of capital markets is significantly more important in the two countries with strong capital markets, the US especially and also the UK, than in the continental countries.

Differences between venture capitalists

The differences found between the venture capital practices in different countries may be due to differences in the nature of the venture capital industry, rather than to between-country differences. The first dimension to be examined concerns differences between countries in the relative importance of different investment stages. If the venture capital industry in a particular country is dominated by early stage investors, it may be that information and valuation

Table 11.9 Assessment of the riskiness of investment

Mean (STD)	USA (N = 73)	UK (N = 66)	Belgium and Netherlands (N = 38)	France (N = 32)
Contribution by management in terms of their managerial skills	4.88 (0.37)	4.76 (0.53)	4.79 (0.58)	4.94 (0.25)
Nature of product market of the company	4.43 (0.75)	4.29 (0.80)	4.58 (0.64)	4.47 (0.72)
Financial contribution by management****	4.10 (0.89)	3.29 (1.09)	3.53 (0.95)	3.94 (0.84)
Expected time horizon to exit of company (stock market/trade sale)	3.57 (1.03)	3.52 (0.93)	3.26 (1.11)	3.74 (0.93)
Expected time horizon to redemption of preference shares	2.68 (1.14)	2.97 (1.02)	2.49 (1.04)	2.69 (1.26)
Nature of the capital market****	3.11 (0.93)	2.57 (1.07)	1.90 (0.86)	2.34 (0.83)
Expected participating dividend yield**	2.11 (1.15)	2.48 (1.04)	2.61 (1.10)	2.59 (1.34)

Note: Significant differences between countries: Kruskall–Wallis Anova by ranks: * $p < 0.1$; ** $p < 0.05$; *** $p < 0.01$; **** $p < 0.001$.

methods used will be different from the practices in industries, dominated by later stage investors. It is equally likely that managers from independent venture capital firms may behave differently from those from venture capital firms dependent on a parent company or on government. Therefore, the interactive effects of country, investment stage preferences and type of venture capital company were examined using ANOVA tests.

If a company is not likely to invest in early stage deals (= an answer of 2 or less on the early stage investment preference question), it was classified as an 'only later stage' investor; if it is also prepared to invest in early stage deals (= an answer of 3 or more on the same question), it was classified as an 'all stage' investor. There are few investors who explicitly exclude later stage deals. Table 11.10 gives the number of venture capital companies, split according to their investment preference. Consistent with the data in Table 11.1, it is clear that US venture capital companies are more interested in investing in early stage deals than the European ones.

Table 11.10 Number of elements in subsamples

	US	UK	Belgium and Netherlands	France	Total
All stages	45	20	13	13	91
Only later stages	28	46	25	19	118
Independent	60	33	21	13	127
Dependent	13	33	17	19	82

Note: Number of elements in subsamples reported here is the total number of elements (if no missing data) and some questions were not included in the survey of one or two of the countries, thus consequently the total number of elements is lower there.

The second dimension to be explored is whether the differences found previously are attributable to differences in governance structure of venture capital companies. Venture capital managers were asked to indicate whether they were independent or dependent/captive (on a financial institution, a non-financial company or on government). Table 11.10 gives the number of companies in each country in each of the categories. More US venture capital companies are independent, while European venture capital companies are more likely to be dependent on a parent company or on government.

ANOVA tests show that, when taking the investment stage preference and governance structure into account, country still explains a significant part of the variation in the answers for most of the items that showed significant country differences. Hence, even when taking the two other dimensions into account, there remain very significant between-country differences in venture capital practices. Due to space constraints, the remainder of this section summarises the significant ($p < 0.1$; 2-sided tests) interaction effects between country and investment stage preferences, and between country and type of venture capital company (dependent versus independent). The *independent* effects of stage preference and venture capital company type and the three-way interaction effects are omitted, the latter being in any case of only marginal and occasional significance.

Due diligence reports

There are several significant interaction effects in the due diligence process. This implies that venture capital companies apply different due diligence processes in the different countries, even when taking their investment preferences and their type into account. Venture capital companies investing in all stages use less independent accountant reports than those investing in early stages only, but there is also an important between-country difference. Continental European venture capitalists, especially French ones, investing in all stages, require significantly more independent accountant or market reports than their colleagues in other countries, especially the UK. British venture capitalists require significantly more independent accountant reports when investing only in later stages, especially compared to their French colleagues. This is a refinement of our previous results. US venture capitalists require much more own market evaluations than in other countries, independent of their investment preference or governance structure. Independent venture capital managers carry out more own market evaluations than dependent ones, and more so in the US than in Continental Europe.

The valuation method

When taking investment preferences and governance structure into account, British investors place much more emphasis on P/E multiples based on historic figures, while French later stage, independent and captive investors prefer third party bids. It is furthermore striking that captive US investors use the dividend yield basis more frequently than captive European investors, while the reverse is true for the independent investors. US later stage and captive investors place relatively more emphasis on replacement cost value of assets, while this is true of independent French venture capital firms. However, replacement cost value of assets is not generally rated as highly as other methods.

Information for valuation

The overall coherence of the business plan, which is the most important information source in France, is even more important for captive than for independent venture capital managers in that country. Later stage investors place a higher emphasis on a qualified audit report, especially in France, and on unaudited financial statements or unqualified audit reports than investors prepared to invest in all stages, especially in the US and in the UK.

The required rate of return

Even when taking investment preference and governance structures into account, it is clear that there are important differences between the required rates of return in the different countries. It is obvious that later stage investors require, on average, a lower overall IRR than all stage investors, except for buy-out investments. Moreover, independent investors require a higher return than dependent investors for all investment stages. It is striking that captive US investors require the lowest return overall and on early stage investments, while their independent colleagues require almost the highest return (after the UK) on these investments.

Later stage investors require more often than all stage investors a standard IRR, regardless of the company's risk profile, but British investors agree least with this statement. Independent investors seek a lower return when the degree of market innovation is higher and when general economic conditions are better, especially in France and in the US. Finally, the required return of investors will vary more with the investment round in the US.

Assessment of the riskiness of a proposal

There are no interaction effects between the country, type of venture ownership or stage preference, with respect to the assessment of the riskiness of the investment.

Discussion and conclusions

Previous evidence has focused on the information and valuation issues which concern venture capitalists in the UK (Wright and Robbie, 1996a). Our results have shown that it is not possible to generalise from UK evidence to other countries. There are important between-country differences with respect to the due diligence and valuation stages of venture capital investment and the relative importance of accounting and financial information in this process. These between-country differences are found to persist even after controlling for between-country differences in the relative importance of investment stages and venture capitalist types.

The valuation methods used to combine the information on risk and required return differ widely across the countries. There did not appear to be a systematic difference in the relative importance of the valuation methods used according to whether countries were more market- or network-oriented. Although it might be argued that countries with less developed capital markets are less likely to utilise valuation techniques consistent with standard corporate finance theory (for example, DCF, dividend yield, and so on), this was not consistently the case.

There were indications that apparently similar systems and markets are, in fact, heterogeneous. For example, PE ratios, which might be expected to be widely used in more developed capital markets where it is possible to make comparisons with other companies for which information is publicly available, were most important in the UK but not in the US. It may be that the use of PE ratios, which are not theoretically based, simply reflects national practices. More research is needed on this subject.

The evidence presented here provides some support for the view that individual relationships are more important in network-based economies than in market-based economies. When gathering information for the valuation process, the personalities of the entrepreneurs, the information provided by the management team and personal references are generally more important in network-oriented countries. However, we have also shown that there is some degree of heterogeneity of behaviour between countries categorised as network- or market-oriented.

Investors in older venture capital markets, such as the US and the UK, rely more heavily upon their own due diligence and market reports. This finding may also be caused by the more financial orientation of venture capital investors in the younger venture capital markets in our study, namely France and Belgium.

Investors in the more established venture capital industries examined here require higher returns for later stage investments (expansion stage or MBO/MBIs). This may be explained by the fact that there is more detailed information on returns realised in the past, thus increasing the pressure on investors to perform above average. When assessing the riskiness of a proposal, the contribution of management is equally important in all countries, not only in the market-based economies. What differs between the countries is the importance of the nature of the capital market in general, which is more important in market-based economies such as the US and the UK. This factor has nearly no influence in countries with weak capital markets, such as France and Belgium. The financial contribution of management is also an important differentiating factor between countries. This factor is particularly important in the US and France compared to the other European countries, notably the UK. This result is important as it represents a departure from the traditional difference between market-oriented and network-oriented countries.

The contribution of management (skills, experience, and so on) was found to be an important factor in reducing the perceived riskiness of a proposal in all countries. In the countries with strong capital markets, the US and UK, the nature of the capital market was found to be a relatively more important factor in assessing the riskiness of a proposal, but relatively little emphasis was placed on this factor.

The results of this research show that the behaviour of venture capital investors varies widely. Some of the differences can be attributed to the dominant corporate governance mechanisms used in the countries, some to the stage of development of the venture industry. Venture capital investors may gain from the sharing of their experiences and practices with investors from other countries. It is possible that the internationalisation of the venture capital industry will induce more common practices over time, but until then this study provides further evidence of the fragmented nature of this industry. Further research is needed in order for these issues to be fully understood.

References

Bleackley, M., M. Hay, K. Robbie and M. Wright (1996), 'Entrepreneurial attitudes to venture capital investment realization: evidence from the UK and France', *Entrepreneurship and Regional Development*, **8**, 37–55.

Brealey, R.A. and S.C. Myers (1991), *Principles of Corporate Finance*, New York: McGraw-Hill.

Bygrave, W. and D. Muzyka (1994), 'Realizing value in Europe: a pan-European perspective', chapter 7 in W. Bygrave, M. Hay and J. Peeters (eds), *Realizing Investment Value*, London: FT-Pitman.

Charkham, J. (1994), *Keeping Good Company: A Study of Corporate Governance in Five Countries*, Oxford: Oxford University Press.

Cooke, T (1988), *International Mergers and Acquisitions*, Oxford: Blackwell, chs 7 and 10.

Elango, B., V. Fried, R. Hisrich and A. Polonchek (1995), 'How do venture capital firms differ?', *Journal of Business Venturing*, **10**, 157–79.

EVCA Yearbook (1996), *A Survey of Venture Capital and Private Equity in Europe*, Zaventem.

Hampden-Turner, C. and A. Trompenaars (1993), *The Seven Cultures of Capitalism*, New York: Doubleday.

Hofstede, G. (1984), *Culture's Consequences: International Differences in Work-related Values*, Beverly Hills, CA: Sage.

Leland, H. and D. Pyle (1977), 'Information asymmetries, financial structure and financial intermediators', *Journal of Finance*, **32**, 371–87.

MacMillan, I., L. Zamann and P. Subbanarasimha (1987), 'Criteria distinguishing successful from unsuccessful ventures in the venture screening process', *Journal of Business Venturing*, **3**, 123–37.

Manigart, S. (1994), 'The founding rates of venture capital firms in three European countries (1970–1990)', *Journal of Business Venturing*, **9** (6), 525–41.

Moerland, P.W. (1995), 'Alternative disciplinary mechanisms in different corporate systems', *Journal of Economic Behavior and Organization*, **26**, 17–34.

Morck, R., A. Shleifer and R. Vishny (1988), 'Management ownership and market valuation: an empirical analysis', *Journal of Financial Economics*, **20**, 293–315.

Murray, G. (1995), 'The UK venture capital industry', *Journal of Business Finance and Accounting*, **22** (8), 1077–106.

Ooghe, H., S. Manigart and Y. Fassin (1991), 'Growth patterns in the European venture capital industry, *Journal of Business Venturing*, **6**, 381–404.

Pike, R., J. Meerjanssen and L. Chadwick (1993), 'The appraisal of ordinary shares by investment analysts in the UK and Germany', *Accounting and Business Research*, **23** (92), 489–99.

Robbie, K. and M. Wright (1996), *Management Buy-ins : Entrepreneurship, Active Investors and Corporate Restructuring*, Manchester: Manchester University Press.

Roure, J., R. Keeley and T. van der Heyden (1990), 'European venture capital: strategies and challenges in the 90s', *European Management Journal*, **8** (2), 243–52.

Sapienza, H., S. Manigart and W. Vermeir (1996), 'Venture capitalist governance and value added in four countries', *Journal of Business Venturing*, **11** (6), 439–69.

Starr, J. and I. MacMillan (1991) 'The assets and liabilities of prior start-up experience: an exploratory study of multiple venture entrepreneurs', in N. Churchill et al. (eds), *Frontiers of Entrepreneurship Research*, Wellesley: Babson College.

Tyebjee, T and L. Vickery (1988),'Venture capital in Western Europe', *Journal of Business Venturing*, **3**, 123–36.

Wright, M. and J. Coyne (1985), *Management Buy-outs*, Beckenham: Croom-Helm.

Wright, M. and K. Robbie (1996a), 'Venture capitalists, unquoted equity investment appraisal and the role of accounting information', *Accounting and Business Research*, **26** (2), 153–68.

Wright, M. and K. Robbie (1996b), *Venture Capital to the Next Millennium*, London: British Venture Capital Association.

Wright, M. and K. Robbie (1998), 'Venture capital and private equity: a review and synthesis', *Journal of Business Finance and Accounting*, **25** (5/6), 521–70.

Wright, M., S. Thompson and K. Robbie (1992), 'Venture capital and management-led leveraged buy-outs: a European perspective', *Journal of Business Venturing*, **7** (1), 47–71.

Wright, M., K. Robbie, Y. Romanet, S. Thompson, R. Joachimsson, J. Bruining and A. Herst (1993), 'Harvesting and the Longevity of Management Buy-outs and Buy-ins: A Four Country Study', *Entrepreneurship: Theory and Practice*, **18** (2), 89–110.

Wright, M., K. Robbie and C. Ennew (1997a), 'Venture capitalists and serial entrepreneurs', *Journal of Business Venturing*, **12**, 227–49.

Wright, M., K. Robbie and B. Chiplin (1997b), *Funds Providers' Monitoring of Venture Capital Firms*, CMBOR Occ. Paper, University of Nottingham: CMBOR.

12. Accounting information system development and the supply of venture capital*

Falconer Mitchell, Gavin Reid and Nicholas Terry

Introduction

One of the most important events in the early life cycle of any entrepreneurial firm which harbours serious growth ambitions is the infusion of external capital (Reid, 1996). This event can lead to significant changes in the firm's ownership composition, and affects its subsequent rate of growth and, consequently, its size and organisational structure. It is within the context of such changes that the managerial demand for information about the firm is stimulated. This study examines the origins and characteristics of developments in the accounting information systems (AIS) of firms which are going through this stage. It does so by investigating the consequences of venture capital[1] intervention for the entrepreneurial firm, particularly as regards the characteristics of its accounting information system.

The significance of positive increments in the firm's supply of external capital for the development of its accounting system depends on characteristics of the evolving circumstances which confront both the owners and managers of the firm. The venture capital investors (VCIs) have put their invested funds at risk, but both at the time of negotiating the subscription agreement,[2] and also subsequently through their ownership stake, they can take steps to 'manage' their risk by making direct and effective demands on the investee for regular information. This can be seen as an attempt to improve contractual efficiency between the investee and investor. Recent studies have shown that VCIs do expect that the power which arises from their investor status makes effective their demands for information from investees as regards its type, quality and frequency (Sweeting, 1991; Mitchell et al. 1995; Wright and Robbie, 1996). Indeed, at the pre-investment stage, special investigations of the capacity of the investee's systems to meet the post-investment requirements of the VCI are frequently undertaken. Any upgrading which is thought to be necessary is then made a condition of the investment. Thus changes in the flow of information from the

* The authors are grateful to the Esmée-Fairbairn trust, the Carnegie Trust and the Centre for Financial Markets Research, University of Edinburgh, for funding the research on which this study is based. This chapter presents the material originally developed for presentation to the conference on 'Private Equity into the Next Millennium', CMBOR, University of Nottingham, 1996.

firm to its new investors become one potential influence on the form of the internal accounting system. Moreover, as decision-making is a central facet of entrepreneurship, it also influences the 'in-house' provision of accounting information. In an uncertain world, the efficacy of decision making is heavily conditioned by the quality of information available to the entrepreneur. Indeed information inadequacy is often associated with business distress and failure in small and medium-sized enterprises (SMEs) (for example, Storey et al., 1987), while better quality information has been associated with success and survival (for example, Hutchison and Ray, 1986).

Prima facie, one would expect the providers of capital to firms which are classed as relatively risky investment opportunities to take steps to ensure that those to whom they commit funds are well served by information which is of relevance to their managerial decisions. It is also probable that this external pressure for development of the AIS is reinforced by those who can most directly influence the supply of information, namely the entrepreneurs/managers of the investee firms. Their motivation to enhance internal accounting methods is strengthened by two specific factors. The first is the need to have appropriate 'decision support' for the allocation of new or existing funds to their most productive uses, such that both *ex ante*, on the basis of projections, and *ex post*, on the basis of outcomes, an improvement is demonstrable. The second is that growth in corporate size, which is contingent upon the planned use of the venture capital provided, often is perceived to reduce or eliminate that personal involvement of the entrepreneur in many aspects of his business, from which he may have derived satisfaction ('psychic income'). Thus increased size creates a problem of control and may lead to a growth/profitability trade-off (Reid, 1995). The need to monitor and report remains, but if it cannot be achieved so readily by direct personal supervision, the entrepreneur satisfies the need for involvement and superintendance directly through the generation of relevant information on performance. The AIS of the firm is one important source of such relevant information for control, and it typically requires modification to cope with those new and more extensive demands placed upon it which arise when the firm grows.

The focus of this chapter is therefore on the impact of capital supply and ownership change on internal information provision. Broader consideration of the determinants of an appropriate AIS is contained in the literature on the contingency theory of management accounting (see Otley, 1980, and Ezzamel and Harte, 1987 for reviews).

This chapter suggests that key contingent variables influencing the AIS and its appropriate development are features of the firm's environment (normally to be conceived of in terms of uncertainty); its technology (normally conceived of in terms of complexity); and its organisational structure (normally conceived of in terms of flexibility). Jones (1985) has used a contingency theory approach to assess the importance of these features as determinants of internal accounting systems in merger situations where ownership has changed. He concluded that, 'overall management accounting systems tended to bear the characteristics of the Universalist theory' that is, that practical management accounting procedures remain similar despite differing contexts in terms of contingent variables. This chapter extends this research by examining one of the factors which, for some firms, may exert a Universalist influence on the AIS. The presumption of part ownership by the VCI, and the institutionalisation of 'standard' information demands on investees, may represent strong formative influences on the genesis of AISs for SMEs going through an important stage of development.

The theoretical backdrop to this chapter is that the investor (VCI) can be treated as a risk-neutral (fully diversified) principal, and the investee as a risk-averse agent, and that both parties have an incentive to achieve an efficient contractual relationship with one another. This can be done by seeking a better sharing of risk and information. The investee has rich information, but is risk exposed. The investor has diversified away much of his risk, but has poor information. Efficient contracting would seek the optimal exchange of information-providing and risk-bearing capacities between investee and investor. First-best contracting may not be possible because, no matter the complexity of the information system, the investee's activities are not completely observed. However, second-best contracting seeks efficiency with information asymmetry being attenuated, and risk-sharing being limited so as to maintain the incentive for effort (see Reid, 1996).

The study

The study on which we report involved gathering data from a sample of 12 VCIs and 12 of their investee firms. The VCIs came from a random sample of those listed in the *Venture Capital Report* (fourth edition) which provides a comprehensive listing of active venture capitalists in the UK. One factor also determining the sample was the willingness of the VCI to allow one of its investee firms to be included. Thus out of a sample frame of 47 VCIs, 20 were randomly selected and 12 of these were prepared to allow the incorporation of an investee in the study. Investees were selected by the VCI on the basis of three criteria. Each investee had to be: (1) willing to grant an interview with its chief executives; (2) possessed of extensive experience of involvement with the VCI; and (3) representative of the VCI's investees, in terms of the nature and size of the VCI stake, its firm size and its industrial sector. A summary of key sample characteristics of investor–investee 'dyads' is given in Table 12.1. It is to be noted that the sample of 12 cases (A through to L) displays considerable variation by size measures (for example, funds managed, turnover), structure (for example, ratio of venture capital executives to investees, venture capital stake) and sectoral activity. It represents well the larger body of investor–investee relations in the UK venture capital industry (Mitchell et al., 1995).

Data were gathered by structured interviews with VCIs and their nominated investees. These interviews were conducted face-to-face between June 1992 and December 1993. Two researchers were involved in each interview, one as interviewer and one as recorder. The interviews varied in duration between one-and-a-half to two-and-a-half hours. They covered risk management and key aspects of the nature of VCIs' demands for accounting information and the nature and development of investees' AISs. All of the VCIs interviewed had gained considerable (typically 12 years) experience in the venture capital industry, and all of the investees were represented by chief executives who had been involved in many aspects of the process of raising venture capital funds for their businesses.

(i) Establishing the information source

All of the VCIs interviewed made effective demands on their investees for accounting information, not only at the time of making the investment, but also subsequently, to ensure a regular flow of monitoring information. The requirements which VCIs placed on the investees to report externally therefore set a minimum standard of systematic accounting information provision within the investee companies. To ensure compliance, the establishment of an appropriate system was a normal condition of investment. Every VCI interviewed (with one exception) undertook a vetting of the investee's AIS. Even the one which did not was at least positive about the idea, saying: 'We want to do this but haven't in the past. In the past we haven't looked at their accounting systems but we realise the venture capitalists need good information not just for me but also for their own decision-making.'

Most of the other 11 VCIs ($n = 9$) assessed the investee's AISs themselves. Of these, two also used auditors' findings (for example, the reviewing of recent letters by managers and the reactions of clients to them).[3] For another two, one relied on the auditor to judge the system in use, and the other commissioned special investigative reviews by independent accountants. In seven cases, the VCIs indicated that they regularly required changes to be made. They cited examples of improvements in various aspects of internal accounting which had been made at their insistence (for example, the development of the sales system, the creation of an effective credit control system, the creation of a costing system). Moreover, one VCI assessed the quality of staff involved in operating the accounting systems, and prompted the recruitment of better staff where necessary. In one case, involving smaller investors, the VCI was even more proactive in influencing internal accounting: 'Sometimes I set them up to begin with . . . I show them my accounting system and several of them use it until they grow. . . .' Thus the concern of VCIs for the availability of reliable and relevant

Table 12.1 Key characteristics of the sample

Case	Venture capital investor (VCI)				Investee			
	Venture funds under management (£m)	Number of venture capital executives	Number of investees	Average Value of Investment Made (£000s)	Industrial sector (SIC)	Turnover (£000s)	Number of employees	Venture Capital stake (%)
A	200	16	25	2000	n.a.	n.a.	n.a.	n.a.
B	28	8	11	400	95	279	8	36%
C	45	2	2	300	22	4000	55	n.a.
D	29	3	13	245	21	7000	193	n.a.
E	175	9	n.a.	n.a.	47	90 000	840	75%
F	50	8	12	1000	48	1700	50	99%
G	60	6	5	4000	34	33 800	735	n.a.
H	2	1	5	25	25	275	7	28%
I	100	7	n.a.	700	94	2750	35	n.a.
J	8	3	6	400	34	1800	27	n.a.
K	88	7	33	n.a.	13	13 500	97	55%
L	150	16	61	500	64	6500	35	n.a.

accounting information was manifested primarily in their readiness to examine and improve the underlying system. However, it was also apparent in three other facets of their behaviour towards investees.

First, in most cases ($n = 9$), the deterrent effect of extra costs of generating and/or processing information was not considered to impose a constraint on obtaining what the VCI wanted to know. Indeed several saw the pursuit of information needs through to their provision as a central facet of their role:

> This is a very real issue. It is very important to get information, and if it does cost more, then so be it. There is no greater crime than to report back, 'don't know'.

> The trend which I've seen over the last 12 years is to be more and more cautious on financial information, to gather more and more information to balance against the price of a deal.[4]

> Information gathering is an essential cost. We are paid a management fee by our clients to monitor our investments.

Although the information which was perceived as necessary would apparently be gathered with little regard to its total cost, a number of VCIs did also express the view that the incremental cost to them of information was seldom high. In view of this, they would ensure that the investee firm had established a system to produce all that was needed. They would not be perturbed at the prospect of imposing any new requirements, for their implementation would, in any case, be funded by the investee. The VCIs' information demands were, however, selective (see following section) and attempts were made to contain the volume of information received, so that overload did not become a problem.

> Processing it is the problem. You can only absorb so much information. We occasionally shout 'stop'.

> We like to think we don't ask for information we can't process. It is important to home in on key variables.

Second, over half ($n = 7$) of the VCIs had obtained direct access to their investees' internal accounting systems. This access had enhanced their capacities both to monitor and to verify the information provided. Finally, ten of the twelve VCIs specifically influenced the audit of the investee company. Six did so by an involvement in the selection of the auditor, with a strong preference being expressed for 'big, reputable' firms. The remaining four were prepared to initiate additional audit work, where problems were apparent which required more external visibility. The two VCIs who did not exert any audit influence did, however, request and study the annual management letter from the auditor.

(ii) Information required

All 12 VCIs had established the requirement for investees to return a fairly conventional package of accounting information every month, and used this as the basis for monitoring their investees' performance. These data were frequently referred to as the 'monthly management accounts'. They typically consisted of three financial statements: the balance sheet; the profit and loss account; and the cash flow statement. These statements also constitute the core financial content of the statutory shareholders' report. However, the VCI's package differed from this report, not only in terms of reporting frequency, but also in several other significant respects. In particular, the level of detail disclosed was greater than that which was statutorily required for external reporting. For example, the profit and loss account supplied would normally incorporate the segmentation of turnover by product line, expenses would be detailed to show the make up of cost of sales and overheads, and a similar breakdown of cash flows would be available. In addition, five of the VCIs specifically mentioned that these financial results would be presented within the context of the investee firm's budget to provide a clear comparison of budgeted against actual magnitudes. Two VCIs also requested the investee company's management to provide a written commentary or narrative on the results contained in the monthly information package. To provide some further indication of investees' future prospects, another two VCIs required a report on their order book positions. Finally, various forms of supplementary information, all directly or indirectly linked to performance, were requested in the light of specific needs of individual VCIs. These included measures of product quality, and capacity utilisation, as well as capital investment proposals and gearing ratios.

Information requirements were, in the main, set and enforced in a fairly standard manner. In all cases investees had, at some stage, to meet the basic demands for information described above, and five of the VCIs allowed no variation in these information demands. The others did allow a measure of flexibility. Four allowed some relaxation in the regularity of reporting (from monthly to a quarterly or half-yearly basis). This required that the relationships they had with investees were well established, and that investees had generated satisfactory track records over this time. Another VCI did not require reports from investees before trading operations had started, and yet another allowed investees to report on differing bases, depending on how reporting demands had evolved over the 1980s.

The investee's AIS: practice and change

The sample of 12 representative investees provided information on both the nature of their AISs and the developments which had occurred therein subsequent to VCIs' involvements with them. Their responses are presented in three sections below (namely, performance measurement, budgetary control and decision-making).

(i) Performance measurement

This aspect of the study focused on the operating performance of the investee. Key components of the profit and loss account (for example, turnover, labour costs, profit), cash flow, and some financial ratios (linking the profit and loss account to the balance sheet) were all specifically discussed. In addition, the investees were requested to identify any other important means by which they assessed their firm's progress and performance. Table 12.2 summarises the responses. The general picture is of a rich flow of information from investee to investor, as would be expected in situations of relatively high risk, in which risk can be 'managed' by attenuating the information asymmetry between investee and investor.

Table 12.2 Performance measurement information used by investees (n = 12)

	Information used internally by investee	Information reported to VCI	Information developed since VCI involvement
Profit and loss components			
Turnover analysis	12	12	1
Labour cost analysis	8	8	1
Net profit	12	12	2
Financial ratios			
Return on equity employed	6	5	3
Return on assets	6	6	1
Sales/assets invested	3	3	1
Other aspects			
Cash flow	12	10	4
Other (see discussion in text)	11	11	8

Turnover, profit and cash flow information were used within all of the investee companies and with only two exceptions (on cash flow) these types of information were also reported to the VCI. Cash flow information did reflect some potential degree of VCI influence in its generation. In four cases its development had only occurred after VCI involvement. The utilisation of the profit and loss account and balance sheet information to derive commonly used financial ratios occurred in roughly half of the firms, and if desired they were typically reported to the VCI. However, only in the case of the return on equity capital employed (a 'shareholder' ratio) was there an indication of a significant number of investees developing the measure in response to requests from their VCIs. The 'other' key performance measures used by investees had largely been associated with the VCI link. They included market share analysis ($n = 1$); stock turnover ($n = 1$); profit margin ($n = 1$); order situation ($n = 1$); debtor analysis ($n = 1$); headcount ($n = 1$); overtime volume ($n = 1$) research milestones ($n = 1$); and proof of bank covenant compliance ($n = 1$).

(ii) Control

To ascertain details of the accounting control system within investee firms, interviewees were asked whether they: (a) produced information to allow them to monitor their business operations; and (b) set financial budgets. If relevant, they had to identify the key components of their budgets, and the basis on which they were reviewed over time (for example, monthly, quarterly, and so on) and used for control purposes. Each was also requested to indicate if the control information produced had been developed since becoming involved with their VCI. The responses are reported by the class of control information in Table 12.3 and by the frequency of budgetary reporting in Table 12.4.

Table 12.3 Control information used by investees

	Used internally by investee	Reported to VCI	Produced since VCI's involvement
(1) Use of monitoring reports	11	10	3
(2) Financial budgets set	12	12	1
(3) Budget components			
Profit and loss account	12	12	3
Cash flow	12	12	3
Balance sheet	12	12	3
Capital expenditure	10	10	3
Headcount	11	11	3
Other	2	2	–

For all classes of control information reported in Table 12.3, the information generated internally by the investee is typically reported to the VCI. In just one case, the monitoring report, this was not done. Generally, the VCI played a significant role in making its demand for information met by the investee. Thus, for most classes of control information, about a third or more of this provision had occurred after the VCI had become involved. The one exception to this was in the setting of financial budgets, a crucial class of control information even for independent SMEs, in which case the influence of the VCI was less.

Table 12.4 Frequency of budgetary reporting by investee

	None	Annual	Bi-Annual	Quarterly	Monthly	Weekly	Daily
(a) Profit and loss Account							
Before VCI involvement	3	5	–	1	3	–	–
After VCI involvement	–	6	1	2	3	–	–
(b) Cash flow							
Before VCI involvement	3	3	1	–	2	2	1
After VCI involvement	–	4	–	–	5	2	1
(c) Balance sheet							
Before VCI involvement	3	5	–	–	4	–	–
After VCI involvement	–	4	1	1	6	–	–
(d) Capital expenditure							
Before VCI involvement	5	6	–	–	1	–	–
After VCI involvement	2	8	–	–	2	–	–
(e) Headcount							
Before VCI involvement	4	4	–	2	2	–	–
After VCI involvement	1	6	–	1	4	–	–
(f) Other							
Before VCI involvement	10	1	–	–	1	–	–
After VCI involvement	10	–	–	1	1	–	–

Table 12.4 emphasises another aspect of information provision, namely its time basis, flow rate, or frequency, as opposed to its volume or variety. Six forms of budgetary reporting are identified, covering a wide range of types from profit and loss account, through balance sheet, to head count. The frequency of reporting is then indicated, both before (first row) and after (second row) VCI involvement with the investee. Overall, annual and monthly reporting are the typical frequencies. For all classes of budgetary reporting, the effect of VCI involvement is almost always to raise the frequency of reporting, in two senses. First, more investees are involved in reporting at any given interval (for example, annual) after VCI involvement, as compared to before. Second, additional intervals for reporting are typically required (for example, bi-annual as well as annual) after VCI involvement, as compared to before. Thus comparing 'before' and 'after' VCI involvement for each budgetary reporting type, the 'after' row frequency is only greater than the 'before' in two cells out of the 21 reported in Table 12.4. For these two instances, in the first (balance sheet) annual reporting has been replaced by bi-annual and quarterly reporting, and in the second (other) annual reporting has been replaced by quarterly reporting. Thus the general picture of increased frequency of reporting as a result of VCI involvement is substantiated.

To conclude our analysis of control, we find that monitoring reports and budgetary control systems were widely used within the investee firms, to an extent which the VCIs affected positively. Financial control through budgetary targets was an important aspect of operations and one that was used with differing degrees of flexibility, as the following qualitative evidence indicates:

> We know what we have in the bank and what we should have next month in the bank. Everything is looked at virtually daily. We're locked into a six month cycle: ... We're on a treadmill that doesn't stop.

> The budget is set annually and we phase it month by month. We might reset the budget depending on the circumstances prevailing at the time.

> We set the budget every 12 months if the actuals run in line with the budget. But if they deviate we review the results, which leads to a new budget.

(iii) Decision making

The investees were asked about the accounting information produced within their organisations for decision making. Once again they were requested to indicate if this type of information was reported to their VCI and whether or not it had been developed subsequent to the VCI involvement with them. Some exploration of the type of information produced was also made. The results on decision types are presented in Table 12.5. The decision types identified are: operating, strategic and capital investment. The results indicate the widespread development of

AIS support for internal decision making. Moreover, in a substantial number of cases this type of information was reported to the investee's VCI. This pattern was most marked in the case of capital investment analysis. Indeed, particularly with regard to longer-run decisions on strategy and investment, the VCI's involvement was linked with the new development of accounting information.

Table 12.5 Decision-making information in investee firms

Decision type	Information used internally	Information reported to VCI	Information developed only since VCI involvement
Operating decisions	11	5	1
Strategic decisions	12	5	5
Capital investment	9	8	4

Two information types for decision making were investigated: output costing and capital investment. Of four output costing procedures considered, it was found that full costing (including a non-production element), which has enjoyed increasing advocacy, particularly for decision making in recent years (Kaplan and Shank, 1990; Shank and Govindarajan, 1989) was in predominant use (two-thirds of the firms). The results on capital investment techniques are displayed in Table 12.6. They broadly mirror the pattern of usage found in more general surveys of practice in larger firms (for example, Pike, 1982). Payback (in all uses) and qualitative assessments (in eight of the nine users) are both widely used and generally influential in investment decisions. Accounting rate of return is used by half of the investees, but is typically not regarded as highly important, while both of the main discounting techniques (IRR, NPV) are used in less than half of the subjects. The four net present value users also used the internal rate of return. When use of the IRR is favoured (typically as computed with Lotus 123 software) it is regarded as important.

Table 12.6 Importance of capital investment techniques

		Importance of technique within firms		
	No. of firms	Low	Medium	High
Payback	9	2	2	5
Internal rate of return	5	–	1	4
Net present value	4	1	1	2
Accounting rate of return	6	1	3	2
Qualitative assessment	8	1	–	7
No response	1	–	–	–

Overview of findings

Tables 12.7 and 12.8 contain summaries of our results, highlighting the key aspects of VCIs' involvements in developing AISs. Table 12.7 considers six VCI policies. The ticks indicate by their presence a fairly strong interest on the part of VCIs in the capabilities their investees have in supplying accounting information. They also indicate considerable variation across cases in the policies underlying the VCIs' demand for accounting information. Half of the VCIs exhibited a relatively comprehensive approach to accessing information by pursuing five of the six policies investigated in this study. By contrast, one third of the VCIs appeared to adopt a more laissez-faire attitude, and only pursued three or less of the six policies.

The representative investees considered in Table 12.8 also exhibit considerable variation in the nature of AIS developments after their VCIs' involvement in terms of performance measurement, after control and decision making. However, the overall extent of change was restricted to just over 25 per cent of the cells in this table. One outlier (D) shows extensive change and another (A) no change, while all of the others had altered in less than half of the aspects investigated. Finally, little systematic variation appears to exist in the pattern of findings concerning the VCI/investee dyads. For example, a higher level of involvement in the investee's AIS does not appear to result in more AIS change. This, of course, may be explained by the varying quality of each investee's AIS prior to a VCI taking a stake in its business.

Conclusions

The results of this study indicate that VCIs view the capabilities of their potential investees' AIS as endogenous to their own decisions as to whether to back the firms. This view may in part reflect their desire to see the management of investee firms supplied with appropriate information for operational purposes, but it is also a function of their own needs for regular information flows for monitoring purposes. The VCIs' power to influence the investees' internal accounting systems has its basis both in their ownership stake, and in the conditions negotiated (and incorporated into) the initial subscription agreement. Thus VCIs can exert this power to influence significantly both the content and the frequency of accounting reports. Their specific information demands do tend to be both conventional and similar, and are typically based on a monthly package of traditional financial statements. However, particularly where problems exist, more information may be demanded on an even more regular basis.[5]

In many cases, the AISs of investees do change when VCIs become involved, not only with respect to performance measurement but also with respect to control and decision-making functions. In this process, the role of the VCI is important, especially as his involvement occurs in the relatively early stage of AIS development, at which point the potential exists for him to have a strong

Table 12.7 VCI policies

VCI policies / Cases	A	B	C	D	E	F	G	H	I	J	K	L	Total
Reporting requirements extend beyond financial statements	–	✓	✓	–	–	–	✓	–	✓	✓	✓	–	6
Access to investee AIS required	✓	✓	–	–	–	✓	✓	✓	✓	✓	–	–	7
No variation allowed in information provided	✓	–	–	✓	✓	✓	–	✓	–	–	–	–	5
AIS vetted	✓	✓	✓	✓	–	✓	✓	✓	✓	–	✓	✓	10
Influence exerted on investee audit	✓	✓	✓	✓	✓	✓	✓	✓	✓	–	–	–	9
No cost deterrent in obtaining information	✓	✓	✓	✓	–	✓	✓	✓	✓	✓	–	–	9
Total number of policies	5	5	4	4	2	5	5	5	5	3	2	1	46

Table 12.8 AIS developments subsequent to VCI involvement

AIS developments subsequent to VCI involvement Cases	A	B	C	D	E	F	G	H	I	J	K	L	Total
Performance measurement													
P&L a/c components	–	–	✓	✓	–	–	–	–	–	–	–	–	2
Financial ratios	–	✓	–	–	–	–	–	–	–	–	✓	–	2
Cash flow	–	–	✓	✓	✓	–	–	–	–	–	✓	–	4
Control													
Use of monitoring reports	–	✓	–	✓	–	–	–	–	✓	–	–	–	3
Setting finance budgets	–	–	–	–	–	–	–	–	–	–	–	–	0
Increasing budget components	–	–	–	✓	–	✓	–	✓	✓	–	–	–	4
Increasing frequency of budget interval for some aspect of the budget	–	–	✓	✓	✓	✓	–	✓	✓	–	–	–	6
Decision Making													
Operating decision information	–	–	–	✓	–	–	–	–	–	–	–	–	1
Strategic decision information	–	–	–	✓	✓	✓	–	✓	–	✓	–	–	5
Capital investment information	–	✓	–	✓	✓	–	✓	–	✓	–	–	–	5
Total number of changes	0	3	3	8	4	3	1	3	4	1	2	0	32

formative impact. Thus the sources and forms of VCI influence contrast noticeably with the variables identified by contingency theorists as being important in their explanations of management accounting practices. The latter emphasise the demands of firm and/or industry specific effects (for example, market environment, organisational structure and technology), whilst VCIs emphasise demands based on 'in-house' standards which are applied to all investees, irrespective of their particular operational circumstances.

While investees are free to adopt their own approaches to internal accounting, the burdens and costs of more than one system might well be impractical for SMEs. This encourages the VCI-driven system to dominate, and thus it tends to determine the path of future development for the SME. In many respects this study therefore supports the notion that the influences of the VCI run counter to those of key contingent variables. This finding provides support for Jones's (1985) concept of a universalist theory of management accounting.

The study also adds weight to the argument for attaching importance to accounting information in managing the investment contract between investor and investee. This can be seen not only at the entry, or investment selection stage, but also in terms of planning the exit route. Moreover, the AIS adopted must be capable of handling periods of difficult, or off-target, trading conditions. The strengths of the AIS become most relevant when there is a requirement for unforeseen additional funds or 're-financing'. Such an event would probably imply some degree of contract re-negotiation, involving issues such as: the re-alignment of equity stakes; and the further refinement of the information interchange represented by the AIS.

Notes

1. Originally, influenced by US practice, referring to high-risk, high-return unquoted equity involvement, but increasingly, in a UK context, having the connotation of development capital. An emerging term is 'private equity', which emphasizes the highly incentivised arrangements agreed between investor and investee.
2. Although many such agreements are standardised, an opportunity exists for customisation (for example, by type and frequency of accounting information requested). To this extent, the chapter casts some light on the sort of provisions that are likely to be found in this essentially confidential document.
3. Such letters may signal to the VCI the sort of information that needs to be sought, or areas where the system can be improved. This role in the development of the AIS is an incentive arrangement permitted by VCIs, allowing investees to go beyond the reporting uses of information (for example, to proactive decision making and strategic planning). Viewed in this way, the AIS plays a role in the trajectory to investment realisation, and begins to play a management IS function.
4. A significant comment, emphasising that the higher the value of the equity at the time of investment, the greater will the firm's performance have to be to raise the value at exit to a level which will enable the target IRR to be realised.
5. When problems occur with investees, the normal procedure is to put them into so-called 'intensive care'. This entails a much greater degree of VCI involvement in the day-to-day operations of the business. The AIS must be sensitive enough to provide early warning of such problems, yet robust enough to allow for an expansion of the role of information beyond simple monitoring.

References

Ezzamel, M. and H. Hart (1987), *Advanced Management Accounting, An Organisational Emphasis*, London: Cassell.

Hutchison, P. and G. Ray (1986), 'Surviving the financial stress of small enterprise growth', in J. Curran, J. Stanworth and D. Watkins (eds), *The Survival of the Small Firm*, Aldershot, Hampshire: Gower, pp. 53–74.

Jones, C.S. (1985), 'An empirical study of the evidence for contingency theories of management accounting systems in conditions of rapid change', *Accounting Organisations and Society*, **10**, 303–28.

Kaplan, R.S. and J.K. Shank (1990), 'Contribution margin analysis: no longer relevant – strategic cost management: the new paradigm', *Journal of Management Accounting Research*, Fall, **1**, 2–15.

Mitchell, F., G.C. Reid and N. Terry (1995), 'The post investment demand for accounting information by venture capital investors', *Accounting and Business Research*, Summer, **25** (99), 186–96.

Otley, D. (1980), 'The contingency theory of management accounting: achievements and prognosis', *Accounting Organisations and Society*, 251–67.

Pike, R. (1982), *Capital Budgeting in the 1980s: a major survey of investment practices in large companies*, London: Chartered Institute of Management Accountants.

Reid, G.C. (1995), 'Early life-cycle behaviour of micro-firms in Scotland', *Small Business Economics*, **7**, 89–95.

Reid, G.C. (1996), 'Fast growing small entrepreneurial firms and their venture capital backers: an applied principal–agent analysis', *Small Business Economics* **8**, 1–14.

Shank, J.K. and V. Govindarajan (1989), *Strategic Cost Analysis*, Boston: Irwin.

Storey, D., K. Keasey, R. Watson and P. Wynarczyk (1987), *The Performance of Small Firms*, Beckenham, Kent: Croom Helm Ltd.

Sweeting, R.C. (1991), 'Early-stage new technology-based businesses : interactions with venture capitalists and the development of accounting techniques and procedures', *British Accounting Review*, **23**, 3–22.

Wright, M. and K. Robbie (1996), 'Venture capitalists and unquoted equity investment appraisal', *Accounting and Business Research*, **26**, 153–68.

13. European IPO markets: a post-issue performance study

Benoît Leleux and Daniel Muzyka

European initial public offerings: an introduction

Secondary markets in Europe have been thrown into a recession of their own in the late 1980s and early 1990s, with a rapid decline in both the number of new firms applying for a listing and the total amounts of financing raised. France declined from 53 IPOs in 1987 to less than 11 in 1991. The United Kingdom plummeted from 128 to 36 IPOs over the same period. While cycles in the volume of new introductions have been witnessed in the past, the current decline seems to be more than cyclical, leading some market authorities to reconsider the very existence of their secondary markets: Britain closed its Unlisted Securities Market to new entrants in late 1994 after having shut down its third market in late 1990, Holland shut its second market in 1993, and other markets, such as Germany, Spain, Italy, Denmark or Belgium have seen very little if any activity over the last three years.[1] Particularly affected are professional investors such as venture capitalists, which have long relied on public equity markets to realize a significant proportion of their investments.[2] Without this harvesting mechanism at their disposal to modulate ownership and reallocate investments and skills, investors are now forced to reconsider the desirability of some investments in light of the reduced exit opportunities set.

Conventional explanations for the rapid decline of the markets include over-regulation, complex listing requirements, the absence of an equity culture in Europe, the lack of competition among national market places (most secondary markets are organized and run by the main exchanges), and a shortage of growth companies. These explanations focus mainly on the supply side of the market. But the lack of supply could be the symptom rather than the cause of the current situation. In particular, insufficient investor interest, and the resulting lack of demand for IPO shares, could as well explain the state of the markets. This chapter posits that long-term underperformance of IPO shares floated in Europe could have contributed to this lack of demand. In particular, abnormally low returns earned on IPO shares in seasoned trades may have affected investors' interest in new issues. The proposition is tested by analyzing the performance of some 307 IPOs in France, the UK, Germany, the Netherlands, and Belgium.

The evidence collected is then interpreted in regard to the information available in the other IPO markets.

The chapter is structured as follows. The first section summarizes the literature on IPO performance. The second section documents the recent trends in volumes of IPOs brought to market and the general activity levels in European markets. It also outlines the main proposition of the paper, namely that IPO underperformance over the long term could have affected the ability of issuers to tap public capital. The third section outlines the methodologies used to analyze long-term performance. In the fourth section the approach is applied to samples of IPO shares in five major European markets: France, the UK, Germany, the Netherlands, and Belgium. The evidence collected is reconciled with results obtained by other researchers to provide a comprehensive overview of IPO markets in Europe. The final section discusses the implications of the findings, indicating future desirable developments.

Pricing and performance of initial public offerings

Three major empirical anomalies in the pricing and performance of IPO shares have been outlined in the literature: (1) the abnormal initial returns, whereby the first market price is on average significantly higher than the offer price. This adjustment is usually interpreted as evidence of 'underpricing' of the shares (Ritter, 1984; Ibbotson, Sindelar and Ritter, 1988; Carter and Manaster, 1990); (2) the 'Hot issue' phenomenon, whereby the general volume of issues brought to market exhibits significant, recurrent, and to some extent predictable variations over time (Ibbotson and Jaffe, 1975; Ritter, 1984); and (3) the long-term underperformance phenomenon, whereby IPO shares seem, on average, to underperform various benchmarks in the three- to six-year post-IPO period (Aggarwal and Rivoli, 1990; Ritter, 1991; Loughran and Ritter, 1993; Keloharju, 1993; Levis, 1993; Loughran et al., 1994).

Most of the research originates in the United States, where information disclosure rules, the dynamism of IPO markets, the homogeneous flotation environment,[3] and the inquisitive nature of the academic community combine to provide the early evidence on IPO pricing and performance. The studies on initial returns have since been replicated in many European settings, supporting the robustness of the phenomenon across a broad range of institutional arrangements. Table 13.1 summarizes the evidence on IPO underpricing in Europe. The results are generally consistent within countries, with minor variations traceable to differences in study periods, sample characteristics, or markets considered.

The evidence on IPO long-term performance is sparse. Keloharju (1993), on a sample of 79 Finnish IPOs floated over the period 1984–89, reports average market-adjusted returns of –21.1 per cent over the first three years of seasoned trade. Hansson and Ljungqvist (1993) document a significantly negative average

Table 13.1 Studies of initial price reaction in European IPO markets: an overview

Study authors	Country	Sample size	Study period	Initial price reactions
Buckland et al. (1981)	UK	297	65–75	9.6%
Davis and Yeomans (1976)	UK	174	65–71	8.5%
McStay (1987)	UK	238	71–80	7.4%
Merrett et al. (1967)	UK	149	59–63	13.7%
Levis (1990)	UK	123	85–88	8.6%
Keasey et al. (1991)	UK	249	84–88	18.5%
Levis (1993)	UK	712	80–88	14.1%
Rees (1992)	UK	489	84–91	NA
Jacquillat et al. (1978)	France	60	66–74	2.7%
Husson and Jacquillat (1989)	France	131	83–86	11.4%
Topsacalian (1984)	France	8	83	29.7%
McDonald and Jacquillat (1974)	France	31	68–71	3.0%
Jenkinson and Mayer (1988)	France	11	86–87	25.0%
Jaffeux (1990)	France	239	83–88	14.5%
Belletante and Paliard (1993)	France	165	83–91	20.7%
Wessels (1989)	Netherlands	46	82–87	5.1 %
Kunz and Aggarwal (1991)	Switzerland	42	83–89	35.8%
De Ridder (1986)	Sweden	55	83–85	40.5%
Keloharju (1993)	Finland	85	84–89	9.5%
Dawson and Reiner (1988)	Germany	97	77–87	21.5%
Hansson and Ljungqvist (1993)	Germany	163	78–91	12.0%
Rogiers and Manigart (1992)	Belgium	28	84–90	10.1 %
Van Hulle et al. (1993)	Belgium	31	84–91	6.6%
Cherubini and Ratti (1992)	Italy	75	85–91	27.1%
Rahnema et al. (1992)	Spain	71	85–90	35.0%
Freixas and Inurrieta (1992)	Spain	58	86–90	22.3%
Alpalhão (1988)	Portugal	62	86–87	54.4%

Note: Average initial abnormal returns documented in European IPO markets. Study authors refers to the authors of the published or working papers. Sample size refers to the total size of the IPO sample used to investigate the initial abnormal returns. Study period indicates the period covered in the study. Initial price reactions, also referred to as initial underpricing in the literature, is the average increase in price between the offer price and the market price prevailing in early secondary trade, with the increase expressed as the percentage gain over the offer price. Studies differ with respect to the market price selected but results have been shown to be relatively robust to the specification of that parameter.

cumulative abnormal return of –13.6 per cent on 118 German IPOs over the period 1978–89. Levis (1993), for 712 IPOs in the United Kingdom over the period 1980–88, reports corresponding abnormal returns of –8.1 per cent. In contrast, Rydqvist (1993) and Kunz and Aggarwal (1991) do not find evidence of underperformance in the secondary markets of Sweden and Switzerland respectively.

The US evidence in this respect is more consistent. Ibbotson (1975) first highlights the presence of negative returns in the two- to four-year seasoning horizon on shares issued over the period 1960–69. Ritter (1991) develops the methodological aspects of long-term performance studies and presents the most statistically convincing account of the phenomenon. Using a sample of 1526 firms going public in the period 1975–1984,[4] Ritter shows that IPOs substantially underperform samples of matching seasoned firms (by industry and firm sizes) from the closing price on the first day of public trade to their third-year anniversary. Variations are highlighted by year of issuance and across industries but the phenomenon appears to be robust. Loughran and Ritter (1993) extend the scope of investigation to larger sampling and investment horizons but report similar underperformance over the long term.

IPO markets in Europe: the post-1987 experience

European IPO markets have been undergoing dramatic changes over the last few years. In particular, the rapid declines in the number of companies brought public and in trade volumes on secondary markets seem to go far beyond the cyclical patterns observed in the past. For example, the French 'Second Marché' went from a high of 53 introductions in 1987 to a low of 11 in 1991. In Britain, the Unlisted Securities Market (USM), established in November 1980 by the London Stock Exchange to promote the financing of small, growth companies, helped some 750 firms to go public in the period to 1991.

The success story did not last, with the importance of the USM as a means of capital financing rapidly declining: companies raised £308 million in 1988, £45 million in 1990, £11.6 million in 1991, and only marginally more in 1992. Several market makers resigned their seats and the USM is bound to close its doors to new entrants in 1994, following the collapse of the Third Market at the end of 1990.[5] The situation in other European centres is not better. Belgium witnessed a total absence of introductions for more than a year. Holland closed its second market in 1993, whereas Italy, Spain, Denmark and Finland all suffer from historically low levels of activity. Germany managed only 5 flotations in 1993.

Some governments, which for years supported the existence of secondary markets as providers of equity capital for the high-growth firms most needed in their economies, have seen some of the most promising enterprises move to NASDAQ to obtain the funds they were unable to raise in Europe, sometimes bypassing entirely the listing process in their own national markets. The European venture capital industry, which in 1991 surpassed its American counterpart for the first time in history, both in terms of new capital raised and total capital available for investments,[6] is increasingly confronted with the problem of not being able to harvest the most promising investments because of disappearing IPO markets, forcing a global rethinking of its investment strategies. The rapid evolution of European IPO markets is demonstrated in Table 13.2.

Table 13.2 Number of IPO flotations on European markets, 1983–91

Country	83	84	85	86	87	88	89	90	91
France	15	25	45	46	53	27	30	15	11
United Kingdom	72	102	121	141	128	134	83	65	36
Germany	10	22	11	25	17	14	24	28	19
Belgium	n.a.	2	4	8	5	3	3	3	0
Italy	7	11	12	42	23	14	7	4	8
Finland	0	9	2	5	16	46	13	0	0
Sweden	51	63	25	25	27	20	21	15	6
Switzerland	2	2	5	23	16	7	1	n.a.	n.a.
Total	157	236	225	315	285	265	182	130	80

Note: Data obtained from studies presented in Table 13.1. Some of the results can also be found in Loughran et al. (1994), table 4. The number of IPO flotations refers indiscriminately to main and secondary markets, as well as regional exchanges.

October 1987 seems to mark a significant turning point in European issuer behaviour. The number of new companies introduced dropped to all-time lows in the years that followed. Cycles in the volume of IPOs have been outlined previously (Ritter, 1984; Ibbotson et al., 1988) but the reversals on European stock exchanges seem to be attributable to structural rather than cyclical factors. Not only have IPO numbers dropped but trading volumes on secondary markets have collapsed, forcing authorities to question the very rationale for the existence of such markets. Conventional explanations for the collapse include over-regulation, complex listing requirements, the absence of an equity culture in Europe, the lack of competition among market places (secondary markets are usually organized by the main exchange authorities), and a shortage of growth companies. These explanations focus mainly on the supply side of the market. But the absence of supply may be the direct consequence of a lack of demand for new shares, either because of regulatory constraints limiting investments by certain categories of investors or because of unsatisfactory performance for IPO investments in the past. This chapter focuses on the latter contributory factor. The main proposition investigated here is that IPO shares in Europe have significantly underperformed over the long term. Such underperformance possibly affects the investors' interest in new issues and the observed lack of supply of new shares in some markets.

Database and research methodologies

This chapter combines the evidence in previous research papers with new analyses of the post-1987 IPO performance in five major European markets (United Kingdom, France, Germany, The Netherlands, and Belgium) for which long-term data could be obtained. The methodological guidelines in Loughran et al. (1994) are followed as closely as possible to facilitate comparisons. The traditional market-adjusted event study method is complemented by cross-sectional regressions (RATS) with robust estimators. This technique, originating in the work of Ibbotson (1975), allows the simultaneous estimation of both abnormal performance and systematic risk of buy-and-hold IPO portfolio strategies.

All IPOs which took place in the five markets considered between November 1987 and March 1991 are identified from stock market information and financial newspapers. The sample period is dictated by three concerns: (1) October 1987 seems to have significantly affected the capacity of European secondary markets to attract new issuers; (2) returns information are only available consistently after 1987; (3) sufficient scope is needed to track long-term performance in the most recent IPOs. Specifics of the issues (offer price, market on which introduction took place, issuer size, number of years since foundation or incorporation at IPO date, and so on) are collected from the same sources. Prices, capital structure changes, and dividend series for both stocks and stock market indices are obtained from Datastream on a monthly basis and used to construct monthly returns series in the 36-month post-offering period. The final sample sizes are 56 for France, 220 for the United Kingdom, 18 in Germany, 8 in Belgium, and 5 in the Netherlands. In most cases, the samples are representative of the population of events: IPOs on the secondary market in France numbered 59 over the period considered, compared with 348 in the United Kingdom over all markets and 10 in Belgium.

The traditional event study performance analysis involves estimating abnormal returns through a standard market adjustment of the form $AR_{i,t} = R_{i,t} - R_{m,t}$, where $AR_{i,t}$ is the market-adjusted abnormal return on share i in post-IPO month t, $R_{i,t}$ is the raw return on share i in month t, and $R_{m,t}$ is the corresponding return on the market index. The choice of an adequate market benchmark potentially influences the reported results. A broad-based second market index is ruled out because of the endogeneity problem: since IPO shares constitute a significant proportion of the index, underperformance of the shares would be reflected in the benchmark index itself, imparting a positive bias in the reported abnormal returns. Accordingly, a comprehensive stock market index is preferred for the adjustments in each country.[7] An average abnormal return is then calculated for each event month following the IPO, using $AR_t = 1/n_t \Sigma_{i=1}^{n_t} AR_{i,t}$, where n_t is the number of shares in the cross-section in post-IPO month t. A first long-run performance measure involves the cumulation of these abnormal returns over time for each individual firm, followed by cross-sectional averages (Dimson and Marsh, 1986):

$$CAR_{s,T} = \frac{1}{n}\sum_{i=1}^{n}\left\{\left[\prod_{t=s}^{T}\left(1+AR_{i,t}\right)\right]-1\right\} \tag{13.1}$$

Conrad and Kaul (1993) highlight the potential bias in this procedure, which aggregates not only returns but also individual estimation errors. The underlying investment strategy also implies monthly rebalancing of the IPO portfolios,[8] a behaviour rarely followed by IPO investors. Consequently, buy-and-hold returns are also preferred (Loughran et al. 1994).

The market adjustment procedure implicitly assumes an average beta of 1.0 for all IPO shares. The evidence in Balvers et al. (1988), Clarkson and Thomson (1990), and Chan and Lakonishok (1992) seems to support such assumption. But Cotter (1992), using IPO daily returns and a 30-day *ex-post* rolling-window beta estimation procedure, shows that IPOs exhibit a slowly decreasing systematic risk pattern, with betas declining from 1.2 on the first month after issue to around 1.0 after 6 to 9 months and 0.6 after 3 years. These results indicate the importance of accounting for shifts in systematic risk levels over the seasoning period. As a consequence, a cross-sectional regression methodology, originating in Ibbotson (1975), is also used to investigate jointly the evolution of systematic risk and abnormal returns over event time.[9] The RATS-type model can be formulated as: $r_{i,n} - r_f = a_n + b_n (r_{m,n} - r_{f,n}) + e_{i,n}$, where $r_{i,n}$ is the return of security i in seasoning month n, $r_{m,n}$ is the market index return measured in the same calendar month as $r_{i,n}$, a_n is the regression constant interpreted as the average abnormal return in seasoning month n, b_n is the systematic risk coefficient, $e_{i,n}$ is the stochastic disturbance term for asset i in seasoning period n, and $r_{f,n}$ is the risk-free return. Holding-period returns are similarly obtained by reinterpreting the n not as a single period but a multi-period index.

The interpretation of a_n as an abnormal performance measure relies on the joint assumption that the market is efficient and that the Sharpe–Lintner CAPM is the appropriate model to describe the cross-sectional variation of returns. Recent empirical works in both Japan and the United States (Ritter and Chopra, 1989; Amihud and Mendelson, 1989) tend to indicate that the empirical slope of the

Security Market Line may be flatter than what is assumed by the model. No similar references could be found for European equity markets, but this limitation should be kept in mind when interpreting the results. The standard OLS estimation procedures are also sensitive to non-normalities in the return distributions. Although OLS estimators remain unbiased and consistent in these circumstances, they lack efficiency. Since fat-tailed distributions have been documented for IPO returns in secondary trading (Ruud, 1993), estimators have to be found which are not only unbiased and consistent but also more efficient than OLS.[10] The trimmed regression quantile (TRQ) method (Koenker and Bassett, 1978; Bassett and Koenker, 1982; Koenker and Portnoy, 1987) is used here at various trimming levels when non-normalities are documented.[11]

A last problem possibly affecting the regressions using long-term performance as dependent variable is that of autocorrelation and heteroscedasticity. As shown by Loughran et al. (1994), new issues of equity tend to cluster in calendar time. This clustering may impart some correlation between returns across firms and time. In all instances, Durbin–Watson, Goldfelt–Quandt, and Breusch–Pagan tests are used to investigate the importance of these problems and the eventual recourse to more adequate methods such as estimated GLS or bootstrapping.

European IPO markets, 1988–93

Organization and flotation mechanisms

Europe offers to issuers a large set of institutional arrangements for going public. Most countries have second and third markets to facilitate the access to public capital. These markets are generally associated with less stringent admission requirements than the main boards, as summarized in Table 13.3. It clearly falls outside the scope of this chapter to investigate in detail the institutional environments prevailing in each European country. But a broad characterization may help in the explanation of some of the results.

Where US markets clearly developed as competitors, European secondary exchanges were usually set up by the main market authorities to facilitate the initial listing of companies with a view to 'grooming' them for the main boards. Secondary markets were never designed to become permanent listing places, a status NASDAQ clearly claims.[12] London was the first European financial place to introduce a secondary market. The USM, later followed by the over-the-counter (Third) market, opened the way to most other secondary markets. Paris, in 1983, opened its Second Marché.

European equity markets offer a wide array of mechanisms for gaining a public listing. The fixed-price, fixed-quantity system prevailing in the United States is complemented by auction-type procedures. France, for example, offers at least three flotation procedures, some of them non-mutually exclusive.[13] The 'Mise

Table 13.3 Admission requirement on secondary European markets

Country	Years in business (in years)	Minimum initial float (in % of equity)	Minimum capitalization (in $ million)
Belgium	0	2.5	1.2
Denmark	n.a.	15.0	0.4
France	2	10.0	9.0
Germany	0	0.0	0.4
Greece	3	13.0	0.4
Ireland	1	0.0	0
Italy	2	10.0	0.6
Portugal	1	10.0	0.7
Spain	0	20.0	0.2
United Kingdom	3	10.0	0
JASDAQ	5	12.5	4.0
NASDAQ	0	*	4.2

Notes:
n.a. refers to not applicable.
* indicates a different standard applied by NASDAQ for the minimum public float at introduction, stated at 100 000 shares instead of a percentage of total equity outstanding.
JASDAQ is the Japanese Association of Securities Dealers Automated Quotation system. Both NASDAQ and JASDAQ figures are provided for comparison purposes only.

Source: The data on admission requirements is from the Graham Bannock & Partners report to the European Union, August 16 1994, quoted in *The Economist*, August 20 1994, p. 60.

en Vente' (MV), or modified competitive auction, is a best-effort, two-stage auction with a minimum price. Conducted under the supervision of the market authorities, the auction results in a pro-rata allocation of the shares at the equilibrium price.[14] The 'Procédure Ordinaire' (PO), or repeated competitive auction, is another price-driven procedure controlled this time by the underwriting syndicate of investment bankers and security houses. Offer prices are successively raised, with bidders resubmitting their respective orders, until a satisfactory equilibrium is reached. The syndicate reserves the right to opt out and to switch to the public sales offer procedure. Again, a minimum price is specified in advance, as well as the maximum increase in price to take place during the auction rounds. The 'Offre Publique de Vente' (OPV), or public sales offer, is a traditional fixed-price, fixed-quantity offer made directly by shareholders to the investing public. The only uncertainty faced by investors is regarding the rationing of shares. An initial price-and-quantity bidding is conducted a week or so in advance of the offering to evaluate the initial strength of the demand for the shares. Based on the indications of interest collected in that round, a definitive offering price is established and shares are ultimately distributed on a pro-rata basis. France is also characterized by the near absence of underwritten procedures, the prohibition of both price and allocation discriminations, the fact that most flotations represent the listing of previously existing shares and not new equity issues, and the broad powers handed over to the market authorities in controlling the introduction process.

In the United Kingdom, the 'Offer for Sale at Fixed Price' is a fixed-price, underwritten offer made to the public, whereas the 'Offer for Sale by Tender' includes a price and quantity bidding stage used to determine the final, unique offer price. In 'Placements', issuing banks act both as distributors and underwriters of the new issues. Shares are initially placed by sponsors to institutional or private clients. The sponsors then purchase the shares from the issuer at the issue price and resell them to the clients. Finally, 'Introductions' can be used by companies listing previously existing shares. Again, as in France, oversubscribed issues are expected to be allocated according to a 'fair' scheme,[15] a concern clearly expressed in most European markets which prohibits the allocation scheme prevalent in the United States.[16]

The Dutch markets add to the choice a rights offer procedure operating as a two-stage process.[17] First, the issuing firm offers to sell shares at a fixed price to holders of 'rights' to them. A market is then established in the rights themselves[18] before these rights are finally exercised. It is interesting to note that the secondary market in Holland was scrapped in 1993. The Portuguese stock exchange is the sole European market to provide issuers with discriminative auctions resulting in different prices being paid by different bidders depending on the auction profile. Auctions, in one form or another, are also used in Belgium, Italy, Spain, Switzerland, and Sweden. Pro-rata allocations, with some technical variations such as the 'block' allocation scheme in France, are used in Finland, Spain, Portugal, and Sweden, in addition to the previously noted France and United Kingdom. Price discrimination is usually prohibited, with Portugal the exception. Fixed-price, fixed quantity offerings are available in most countries, with significant variations in the procedures used to determine the offer prices.[19]

A number of authors have posited the existence of a relationship between the choice of flotation mechanism and the performance of IPO shares, both in the short and the long term. Auction-related mechanisms have been shown to potentially reduce the winner's curse problem inherent in fixed-price procedures. Furthermore, the different mechanisms have been associated with differing abilities to capture the temporary 'overoptimism', or fad's component, in IPO markets.[20] The next section investigates both the long-term performance of IPO shares and the relationship between initial price reactions and long-term performance on five European IPO markets.

European IPO performance in the short and the long run

Initial abnormal returns Tables 13.1 and 13.2 summarize the evidence on both initial abnormal returns and the distribution of IPO issues over time in Europe. The potential effect of the choice of flotation mechanism on initial price reactions is highlighted in Table 13.4 for French IPOs. Fixed-price procedures appear to exhibit higher initial abnormal returns on average than auction-related procedures. This evidence can be the consequence of either intertemporal shifts in the type or quality of firms going public and/or the mechanism they select to float the shares. Levis (1993), in his exhibit 3, shows similar results for the United Kingdom.

Keasey et al. (1991), in a sample of 249 IPOs using the placement method over the period 1984–88, observe an average abnormal return of 18.48 per cent (market adjusted) and relate it to a number of variables capturing the ex-ante uncertainty in each issue. Levis (1990), sampling 123 offers for sale over the period 1985–88, observes abnormal first-day returns of 8.64 per cent, explained mostly by the combined effects of the winner's curse and the prepayment mechanism applied in the UK IPO market. In Germany, Uhlir (1989), sampling 97 firm-commitment IPOs over the period 1977–87, documents market adjusted initial returns of 21.5 per cent, statistically different from 0, whereas Hansson and Ljungqvist (1993), over the period 1978 to 1991, report only an average 12 per cent. In Belgium, Rogiers and Manigart (1992) find an average initial abnormal return of 10.2 per cent on a sample of 28 IPOs between 1984 and 1990, results confirmed by Van Hulle et al. (1993). In Amsterdam, Wessels (1989) shows that only the fixed price procedure generates significant abnormal returns: rights offers and the offers by tender are not associated with abnormal returns. Keloharju (1993), sampling Finnish IPO markets over the period 1984–91 shows a mean initial excess return of 6 per cent. The Swiss market, investigated by Kunz and Aggarwal (1991), also shows initial underpricing of 35.8 per cent, a pattern documented for Spain by Freixas and Inurrieta (1992), with market-adjusted initial returns of 22.3 per cent, and Portugal by Alpalhão (1988), where average initial returns in excess of 63 per cent are documented.[21]

Long-term performance of European IPO shares

This section analyses the performance of shares issued in France, the United Kingdom, Germany, Belgium, and the Netherlands in the post-IPO period.[22] Cumulative abnormal returns over a 36-month seasoning period are reported for the five countries in Figure 13.1. These figures do not attempt to control for the possible flotation mechanism effect. The long-term underperformance first reported by Ritter (1991) for the United States is evident in at least three countries analyzed (France, UK and the Netherlands). Inferences for Belgium and Germany are constrained by sample sizes. The 36-month average cumulative

Table 13.4 French IPO offerings by issue year (1983–91) and average abnormal initial returns

Offer procedure	83	84	85	86	87	88	89	90	91	Husson & Jacquillat (1989)	Belletante & Paliard (1993)
Procedure Ordinaire	9	2	1	2	4	17	4	3	3	4.2%	4.3%
Mise en Vente	1	7	23	16	12	1	6	0	4	3.9%	16.4%
Direct OPV	3	6	6	9	29	8	8	12	4	11.4%	28.0%
Indirect OPV	2	10	15	19	8	1	12	0	0	17.4%	26.4%
Total	15	25	45	46	53	27	30	15	11		

Note: Data from Husson and Jacquillat (1989), Jacquillat (1989), and various COB and SBF annual reports. The average abnormal initial returns are measured from the offer price to the market price prevailing in early trade. The 'Procedure Ordinaire' is a modified competitive auction with uniform price. The 'Mise en Vente' is a repeated auction with both minimum price and maximum price increase during the various rounds of auctions. The 'OPV' procedure is a fixed-price, fixed-quantity mechanism, with a distinction made between flotations conducted with that method as a first choice (direct) and those conducted after first attempting an alternative auction-type procedure (indirect).

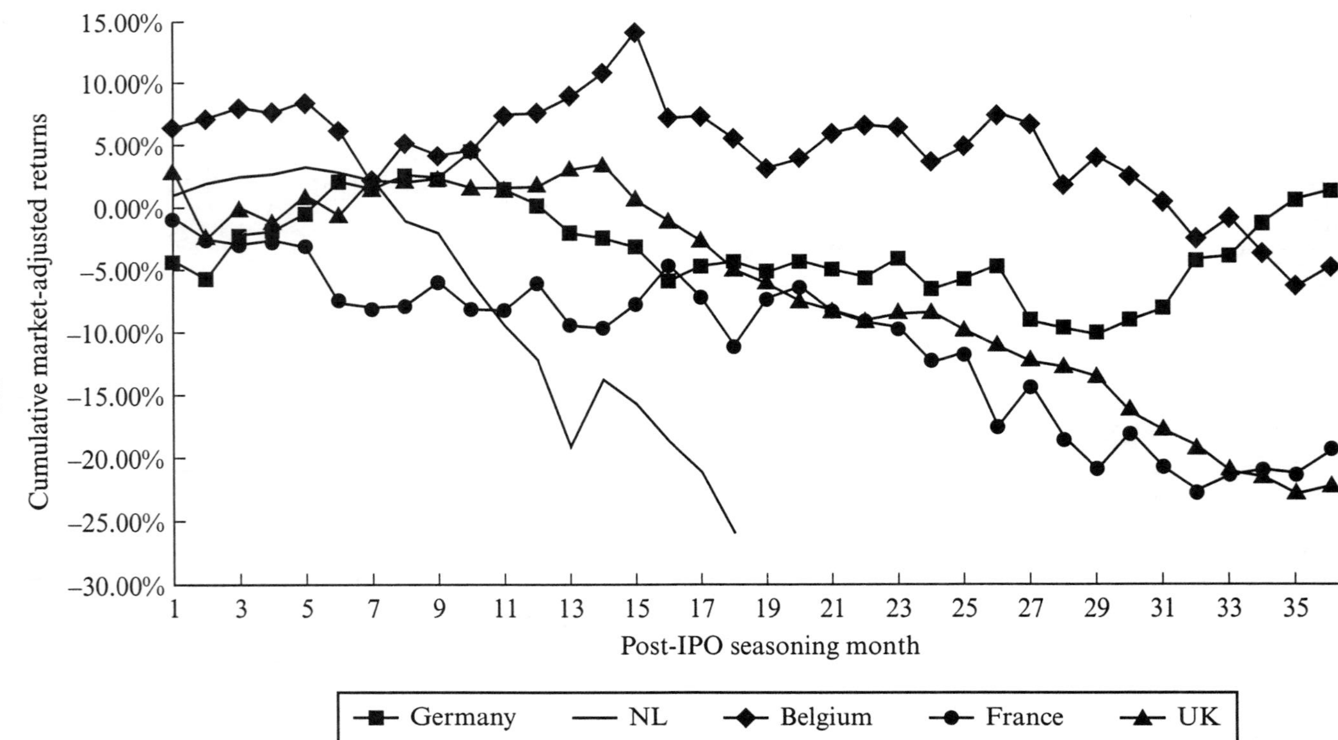

Figure 13.1 Cumulative market-adjusted abnormal returns, all five countries

market-adjusted returns for France and the UK are reported respectively at –29.2 and –21.8 per cent.

Table 13.5 *Post-IPO buy-and-hold mean market-adjusted returns in five European markets*

Holding period	France *n* AR *t*-test (Prob > |*t*|)	United Kingdom *n* AR *t*-test (Prob > |*t*|)	Germany *n* AR *t*-test (Prob > |*t*|)	Netherlands *n* AR *t*-test (Prob > |*t*|)	Belgium *n* AR *t*-test (Prob > |*t*|)
6 Month	56	191	15	5	8
	–4.6%	–0.4%	7.8%	–0.2%	2.2%
	–2.05	–0.21	n.a.	n.a.	n.a.
	(0.04)	(0.81)	n.a.	n.a.	n.a.
12 Month	52	162	15	5	8
	–7.7%	0.3%	4.3%	–13.6%	4.6%
	–2.25	0.06	n.a.	n.a.	n.a.
	(0.03)	(0.95)	n.a.	n.a.	n.a.
24 Month	46	148	12	3	8
	–12.8%	–16.2%	7.5%	–25.6%	0.2%
	–2.22	0.77	n.a.	n.a.	n.a.
	(0.03)	(0.44)	n.a.	n.a.	n.a.
36 Month	32	99	4	n.a.	3
	–30.3%	–19.2%	12.2%	n.a.	9.9%
	–3.93	–2.07	n.a.	n.a.	n.a.
	(0.001)	(0.04)	n.a.	n.a.	n.a.

Note: Returns information from Datastream on-line services. AR refers to the average market-adjusted buy-and-hold returns for the market analyzed. *t*-tests are for the null hypothesis that the mean market-adjusted holding-period returns are equal to zero. *n* is the sample size in each category. (Prob > |*t*| indicates the significance levels of the *t*-ratios obtained. *t*-tests are not reported for categories with less than 20 observations because of the difficulty in interpreting the results.

The econometric limitations inherent in the cumulation method[23] warrant the evaluation of holding-period rates of return, corresponding to the market-adjusted returns to strategies consisting in buying IPO shares on the first day of the first full month of trade following the flotation and holding them for pre-determined periods of time (6, 12, 24, and 36 months). The returns to such strategies are reported in Table 13.5. Sample sizes again prohibit statistical tests for Belgium, Germany and the Netherlands. The results for France and the United

Kingdom provide additional support for the existence of abnormally negative returns over the 36-month post-IPO interval. The –30.3 per cent observed in France and the –19.2 per cent in the United Kingdom are all statistically different from zero at the usual levels of confidence. The UK figure is in line with previous findings by Levis (1993) who reported average abnormal returns of –11.4 per cent for 483 IPOs over the period 1980–88. The figures do not differ much from those obtained using the cumulation approach.

Long-term studies are potentially exposed to a survivorship bias, or selective censoring through attrition: samples at various intervals may not be comparable because of natural attrition through bankruptcy, firms going private, or change of listing venue. Following Ritter (1991), this study tracks share performance even when a company shifts to an alternate market. No going-private transactions occurred in the sample over the 36 months of seasoning. Concerns about truncation of the sample for firms issued in early 1991 are alleviated by the relatively limited IPO activity in the period. No bankruptcies were observed in the French sample over the 36-month period of investigation and only six in the UK. These figures remain very low compared to the attrition observed for example by Ritter (1991), where some 25 per cent of the firms tracked disappeared within 36 months of the IPO, a finding that can be related to significant differences in the characteristics of the firms going public. As outlined in other studies,[24] European firms tend to be older and with more mature operations than the typical IPO firm in the United States.

The holding-period method controls for both the error cumulation problem and the rebalancing assumption in the cumulative returns method. Unfortunately, it also assumes that IPO shares on average exhibit systematic risks close to or in excess of 1.0, a point still debated. For this purpose, a cross-sectional regression methodology is also used to simultaneously evaluate abnormal returns and systematic risk. Goodness of fit tests on the residuals of the OLS estimations indicate the existence of significant deviations from normality, as argued by Ruud (1993). Such non-normalities warrant the use of robust estimators of the regression coefficients. The estimated regression coefficients are presented in Table 13.6 for the two markets (UK and France) for which sample sizes are large enough to support robust estimations. The results are very similar to those presented in exhibit 6 using the simpler market-adjustment methodology. The 36-month abnormal returns, controlling for systematic risk, stand at –31.1 per cent for France, versus –29.2 per cent previously. The UK figures are now –27.1 per cent, versus –21.8 per cent previously. The cross-sectional estimates of the systematic risk of the portfolio holding strategies with various investment horizons never differ significantly from 1.0. No trend or pattern could be outlined in the time-series pattern of systematic risk.

Table 13.6 *Buy-and-hold abnormal performances (France and United Kingdom) cross-sectional regression methodology using both OLS and TRQ estimators*

Holding period	Country analyzed	Regression method	Abnormal returns (%)	Standard deviation	*t*-test	Systematic risk	Standard deviation
6 Month	France	OLS	–4.1	0.021	6.09***	0.79	0.13
		TRQ5	–4.5	0.019	–2.31*	0.66	0.02
		TRQ10	–4.5	0.020	–2.22*	0.74	0.12
	United Kingdom	OLS	1.1	0.023	0.79	0.74	0.18
		TRQ5	1.8	0.021	0.68	0.68	0.16
		TRQ10	2.1	0.021	0.67	0.70	0.16
12 Month	France	OLS	–8.1	0.034	–2.33**	0.85	0.13
		TRQ5	–8.3	0.033	–2.53**	0.83	0.12
		TRQ10	–9.2	0.034	–2.65**	0.78	0.13
	United Kingdom	OLS	–2.3	0.048	–1.01	0.80	0.20
		TRQ5	–2.2	0.042	–0.92	0.80	0.17
		TRQ10	–1.6	0.042	–0.90	0.79	0.17
24 Month	France	OLS	–13.4	0.059	–5.96***	0.99	0.16
		TRQ5	–14.1	0.052	–2.69***	0.94	0.15
		TRQ10	–13.6	0.056	–2.44**	0.93	0.16
	United Kingdom	OLS	–12.1	0.158	–2.12**	1.12	0.46
		TRQ5	–22.2	0.103	–2.45**	1.31	0.37
		TRQ10	–16.4	0.107	–1.82*	1.05	0.38
36 Month	France	OLS	–31.1	0.091	–3.41***	0.81	0.24
		TRQ5	–27.0	0.085	–3.18***	0.79	0.22
		TRQ10	–27.0	0.085	–3.17***	0.78	0.23
	United Kingdom	OLS	–27.1	0.126	–2.84***	0.71	0.61
		TRQ5	–25.8	0.136	–3.02***	0.74	0.37
		TRQ10	–26.7	0.140	–3.12***	0.70	0.38

Notes:
Holding period refers to the time between the IPO flotation (buy) and the end of the holding period (sell). Regression method indicates the statistical method used to evaluate the parameters of the cross-sectional regressions. Standard deviation relates to the regression coefficients. Systematic risk refers to the cross-sectional systematic risk coefficient, with its standard deviation.
Significance levels: *** at the 1% level; ** at the 5% level; * at the 10% level.
The *t*-tests used to investigate the hypothesis that systematic risk coefficients are different from 1.0 are never significant at the usual levels of confidence.
TRQ stands for trimmed regression quantile estimators, with trimming levels of 5 and 10 per cent respectively.

These long-term performance results reinforce previous similar findings by Rydqvist (1993) in Sweden, Kelohaju (1993) in Finland, Rydqvist (1993) in Germany, or Levis (1993) in the UK.

Flotation method, underpricing, and long-term performance

As mentioned previously, Europe offers a broader choice of flotation mechanisms to the potential issuer than the United States. The mechanisms differ not only in terms of their underlying sales principle (fixed-price versus auctions) but also in the rules used for allocating shares (pro-rata, block allocation, and so on), the ability to discriminate among investors' orders, the type of support provided by underwriters (underwritten versus best-effort), and the level and type of intervention by market authorities. For example, IPOs in France's secondary market are rarely underwritten, most often represent the listing of previously existing shares and not capital raising efforts, and use all available procedures with some frequency. Most issues are also largely oversubscribed, sometimes more than a hundred times.[25]

Table 13.7 Buy-and-hold performance by flotation method used (France and United Kingdom)

Holding period	France MV (*p*-value)	 PO (*p*-value)	 OPV (*p*-value)	UK I (*p*-value)	 O (*p*-value)	 P (*p*-value)
12 Month	–6.28%	–14.05%	–4.45%	–3.38%	11.87%	–1.46%
	(0.246)	(0.032)**	(0.382)	(0.841)	(0.081)*	(0.752)
24 Month	–14.44%	–14.70%	–11.34%	–12.59%	10.25%	–34.8%
	(0.512)	(0.086)*	(0.190)	(0.621)	(0.341)	(0.431)
36 Month	n.a.	–23.56%	–32.89%	–22.55%	–11.5%	–19.92%
	n.a.	(0.114)	(0.004)	(0.601)	(0.581)	(0.05)**

Notes:
Holding period refers to the length of time between the first day of trade in the first full month of trade following the flotation (buy) and the sale of the IPO portfolio.
Significance: *** stands for significance at the 1% level, ** at 5% and * at 10%.
MV stands for 'Mise en Vente', a competitive auction procedure, PO for 'Procédure Ordinaire', a repeated auction flotation mechanism, OPV for 'Offre Publique de Vente', a fixed-price fixed-quantity procedure, I for Introductions, O for Offer for Sales (by tender of fixed-price), and P for Placements.
n.a. means not applicable, referring to situations where the sample sizes do not permit proper analyses.

Source: Returns information from Datastream.

Table 13.7 compares the buy-and-hold performance of shares issued under various mechanisms in the UK and France. Although performance differences are apparent by issuing method, the differences are not statistically significant. Part of the problem may stem from data aggregation: Offers for Sale in the UK, for example, regroup both fixed-price and auction-type mechanisms. In France, the OPV category also includes both straight fixed-price introductions and two-stage offerings, where the initial introduction using an auction failed and a fixed-price offering was resorted to only as a last resort. Small sample sizes prevent further disaggregation here.

The relationship between initial price reaction and long-term performance is investigated in Table 13.8. A large body of IPO literature has implications for this relationship. The 'fads' hypothesis in Ritter (1991) attributes the initial abnormal returns to overenthusiastic investors bidding prices up to unsustainable heights. Assuming that the market is efficient at least in the long run, a correction is bound to take place, translating into a negative correlation between initial returns and long-term performance. The 'signaling by underpricing' models of Welch (1989), Grinblatt and Hwang (1989), and Allen and Faulhaber (1989) stress the signaling potential of initial pricing, with high quality issuers separating from their lower quality counterparts by their ability to underprice more because they expect to recoup the costs on secondary share issues. Under the 'strategic behavior' proposition, issuers not only time their offerings to be close to market peaks[26] but also select the most appropriate flotation mechanism to reduce their overall cost of capital. This explanation has ambiguous implications for the relationship between initial price reaction and long-term performance because of the mediating effect of the choice of flotation mechanism.

Table 13.8 Coefficient estimators for the cross-sectional regressions on long-term performance

	France			UK		
	LTPERF12	LTPERF24	LTPERF36	LTPERF12	LTPERF24	LTPERF36
Explanatory variable	Coefficient *p*-value	Coefficient *p*-value	Coefficient *p*-value	Coefficient *p*-value	Coefficient *p*-value	Coefficient *p*-value
LCAPIT	0.007	–0.007	0.077	0.078	0.205	0.081
	0.834	0.900	0.308	0.001***	0.492	0.199
UNDERP	0.766	0.890	0.760	–0.029	–0.072	–0.052
	0.126	0.275	0.447	0.09*	0.759	0.180
INTERCEPT	–0.266	–0.045	–1.881	–1.102	–2.402	–1.219
	0.694	0.275	0.209	0.002***	0.584	0.184
Sample size	52	40	32	162	148	90
R^2	0.04	0.03	0.06	0.06	0.07	0.05

Notes:
LTPERF12 represents the abnormal performance of a 12-month buy-and-hold investment strategy. LPPERF24 and LTPERF36 are similarly defined for periods of respectively 24 and 36 months. The figures in the table refer to the regression coefficients for the respective explanatory variables using OLS estimators. *p*-values indicate the level of significance of the regression coefficients. Significance: *** stands for significance at the 1% level, ** at 5%, and * at 10%.

Source: Returns information from Datastream on-line services.

These implications are tested for the two largest markets, the UK and France. Regressions are run with long-term holding-period abnormal returns as dependent variables and both the logarithm of the size of the firm (measured as the market value at the first market price) and the initial price reaction as explanatory variables. The results are presented in Table 13.8. Tests for correlation and hereroscedasticity do not indicate the existence of problems. The more efficient OLS technique is then preferred to EGLS or bootstrapping. None of the regression coefficients are statistically different from zero for France. The signs of the estimated coefficients for the effect of initial underpricing are all positive, providing some weak support for the signaling-by-underpricing explanation. In the UK, both the size of the firm (p-value = 0.001) and the initial price reaction (p-value = 0.09) are significantly related to the performance of buy-and-hold strategies over the first 12-month interval. The underpricing coefficient is negative, contrary to what is found in France. For longer portfolio strategies, none of the coefficients are statistically significant. Overall, the evidence is inconsistent and weakly significant. It is thus difficult to support either of the proposed models.

Conclusions from the analysis

The analyses conducted above do not consider the transactions costs incurred in setting up the buy-and-hold IPO portfolios. Doing so would only reinforce the evidence of long-term under-performance in European IPOs post-1987, in line with the results presented by both Ritter (1991) and Aggarwal and Rivoll (1990) for the United States. The support for abnormally low long-term returns is particularly strong in France and the UK, whereas the evidence for Germany, the Netherlands, and Belgium is difficult to analyze due to limited sample sizes. Further analyses on the effect of the year of introduction (proxying for general market conditions) on the long-term performance support the robustness of the findings with respect to that factor. The results are not presented here.

General conclusions and implications

The multi-country survey and analysis of IPO long-term performance in Europe presented here supports the initial proposition that European IPO shares exhibit the pattern of long-term under-performance previously highlighted in the United States. The pattern is robust with respect to the methodologies used to measure the abnormal returns (market-adjusted event study methodologies and cross-sectional regression methods), the countries investigated, the types of flotation mechanisms used, the years of issuance, or the markets on which the shares were introduced. The overall magnitude of the phenomenon is comparable to figures reported in the United States by Ritter (1991) and Loughran and Ritter (1993). The choice of flotation mechanism seems to affect long-term performance, but the overall pattern remains. The systematic risk profile of IPO shares in secondary trading, estimated using robust estimators of cross-sectional regression parameters, supports the conservative nature of the market-adjustment procedures.

The primary objective of the chapter was to provide a comprehensive overview of the IPO markets in Europe post-1987 in an attempt to highlight possible explanations for the current dismal status of secondary markets. Traditional explanations focus on the supply side of the market for IPOs. But limited supply could as well be the direct consequence of inadequate demand for shares resulting for example, from regulatory constraints on institutional investments in small capitalization stocks or poor historical returns on IPO investments. This chapter focuses on the second component of that demand equation, highlighting significant underperformance of IPO shares in secondary trading.

Underperformance clearly does not explain the whole situation. Similar underperformance results have been highlighted in the United States without preventing record-breaking numbers of firms going public in 1992–94. Accordingly, underperformance is unlikely to be the single causal factor. As mentioned above, institutional restrictions on investments in small firms are likely contributory factors as well: few mutual funds have been set up so far specializing on small (market) capitalization growth firms, limiting the development of a competent pool of analysts following small capitalization stocks in Europe. This limited level of knowledgeable monitoring of growth firms may affect the ability of risk sensitive investors to actively purchase these securities. Such interpretation is supported by the shift observed in issuing behaviour by promising European concerns. Where a few years ago, most would have considered a national listing as a natural first step in the public domain, the number of firms bypassing their home markets entirely and going public in the United States is increasing rapidly. Venture capitalists, especially, seem to have refocused their flotation objectives towards a NASDAQ base, either out of concern about the ability of many European stock exchanges to provide the right environment and liquidity to harvest some of their investments, or simply because of the easy availability of well-identified and recognized industry analysts and followers making the information creation and dissemination phases much more efficient.[27]

A byproduct of this concern for information production and analyst follow-up is the high level of interest generated by the possible creation of a pan-European market for growth firms, a European NASDAQ of sort, either based on and connected to the American system or self-standing. Although sovereignty concerns would obviously create implementation problems, the extraterritorial nature of the computerized trading network could in effect create the first international market for IPO shares.

The question of what causes the long-term underperformance of IPO shares is also left unanswered here. Can the phenomenon be ascribed to 'fads' (Ritter, 1991), investor sentiment (Rajan and Servaes, 1993), or the superior ability of issuers to time their offerings and take advantage of 'windows of opportunities'

(Loughran and Ritter, 1993)? The last study shows that underperformance persists for as long as six years after the initial offerings. Is there a point at which the trend reverses itself? Is that trend the result of systematic overpricing of stocks due to a lack of sufficient information with which to set initial prices? Is there initial overpricing due to excessive 'packaging' of information during the pre-IPO process? Are we properly conceptualizing the notion of risk in growth firms? The assumptions made above imply a high level of market risk exposure for the newly floated shares. Although total risk is clearly high in individual securities, the proportion attributable to the market may be limited. In other words, the systematic risk of IPO shares may not necessarily be larger than 1.0. The cross-sectional estimations conducted here did not highlight betas in excess of 1.0 but it is easily conceivable that they could be smaller that 1.0, in which case market adjustments (or even adjustments to the returns of 'comparable' portfolios of seasoned firms, as in Ritter, 1991) may bias the results downward.

We suggest that a better understanding of the risk in IPO shares and measures aiming at the simplification of the going-public requirements are critical developments required to reestablish dynamic initial public offering markets in Europe. Investors (and their regulatory authorities) need to be convinced that small capitalization stocks do indeed provide a desirable diversification for their portfolios for an active market to reemerge in small cap firms. This will require a significant dose of political will from authorities in each country, but the costs of inaction are too high to be ignored any longer.

Notes

1. See the report produced for the European Union by Graham Bannock and Partners on August 16, 1994. A summary can also be found in *The Economist*, August 20 1994, p. 60.
2. The 1993 European Venture Capital Association meeting in Venice focused almost exclusively on the problem, considered one of the most challenging facing the venture community in recent years.
3. For example, fixed-price, fixed-quantity flotation mechanisms have been the rule in the United States since World War 1, a norm maintained by both the NASD and the SEC. In Europe, dozens of mechanisms are available to issuers, including various forms of auctions (with uniform or discriminative pricing).
4. Firms with IPO prices above $1 per share and gross proceeds above $1 million in 1984 terms.
5. See, for example, the article in the *Financial Times* on November 30 1992 entitled 'The Lingering Death of a Whizzkid's Haven' for more details on the evolution of the USM.
6. For a better view of the evolution of the venture capital industry in Europe, see the annual reports of the European Venture Capital Association (EVCA) or the proceedings of its 1993 conference in Venice (Italy).
7. The Datastream Paris Total Market index is used for France, the Financial Times All Shares index in the United Kingdom, the Frankfurter Algemeine Zeitung (FAZ) index for Germany, the General Koersindex in the Netherlands, and the Brussels General index for Belgium.
8. Shares that performed well in the last period are sold in part to repurchase shares that have not been doing so well.
9. Cross-sectional regression methodologies and robust estimators are both seriously constrained by sample size. For this reason, they are only used for the two largest samples, namely France and the United Kingdom.

10. These efficiency gains come at a cost though: if the underlying distributions are indeed Gaussian, then the robust estimators are less efficient than standard OLS estimators. In the case at hand, deviations from normality are sufficiently well documented to warrant a shift to robust estimators.
11. Judge et al (1988) describe in more detail the formulation of the objective functions and the aggregation of the quantile statistics for the TRQ robust estimation procedure.
12. Witness, for example, the number of software and computer industry growth firms such as Apple or Microsoft that obtained listings on the NASDAQ in the 1980s and never expressed a desire to move to main boards even when their size and reputation would have permitted it.
13. Auction-related mechanisms sometime fail due to constraints on rationing. When this happens, fixed-price, fixed-quantity procedures can still be resorted to as mechanisms of last resort to sell the shares to the public.
14. To be absolutely correct, the offer price is actually set, after truncation of the revealed demand curve, at a level below the one that would clear demand and offer for the shares. Van Hulle et al. (1993) refer to this procedure as a 'dirty' equilibrium.
15. For a more detailed exposition of the IPO mechanisms in London, see Levis (1990, 1993).
16. American underwriters have broad discretion when allocating IPO shares to their clients. As outlined for example by Spatt and Srivastava (1991), such flexibility provides underwriters with the degree of leverage required to incite potential investors to reveal their private information regarding the value of the shares to be issued. Such leverage is often not present in Europe.
17. See Wessels (1989) for more details on the Amsterdam Stock Exchange and the going-public procedures available to issuers.
18. The market is established initially between incumbent shareholders willing to sell their rights and investors looking for an opportunity to buy shares at the fixed stated price.
19. Loughran et al. (1994) present, in their table 3, an international comparison of the distribution of flotation mechanisms used over the world.
20. Jacquillat (1989), Bikhchandani and Huang (1989) and Spatt and Srivastava (1991) examine various aspects of the debate over the efficiency of both fixed-price and price-driven procedures. Leleux and Paliard (1994) empirically examine the relationship between issue mechanism and IPO performance on the French market, as does Levis (1993) in the UK.
21. Recall that the procedures in effect in Portugal allow price discrimination, such that bidders end up paying different prices for the shares. The average initial returns are calculated with respect to the minimum offer price when different prices were paid by different investors.
22. The long-term returns are calculated from the market price prevailing the first day of the first full month of trade to the end of the seasoning period considered. They do not include the abnormal initial returns occurring between offer price and first market price.
23. The limitations are discussed in the methodology section.
24. Belletante and Paliard (1993) show that French firms for example are much older at introduction than the typical American IPO firm.
25. Leleux and Paliard (1994) focus on the problematic of the mechanism selection process in France, emphasizing constraints on rationing when auctions are used and the corporate control implications of public issues.
26. Loughran et al. (1994) provide an international analysis of the timing hypothesis.
27. The concerns over liquidity and analyst followings were expressed publicly in various instances, such as the annual meetings of the European Venture Capital Association (EVCA) or the European Foundation for Entrepreneurship Research (EFER).

References

Aggarwal, R. and P. Rivoll (1990), 'Fads in the initial public offering market?', *Financial Management* **19** (4), 45–57.

Allen, F. and G. Faulhaber (1989), 'Signaling by underpricing in the IPO market', *Journal of Financial Economics*, **23** (2), 303–23.

Alpalhão, R.M. (1988), 'Opertas públicas iniciais: o caso Portuguès' (Initial public offerings: the Portuguese case), Working paper, Universidade Nova de Lisboa.

Amihud, Y. and H. Mendelson (1989), 'The effects of beta, bid-ask spread, residual risk, and size on stock returns', *Journal of Finance*, **44**, 479–86.

Balvers, R., B. McDonald and R. Miller (1988), 'Underpricing of new issues and the choice of auditor as signal of investment banker reputation', *Accounting Review*, **63** (4), 605–22.

Bassett, G. and R. Koenker (1982), 'An empirical quantile function for linear models with i.i.d. errors', *Journal of the American Statistical Association*, **77**, 407–15.

Belletante, B. and R. Paliard (1993), 'Does knowing who sells matter in IPO pricing? The French second market experience', *Cahiers Lyonnais de Recherche en Gestion*, **14**, 42–74.

Bikhchandani, S. and C.-F. Huang, (1989), 'Auctions with resale markets: an exploratory model of treasury bill markets', *Review of Financial Studies*, **2**, 311–40.

Buckland, R., P.J. Herbert and K.A. Yeomans (1981), 'Price discount on new equity issues in the UK and their relationship to investor subscription', *Journal of Business Finance and Accounting*, **8** (l), 79–95.

Carter, R. and S. Manaster (1990), 'Initial public offerings and underwriter reputation', *Journal of Finance*, **45** (4), 1045–67.

Chan, L.K.C. and J. Lakonishok (1992), Robust measurement of beta risk, *Journal of Financial and Quantitative Analysis*, **27** (2), 265–82.

Cherubini, U. and M. Ratti (1992), *Underpricing of Initial Public Offerings in the Milan Stock Exchange, 1985–1991*, Rome: Banco Commerciale Italiana, Economic Research Unit.

Clarkson P. and R. Thompson (1990), 'Measurement of beta risk within the differential information model', *Journal of Finance*, **45**, 431–53.

Conrad, J. and G. Kaul (1993), 'Long-term market overreaction or biases in computed returns', *Journal of Finance* **45** (2), 39–63.

Cotter, J.F. (1992), 'The long-run efficiency of IPO pricing', Working paper, NC: University of North Carolina at Chapel Hill.

Davis, W. and K.A. Yeomans (1976), 'Market discount on new issues of equity: firm size, method of issue, and market volatility', *Journal of Business Finance and Accounting*, **3**, 27–42.

Dawson, S.M. and N. Reiner (1988), 'Raising capital with initial public share issues in Germany, 1977–1985', *Management International Review*, **28** (l), 64–72.

De Ridder, A. (1986), 'Access to the stock market: an empirical study of the efficiency of the British and Swedish primary markets', Working paper, The Federation of Swedish Industries.

Dimson, E. and P. Marsh (1986), 'Event study methodologies and the size effect', *Journal of Financial Economics*, **17**, 113–42.

Freixas X. and A. Inurrieta (1992), Infravaloracion en las salidas a bolsa, Preliminary Working Paper, Spain: FEDEA.

Grinblatt, M. and C.Y. Hwang (1989), 'Signalling and the pricing of new issues', *Journal of Finance*, **44** (2), 393–420.

Hansson, B. and A. Ljungqvist (1993), 'Mispricing of initial public offerings: evidence from Germany', Working Paper Series 19/1993, Department of Economics, University of Lund, Sweden.

Husson, J. and B. Jacquillat (1989), 'French new issues, underpricing, and alternative methods of distribution', in Guimaraes et al. (eds), *A Reappraisal of the Efficiency of Financial Markets*, Berlin, Germany: Springer-Verlag.

Ibbotson, R.G. (1975), 'Price performance of common stock new issues', *Journal of Financial Economics*, **2** (3), 235–72.

Ibbotson, R.G. and J.F. Jaffe (1975), 'Hot issue markets', *Journal of Finance*, **30** (4), 1027–42.

Ibbotson, R.G., J. Sindelar and J.R. Ritter (1988), 'Initial public offerings', *Journal of Applied Corporate Finance*, **1**, 37–45.

Jacquillat, B.C. (1989), *L'Introduction en Bourse*, (Coming to the stock market) Paris, France: Presses Universitaires de France.

Jacquillat, B.C., J.G. McDonald and J. Rolfo (1978), 'French auctions of common stock: new issues, 1966–1974', *Journal of Business Finance*, **2**, 305–22.

Jaffeux, C. (1990), 'Essai d'explication de la sous-evaluation des titres à leur introduction sur le second marché, (An attempt to explain the under-valuation of shares on their introduction to the stock market) *La Revue Banque*, **509**, 952–8.

Jenkinson, T. and C. Mayer (1988), 'The privatization process in France and the United Kingdom', *European Economic Review*, **32**, 482–90.

Judge, G., C. Hill, W. Griffiths, H. Lutkepohl and T.C. Lee (1988), *Introduction to the Theory and Practice of Econometrics*, New York, NY: John Wiley and Sons, Inc.

Keasey, K., H. Short and R. Watson (1991), 'Capital market efficiency and the underpricing of new issues on the UK unlisted securities markets', in J. Roure and S. Birley (eds), *Growth Capital and Entrepreneurship*, Barcelona, Spain: IESE.

Keloharju, M. (1993), 'The winner's curse, legal liability, and the long-run price performance of initial public offerings in Finland', *Journal of Financial Economics*, **34**, 251–77.

Koenker, R. and G. Bassett (1978), 'Regression quantiles', *Econometrica*, **46**, 33–50.

Koenker, R. and S. Portnoy (1987), 'L-estimation for linear models', *Journal of the American Statistical Association*, **82**, 851–7.

Kunz, R. and R. Aggarwal (1991), *Explaining the Underpricing of Initial Public Offerings: Evidence from Switzerland*, Working Paper, Georgetown University School of Business Administration.

Leleux, B. and R. Palliard (1994), 'The posted-price paradox: evidence on the flotation mechanism selection process in France', Working Paper, The European Institute of Business Administration (INSEAD), Fontainebleau, France.

Levis, M. (1990), 'The winner's curse problem, interest costs and the underpricing of initial public offerings', *Economic Journal*, **100** (399), 76–89.

Levis, M. (1993), 'The long-run performance of initial public offerings: the UK experience 1980–1988', *Financial Management*, (Spring), 28–41.

Loughran, T. and J.R. Ritter (1993), *The Timing and Subsequent Performance of IPOs: The U.S. and International Evidence*, Working Paper, University of Illinois at Urbana-Champaign.

Loughran, T., J.R. Ritter and K. Rydqvist (1994), 'Initial public offerings: international insights', *Pacific-Basin Finance Journal*, **2** (2), 165–99.

McDonald, J.G. and B.C. Jacquillat (1974) 'Pricing of initial equity issues: the French sealed bid auction', *Journal of Business*, **33** (January), 37–47.

McStay, K.P. (1987), 'The efficiency of new issue markets', PhD Thesis, Department of Economics, University of California.

Merrett, A.J., M. Howe and G.D. Newbould (1967), *Equity Issues and the London Capital Market*, London, UK: Macmillan.

Rahnema, A., P. Fernandez and E. Martinez-Abascal (1992), *Initial Public Offerings: The Spanish Experience*, Barcelona, Spain: IESE.

Rajan, R. and H. Servaes (1993), 'The effect of market conditions on initial public offerings', University of Chicago Working Paper.

Rees, W. (1992), Initial public offerings in the UK: 1984–1991', University of Strathclyde Working Paper, Glasgow.

Ritter, J.R. (1984), 'The "Hot Issue" market of 1980', *Journal of Business*, **57** (2), 215–40.

Ritter, J.R. (1991) 'The long-run performance of initial public offerings', *Journal of Finance*, **46** (1), 3–28.

Ritter, J.R. and N. Chopra (1989), 'Portfolio rebalancing and the turn-of-the-year effect', *Journal of Finance*, **44**, 149–66.

Rogiers, B. and S. Manigart (1992), *Empirical Examination of the Underpricing of Initial Public Offerings on the Brussels Stock Exchange*, Gent, Belgium: Vlerick School for Management.

Ruud, J.S. (1993), 'Underwriter price support and the IPO underpricing puzzle', *Journal of Financial Economics*, **34**, 135–51.

Rydqvist, K. (1993), 'Initial public offerings in Sweden', Working Paper, Stockholm School of Economics.

Spatt, C. and S. Srivastava (1991), 'Preplay communication, participation restrictions, and efficiency in initial public offerings', *Review of Financial Studies*, **4** (4), 709–26.

Topsacalian, P. (1984), 'Second marché: sous évaluation des titres à l'introduction' (Second market: undervaluation of shares on introduction), *Analyse Financière*, **4**, 52–61.

Uhlir, H. (1989), 'Going public in the Federal Republic of Germany', in Guimaraes et al. (eds), *A Reappraisal of the Efficiency of Financial Markets*, Berlin: Springer-Verlag.

Van Hulle, C., M. Casselman and M.O. Imam (1993), 'Initial public offerings in Belgium: theory and evidence', *Tijdschrift Voor Economie En Management*, **38** (4), 385–423.

Welch, I. (1989), 'Seasoned offerings, imitation costs, and underpricing of initial public offerings', *Journal of Finance*, **44** (2), 421–49.

Wessels, R. (1989), 'The market for IPOs: an analysis of the Amsterdam stock exchange (1982–1987)', in Guimaraes et al. (eds), *A Reappraisal of the Efficiency of Financial Markets*, Berlin: Springer-Verlag.

14. Venture capitalists, serial entrepreneurs and serial buy-outs

Mike Wright, Ken Robbie and Christine Ennew

Introduction

For almost two decades there has been a worldwide growth in interest in entrepreneurship and the financing of entrepreneurial ventures (see the discussion in Chapters 2 to 4). Much of this interest has focused on encouraging 'nascent entrepreneurs' to become entrepreneurs, through either the creation or purchase of an entrepreneurial venture together with the development of various enabling sources of funds. However, as experience of entrepreneurship and venture capital develops, an increasingly important issue to emerge concerns the dynamic aspects of these phenomena. That is, to what extent do entrepreneurs become involved in subsequent ventures and what happens to entrepreneurial enterprises once the original parties wish to harvest their investment. These issues are of particular importance as venture capital and the associated buy-out and buy-in markets mature and the longevity and life cycle of such entrepreneurial organisational forms begins to emerge (Bygrave et al., 1994; Relander et al., 1994). The extent of realizations of venture capital and buy-out investments is already substantial in the US market (see, for example, Devlin, 1992, and Petty et al., 1992), in the UK (EVCA, 1995, CMBOR, 1996) and in some of the more developed continental European markets (Chapter 3).

Growing research effort is being devoted to entrepreneurs in general who found more than one venture (MacMillan, 1986; Starr and Bygrave, 1991), though there has been little systematic effort to delineate the general forms that habitual or multiple entrepreneurship might take. Although this chapter presents a typology of habitual entrepreneurship, our main concern is with those individuals who have exited from their first venture before embarking upon a subsequent one. Each of these ventures may have involved either the purchase of an existing venture or establishment of a new one. This broad definition is employed since the focus is primarily upon venture capitalists' approaches towards serial entrepreneurs and in this context it is necessary to recognise the range of entrepreneurial activity.

While entrepreneurs exiting from one venture may have accumulated sufficient funds to invest in subsequent ones, they are also likely to make use of venture capital, especially if they have accessed this source of funding before. In the US there has been evidence for some time that previously backed entrepreneurs are important in generating venture capital deal flow (Silver, 1985) with consideration of previous entrepreneurial experience an element of the deal screening process (for example, MacMillan et al., 1987). However, there has been little explicit attention to the process by which venture capitalists screen entrepreneurs who have exited from a previous venture and the criteria they use. Moreover, while there is some evidence concerning the extent to which founders of new businesses have previously started a venture (see Birley and Westhead, 1994 for a review), there is little evidence concerning the extent to which entrepreneurs exiting from one venture are backed a second or subsequent time by their initial financial partner.

Although not all entrepreneurs leave a company when it exits from a venture capitalist's portfolio, many do. Some of these entrepreneurs will seek to start new ventures, a number will retire, while others will go to work for someone else (Ronstadt, 1988). In addition, venture capitalists may consider that exiting entrepreneurs who are either unsuitable for a further venture or who do wish to pursue such a route may usefully be employed in some form of advisory role such as a non-executive director or consultant. Among the large number of failed ventures in the recession of the 1990s, there may be entrepreneurs who have attractions for venture capitalists since the failure may have been beyond their control or they may have gained valuable experience through the failure (Vesper, 1980).

Serial entrepreneurs can re-enter the venture process in various ways. Much of the debate in this emerging aspect of entrepreneurship has focused on the use of capital proceeds from one venture in the start-up of a new firm. However, for the formal venture capital industry the funding of exiting entrepreneurs in the acquisition of existing businesses through a secondary management buy-out or management buy-in may be as important in terms of the volume of investments and possibly even more important in value terms. Indeed, an increasingly important subset of the phenomenon of repeat buy-outs and buy-ins concerns multiple or serial ownership change of the same business entity. Increasing numbers of buy-outs and buy-ins are floated on stock markets or sold to other groups (CMBOR, 1996). As part of this trend, recent years have seen an increase in the number of buy-outs and buy-ins in the UK which have exited by means of a secondary or serial management buy-out or buy-in. In 1996, serial buy-outs and buy-ins accounted for 13.3 per cent of all exits, a marked increase from the 8.5 per cent in 1994, and 11.4 per cent in 1995.

These transactions represent a number of options which may involve complete, partial or no change in incumbent management and/or complete, partial or no chancre in venture capital providers. A secondary transaction with no change in management and partial or full change in the venture capital firms providing funds may occur where some or all of the venture capital firms seek to realise their investments. In such circumstances, one or more of the exiting venture capital firms may be replaced by new incoming funds providers. Alternatively, some or all of the incumbent management team may be replaced by new entrepreneurs, possibly at the instigation of the venture capital firm as a result of poor performance. In some cases, there may be a change in both some management and some of the funds providers. As a result of these combinations of changes, the ownership and financial structure of the business changes to create a secondary or serial buy-out or buy-in.

This chapter examines the role of serial entrepreneurs and serial buy-outs in the venture capital industry as follows. The next section reviews the relevant literature relating to the nature of serial entrepreneurship and the venture capital screening process. The discussion provides an extension of the relatively limited existing literature by developing a conceptual typology of habitual and of serial entrepreneurship based on a broad definition of entrepreneurship which includes both the foundation and acquisition of new ventures. This is followed by a discussion of the importance of previous entrepreneurial experience within the venture capital screening process. This section extends previous models of the venture capital process by showing that the possibility for reinvestment in exiting entrepreneurs adds a dynamic dimension previously ignored. Issues relating to serial buy-outs and buy-ins are then examined in the context of the longevity of venture capital investments. The fourth section outlines the data sources and methodology used in this study. The fifth section presents the results of the surveys of venture capitalists perspectives in relation to serial entrepreneurs and quantitative and case study evidence relating to serial buy-outs and buy-ins. The final section presents the conclusions and implications of the research.

Habitual and serial entrepreneurs

Within the continuing debate as to what is meant by entrepreneurship (see, for example, Low and MacMillan, 1988; Gartner, 1985), there is growing recognition that the entrepreneurial act may not simply involve the creation of a single venture but that a full career may see an entrepreneur become involved in a number of ventures. Serial entrepreneurship is essentially a subset of the wider phenomenon of multiple or habitual entrepreneurship, different forms of which can be categorised as in Table 14.1.

In general, entrepreneurship may involve activities within an existing organisation or the formation of a new one (Cooper and Dunkelberg, 1986; Robbie and Wright, 1996). In particular, the relatively recent development of management buy-outs and buy-ins suggests the possibility for entrepreneurial acts in organisations which already exist (Kelly et al., 1986; Bull, 1989; Wright et al., 1992; Zahra, 1995). In addition, examination of the characteristics of the leading individuals in buy-out and buy-in transactions identifies similar features to those found in respect of entrepreneurs who start new ventures, with buy-in entrepreneurs generally having more proactive features than their counterparts in buy-outs (Ennew et al., 1994) Entrepreneurship may also involve cases where the entrepreneur becomes an owner of the organisation or is a manager with little or no ownership stake as in corporate entrepreneurship (Block and MacMillan, 1993; Stopford and Baden-Fuller, 1994).

Table 14. 1 Categorization of multiple or habitual entrepreneurship

	Multiple entrepreneurship involving existing firms	Multiple entrepreneurship involving new firms
Ownership change between ventures	Quadrant 1 Serial MBO/MBI	Quadrant 2 Serial start-up
No ownership change between ventures	Quadrant 3 Multiple corporate entrepreneurship	Quadrant 4 Portfolio entrepreneurship

Habitual and multiple entrepreneurship focuses on the dynamics of these entrepreneurial actions. However, there has hitherto been little attempt to identify the differing types of habitual entrepreneurial activity. In their pioneering study, Starr and Bygrave (1991) take a general view of multiple venture experience. Hall (1995) in discussing habitual or multiple business founders distinguishes portfolio owners (Quadrant 4 of Table 14.1), where ownership of the first venture is maintained when a subsequent venture is embarked upon, from serial owners who dispose of one venture before founding another (Quadrant 2). Although there is some evidence to show that habitual portfolio entrepreneurship is extensive (for example, Birley and Westhead, 1994), there is little empirical research which distinguishes between portfolio and serial entrepreneurs or which embraces other forms of entrepreneurship beyond start-ups. Kolvereid and Bullvag (1993) examine portfolio entrepreneurs who start more than one business, but explicitly exclude serial entrepreneurs. Westhead and Wright (1998) compare the characteristics, motivations and performance of novice, serial and portfolio entrepreneurs. It should be borne in mind, however, that the portfolio/serial categorisation may be too simplistic in the light of recent developments in entrepreneurship theory and should perhaps be broadened to include activities relating to existing firms. Multiple corporate entre-preneurship (Quadrant 3) may occur within the same firm or by the entrepreneurial managers concerned moving to another firm, in both cases to engage in further acts of new resource deployment. Conversely, serial entre-preneurship could involve the purchase of an existing firm after the first venture is sold (Quadrant 1). Serial entrepreneurial behaviour may be considered to be firstly a desire to exit from an initial venture when entrepreneurial opportunities are perceived to have been exhausted and to search for new possibilities through entry into a subsequent venture.

Table 14.2 Categorization of second venture types

	Second venture		
First venture	Secondary MBO	MBI	Start-up
MBO	Sale and subsequent buy-back	Cash-out and use funds to buy-in with venture capital funds	Cash-out and use own funds to start-up
MBI	Ditto	Cash-out and repeat the venture	Cash-out and attempt a new business
Start-up	Ditto	Cash-out and find a turnaround vehicle	Cash-out from success and start major new business with own funds or fail in first venture and try again

Quadrants 1 and 2 of Table 14.1 can be expanded to identify more specifically the different forms of serial entrepreneurship as shown in Table 14.2. Essentially the categories of second time entrepreneurship may be represented as:[1] repeating entrepreneurial experience with the same enterprise that is, selling out from whatever form the initial venture took and then buying it, or part of it, back (a secondary, MBO); repeating entrepreneurial experience by leading a new venture involving a company which already exists and which may (a pure management buy-in, MBI) or may not (a buy-in/buy-out, BIMBO) involve incumbent management in equity ownership; and repeating the entrepreneurial experience with an entirely new company (a start-up).

Repeating an entrepreneurial experience with an entirely new company is generally regarded as the classic case of serial entrepreneurship (Birley and Westhead, 1994). However, serial entrepreneurship may also entail re-establishing a relationship with a previously owned company. An entrepreneur may remain with an initial venture when it is sold and subsequently buy it back as either the acquisition fails to fit or the parent experiences major trading difficulties. Alternatively, the entrepreneur may perceive an opportunity to buy-out part of the business which she/he considers to have growth prospects but which does not fit strategically with the new parent. Entrepreneurs may also seek to reestablish ownership to make good their sense of loss from having sold out in the first place (Petty et al., 1992).

Management buy-ins provide a further medium for serial entrepreneurship. Evidence indicates that well over a quarter of buy-in team leaders had previously owned a significant equity stake in a company in which they had been employed. Although such investments have many of the features of start-ups they do involve an existing organisational structure. Typically, significant entrepreneurial input is required to turn round an enterprise subject to a buy-in (Robbie and Wright, 1996). However, entrepreneurs entering buy-ins may be faced with potentially severe asymmetric information and adverse selection problems. Previous experience with a buy-in may alert entrepreneurs to the existence of these problems, though they may still be unable to assess the nature of them ex ante in a new venture. For these reasons experienced entrepreneurs may seek to complement less entrepreneurially experienced incumbent management, creating a hybrid buy-in/buy-out (so-called BIMBO).

As Table 14.2 indicates, serial entrepreneurs may pursue a similar kind of second venture to their first or may shift their focus of attention. Shifts may occur, for example, where entrepreneurs having exited from and turned round a buy-out may seek a similar challenge by buying into an already existing company or, perhaps less likely given their experience, creating a new company. Similarly, entrepreneurs having started-up and grown a company may seek to buy into an underperforming company with growth prospects in order to achieve a larger entity relatively quickly, rather than starting totally afresh. Where serial entrepreneurship involves successive buy-ins, successive buy-outs or some combination of the two, then venture capital is likely to be involved; this in turn raises issues concerning the process by which serial entrepreneurs are evaluated both by their initial venture capitalist and by other potential venture capital funders.

Venture capitalist assessment

As seen in Chapter 1, a number of studies have developed models of the venture capital appraisal process. In general this research does not explicitly distinguish the criteria used by those venture capitalists who prefer to invest in experienced entrepreneurs and those who do not. The existence of entrepreneurs who are exiting from venture capitalists' own portfolios adds a further source of deal generation and also raises issues concerning the nature of the process by which venture capitalists assess exiting entrepreneurs with a view to reinvestment. The stages in the venture capital process as regards serial entrepreneurs can be conceptualised as involving: exit of the entrepreneur at the time of venture capitalist exit or afterwards with assessment by the venture capitalist for potential reinvestment; post-exit monitoring by the venture capitalist if reinvestment does not occur on exit; screening of entrepreneurs, together with novice entrepreneurs and entrepreneurs exited from other venture capitalists' portfolios, with a view to investment; and overall deal screening, appraisal, negotiation and completion.

Several studies examine the relative importance of the factors taken into account in the screening process for new venture investment (for example, Bruno and Tyebjee, 1985; MacMillan et al., 1985, 1987). An entrepreneur's past experience is undoubtedly of importance, although it is only one among many criteria used in the screening process. MacMillan et al. (1987) show that the most important criteria used by venture capitalists in screening investment proposals were entrepreneurial personality and experience, with lesser dependence being placed on market, product and strategy. The particular attraction of past experience in the context of screening is the potential reduction in adverse selection problems because of the information contained in past and potentially similar experience. Where such experience relates directly to entrepreneurial activity it will be of particular value. Hence, it may be expected that venture capitalists who express a preference for investing in experienced entrepreneurs will place greater emphasis on previous entrepreneurial experience than those who do not have such a preference. Furthermore, venture capitalists will evaluate first time entrepreneurs and serial entrepreneurs differently.

Of course, it is important to recognise the assets and liabilities of past experience (Starr and Bygrave, 1991, 1992; Starr et al., 1993). Previous venture experience may have both positive and negative features. Positive features include reputation, expertise and networks of contacts. Negative features include reduced motivation to work as hard or to take on risky projects, and fixation on previous success/failure factors (blinders) which may not be appropriate for the new venture. These studies suggest that the negative features of experience are likely to lead to experienced entrepreneurs not implementing resourceful strategies arid using resources parsimoniously. Wright et al. (1997) provide some case study evidence that a change in motivation may occur between the first and subsequent ventures owned by serial entrepreneurs. After founding a business, some entrepreneurs may be less willing to undertake riskier ventures and may reduce the percentage of their wealth that they are prepared to commit to a new venture. In the context of repeat management buy-outs the danger may be that entrepreneurs take the same actions in an attempt to repeat their previous success though the conditions surrounding the enterprise may have changed. It may be expected that if the process is working effectively, venture capitalists will assess both the assets and the liabilities of an individual entrepreneur's previous experience and invest in only those cases where the former exceed the latter.

Starr and Bygrave also propose that the positive experience of previous entrepreneurial ventures should make it easier to raise start-up financing *per se* and in larger amounts. However, they do not distinguish between raising further finance from existing sources or from alternative possibilities, which may be important. At the initial investment stage, entrepreneurs are unlikely to be fully conversant with the workings of venture capitalists, hence among other things the widespread use of financial intermediaries. For the venture capitalist, there is a potential adverse selection problem in contracting with novice entrepreneurs which the above screening mechanisms are designed to obviate. At the initial stage, venture capitalists may see themselves as able to negotiate relatively advantageous terms compared to the entrepreneur. In recontracting with entrepreneurs who have exited from their own firm's portfolio, venture capitalists are potentially faced with a situation where the entrepreneur is more aware than previously of the effectiveness of the venture capitalist's monitoring and of how (dis)advantageous was the initial contract. There is essentially a multi-period game whereby serial entrepreneurs will seek to shift the distribution of expected gains in their favour.

Case study evidence by the authors (Wright et al., 1997) suggests that habitual entrepreneurs often change their venture capital backer. Experienced habitual entrepreneurs, owning larger businesses the second time around, may obtain finance from venture capitalists for the first time in order to ensure further business development. In other cases, some habitual entrepreneurs who had previously obtained finance from a venture capitalists, may not utilise this form of finance in a subsequent venture. The cases suggest that venture capitalists tend to be dropped if the subsequent business is smaller and/or if there had been problems in the relationship.

With respect to entrepreneurs who have exited from other venture capitalists' portfolios, the contracting problem is more complicated as the entrepreneur now has knowledge about the venture capital negotiating process in general, though not of the venture capitalist to whom an approach is being made for the first time. Moreover, while venture capitalists may know the entrepreneurs who have exited from their own portfolios, they are still faced by potential adverse selection problems in respect of entrepreneurs who have exited from other venture capitalists' portfolios. Hence it may be expected, therefore, that as a result of the potential for recontracting problems, venture capitalists will be cautious about reinvesting in experienced entrepreneurs from their own portfolios. Venture capitalists will also be cautious about investing in entrepreneurs who have exited from other venture capitalists' portfolios because of recontracting problems relating to both asymmetric information and the entrepreneurs' knowledge of the negotiation process.

Ultimately, the key question is whether entrepreneurial experience affects performance. The implications of ownership experience for the performance of serial entrepreneurs are surrounded by a degree of ambiguity. Vesper (1980) found that a variety of entrepreneurial and functional experience, including prior failure, was an indicator of better performance. Stuart and Abetti (1990) find that the most significant influence on performance was the level of managerial experience in previous ventures. Studies which have specifically examined cases of experienced versus novice entrepreneurs are less sanguine. Birley and Westhead (1994) found no evidence to suggest that new businesses established by habitual founders are particularly advantaged compared to their more inexperienced counterparts. Kolvereid and Bullvag (1993) examine differences between novice and experienced business founders where experienced entrepreneurs still own their original business. They are also unable to identify performance differences between the two types of entrepreneur. Westhead and Wright (1997) compare the characteristics, motivations and performance of novice, serial and portfolio entrepreneurs. They find significant differences between the three types of entrepreneurs in respect of characteristics and motivations, but show there is little difference in performance. There are no indications from these studies that entrepreneurs in established subsequent ventures had been subject to scrutiny by venture capitalists as to previous experience and performance. The earlier discussion suggests that, in the case of serial entrepreneurs, during the screening process venture capitalists will need, and be more able, to satisfy themselves that experienced entrepreneurs still have the motivation to perform, and that experienced entrepreneurs will perform at least as well as they did before and at least as well as inexperienced entrepreneurs. It may be expected that venture-backed serial entrepreneurs are expected to perform both at least as well as they did in their own first venture and as well as novice entrepreneurs.

Serial buy-outs

Wright et al. (1994) argue that the longevity of a management buy-out or buy-in is influenced by three main factors – the aims and objectives of incumbent management, the aims and objectives of the financiers and the exigencies of the market which may mean that the firm itself has to change its ownership structure in order to be able to adapt and survive. Incumbent management may seek to grow the business through flotation on a stock market. Alternatively, they may see their career developing through selling the buy-out or buy-in to another group and subsequent advancement within the parent company. They may also see themselves exiting at these stages and either founding or buying into a new venture, becoming serial entrepreneurs in the process (Westhead and Wright, 1998; Wright et al., 1997).

Management may, however, seek to retain the business as a privately-owned independent entity in the long term. This, too, may be for differing motivations. Management may simply require more time to finish the restructuring and entrepreneurial actions they began at the time of the initial buy-out or buy-in, but which for various reasons outside their control they were unable to complete in the time horizon required by the funding venture capitalist. A second explanation lies in the motivations of management in that they may take the view that their objectives can best be met by becoming a long-term privately-owned independent business, which avoids the scrutiny of stock market analysts and minimises the threat of a hostile takeover. Although the management in such cases will need to identify means of buying-out the equity stakes of the investors in the second venture whilst remaining independent, such serial buy-outs and buy-ins may be a new means of extending the already complex notion of family businesses (Westhead, 1997). A variation is where senior management who conducted the initial buy-out seek to retire or exit for other reasons but where second tier management are in place and are able to move into the position of being lead management.

Evidence from representative samples of the buy-out and buy-in populations concerning the motivations and objectives of management at the time of the initial transaction emphasises the importance attached to wanting to control one's own business and a long-term faith in the company (Wright et al., 1990). This evidence also indicates that flotation and trade sale are clearly the preferred exit routes (Robbie and Wright, 1996).

To generate a targetted rate of return, venture capitalists typically seek a dividend and capital gain on their investment within a particular time period. For the venture capitalist, evidence suggests that trade sales followed by stock market flotations are the preferred means of harvesting their investments in buy-outs and buy-ins (Wright et al., 1993). However, although a preferred exit route may be established at the time of the first deal, venture capitalists are typically flexible about the actual exit route, keeping it under review as the company develops (Relander et al., 1994). The pressure on venture capitalists to realise their investment in a particular venture may be greater where a closed-end fund is reaching the end of its life since the venture capitalist will be obliged to return cash to its investors. Successful companies may exit by these routes within a three to five year period as they are attracted to strategic partners and/or to stock market investors. More problematical are investees which are either performing poorly or not performing strongly enough to be attractive prospects for trade sales or flotations. Such cases include investees with little prospects of growth (so-called 'living dead' investments, Ruhnka et al., 1992) or those with growth prospects which have yet to be realised (so-called 'good rump' (of portfolios), Wright et al., 1993). A serial buy-out or buy-in may be a means by which initial investors facing time pressures to exit can achieve their objectives, but it may be expected that in general it is not the preferred exit route. It is also expected that the time elapsed since the first buy-out at the time a secondary transaction takes place will in general be greater than that in respect of flotations and trade sales.

A major issue arises which concerns why other venture capitalists will be attracted to investing in companies from which the initial venture capitalist is exiting. Asymmetric information arguments would suggest that venture capitalists will be suspicious of the motives of other venture capitalists wishing to sell. As a result the market may be expected to break down. However, where initial venture capitalists are able to signal information that companies fall into the 'good rump' rather than the 'living dead' category and have good prospects, or there are fund structure reasons for sale (for example, the implications of the life of a closed-end fund), the conditions may be established for the market to function.

A further dimension concerns the position of management. Although the company may have good prospects, the problem may lie with the incumbent management. In such cases, the venture capitalist may seek to replace existing management. Where such actions involve major changes to the ownership structure, for example where a new incoming entrepreneur needs to be given a significant equity stake to persuade him/her to undertake the transaction, a serial buy-in is created.

With respect to the company itself, it is clear that companies with strong growth prospects and of an appropriate size may seek a listing on a stock market as a means of accessing new capital. Companies which are relatively small in their markets may seek to become part of a larger group in order to achieve a critical mass. Those with some form of strong market position may be attractive to strategic buyers where the acquirer envisages prospects for synergy. Other companies may fit the classic buy-out and buy-in idea of being in niche markets, may have stable markets but may have little prospects for growth. In such cases, continued independent existence may be feasible, a serial buy-out or buy-in being necessary to meet the objectives of management and financiers. It may be expected that serial buy-outs and buy-ins are more likely than buy-outs and buy-ins generally to be in niche markets such as traditional mechanical engineering and metals sectors.

Data and methodology

In order to assess the extent and nature of usage of serial entrepreneurs, data were collected by means of two postal questionnaires.[2] The first survey was carried out at the end of 1992 and beginning of 1993. A draft questionnaire was developed and subsequently piloted with a number of venture capitalists, advisors, and academics. The scales used in the questionnaire concerning the criteria used to assess entrepreneurs were developed from a review of the existing literature and from discussions with the main participants in the venture capital industry. Following analysis of the replies, modifications were made to the content and structure of the questionnaire.

The first questionnaire was mailed to the 113 institutions then listed as full members of the British Venture Capital Association. The questionnaires were sent to Chief Executives of the venture capital firms or senior colleagues with whom CMBOR has regular contact through its buy-out and buy-in surveys.

Mailing of the questionnaires was undertaken in early December 1992. A follow-up reminder was sent in January 1993. In total, 55 completed and usable replies were received, representing a response rate of 48.7 per cent. Ten respondents were CEOs, 22 were directors and the remainder were assistant directors or equivalent. A further 13 replies were received with reasons for non-completion stated. These reasons generally related to the immaturity of a particular venture capitalist's portfolio, a deliberate policy not to answer questionnaires or that the companies were no longer involved in venture capital. Comparative demographics of respondents and non-respondents are shown in Table 14.3 where data could be identified. The only significant difference between the respondents and non-respondents for whom data were available related to the total value of investments at cost.

Table 14.3 Characteristics of respondents and non-respondents

	No. investments per year	Value of investments (£m)	Age of venture capital firm (years)	No. of investment executives
Respondents:				
Mean	29.2	125.9	12.6	12.3
Std. dev.	135.0	334.7	11.7	30.0
Median	8	25.5	9.5	5.5
Non-respondents:				
Mean	12.0	39.8	12.5	6.7
Std. dev.	16.9	59.6	10.2	4.6
Median	6.5	18.5	9.5	6.0

Notes:
n for respondents = 54; n for non-respondents = 42.
t-tests for differences between respondents and non-respondents were insignificant at conventional levels except in respect of value of investments where $t = 1.85$ (significant at 7% level).

Analysis of the responding institutions revealed that they covered a substantial proportion of the UK venture capital industry. Virtually all the principal and longest-established venture capitalists in the UK had participated in the study. The venture capital firms in the sample had made 2354 venture capital investments over the period 1990–92 worth over £3.5 billion.

A second questionnaire was developed which was specifically targeted at those venture capitalists who had experience of serial entrepreneurs as revealed by the first survey. The scales covered in this second questionnaire were derived from the existing literature relating to habitual entrepreneurship, notably Starr and Bygrave (1991), who suggest a number of positive and negative aspects of entrepreneurial experience. This questionnaire was piloted as for the first, and during this process considerable resistance to the provision of data on numbers and types of serial entrepreneurs funded by venture capitalists was identified. The problem essentially was due to the time involved in searching documentation for such information. As a result this question was dropped and accordingly we are unable to provide data on this aspect of serial entrepreneurs.

The second questionnaire was mailed to the 40 venture capitalists in the first sample who stated on the first questionnaire that they had either invested in an entrepreneur who had exited from their own and/or another venture capitalist's portfolio. This survey yielded 23 usable responses. Evidence from returned but uncompleted questionnaires and from the researchers follow-up telephone contacts with potential respondents, indicated that although these venture capitalists had experience with serial entrepreneurs they considered it to be too limited to draw general conclusions.

The methodology adopted to examine serial buy-outs and buy-ins was also a two-stage one. The first stage utilises the authors' database of management buy-outs and buy-ins in the UK. This database, which constitutes the effective population of management buy-outs and buy-ins in the UK, covers transactions from before 1980 until the present. The database is continually updated from a number of sources. Primarily, the data is compiled from a twice yearly survey of all financiers of management buy-outs and buy-ins in the UK. Other sources of data include intermediaries, systematic searches of company accounts, Extel Financial News and the financial press. Once entered into the database, companies are subsequently monitored with exits being identified through similar sources to the above, plus flotation documents where relevant. This data capture and monitoring procedure for the database enables both initial and serial buy-outs and buy-ins involving the same company to be identified.

This stage of the analysis shows that serial buy-outs are considerably more prevalent than serial buy-ins (Table 14.4). Of a sample of 178 serial deals of the 189 such transactions identified by CMBOR, where sufficient information was available 87 per cent involve serial buy-outs. There may be changes from buy-outs to buy-ins, and vice versa, between the first and second deals, although the most common situation is when a first buy-out becomes a serial buy-out. In a sixth of cases (16.1 per cent) a first buy-out becomes a serial buy-in. Over two thirds of first time buy-ins (69.6 per cent) become serial buy-outs.

In order to examine the rationale for serial buy-outs, the second stage involved case studies of 13 serial management buy-outs and buy-ins, during the period July to September 1996. Face-to-face interviews were conducted with either the Chief Executive, Managing Director or, in one case, the Finance Director. The research was conducted using a structured questionnaire which was sent after the directors had agreed by telephone to participate in the study. All the companies interviewed had undergone their serial management buy-out within the last five years, with the majority occurring within the last three.

Table 14.4 First and serial buy-outs and buy-ins

	Serial buy-out	Serial buy-in	Total sample
First buy-out	130	25	155
First buy-in	16	7	23
Total sample	146	32	178

Source: CMBOR/Barclays Private Equity/Deloitte & Touche Corporate Finance.

Results: serial entrepreneurs

The initial discussion of results concentrates on providing a general overview of the nature of serial entrepreneurship as revealed by the two surveys. Thereafter, specific analysis is presented to address the propositions advanced earlier.

Overview

The use of exiting entrepreneurs in further ventures by the same institution appears limited. A number of institutions responding to the survey considered that it was too soon for them to have had significant, if any, experience of using exited entrepreneurs again,[3] although others also stated that the data were not available.[4] The 28 institutions who responded to this part of the first survey indicated that less than 5 per cent of previously funded entrepreneurs were funded in any subsequent venture by the same institution. Indeed, over three quarters (77.1 per cent) of the lead entrepreneurs in previously backed investments were not used again by the venture capitalist in any capacity. Where previously funded lead entrepreneurs were used, it was usually in an informal advisory/consultancy (13.1 per cent) role or as a non-executive director in a new venture (5.5 per cent).

The most important reason given by venture capitalists for the low extent to which they invested again in entrepreneurs who had previously been supported was the view that no suitable candidates had emerged. This factor seems particularly important among smaller companies[5] which might reflect the ability of larger organisations to attract a good pool of potential entrepreneurs. The second most important reason cited was that venture capitalists had not actively pursued entrepreneurs who had exited with a view to making new investments with them. The operation of formal policies of not reinvesting in the same entrepreneur or of only using them in other consultancy/non-executive/due diligence roles was generally seen as unimportant. There was no evidence of any significant difference in the degree of importance attached to any of these three factors by small and large venture capitalists.

Evidence from the second survey suggests that even when proposals are received from potential serial entrepreneurs they are often found wanting. Twelve respondents had declined to invest in a proposal brought by an entrepreneur who had exited from their portfolio. Proposals which were viewed as not being viable (mean 4.46, standard deviation (STD) 0.93, on a scale where 5 = very important to 1 = irrelevant/very unimportant) or which did not meet current investment criteria (mean 4.09, standard deviation 0.94) received the highest scored reasons for being turned down. Personal (mean 2.82, standard deviation 1.25) and financial motivations (mean 2.91, standard deviation 1.45), unreasonable negotiating demands (mean 2.82, standard deviation 1.54), and attempts to repeat a previously successful approach in an inappropriate situation (mean 3.00, standard deviation 0.89) were all viewed to be of little importance. There was some slight indication that serial entrepreneurs may be rejected as they attempt a venture which is beyond their skills (mean 3.08, standard deviation, 0.90).

Funding serial entrepreneurship is not restricted to the funding of an organisation's own exited entrepreneurs; it may also be manifested in the funding of entrepreneurs who have exited from ventures funded by competitors. Slightly over half the sample of venture capitalists (52.9 per cent) had made use of entrepreneurs who had exited from investments funded by other venture capitalists. The median use of entrepreneurs had been three, although there was considerable variation around this level. Almost half (48.0 per cent) of lead serial entrepreneurs were used to lead a buy-in, BIMBO or buy-out. Well over half (55.6 per cent) of other entrepreneurial team members were being used in a formal supporting executive director role with Finance Directors being particularly prominent.

Almost three-quarters of venture capitalists in the sample (40 out of 55) claimed to prefer to finance an entrepreneur who has played a major role in a previous venture. The most important reason for preferring entrepreneurs with previous venture experience are shown in Table 14.5. The most important reason emerges as being that previous experience provides a track record, followed by demonstrated motivation. Some importance was attached to the view that such managers were more likely to achieve success again.

There is no evidence to suggest that there is any systematic relationship between preference for using serial entrepreneurs and the characteristics of the individual venture capitalist as the results in Table 14.6 show.[6] However, it is noticeable that those venture capitalists preferring serial entrepreneurs do appear generally to have a larger volume of funds under investment and to be rather older than those venture capitalists that do not prefer to use serial entrepreneurs. This may simply reflect the fact that the longer established (and often larger) venture capitalists have had more opportunity and experience in relation to second-time entrepreneurs.

Table 14.5 Reasons for preferring to finance a manager with previous venture experience

	Mean	STD
Wider management experience	3.13	1.53
Demonstrated motivation	3.24	1.57
Track record available	3.47	1.73
Aware of venture management pressures	2.84	1.38
Greater commercial awareness	3.07	1.51
More likely to achieve success again	3.04	1.57
Career entrepreneur	2.44	1.33
Financial commitment higher	2.35	1.32
Commercial motivation greater than financial	2.31	1.32
Number of respondents	40	

Table 14.6 Characteristics of venture capitalists and their preferences for second-time entrepreneurs

	Prefer serial entrepreneur	Do not prefer	Multivariate F-ratio	Univariate F-ratio	Sig. level
Investment patterns (% of investments)			1.48		0.213
Seed/start up/early stage	0.18	0.17	–	0.01	0.90
Expansion/development	0.31	0.22	–	1.77	0.19
Management buy-out	0.26	0.36	–	2.49	0.12
Management buy-in	0.13	0.13	–	0.01	0.92
Secondary purchase/ replacement	0.12	0.04	–	2.70	0.11
				T-ratio	Sig. level
Other					
Age (years)	14.44	9.28	–	1.08	0.286
No. of investment executives	13.48	6.43	–	0.87	0.386

It was shown earlier that many venture capitalists do not actively pursue entrepreneurs who have exited with a view to investing in new deals. Evidence from the questionnaire responses suggests that the nature of any continuing or developing relationship is mainly of an informal/social or ad hoc nature. Other more systematic approaches such as active procedures to monitor post-venture activities, formal assessment of managers' performance and feedback of performance into proposal evaluations were identified as relatively unimportant means of developing the relationship. Indeed, only 17 per cent of venture capitalists who responded to the questionnaire claimed that they carried out an evaluation of a manager's performance at the time they exited.

Screening of serial entrepreneurs

The examination of issues surrounding the screening and evaluation of entrepreneurs and differences according to the type of entrepreneur and the preferences of the venture capitalist requires a comparison of two groups of venture capitalists across a set of screening criteria. Clearly the list of criteria used in investment appraisal are not independent and relationships between some, if not all, criteria would be expected. Consequently, simple univariate tests on each criterion would be inappropriate. Accordingly a multivariate approach was preferred which accommodates the effects of interdependence between criteria. The first stage in this analysis was to subject both sets of investment appraisal factors to a principal components analysis to identify underlying dimensions/relationships between these factors. With respect to the general investment appraisal factors the principal components analysis identified five factors accounting for 70 per cent of the variance. A varimax rotation suggested that two factors were related to track record; one of these reflected ownership experience while the other represented management experience. The third factor was related to personal attributes such as age, knowledge and family background. The fourth factor represented links to the funding institution and the final factor (a single variable factor) concerned financial commitment. The principal components analysis for screening factors on management buy-ins produced a single factor comprising all variables. Thus it was decided that this set of variables should be treated as measuring a single dimension.

The five investment appraisal factors and the one management buy-in screening factor were then subject to a multivariate analysis of variance (MANOVA) with preference for use of a serial entrepreneur as the independent variable. The results of these analyses are shown in Tables 14.7 and 14.8. Table 14.7 presents the results for general screening factors. In most instances there is no evidence of any significant differences in the rating applied to each factor across the two groups of venture capitalists. However, in relation to previous ownership experience there are some differences which might be considered marginally significant. As might be expected previous ownership experience, length of ownership career and number of previous ventures all obtain high significantly higher ratings from those venture capitalists who prefer to use serial entrepreneurs.

Table 14.7 Multivariate analysis of variance for investment appraisal criteria

	Means		Tests		
	Prefer serial entrepreneur	Do not prefer	Multivariate F-ratio	Univariate F-ratio	Significance
Ownership			2.45	–	0.074
Previous ownership experience	2.85	2.14	–	2.48	0.098
Length of ownership career	2.58	1.79	–	4.09	0.048
Number of previous ventures	2.5	1.79	–	5.69	0.021
Management			1.10	–	0.340
Managerial experience	4.53	4.71	–	0.84	0.362
Managerial success	4.85	4.79	–	0.19	0.661
Personal background			1.07	–	0.389
Qualifications	2.53	2.86	–	1.10	0.297
Knowledge of industry	4.35	4.79	–	2.88	0.095
Stable family background	2.28	2.76	–	2.49	0.120
Age	2.78	3.07	–	1.18	0.281
Motivation	4.62	4.71	–	0.12	0.732
Institutional links			1.15	–	0.323
Level of funding sought	2.60	2.43	–	0.20	0.656
Previous relationship with manager	2.90	2.28	–	2.30	0.135
				0.43	0.67
Financial commitment*	3.80	3.93	–	0.43	0.67
N	40	14	–	–	–

Note: * Reported test statistic is T-ratio because financial commitment is a univariate measure.

Table 14.8 presents the results for the analysis of management buy-in screening. The overall analysis suggests that there are no significant differences between the two groups although there is some evidence to suggest a marginally significant difference in relation to the assessment of managers' contributions to target achievements, with those entrepreneurs preferring to use serial entrepreneurs scoring this factor significantly higher than those who do not. There is some tentative indication of a preference for the use of serial entrepreneurs among the older and larger venture capital organisations but there is little evidence to suggest that this preference is then reflected in any substantive differences in investment appraisal across the two groups.

Respondents were also asked to score ten factors derived from the existing literature, which may be important in assessing the investment potential of first time and serial entrepreneurs. As Table 14.9 shows, there is a high degree of

Table 14.8 Multivariate analysis of variance for investment appraisal criteria

	Prefer serial entrepreneur	Do not prefer	Multivariate F-ratio	Univariate F-ratio	Significance
Screening for MBI			1.66	–	0.118
Years of management experience	3.40	3.57	–	0.15	0.702
Age	2.75	2.64	–	0.10	0.755
Personal ambition	3.87	3.86	–	0.00	0.969
Entrepreneur's desire for job security	2.15	1.86	–	0.71	0.402
Independence and motivation	3.05	2.93	–	0.10	0.758
Commercial awareness	4.02	3.92	–	0.05	0.824
Previous experience – similar site venture	3.43	3.21	–	0.29	0.592
Experience in sector	3.90	4.07	–	0.14	0.704
Achievement of targets in previous ventures	3.57	3.29	–	0.53	0.469
Manager contribution to target achievements	3.63	2.86	–	3.56	0.064
Experience as lead manager	3.38	2.79	–	1.91	0.172

Table 14.9 Assessment of serial and first time entrepreneurs' investment potential

	Mean (serials)	Mean (first time)	T-ratio	Sig.
Achievement of sales/finance targets	3.85	4.05	1.12	0.27
Ability to meet timescales	3.53	3.71	1.20	0.23
Creation of commercial opportunities	3.85	3.69	–0.80	0.42
Leadership skills	4.18	4.31	0.77	0.44
Management skills	4.00	4.29	1.93	0.05
Financial commitment	3.40	3.38	–0.12	0.91
Enterprise driven	3.23	3.45	1.47	0.14
Financially driven	3.38	3.52	1.09	0.28
Ability to cope with venture stress	3.38	3.71	1.88	0.06
Time to exit	3.16	3.03	–1.02	0.31
Number of respondents		47		

similarity in the ways in which the two types of entrepreneur are assessed, with only management skills and ability to cope with stress being identified as significantly more important in the assessment of first time entrepreneurs than in the assessment of career entrepreneurs. In both cases, the three most important factors were leadership skills, management skills and the achievement of sales/finance targets. For both types of entrepreneurs also, time to exit was the least important factor. For first time entrepreneurs, relatively more importance was placed on ability to cope with venture stress and being enterprise driven than was the case for career entrepreneurs. Correspondingly, venture capitalists placed relatively more emphasis on the creation of commercial opportunities, an ability to meet timescales, being financially driven and financial commitment for serial entrepreneurs.

This suggests that the weights associated with different screening criteria do not differ substantially between first-time and serial entrepreneurs, despite the potential for adverse selection problems to be lower for the latter group.

Assets and liabilities of serial entrepreneurship

Using a scale containing variables derived from Starr and Bygrave (1991) and responses from the second questionnaire, venture capitalists generally report that the previous entrepreneurial experience of serial entrepreneurs *in whom they have invested* is an asset rather than a liability (Table 14. 10), with the ability to build on expertise in running an independent business and on reputation as a successful entrepreneur scoring particularly highly. Ability to identify business networks appropriate to a particular situation and ability to adapt expertise to new circumstances also score highly. The main factor relating to the negative aspects of previous experience to score highly was that serial entrepreneurs were generally reported as being unable to recognise their own limitations. Reliance on networks which were successful in a first venture, which may be positive or negative, also scored reasonably highly. Note that these responses relate to serial entrepreneurs in whom venture capitalists had invested, suggesting an awareness by them of the positive and negative aspects of experience with those with negative attributes not receiving subsequent backing.

Recontracting issues

It was suggested earlier that venture capitalists may be cautious about reinvesting in serial entrepreneurs as a consequence of the knowledge and experience of the negotiating process which those entrepreneurs have. Tentative support for the view that caution is exercised in respect of reinvesting in entrepreneurs from the venture capitalists' own portfolio is provided by the descriptive statistics presented earlier which reveal a low level of use of previously funded entrepreneurs. Indeed, where venture capitalists had made use of entrepreneurs whom they had previously backed, it was relatively unusual for them to be used as participants in buy-outs, buy-ins or start-ups. The use made of entrepreneurs in management buy-outs, buy-ins and BIMBOs accounted for only 2.6 per cent of former lead entrepreneurs and 0.5 per cent of other entrepreneurial team members. More in evidence was the role of the exiting entrepreneur in an

Table 14.10 *View on serial entrepreneurs' initial experience brought to second venture*

	Mean	STD	Median
Build on expertise in running an independent business	4.00	0.55	4.00
Ability to build on reputation as a successful entrepreneur	3.90	0.72	4.00
Ability to identify business networks appropriate to a particular situation	3.81	0.81	4.00
Able to adapt expertise to new circumstances	3.52	0.81	4.00
Fixation on repeating the same actions even though conditions may have changed	2.95	0.97	3.00
Unwillingness to take independent advice from investor	2.81	1.12	3.00
Reliance on network relationships which were successful in first venture	3.29	0.90	3.00
Overestimate their own contribution to the success of a venture: by refusing to delegate	2.86	0.91	3.00
Overestimate their own contribution to the success of a venture: by refusing to recruit experts	2.67	0.86	3.00
Unwillingness to maintain tight control on limited resources	2.43	0.81	2.00
Unable to recognise own limitations	3.33	1.03	3.00
Unwillingness to undertake important tasks which they now see as 'beneath them'	2.71	0.90	2.00

Note: $n = 21$; scores based on a range from 1 to 5 where 5 = strongly agree to 1 = strongly disagree.

Source: CMBOR/Barclays Private Equity/Deloitte & Touche.

informal or part time context. Thus for both lead entrepreneurs and other members the single most important area of subsequent involvement was in an informal advisory role. There was little evidence of any systematic variation in the use of previously funded entrepreneurs across different institutions. While generally, the larger venture capital firms made more use of previously funded entrepreneurs (particularly in buy-outs and in the role of director), the observed differences were not statistically significant.

However, over 50 per cent of respondents to the first survey indicated that they used entrepreneurs who had previously been funded by another venture capitalist; almost half of these entrepreneurs were funded for (genuine serial entrepreneurship – that is, leading a buy-in buy-out or BIMBO. When compared to usage of entrepreneurs from the venture capitalists' own portfolio, there is evidence of a substantial difference and this would tend to suggest that venture capitalists see recontracting as less problematic with entrepreneurs previously funded by a different venture capitalist.

Further evidence concerning reinvestment practice comes from the second survey. Major differences between first time and serial entrepreneurs in negotiations were identified and provide some support for the concerns venture capitalists were suggested to have about serial recontracting (Table 14.11). The ability of serial entrepreneurs to understand the venture capital process better received the highest score.

Table 14.11 Differences of serial entrepreneurs from first time entrepreneurs in negotiating investments

	Mean	STD	Median
Able to foresee your negotiating techniques	4.41	0.73	5.00
Able to obtain higher equity stake	3.86	0.71	4.00
Unwilling to risk high proportion of personal wealth	3.72	0.88	4.00
Able to find other founders	4.14	0.64	4.00
Run an auction of other founders	3.36	0.85	3.00
Insist on the use of particular debt funder	3.09	0.87	3.00
Insist on veto of syndicate membership	3.27	0.83	3.00
Less reliant on other intermediaries	3.86	0.83	4.00
Insist on hands-off monitoring by the venture capitalist	2.86	0.89	3.00
Insist on greater say in timing and nature of exit	3.18	0.66	3.00
Understand the venture capital process better	4.50	0.60	5.00

Notes: $n = 22$; scores based on a range from 1 to 5, where 5 = more likely to be the case with serial entrepreneurs to 1 = less likely to be the case with serial entrepreneurs.

Difficulties in negotiations were signalled by the ability of serial entrepreneurs to foresee the venture capitalists' negotiating techniques, their ability to find other funders and their ability to obtain a higher equity stake, which were the second, third and fourth highest scores, respectively. Other potential problem areas, such as running an auction of funders, insisting on a greater say in the timing and nature of exit, and vetoing syndicate membership, figured less highly, and insisting on hands-off monitoring scored lowest.

In cases where venture capitalists negotiated with experienced entrepreneurs who had exited from another venture capitalist's portfolio there was little evidence to suggest a preference for this kind of individual, even though there seems to be a higher incidence of such investment. There was slight agreement with the view that an entrepreneur who was seeking to change venture capitalist is likely to be a potential problem so there was need for great caution (mean 3.17

on a scale where 5 = strongly agree to 1 = strongly disagree). There was no clear agreement or disagreement that venture capitalists saw themselves as more able to negotiate acceptable terms with an entrepreneur in whom they had not invested before (mean 3.00, standard deviation 0.67). Venture capitalists expressed some slight disagreement that they had had more suitable proposals from entrepreneurs who had exited from other venture capitalists' portfolios than from their own (mean 2.23, standard deviation, 1.09). Venture capitalists may or may not have considered investing in the individuals concerned the first time around (mean 2.70, standard deviation 0.66) and did not particularly take the view that entrepreneurs changing venture capitalist were demonstrating initiative which suggested that they were motivated to succeed in a second deal (mean 2.70, standard deviation 0.77).

Thus, as was the case with the results of the first survey, the data from the second survey appears to provide some support for recontracting problems when venture capitalists deal with entrepreneurs from their own portfolios but the extent of such difficulties seems rather less in the case of entrepreneurs from the portfolios of other venture capitalists.

Performance

The results of the second survey suggest that in terms of performance in the second venture in comparison to that in the first, there was little evidence of much difference; there was a slight indication that profit performance was better in the second than in the first (mean = 3.16; standard deviation = 0.69), but that sales growth was worse (mean = 2.90; standard deviation = 0.57). However, venture capitalists scored their preparedness to support serial entrepreneurs in a third venture in the same capacity reasonably highly (mean 3.53 out of 5 on a 1 to 5 point scale where 5 = strongly agree, standard deviation = 0.96). Venture capitalists did not report serial entrepreneurs performing better than first time entrepreneurs in whom they invested in the same period (mean = 2.95; standard deviation = 0.85).

Results: serial management buy-outs and buy-ins

The first section presents the quantitative evidence while the second discusses the findings from the case studies.

Quantitative evidence

Trends Serial buy-outs and buy-ins have occurred in increasing numbers over the last decade (Table 14.12). A first peak of activity occurred in the late 1980s, after which there was a marked decline at the beginning of the 1990s. From 1993 onwards numbers have increased noticeably. Indeed, over a half of all the 189 serial buy-outs and buy-ins identified by CMBOR have been completed in the last four years. In 1996, the peak year to date, they accounted for 5.7 per cent of all new buy-out and buy-in completions.

Table 14.12 Development of serial buy-outs and buy-ins

Year	Number	Percentage
1984	1	0.6
1985	2	1.1
1986	3	1.6
1987	3	1.6
1988	16	8.5
1989	18	9.5
1990	15	7.9
1991	8	4.2
1992	14	7.4
1993	23	12.1
1994	21	11.1
1995	30	15.9
1996	35	18.5
Total	189	100.0

Source: CMBOR/Barclays Private Equity/Deloitte & Touche.

Serial buy-outs and buy-ins appear to be slightly more prevalent among medium-sized deals; some 12 per cent having an initial transaction value in the range £5–10m compared to 7 per cent of all buy-outs and buy-ins. There are some notable divergences between the original sources of serial buy-outs and buy-ins and buy-outs and buy-ins in general. There is evidence that divestments are more prevalent among serial buy-outs and buy-ins than for buy-outs and buy-ins generally, whilst the reverse is true in respect of buy-outs involving private/family businesses (Table 14.13). There is little difference for receivership, privatisation and going private sources.

There are also marked differences in the industrial characteristics of serial buy-outs and buy-ins and the population of buy-outs and buy-ins as a whole (Table 14.14). Serial buy-outs and buy-ins are represented to a greater extent than might be expected given the industry distribution of all buy-outs and buy-ins especially in mechanical engineering, metals, shipbuilding and vehicles, and primary industries. To a lesser extent, serial buy-outs are also over-represented in the chemicals, electrical engineering, timber and furniture sectors, and transport and communication sectors. The corollary is that there are lower proportions of serial buy-outs and buy-ins than might be expected in business and financial services, textiles, leather and footwear and wholesale distribution.

Table 14.13 Initial deal sources of serial buy-outs and buy-ins

Source	Serial	All
Receivership	9.0	8.6
Divestment	61.2	55.4
Private/family	24.5	31.2
Privatisation	4.4	4.0
Going private	0.9	0.8
Total	100.0	100.0

Source: CMBOR/Barclays Private Equity/Deloitte & Touche.

Table 14.14 Industry distributions of serial buy-outs and buy-ins.

	Serial	All
Primary industries and energy	4.0	1.0
Food and drink	3.3	3.6
Chemicals and man made fibres	3.9	2.1
Metals	8.5	4.6
Mechanical and instrument engineering	10.7	8.9
Electrical engineering and office machinery	9.6	8.8
Shipbuilding and vehicles	7.9	3.6
Textiles, leather, footwear	1.1	4.4
Timber, furniture	3.4	2.6
Paper, printing, publishing	6.2	6.7
Other manufacturing	5.6	6.3
Transport and communication	5.6	4.6
Wholesale distribution	6.2	8.6
Retail distribution	6.2	6.1
Business, financial and other services	15.7	24.0
Other	2.1	4.1
Total	100.0	100.0
Sample number	178	6592

Source: CMBOR/Barclays Private Equity/Deloitte & Touche.

Exits from first buy-outs The average age at which first buy-outs and buy-ins became secondary deals was 5 years, 10 months. However, the age at which first buy-outs and buy-ins become secondary deals varies considerably (Table 14.15). A quarter had occurred when the first buy-out or buy-in was three years old or less with a half occurring within five-and-a-quarter years. In three-tenths of cases, the first buy-out or buy-in had been established for between six and ten years, with the buy-out or buy-in being in excess of ten years old in slightly over a tenth of cases (11.2 per cent).

Table 14.15 Age at time of serial buy-out or buy-in

Age at time of serial buy-out/buy-in (years)	Percentage of sample	Cumulative percentage of sample
Less than 1	1.7	1.7
1–2	9.6	11.8
2–3	12.9	24.2
3–4	10.7	34.8
4–5	10.7	45.5
5–6	11.8	57.3
6–7	7.3	64.6
7–8	12.4	77.0
8–9	8.4	85.4
9–10	3.4	88.8
At least 10	11.2	100.0

Note: Based on 178 companies for which data are available.

Source: CMBOR/Barclays Private Equity/Deloitte & Touche.

The resurgence of activity in the last two years reflects this wide range of first buy-out ages at the time that a serial buy-out or buy-in takes place (Table 14.16). Whilst some recent serial deals involved first buy-outs and buy-ins completed since 1990, seven-tenths of those where the buy-out or buy-in was more than ten years old have been completed in 1995 and 1996.

Case study evidence

The wide distribution of ages at which secondary deals occur suggests that there are varying reasons for selecting a serial buy-out or buy-in. Using evidence from the case studies, as discussed in the data section, we provide insights into this process. The features of the cases are summarised in Table 14.17.[7]

Table 14.16 *Year of buy-out by year of serial buy-out*

Year of original buy-out	Year of serial buy-out										
	Pre-1988	1988	1989	1990	1991	1992	1993	1994	1995	1996	Total
Pre 1982	2	5	3			1			2	1	14
1982	4		1			2	3		1	3	14
1983		1	2	3	1			2		1	10
1984	2	1	3	2		2			2		12
1985	1	3	3	2	1	3	3	1		1	18
1986		4		3			1	4	3	2	17
1987		1	4	4	1	1	7	2	4	3	27
1988		1	1	1	1	1	1	4	1	4	15
1989			1		1		3	3	2	2	12
1990					2	2	2	2	5	2	15
1991					1	2	1		3	3	10
1992							2	1	2	5	10
1993								1	3	1	5
1994								1	2	1	4
Total	9	16	18	15	8	14	23	21	30	29	183

Notes:
1996 to October, details of 6 more not included.

Source: CMBOR/Barclays Private Equity/Deloitte & Touche.

First buy-out/buy-in exit preferences The most preferred exit routes from the first deal for the management involved in serial buy-outs had been in order of declining importance, flotation, trade sale, and share buy-back. None of the companies interviewed had considered a serial buy-out or buy-in as a possible exit route at the time of the first deal.

Six of the interviewees had expressed a preference for a flotation in order to have a continuing influence in the company, to realise part of their investment, to raise finance for the company more easily and to add prestige to themselves and the company.

Four interviewees had preferred a trade sale for reasons which focused on an aversion to dealing with institutional investors, the lack of their company's suitability for a flotation and because it provided an opportunity to remain with the company as managerial employees.

Only one company had stipulated at the time of the first buy-out that they preferred to exit through a share buy-back. This was agreed in principle by the

Table 14.17 The serial buy-outs interviewed

Company	1st deal	Year	Reason	2nd deal	Year	Reason
A	MBO	1986	Non-core activity	MBO	1994	Contested a trade sale
B	MBO/I	1990	Retirement	MBO	1995	Term loans due
C	MBO	1984	Retirement	MBO	1989	Venture capital firm wanted exit
D	MBO	1990	Pending receivership	MBO	1995	Refinancing
E	MBO	1985	Non-core activity	MBO	1993	Share buy-back
F	MBO	1990	Receivership	MBO	1994	Institutions outbid trade buyers
G	MBO	1990	Management retired	MBI	1994	Team leader dismissed
H	MBO	1986	Alternative to closure	MBO	1995	Funds for future growth
I	MBO	1987	Non-core activity	MBO	1992	Share buy-back
J	MBO	1992	Non-core activity	MBO	1994	Share buy-back
K	MBO	1981	Non-core activity	MBI	1995	Retirement
L	MBO	1988	Group divestment	MBO	1996	One investor sought exit
M	MBO	1988	One of the owners left	MBO	1996	Conflicts of interest

venture capital firm with the option that if the management could not raise the funds within four years an alternative exit would be proposed. Two years after the buy-out, management had raised sufficient funds through personal finance and loans to provide the venture capital firm with a satisfactory return. The other interviewees had not made specific exit plans.

The consensus among the companies interviewed was that the venture capital firms supported their exit strategies as long as their realisation criteria were met. The management had less influence over the timing of an exit from the first buy-out, which was often stipulated by the type of venture capital fund. However, it was also clear from the interviews that at the time of completing the original buy-out no serious consideration was given to alternative exit routes if the first preference was not met. This was especially important as the recession of the early 1990s delayed many planned exits. Had the original exit not been delayed, managers were of the view that they would not have considered a serial buy-out. The delayed exit also exposed inadequacies in financing structures that had not taken into account the future financing needs of the companies.

Initiation of exit from the first deal In seven of the 13 companies interviewed, the exit process from the first buy-out was initiated by the venture capital firm and in the remaining cases by management.

Venture capital firms may initiate an exit from the first buy-out for several reasons. In two of the cases, the investors' closed end funds were reaching the end of their life leading to pressure to realise remaining investments in their portfolios. A second set of reasons concerned the time constraints stipulated by some of the venture capital firms during the initial negotiations which they made clear they intended to keep. The requirement for further finance by some of the companies, which the venture capital firm was not prepared to provide, often because of unsatisfactory performance, also contributed towards them initiating this kind of exit.

Management teams may also have a number of reasons for initiating an exit. In one of the companies there was a split in the management team's views about the future strategy of the company, such that a serial buy-out involving some of the management quitting the company was the only option to resolve the problem. In another case, the exit was initiated through management's desire to retire after having been with the buy-out for 14 years. A further case involved conflicts which arose in the management team following attempts to obtain further finance to repay the institutional investors' term loans. As a result, some of the team members looked to a serial buy-out which would exclude those members who were seen to have been disruptive to the company.

Serial buy-out or buy-in as an exit route A number of factors led the search for an appropriate exit route to settle on a serial buy-out or buy-in.

In three companies, further finance was required to continue their growth strategy. Company D experienced problems in meeting repayment schedules coming out of recession and decided to seek further finance to enable them to penetrate export markets. The venture capital firm took the view that in order to acquire the funding another venture capital firm should be approached. As a result the management's equity stake was diluted. A similar situation occurred in company G; except when further finance was requested, the venture capital firm replaced the manager with an inexperienced buy-in team. This resulted in the dismissed manager being reinstated to form a serial buy-out/buy-in. Company H was also seeking further growth finance but as it was the only investment in the venture capital firm's fund it was suggested that another venture capital firm should be sought who was more familiar with the company's industry.

Three of the companies underwent a serial buy-out to buy-back the venture capital firm's equity stake. At company E the buy-out had been in existence for eight years when the venture capital firm decided it wanted to exit and this was achieved through the venture capital firm proposing a special dividend to meet the valuation placed on the company's shares. Company I had initially planned to float, but when this did not look likely the venture capital firm discussed a potential trade sale. This did not appeal to management who felt that as they were still 20 years from retirement they had much to offer the company. The management approached the venture capital firm with a buy-back proposal and raised the £2 million in loans to meet the venture capital firm's price. Company I had planned a buy-back at the time of the first buy-out and this was achieved two years earlier than planned because of strong performance.

In two companies, both management teams made attempts to find trade buyers but a serial buy-out was found to offer the highest valuation for the venture capital firm. Company A received an unsolicited offer from a trade buyer which was rejected as insufficient. Further offers were pursued, with the venture capital firm keen to achieve an exit by this route as they were constrained by the limited life of their funds. At the same time management expressed a desire to undertake a serial buy-out but were dissuaded by the venture capital firm on the grounds that this could reduce interest from potential trade bidders. After a period of time it became evident that the venture capital firm would not achieve the valuation they were seeking from a trade bidder and it was decided that a serial buy-out could go ahead if management could raise the agreed level of finance. The successful Company F's management had originally targeted a trade sale as an exit route, but their advisers suggested that it would also be prudent to consider a buy-out refinancing. When the offers were received it became evident that venture capital firms were offering the highest price for the equity. As a result, the management decided to sell part of their equity stake to a venture capital firm and undergo a serial buy-out.

In a further two companies the serial buy-out arose as a consequence of venture capital firms seeking to exit because of the pressures of limited life closed-end funds. In case C, management, having been prompted to find a trade buyer by the venture capital firm and succeeding in doing so, realized during the negotiations that they could raise the finance themselves. Once approached, the venture capital firm supported a serial buy-out. Management had achieved significant growth and took the view that it was preferable to continue along this route rather than becoming managerial employees in a large group. In company

L, plans for a flotation were thwarted for technical reasons and two trade sale attempts failed to reach agreement. A serial buy-out was adopted as a means of meeting the venture capital firm's time constraints.

The serial buy-outs in the remaining three companies arose because of managerial issues. In company K, the buy-out leader retired and with no managers with sufficient expertise to ensure succession attempts were made to find a trade buyer. These failed because of concerns that a trade sale would threaten the continuity of the business. As a result, the venture capital firm proposed the introduction of an outside manager to create a serial buy-in with the retiring manager retaining a preference shareholding. In company M, the management team split on agreed terms, the departing manager taking over the non-core activities in a second buy-out and the remaining management retaining the core interests. In contrast, friction in the two-man management team in company B was highlighted when new venture capital firms approached for finance to repay terms loans were prepared to support only one manager. The result was a replacement of the original venture capital firm and the departure of the other manager.

Differences between first and second deals Management generally took the view that the greater experience they now had meant that they were more efficient and effective in following their planned strategy than they had been in their first buy-out when managers were often only focused on their own function. The benefits of experience were also evident in management's negotiations with financing institutions the second time around. There was also greater satisfaction with the contribution of non-executive directors in the second transaction. Those companies which had experienced no growth during the recession were all now showing significant growth.

The management teams involved in serial buy-outs had either changed completely or partially. In six companies, there had been partial changes consisting of either some members leaving and not being replaced, or the bringing in of new members. Excluding those managers who became buy-in members, the changes that occurred were: dismissal of members of the management in three companies; retirement of members in two companies; voluntary departures in four companies; and the forced sale of managerial equity stakes by the venture capital firm in one case.

Managements' motivations appear to have changed somewhat in the second buy-out from aiming to realise significant gains in the first. Management generally reported their main reason for undergoing a serial buy-out as an aversion to becoming managerial-employees and a desire to remain with and exert a continuing influence in their company by aiming to keep it independent, in many cases indefinitely. To this end, management reported a greater influence in determining exit horizons in the second buy-out than they had in the first.

None of the financial structures in the second deals in the sample included a ratchet, although this may not necessarily be the case in all buy-outs of this kind.[8] It was also the case that none of the companies interviewed had met their ratchet targets in the first buy-out. In most companies, management retained a majority equity stake in the second buy-out, but in some cases this had been reduced from the first buy-out either because of poor performance or because of the dilution effect of the issue of shares to incoming venture capital firms.

Exits from the second deal Of the 13 companies interviewed, four reported that they were seeking a stock market flotation as a means of exiting from the second buy-out and that they intended to do so within the next two to three years. Three of the four involved companies whose second deal had a transaction value in excess of £10 million.

Only two of the companies had considered a trade sale as the proposed exit route, one of which was already negotiating the terms of their trade sale two years after the second buy-out. The other company reported that it would only pursue a trade sale if the correct price is offered. If this is not the case the aim is to achieve a third management buy-out.

The management in six of the companies intended to stay with the company until retirement. Given that most of these managers had between 15 and 20 years of their career still to run, this indicates that the maintenance of the company as a long term privately owned independent business was a major objective. All these management owned majority equity stakes in their companies and were prepared to undertake further refinancing (that is, a tertiary buy-out) in order to maintain their independence. The remaining company had no explicit exit strategy other than to develop the company. There was some evidence that managers intending to remain as private independent companies were seeking growth through organic development whereas those seeking a stock market flotation also placed emphasis on acquisitions.

Discussion and conclusions

The results of this study have implications for both academics and practitioners. The study of serial entrepreneurs suggests that the extent to which venture capitalists use previously funded entrepreneurs is relatively low compared to the number of investments harvested. This relatively low use of entrepreneurs in subsequent investments may be at least partially attributable to type of harvesting (for example, entrepreneurs are more likely to leave their venture at the time of its sale to another company than at the time of an IPO); contractual arrangements made following the sale of a business between the selling entrepreneurs and the new owners (for example, new management contracts, legal restraints on setting up competing businesses); the attitudes of entrepreneurs to being involved in second time ventures; and their assessment of the venture capital firm and process. Thus entrepreneurs who sell their business may retain a formal management position with the new owners or decide to pursue some totally different activity not involving a venture capitalist or wish to pursue a venture but with an alternative financing structure. Higher levels of personal wealth resulting from a successful sale of their first business may enable the second time entrepreneur to avoid the use of venture capital finance in the initial stages of a second venture although she/he may require such finance at a later point to fund growth depending on the initial size and stage of the new venture. Additionally, there may have been a significant change in the relative bargaining powers of the entrepreneur and venture capitalist which may make it more difficult for the venture capitalist to accept, for instance, the equity shares being demanded by the now financially wealthy second time entrepreneur.

The results lend some support to Starr and Bygrave's (1991, 1992) observation about the assets and liabilities of experience. There was some concern on the part of venture capitalists, as to whether exiting entrepreneurs can perform a second time either because they lose motivation or are unable to repeat the initial conditions. The study showed that in terms of appraisal of entrepreneurs, both in general and in respect of those experienced entrepreneurs exiting from initial investments, venture capitalists generally claimed to prefer to finance an entrepreneur who had played a major role in a previous venture. Multivariate analysis showed that previous ownership, length of entrepreneurial career and number of previous ventures were rather more important for those venture capitalists who expressed a preference for serial entrepreneurs. Previous experience was viewed as being important in providing a track record, followed by demonstrated motivation. Some importance was attached to the view that experienced entrepreneurs were more likely to achieve success again, although this factor was not rated as highly as entrepreneurial ambition and motivation. Although previous ownership experience is of some importance it is not of itself a critical factor, since indications are that venture capitalists will need to be satisfied that experienced entrepreneurs still have the motivation, ambition and managerial skills to succeed in a subsequent venture. These points may be especially true of entrepreneurs exiting from a management buy-out, who typically may be reacting to the presentation of a one-off opportunity in the enterprise in which they find themselves. The views of those venture capitalists who had experience of serial entrepreneurs indicated a generally positive view of previous experience, apart from entrepreneurs' inability to recognise their own limitations. This suggests that venture capitalists have been careful at screening out those entrepreneurs who do not meet these criteria.

The effects of the extent and nature of scrutiny of experienced and novice entrepreneurs is reflected in the evidence relating to venture capitalists' perceptions of performance. While experienced entrepreneurs performed slightly better on average in their second ventures in terms of profits, it is less clear that they performed better than novice entrepreneurs in whom the venture capitalists invested during the same period. These findings are consistent with more general studies of habitual entrepreneurs by Birley and Westhead (1994) and Kolvereid and Bullvag (1993).

The use made of other venture capitalists' ex-entrepreneurs may reflect such factors as the ability of more seasoned entrepreneurs to purchase their finance in a more sophisticated way, the type of finance required, concerns over the way the harvesting process was managed, disputes over equity ratchets or more fundamental problems in the personal relationship between the venture capitalist and the entrepreneur. The departing venture capitalist will also be more aware of the limitations of the entrepreneur which may not be so apparent to the new venture capitalist who will have been impressed by the track record. Additionally, the departing venture capitalist through having personal experience of the entrepreneur may make a different judgement from another venture capitalist about the abilities of the entrepreneur to move from, say, a management buy-out to a management buy-in where different types of managerial and entrepreneurial skills are required. Nevertheless, the evidence implies that the lack of systematic follow-up of entrepreneurs backed by a venture capitalist may be presenting opportunities for competitor venture capital firms rather than allowing the original backer to generate new investments.

There was evidence from the follow-up survey of venture capitalists with experience of serial entrepreneurs of caution in renegotiating with experienced entrepreneurs from their own portfolios, notably because of entrepreneurs' greater awareness of the venture capitalists' negotiating techniques, greater understanding of the process, and ability to obtain a higher stake. However, reasons for rejection appeared to be more related to the absence of a viable proposal or changes in investment criteria rather than unreasonable demands by entrepreneurs, but this also needs to be seen in terms of the changes over time in the type of deal sought by the venture capital firm and their targeted returns. Venture capitalists appeared to be more cautious than expected in negotiating and investing in entrepreneurs from other venture capitalists' portfolios.

The study of serial buy-outs and buy-ins has identified some notable differences compared with buy-outs and buy-ins generally, especially with respect to their original sources and their industrial distribution. Serial buy-outs and buy-ins are represented to a greater extent than might be expected given the industry distribution of all buy-outs and buy-ins especially in mechanical engineering, metals, shipbuilding and vehicles, and primary industries.

Serial buy-outs and buy-ins are not the first choice exit at the time of the original buy-out, but will become a live exit option when other exit possibilities have failed to occur as planned, where management seek continuing independence and where the venture capital firm may be under pressure to exit, especially if managing a closed-end fund. Some serial buy-outs and buy-ins have strong growth prospects while many appear to be in fairly stable market niches. This position is reinforced by the greater prevalence than might be expected of serial buy-outs and buy-ins in engineering and metal manufacturing sectors.

Given the maturity of the overall buy-out market and the high proportion of buy-outs and buy-ins which have not exited by a trade sale or flotation, our findings suggest that there may be further opportunities for secondary deals among long-established first buy-outs and buy-ins where succession problems are developing, and there is a desire to maintain the independent private existence of the company.

To the extent that serial entrepreneurs and serial buy-outs are becoming more in evidence, further research may usefully be directed at consideration of the views of venture capitalists in relation to the characteristics and motivations of the entrepreneurs involved and their approaches to serial buy-outs and buy-ins. Examination of issues concerning the processes by which entrepreneurs enter into subsequent ventures, from the perspective of the entrepreneurs, may help in understanding the phenomenon. These issues relate to consideration of whether entrepreneurs move directly to a subsequent venture or only arrive at it after a period of search or employment in a larger group. There is also a need to examine the nature of the serial entrepreneur's search process and, in order to counterbalance the views of venture capitalists, the extent to which and the reasons why serial entrepreneurs do or do not retain advisers and financiers who were involved in the initial ventures in subsequent ones.

In addition, although four broad categories of habitual entrepreneur were identified at the outset, this chapter has only examined one subset. There would thus appear to be further scope for examination of the other types, comparison of the characteristics of the entrepreneurs involved and analysis of their performance effects. For example, are leaders of serial buy-outs/buy-ins simply venture repeaters (Wright et al., 1997) or do some belong to a different category? Also, does the very different asymmetric information issue compared to the other subsets of habitual entrepreneur significantly reduce the risks to the venture capital investor?

The results of the study have a number of implications for practitioners. First, the findings emphasise the importance of not considering previous venture experience in isolation, but in the context of other key investment variables. Second, the lack of strongly greater performance from serial versus novice entrepreneurs, which is consistent with that from other studies, further emphasises the care to be taken in assessing experienced entrepreneurs. Third, the relatively low degree of formal and rigorous post-exit assessment and monitoring by venture capitalists suggests that they may be missing important opportunities to invest in experienced entrepreneurs. Fourth, serial buy-outs and buy-ins present a new and rapidly developing opportunity for venture capital firms to back experienced entrepreneurs.

Notes

1. These are the three main forms of serial entrepreneurship although it is recognised that serial entrepreneurs may make minority and/or part-time investments as business angels and may have a comparative advantage over formal venture capitalists in making helpful contributions in operational and strategic functional areas of an enterprise's activity, though there may be difficulties in the process of searching and matching investors with investments (Harrison and Mason, 1992).
2. Both instruments are available from the authors on request.
3. *t*-tests were conducted for significant differences between the characteristics of respondents who provided information on their usage of serial entrepreneurs and those who did not. There was no evidence of differences between the two groups at conventional levels of significance. Absolute *t*-values ranged from 0.09 to 1.55.
4. To test whether this was significantly related to size of portfolio we tested for significant differences and found that although non-respondents were larger they were not significantly so.
5. Small organisations are those with less than the median number of executives. The difference between the mean score in respect of no suitable candidates having emerged was significantly smaller for larger organisations (mean score 3.5, standard deviation 1.4) than for smaller ones (mean score 4.9, standard deviation 0.37), with a *t*-value of –3.52.
6. Because of the interdependent nature of the proportions of venture capitalists' portfolios which are invested in each investment stage, we use multivariate analysis of variance (MANOVA) to test for differences between those venture capitalists who prefer serial entrepreneurs and those who do not.
7. Because of confidentiality undertakings, information on the cases is presented anonymously.
8. See, for example, the case of Maccess in Wright and Robbie (1990). In this case there was a negative ratchet.

References

Birley, S. and P. Westhead (1994), 'A comparison of new businesses established by "novice" and "habitual" founders in Great Britain', *International Small Business Journal*, **12** (1), 38–60.

Block, Z. and I. MacMillan (1993), *Corporate Venturing*, Boston, MA: Harvard Business School Press.

Bruno, A. and T. Tyebjee (1985), 'The entrepreneur's search for capital', *Journal of Business Venturing*, **1**, 61–74.

Bull, I. (1989), 'Management performance in leveraged buy-outs: an empirical analysis', *Journal of Business Venturing*, **4**, 263–79.

Bygrave, W., M. Hay and J. Peeters (eds) (1994), *Realizing Investment Value*, London: FT-Pitman.

CMBOR (1996), 'Trends in UK management buy-outs', *Management buy-outs – quarterly review from CMBOR*, Centre for Management Buy-out Research, University of Nottingham.

Cooper, A., and W. Dunkelberg (1986), 'Entrepreneurship and paths to business ownership', *Strategic Management Journal*, **7**, 53–6.

Devlin, K. (1992), 'M&A no match for powerful IPO market', *Venture Capital Journal*, **32** (2), 27–31.

Ennew, C., K. Robbie, M. Wright and S. Thompson (1994), 'Small business entrepreneurs and performance: evidence from management buy-ins', *International Small Business Journal*, **12** (4), 28–44.

European Venture Capital Association (EVCA) (1995), *Venture Capital in Europe*, Zaentem: EVCA.

Gartner, W. (1985), 'A conceptual framework for describing the phenomenon of new venture creation', *Academy of Management Review*, **10** (4), 685–706.

Hall, P. (1995), 'Habitual owners of small businesses', chapter 15 in F. Chittenden M. Robertson and I. Marshall (eds), *Small Firms: Partnerships for Growth*, London: Paul Chapman Publishing.

Harrison, R. and C. Mason (1992), 'The roles of investors in entrepreneurial companies: a comparison of informal investors and formal venture capitalists', in N. Churchill et al. (eds), *Frontiers of Entrepreneurship Research*, Wellesley, MA: Babson College.

Kelly, J.M., R.A. Pitts and B. Shin (1986), 'Entrepreneurship by leveraged buy-out: some preliminary hypotheses', in N. Churchill et al. (eds), *Frontiers of Entrepreneurial Research*, Wellesley, Ma: Babson College.

Kolvereid, L. and E. Bullvag (1993), 'Novices versus experienced founders: an exploratory investigation', in S. Birley and I. MacMillan (eds), *Entrepreneurship Research: Global Perspectives*, New York: Elsevier Science Publishers, pp. 275–85.

Low, M. and I.C. MacMillan (1988), 'Entrepreneurship; past research and future challenges', *Journal of Management*, **14** (2), 139–61.

MacMillan, I.C. (1986), 'To really learn about entrepreneurship, let's study habitual entrepreneurs', *Journal of Business Venturing*, **1** (3), 241–3.

MacMillan, I.C., R. Siegel and P.N.S. Subbanarasimha (1985), 'Criteria used by venture capitalists to evaluate new venture proposals', *Journal of Business Venturing*, **1** (1), 119–28.

MacMillan, I.C., L. Zemann and P.N.S. Subbanarasimha (1987), 'Criteria distinguishing successful from unsuccessful ventures in the venture screening process', *Journal of Business Venturing*, **3**, 123–37.

Petty, J.W., J. Suhlman, W.D. Bygrave (1992), 'Mergers and acquisitions: a means of harvesting the venture', in N. Churchill et al. (eds), *Frontiers of Entrepreneurship Research*, Wellesley, MA: Babson College, pp. 662–75.

Relander, K., A. Syrjanen and A. Miettinen (1994), 'Analysis of the trade sale as a venture capital exit route', chapter 6 in W. Bygrave, M. Hay and J. Peeters (eds), *Realizing Investment Value*, London: FT-Pitman, pp. 132–62.

Robbie, K. and M. Wright (1996), *Management Buy-ins: Entrepreneurship, Active Investors and Corporate Restructuring*, Manchester: Manchester University Press.

Ronstadt, R. (1988), 'The corridor principle', *Journal of Business Venturing*, **3**, 31–40.

Ruhnka, J., H. Feldman and T. Dean (1992), 'The "living dead" phenomenon in venture capital investments', *Journal of Business Venturing*, **7** (2), 137–56.

Silver, A.D. (1985), *Venture Capital: The Complete Guide for Investors*, New York: John Wiley and Sons.

Starr, J. and W. Bygrave, (1991), 'The assets and liabilities of prior start-up experience: an exploratory study of multiple venture entrepreneurs', in N. Churchill et al. (eds), *Frontiers of Entrepreneurship Research 1991*, Wellesley, Ma: Babson College.

Starr, J. and W.D. Bygrave (1992), 'The second time around: the outcomes, assets and liabilities of prior start-up experience', in S. Birley and I. MacMillan (eds), *International Perspectives on Entrepreneurship Research*, New York: Elsevier Science Publishers, pp. 340–63.

Stopford, J. and C. Baden-Fuller (1994), 'Creating corporate entrepreneurship', *Strategic Management Journal*, **15**, 521–36.

Stuart, R.W. and P.A. Abetti (1990), 'Impact of entrepreneurial and management experience on early performance', *Journal of Business Venturing*, **5**, 151–62.

Vesper, K. (1980), *New Venture Strategies*, Englewood Cliffs, NJ: Prentice-Hall.

Westhead, P. (1997), 'Ambition, "external" environment and strategic factor differences between family and non-family companies', *Entrepreneurship and Regional Development*, **9**, forthcoming.

Westhead, P. and M. Wright (1998), Novice, serial and portfolio entrepreneurs: are they different?', *Journal of Business Venturing*, **13** (3), 173–204.

Wright, M., B. Chiplin, S. Thompson and K. Robbie (1990), 'Management buy-outs and large–small firm relationships', *Management International Review*, **30** (1), 55–72.

Wright, M. and K. Robbie (1990), 'The case of Maccess', in S. Turley and S. Taylor (eds), *Cases in Financial Reporting*, Deddington: Philip Allan.

Wright, M., K. Robbie, Y. Romanet, S. Thompson, R. Joachimsson, J. Bruining and A. Herst (1993), 'Harvesting and longevity in management buy-outs and buy-ins: a four country study', *Entrepreneurship: Theory and Practice*, **18** (2), 89–110.

Wright, M., K. Robbie, S. Thompson and K. Starkey (1994), 'Longevity and the life-cycle of management buy-outs', *Strategic Management Journal*, **15** (3), 215–27.

Wright, M., K. Robbie and C. Ennew (1997), 'Serial Entrepreneurs', *British Journal of Management*, **8** (3), 251–68.

Wright, M., S. Thompson and K. Robbie (1992), 'Venture capital and management-led leveraged buy-outs: European evidence', *Journal of Business Venturing*, **7** (1), 47–71.

Zahra, S. (1995), 'Corporate entrepreneurship and financial performance: the case of management leveraged buy-outs', *Journal of Business Venturing*, **10** (2), 225–47.

Index